INSTRUCTOR'S MANUAL

to accompany

Ramage / Bean / Johnson

Writing Arguments
A Rhetoric with Readings
Eighth Edition

&

Writing Arguments
A Rhetoric with Readings
Brief Edition,
Eighth Edition

&

Writing Arguments
A Rhetoric with Readings
Concise Edition,
Fifth Edition

Tim N. Taylor
Eastern Illinois University

Longman

New York Boston San Francisco
London Toronto Sydney Tokyo Singapore Madrid
Mexico City Munich Paris Cape Town Hong Kong Montreal

This work is protected by United States copyright laws and is provided solely for the use of instructors in teaching their courses and assessing student learning. Dissemination or sale of any part of this work (including on the WorldWideWeb) will destroy the integrity of the work and is not permitted. The work and materials from it should never be made available to students except by instructors using the accompanying text in their classes. All recipients of this work are expected to abide by these restrictions and to honor the intended pedagogical purposes and the needs of other instructors who rely on these materials.

Instructor's Manual to accompany Ramage/Bean/Johnson, *Writing Arguments: A Rhetoric with Readings,* Eighth Edition, *Writing Arguments: A Rhetoric with Readings,* Brief, Eighth Edition, and *Writing Arguments: A Rhetoric with Readings,* Concise, Fifth Edition

Copyright ©2010 Pearson Education, Inc.
All rights reserved. Printed in the United States of America. Instructors may reproduce portions of this book for classroom use only. All other reproductions are strictly prohibited without prior permission of the publisher, except in the case of brief quotations embodied in critical articles and reviews.

1 2 3 4 5 6 7 8 9 10–BIR–12 11 10 09

Longman is an imprint of

www.pearsonhighered.com

ISBN 10: 0-205-63410-9
ISBN 13: 978-0-205-63410-1

CONTENTS

PREFACE

Composing this *Instructor's Manual* was much like marking my own analyses on a palimpsest. Based from John Ramage and John Bean's previous work and building particularly from June Johnson's fine work with the *Instructor's Manual*, 6th edition, I offer my own perspectives on the varied arguments within *Writing Arguments*, 8th edition. For the most part, the new edition of the *Instructor's Manual* (IM) won't look significantly different in organization or character from the previous editions except for two significant additions.

Like the previous editions, the IM has these basic components:

- Three detailed syllabi reflect three different course designs and goals—Generic Emphasis on Skills and Strategies, Emphasis on Claim Types, and Emphasis on Genres and Research.
- A lesson and a sequence of exercises explain and explore the Toulmin system—the concepts of claim, reasons, warrants, grounds, backing, conditions of rebuttal, and qualifiers.
- There are detailed responses to each chapter's For Class Discussion questions.
- At the end of the claim type (stasis) chapters, the IM provides a list of anthology readings that can illustrate a claim type either as a major claim or as a contributing claim to a hybrid argument.
- For instructors who use the anthology of arguments, the analysis of every argument is organized in this way: 1. the core of the argument; 2. the major or dominant stases of the argument; 3. the argument's use of evidence or argumentative strategies; 4. weaknesses of the argument; 5. the appeals to *ethos* and *pathos*, and sometimes how the argument exemplifies *kairos*; and 6. the argument's genre.

The 8th edition of the IM does have some additions, however. It provides a new sample syllabus, "Emphasis on Rhetorical Analysis, Research as Discovery, and Civic Argumentation" (pages 35-40). And the IM provides nine sample writing assignments (pages 41-62). Some of those assignments connect directly to the fourth sample syllabus, but others could be modified and used in any composition course focused on argumentation and research.

I hope the manual offers substantial assistance and suggestions that help instructors and students explore the intricacies of argument.

Acknowledgements
I am grateful to June Johnson and John Bean for giving me the opportunity to revise the *Instructor's Manual* for *Writing Arguments*. Also, I would like to thank my family—Diana, Hannah, and Quinn—for keeping me grounded and being supportive during my hectic writing schedule and professional obligations.

Tim N. Taylor
Eastern Illinois University

Copyright © 2010, Pearson Education, Inc., Publishing as Longman

I. GENERAL ISSUES IN USING THIS TEXT

THE GOALS AND PHILOSOPHY OF *WRITING ARGUMENTS*

The goal of *Writing Arguments* is to equip students to write arguments that are fully developed, rhetorically situated, and critically thoughtful. The philosophy underlying the textbook posits that argument is both a product and a process—an activity more complex and productive than the conventional view of argument as pro-con debate. In this view, argument is not a way of rationalizing claims to which writers are committed before the arguing occurs. Rather, the authors see argument as a process of exploring various points of view in order to arrive gradually at the best conclusions. In sum, the act of writing and the act of arguing are part of a journey toward conclusions that often can't be foreseen.

The model for the arguing process, as explained in Chapter 1, is a well-functioning committee charged with solving a problem. The classroom equivalent of the well-functioning committee is the collaborative group. *Writing Arguments'* numerous "For Class Discussion" exercises provide opportunities for productive group work that encourages students to see arguments as contributions to a dynamic social conversation about an issue that matters, in contrast to perceiving argument as an unproductive, heated verbal battle.

The last few editions of *Writing Arguments* have provided a greater emphasis on the rhetorical situation, genre, and the social dimension of argument. The text directs students' attention to the forum in which an argument first appears, asking students to think about the limits and purposes of genre, the political orientation of magazines and journals, the writer's occasion and goal, and the values of the intended audience. It's important for instructors to encourage students to think of themselves as members of various rhetorical communities (for example, dormitories or apartments, classrooms, university organizations, religious groups, workplaces, civic organizations) and to see how the occasion for argument grows out of their lives in these communities—their desire to make a difference on an issue that divides or troubles the community. The text teaches students to contextualize their arguments, to see themselves as agents of change and their audiences as decision-makers or mediators who need to be persuaded to revise their views and possibly to act.

In addition, students need to consider the constraints on audiences that prevent change or block action. The text's emphasis on audience and rhetorical situation will lead to a dynamic, dialectical understanding of the social role of argument. (To further explore the authors' value of constraints against action, see Lloyd F. Bitzer's article "The Rhetorical Situation," *Philosophy and Rhetoric* 1.1 [1968]: 1–14. Print.; see also James Crosswhite's emphasis on claims and questioning claims and on argument as social conflict and social criticism in *The Rhetoric of Reason: Writing and the Attractions of Argument.* Madison, Wisconsin: U of Wisconsin P, 1996. Print.)

Copyright © 2010, Pearson Education, Inc., Publishing as Longman

A RATIONALE FOR THE STRUCTURE OF THIS TEXT

A Note on Different Editions

This *Instructor's Manual* provides guidance for anyone using the concise, brief, or comprehensive edition of *Writing Arguments*, 8th edition. However, all page numbers referenced in the IM refer to pages in the brief edition, *Writing Arguments: A Rhetoric with Readings*. Regardless, instructors using the comprehensive or concise editions should also find the IM useful. The structure of the brief textbook is divided into five main parts, while the brief edition has Sections I-IV with appendices, and the concise edition has Sections I-III with appendices. What follows is a detailed description of the six sections from the comprehensive text.

Part One: "Overview of Argument"

Part One, combined with Part Two, forms a self-contained mini-text suitable for an introductory course in argument. Indeed, some teachers will choose to emphasize just these two parts for a freshman course, especially if the course is offered on the quarter system.

Part One (Chapters 1–2) is introductory. These chapters present the notion of argument as a process of clarification and inquiry—persuasion and truth seeking. Chapter 2 treats reading as an active meaning-making activity drawing on students' capacity to probe issues more deeply through believing and doubting. Particularly, the chapter teaches students how to write summaries as a means of "listening" to arguments and how to raise questions about facts and values as a means of maintaining critical distance. The chapter also shows students how understanding an argument's genre helps contextualize the argument and how identifying disagreements among sources can become a productive first step toward investigating an issue and joining the argumentative conversation themselves. In preparation for writing their own arguments, Chapter 2 asks students to consider who writes arguments, what their specific purposes may be, and for whom they are writing. Like writers who present their arguments in media and in political, business, academic, and regional contexts, student writers need to discover their own occasions for argument, their investment in issues, and their consciousness of the stakes involved.

Part Two: "Writing an Argument"

Part Two examines the principles of argument. Chapters 3–7 show that the core of an argument is a claim with reasons. These reasons are often stated as enthymemes, the unstated premise of which must sometimes be brought to the surface and supported. Discussion of Toulmin logical classifications shows students how to discover both the stated and unstated premises of their arguments and to provide structures of reasons and evidence to support them. Instructors can help students grapple with Toulmin schemes for arguments to help them shape argument frames with audience-based reasons that connect with specific audiences. Chapters 4 and 5 explain kinds of evidence and the importance of using evidence rhetorically, framing it to reach specific audiences. Chapters 6 and 7 continue the emphasis on rhetorical context, focusing on the writer's relationship with an audience, on using appeals to *ethos* and *pathos* effectively and responsibly while understanding the important ancient concept of *kairos*, and on accommodating or refuting opposing views. Chapters 6 and 7 also introduce students to a repertoire of arguing strategies,

Copyright © 2010, Pearson Education, Inc., Publishing as Longman

discussing the power of visual elements and importance and applicability of "dialogic argument," drawing from delayed thesis and Rogerian foundations to show the varieties of argument that strive for conciliation.

The writing assignments following Parts One and Two provide a coherent sequence of tasks that build argumentative skills sequentially. A first-year course could be built entirely on these tasks.

Part Three: "Analyzing Arguments"
Part Three focuses on the rhetorical analysis of arguments. Chapter 8 provides a substantial treatment of the act of reading verbal arguments rhetorically. Chapter 9 probes visual elements in depth, concentrating on helping students analyze visual rhetoric, create visual arguments, and incorporate images and graphics into their arguments.

Part Four: "Arguments in Depth: Five Types of Claims"
Part Four treats five types of claims or *stases* of argument: categorical or definitional; causal; resemblance; evaluation or ethical; and proposal claims.

The claim type or stasis approach employed in Part Four introduces students to three different kinds of argumentative "moves" or thinking strategies that recur in various combinations in almost all arguments: (1) a criteria-match strategy in which the writer establishes criteria for defining or evaluating a given class Y and then argues that a specific X meets or does not meet the criteria; (2) a causal strategy in which the writer argues that X leads to Y; (3) and a resemblance strategy in which the writer argues through analogy or precedent that X is like Y. (For a more developed justification of the stasis approach, see Fahnestock, Jeanne and Marie Secor, "Teaching Argument: A Theory of Types," *CCC*, 34 [February 1983], 20–30. Print. See also Sharon Crowley and Debra Hawhee, *Ancient Rhetorics for Contemporary Students*, 4th ed. Boston: Allyn and Bacon, 2009. Print.)

Chapter 10 introduces students with the idea of claim types as a way for arguers to determine where their most fundamental point of disagreement with their audience lies while also noting, in detail, that arguments rarely exemplify a single stasis. Rather, the section guides students to see that most arguments illustrate a hybrid of different types of claims for the purpose of truth-seeking and persuasion. Nevertheless, nurturing the ability to ascertain points of disagreement among arguers will help students build the best argument for their own rhetorical situations. The study of these stases will also help them generate strong supporting material because each type of claim calls for a characteristic pattern of support, and learning these patterns of development for the different types of claims can become a powerful generative tool. Students then look at each type of claim in more depth throughout Part Four.

The chief strength of a stasis approach is its heuristic power and its systematic development of thinking and arguing skills. Its potential weakness is that students might begin to expect all arguments to fit neatly into one of the stases, which is why the section "Hybrid Arguments: How Claim Types Work Together in Arguments" is essential for showing that most arguments are a composite of claim types. To further obviate the challenge of students wanting arguments to fit a certain mode of argumentation, the text treats the claim types more as means of invention and exploration rather than as means of classification (see Frank D'Angelo's discussion of the

Copyright © 2010, Pearson Education, Inc., Publishing as Longman

connection between rhetorical forms and conceptual structures of cognition in *A Conceptual Theory of Rhetoric*, Cambridge, Mass.: Winthrop, 1975. Print.). However, it is also important to introduce students to how claim types usually work together in arguments—a causal reason supporting a proposal claim, an evaluation supported by causal arguing and resemblance claims, for instance—to show student-writers how many arguments exemplify hybrids of claim types. Writing assignments are integrated into each of the five claim-type chapters in Part Four (Chapters 11–15), and each assignment offers a variety of options for selecting an issue question that can be developed through the type of claim under discussion.

Part Five: "The Researched Argument"
Part Five examines researched arguments, teaching students to think of research rhetorically. Chapter 16 teaches students how to use their own research questions to guide their research with the idea that they will enlist evidence from sources in their own arguments to support contestable claims. Finding and processing this information, however, begins with learning how to use a library and the Internet, particularly how to unlock the vast wealth of information that these resources contain and that writers of argument often need. Chapter 16 encourages students to think rhetorically about the sources they use—to consider the differences in content and reliability of information found through restricted, licensed databases and through the free access parts of the Internet, the World Wide Web. The chapter explains to students how to evaluate Web sources. Chapter 17 focuses on using, integrating, and documenting sources effectively and ethically. It covers all the conventional material about citations, documentation, plagiarism, and so forth, but it also focuses on *how* to use sources. It shows, for example, how two writers might summarize the same article in different ways to meet the rhetorical demands of different issue questions or different claims.

For courses that end with a major researched argument, a term project that grows out of Option 4 in "Writing Assignments for Chapters 1–3" (71-2) is a good reference point for designing a large assignment. This option asks students to identify an issue of interest to them on which they are currently puzzled and undecided. The research project requires them to research the issue, weigh all sides, take a stand, and write a major argument supporting their position.

Appendixes
The text has two appendixes. The first treats informal logical fallacies and can be introduced at any stage in the course. The second discusses collaborative learning, including various strategies for working effectively in groups. It concludes with several group tasks: how to conduct a class "norming session" on arguments and how to conduct a classroom debate. This appendix could be introduced in conjunction with Chapter 3 at the point where students are encouraged to talk about their ideas in small groups as one strategy for improving their writing processes.

Part Six: "An Anthology of Arguments"
Part Six provides a selection of professional arguments covering twelve topic areas. In selecting the readings in these topic areas, the text's aim is to offer a wide spectrum of views and a wide variety of genres of argument. These readings illustrate some of the subtlety and complexity of real-world arguments, and they also demonstrate one of the main points of the text: argument as a multi-sided conversation rather than pro-con debate. Additionally, throughout the rhetoric section of the text there are several dozen arguments—both student and professional—that

Copyright © 2010, Pearson Education, Inc., Publishing as Longman

illustrate the strategies under discussion. Several of the topics raised in the rhetoric chapters are amplified in the readings in the anthology—online activity, video games, immigration, women and science, sustainability, and biotech agriculture are all issues that appear in readings throughout the rhetoric.

This *Instructor's Manual*—in the sample syllabi and at the ends of the chapter guides—provides numerous suggestions of how to incorporate these readings into an argument course; however, teachers will make different uses of these readings. Those who devote the majority of class time to student writing and the sharing of drafts might have only limited time for discussing readings. Such teachers might choose to use Part Six sparingly since they base their courses primarily on student writing rather than on reading and analysis of arguments.

Other teachers might use the anthology extensively. There are several ways to do so. The readings can be used to teach the process of reading arguments as discussed in Chapter 2. Analyzing why arguers disagree with one another—through disagreement about facts and values and assumptions—is solid training in critical thinking and sophisticated reading. And this activity also expands students' perspectives on the world around them and argumentation in general.

Additionally, the readings can be used as sample arguments for close analysis. Following the strategies discussed throughout the text, students can examine the organization of the arguments, the rhetorical strategies or stases employed, the effectiveness of the argument's *logos*, the author's creation of *ethos* and *pathos*, consideration of *kairos,* enthymemes and warrants, and the integrity of its evidence in response to Richard Fulkerson's analytical tool of STAR (Sufficiency, Typicality, Accuracy, and Relevance). To aid instructors using this approach, the *Instructor's Manual* includes comprehensive analyses of all the readings.

For those instructors looking for arguments that represent the different claim types, at the end of each claim-type chapter, the *Instructor's Manual* provides a number of suggested arguments in the anthology that employ the stasis under consideration, either as the major claim or as one of the chief supporting lines of argument.

One fruitful strategy for having students grapple with readings in any section of the text is to use the "Guide Questions for the Analysis and Evaluation of Arguments (pages 425-27). The Guide Questions provides three lists that cater to how an instructor is working with argumentatively rich texts. List 1, "Questions for Analyzing and Evaluating a Conversation," guides readers to examine the argumentative conversation among sources. List 2, "Questions for Analyzing and Evaluating an Individual Argument Rhetorically," helps students break down individual arguments. And List 3, "Questions for Responding to Reading and Forming Your Own Views," leads students to compose their own arguments based on reading material.

Copyright © 2010, Pearson Education, Inc., Publishing as Longman

DESCRIPTION OF WRITING ASSIGNMENTS IN THE TEXT

The text provides many options for writing assignments, enabling instructors to create assignment sequences suitable to their needs and purposes. A summary of these assignments will help instructors get a quick overview of the available options.

Writing Assignments for Part One (Chapters 1—2) (50-51)

Any one of these assignments provides a good initial writing task for the course. The assignments, which assume no knowledge of the text beyond Chapter 2, will enable instructors to assess their students' skills. The assignment options include the following:

Option 1: An argument summary
Option 2: A formal exploratory essay examining your thinking about an issue or a problem while incorporating various sources of disagreement within the argument or issue

Exploratory Tasks in Chapter 2

Exploratory Tasks—Set 1: Finding Issues to Explore (25-26, 29-30)

This set of exploratory tasks helps students develop ideas for argument essays. Using brainstorming, freewriting, and idea-mapping, students create a fund of ideas from which they can draw as the course progresses.

Exploratory Tasks—Set 2: The Believing and Doubting Games (30-31)

Using this analytical reading tactic espoused by Peter Elbow, students can fully inhabit views they may not be accustomed to inhabiting. Using this strategy for approaching important arguments, writers can create summaries that provide the overall focus of articles and arguments.

Exploratory Tasks—Set 3: Thinking Dialectically (45-46)

These questions provided help students explore an issue from two perspectives. These questions make students consider what creates disagreement, whether it stems from analysis of data/facts, assumptions, values, belief, or dogma.

Writing Assignments for Part Two (Chapters 3–7)

These assignments can be used as introductory exercises to help students develop skills working with evidence that they will need for longer arguments and to give students their first opportunity in the course to construct a whole argument. The microtheme, supporting reasons argument, classical argument, and the dialogic argument can be used as a formal assignment, giving students an opportunity to think about audience-based reasons, framing their evidence, and responding to alternative views. The shorter assignments can be evaluated as part of participation or count similar to a journal-like writing assignment. The options for writing assignments provided within the text are as follows:

Chapter 3: An issue question and a working thesis statement (71-72)
Chapter 4: A plan of an argument's details based on a working thesis statement (87-88)

Copyright © 2010, Pearson Education, Inc., Publishing as Longman

Chapter 5: A microtheme or a supporting-reasons argument (104-05)
Chapter 6: A revision based on revising for *ethos*, *pathos*, and audience-based reasons (123)
Chapter 7: A classical argument or a dialogic argument aimed at conciliation (140)

Writing Assignments for Part Three (Chapters 8–9)

Assignment for Chapters 8 and 9

To give students practice at strong analytical reading and see arguments rhetorically, Chapter 8 provides an assignment that works in rhetorical criticism—the Rhetorical Analysis essay. Writers analyze an argument and provide their own evaluations on the cogency and effectiveness of the arguments. Likewise, in Chapter 9, the text provides these opportunities for analysis and argumentation:

Chapter 8: A rhetorical analysis (158-59)
Chapter 9, Option 1: A rhetorical analysis of a visual argument (198)
Chapter 9, Option 2: A poster argument (198)
Chapter 9, Option 3: A microtheme using a quantitative graphic (198)

Writing Assignments for Part Four (Chapters 11–15)

Chapters 11–15 in Part Four each include a writing assignment with accompanying discovery and exploration exercises. The assignments are closely integrated into the content of the chapters so that assigning the writing tasks for each chapter will ensure close reading and study of the text.

Assignment for Chapter 11, "A Definitional Argument" (225-28)

In this chapter, students are introduced to categorical arguments that place some thing or event or person in a certain class: for example, does skateboarding qualify as a "true sport"? Or: is time management a major problem for college students? The chapter's assignment asks them to use the criteria-match strategy to define a controversial concept such as "cruelty to animals," "true athlete," or "act of courage" and then to argue whether or not a borderline case meets the criteria.

Assignment for Chapter 12, "A Causal Argument" (249-53)

Students are asked to create an argument identifying "surprising" or "disputed" causes or consequences of a phenomenon.

Assignment for Chapter 13, "A Resemblance Argument" (271-73)

Students are asked to write a letter to the editor in which they try to influence public opinion on some issue through the use of a persuasive analogy or precedent.

Assignment for Chapter 14, "An Evaluation or Ethical Argument" (296-300)

Using a controversial or surprising issue or problem or phenomenon, students are asked to develop an evaluation argument while contending with alternative and hostile views to your argument.

Copyright © 2010, Pearson Education, Inc., Publishing as Longman

Assignment for Chapter 15, "A Proposal Argument" (323-27)

Students are asked to identify a problem, propose a solution, and argue persuasively that the proposal should be adopted. Students are offered several choices of proposal arguments:

Option 1: A practical proposal addressing a local problem (323-24)
Option 2: A policy proposal as a guest editorial (324)
Option 3: A researched argument proposing public policy (324)
Option 4: A one-page advocacy advertisement (324)

Writing Assignments in Part Six (Anthology of Arguments)

The "Optional Writing Assignments" in Part Six at the end of each of the anthology units are assignments designed to engage students in the issues under dispute in the readings. Alternatively, instructors could ask students to write rhetorical analysis arguments following the guidelines explained in Chapter 8.

Instructors will undoubtedly think of many other ways to create writing assignments in response to the readings.

The pages following the sample syllabi in the *Instructors' Manual* also provide eight sample writing assignments that can be adapted, modified, and used by instructors: I-Search Essay, Web Site Evaluation Essay, Rhetorical Analysis Essay, Synthesis Essay, Arguing about Images, Position Essay with Prospectus, Proposal with Prospectus, and a Recommendation Report Case.

These assignments are to serve as examples for instructors to create their own writing prompts.

Copyright © 2010, Pearson Education, Inc., Publishing as Longman

II. DESIGNING YOUR COURSE

AN OVERVIEW OF COURSE DESIGNS

The text's organization makes it relatively easy to design a course syllabus. Before doing so, however, an instructor needs to make preliminary decisions about the particular objectives of the course, about the number and kinds of writing assignments to include, about use of class time, and about the amount of textbook material to cover.

Creating a course in writing arguments is a challenging, individualized project. To design your course, you need to make decisions on a number of key points, rather like ordering coffee at an upscale coffee bar. A customer might say, "I want a double tall, decaf, nonfat latte, no foam." Instructors have similar freedom in designing an argument course. You can design a high Toulmin, low Toulmin, or even non-Toulmin course; you can go heavy on claim types or light on claim types; you can include lots of writing process time in your course, or you can devote class hours to analyzing readings. One of the great benefits of using *Writing Arguments* is that instructors will find it comprehensive yet flexible and adaptable to individual and institutional objectives. Thus the three sample syllabi that follow all show different kinds of emphases. This *Instructor's Manual* will help you tailor a course to your needs.

KEY DECISIONS

Before offering syllabi for several different argument courses, there are many large decisions that instructors must make at the level of course design. The following points are the five big decisions that face instructors as they design their argument courses:

- Approach to argumentation: Which of the following approaches will the course target, emphasize, and/or combine: the enthymeme as a rhetorical and logical structure; the classical appeals to *logos*, *ethos*, and *pathos*; the Toulmin system; and stasis theory?
- Subject matter for writing assignments: Will students choose their own issues or will the whole class write about the same issues? Will topics grow out of local issues (personal/school/workplace) or national/global issues?
- Choice and use of readings: Will this course devote considerable class time to the discussion of readings? Will readings be used as material for rhetorical analysis of arguments and/or as models of argumentative strategies and types? Or will the focus be primarily on content so that a set of readings introduces students to various perspectives on a controversial issue? In the latter case, will students be asked to write their own arguments on the issue, thereby joining the controversial conversation?
- Inclusion of writing process time: How much time should be built into the course for generating ideas for arguments, for writing drafts, for peer reviewing, and for revising and editing?
- Principle of sequencing assignments: Will assignments be sequenced from short to long, from simple to complex? Will assignments vary by claim type (definition, cause, proposal, and so forth), by topic/readings (Responses to Terrorism, Steroids, the Media), or by audience/genre (classical argument for neutral audience, delayed thesis argument for a hostile audience, letter to the editor, op-ed piece, white paper), or by kinds of

Copyright © 2010, Pearson Education, Inc., Publishing as Longman

evidence (argument based on personal experience, argument based on a few research sources, major researched argument)?

A strong course in argument can be constructed from any of these choices, and *Writing Arguments* can be used effectively with a wide variety of course designs. What follows are three possible course syllabi, each developed for a writing course with a different emphasis. Each syllabus includes more class activities and small assignments than most instructors can cover in one course (including some additional lessons applying and extending the concepts in the main text), but the idea is to give instructors a full menu from which to design their individual courses.

Copyright © 2010, Pearson Education, Inc., Publishing as Longman

SAMPLE SYLLABUS #1: GENERIC EMPHASIS ON SKILLS AND STRATEGIES

Course Design Decisions

- This course emphasizes the enthymeme, *logos*, *ethos*, and *pathos*. It downplays Toulmin and includes a minimalist use of stasis theory.
- Students choose their own topics for their arguments.
- This course uses readings as content for rhetorical analysis and as models of argument types.
- Writing process time is built into the course: for invention exercises, for peer reviews, and for revision exercises.
- This course takes a skill-building approach that sequences assignments from simple to complex as students enlarge their repertoire of argumentative moves, directing their arguments toward more resistant audiences and working with different types of claims.

Scope of the Course

This course is intended to give students a comprehensive introduction to argument. It emphasizes the enthymeme and *logos*, *ethos*, and *pathos*. It touches on the Toulmin approach only to pick up the idea of assumptions (warrants) that connect reasons to claims, pointing out to arguers that they may need to address and support these assumptions directly in their arguments. Although it does not focus on stasis theory, it does give students practice with writing arguments using several different claim types: definitional arguments or evaluation arguments and proposal arguments. This course emphasizes building students' reading, critical thinking, and writing skills sequentially before plunging them into the production of long pieces of writing. It can entail weekly short or informal writing assignments. It involves ***seven*** formal writing assignments, one of them a visual argument, and includes the idea that students will be engaged in ongoing revision of their essays. Intended for a sixteen-week course, this syllabus may be adjusted for a quarter-length course by eliminating or modifying the two-week unit on visual argument and eliminating the two-week unit on criteria-match strategy, definitional arguments, and evaluation arguments. This course interweaves groups of readings from the anthology for rhetorical analysis and for models of complex argumentative conversations; however, instructors can also include their own selection of readings either from the anthology or from their own regional newspapers and from the magazines and journals they find most helpful.

Formal Writing Assignments

1. Exploratory essay analyzing the sources of disagreement on the same issue
   3 pages (Chapter 2, page 50-51)
2. Classical argument based on a claim and evidence drawn from personal experience
   3–5 pages (Writing Assignment, Chapter 7, page 140)
3. Dialogic Argument addressing a resistant audience
   3–5 pages (Writing Assignment, Chapters 7, page 140)
4. Poster argument
   1 page (Writing Assignment, Chapter 9, page 198)
5. Definitional argument or an evaluation argument, defending both the criteria and the match
   4–5 pages (Writing Assignment, Chapter 11, pages 225-28, or
   Writing Assignment, Chapter 14, pages 296-300)
6. Policy proposal as a guest editorial
   2–4 pages (Writing Assignment, Chapter 15, page 324)
7. Researched policy proposal
   5–7 pages (Writing Assignment, Chapter 15, page 324)

Copyright © 2010, Pearson Education, Inc., Publishing as Longman

Week 1: Introduction to Argument as Process and Product

Objectives

- To help students understand that an argument must begin with an issue question and must have as its core a claim with reasons
- To help students begin to see argument as a process of clarification and inquiry—searching for the best solutions to problems
- To help students recognize issue questions
- To help students formulate ***because*** clauses to support a claim

Readings

- Chapters 1, 3, and 4

Formal Writing Assignment

No formal writing assignment this week

Class Activities

- Group and class discussions of the students' analysis of implicit arguments (Chapter 1)
- Group discussion of Gordon Adam's petition; freewrite after group's discussion; class discussion (Chapter 1)
- Class discussion distinguishing issue questions from information questions and genuine arguments from pseudo-arguments (Chapter 3)
- Group or pairs work generating ***because*** clauses for students' claims (Chapter 4)

Possible Short or Informal Writing Assignments

- A short analysis of an implicit argument in an advertisement, a billboard, or a poem: What is the main claim? What reasons and evidence are present to support the claim?
- A response to Gordon Adams, accepting or rejecting his petition

Week 2: Strategies for Reading Arguments as a Bridge to Writing Arguments

Objectives

- To help students improve their ability to comprehend and interact with difficult reading material
- To help students listen to alternative viewpoints and expand their thinking by learning to summarize, agree with, and question arguments they read
- To help students recognize how genre shapes expectations about the form, depth, and complexity of arguments
- To help students cope with ambiguity and disagreement by identifying the points of disagreement as differences in interpretations of facts, values, or uses of analogies
- To help students explore these differences as a step toward asking their own questions about an issue

Readings

- Chapter 2 and 8
- Possible anthology articles to evaluate for disagreements in interpretations of facts, values, and assumptions are listed in this *Instructor's Manual* at the end of Chapter Guide 2; this list provides pairs of articles that talk to each other and conflict over facts and values. The diverse units in Part Six of the text encompass particularly rich, multi-sided argumentative conversations.

Formal Writing Assignment

Exploratory essay analyzing the sources of disagreement on the same issue (Chapter 2, pages Writing Assignment, page 50-51)

Class Activities

- Group and class discussion of the articles assigned; discussion of the articles' framing of the issue, interpretation of facts, and values and assumptions
- Discussion of summary writing and possible peer reviewing of students' own summaries
- Peer reviewing of students' essays on sources of disagreement

Copyright © 2010, Pearson Education, Inc., Publishing as Longman

Possible Short or Informal Writing Assignments

- Believing and doubting, using assertions related to the anthology essays or supplied by the instructor
- A 250-word summary of one article

Week 3: Helping Students Become Engaged Arguers

Objectives

- To equip students with a whole repertoire of strategies for generating claims that they will want to argue
- To help students think in terms of mustering the most effective evidence for their claims and reasons
- To help students apply the STAR criteria (Sufficiency, Typicality, Accuracy, and Relevance) to the evidence they use to support their claims
- To help students understand the concept of angle of vision as the values, beliefs, and perspectives filtering writers' uses of evidence
- To help students use evidence rhetorically by employing various ways to frame their evidence to guide their audience's response

Readings

- Chapters 2, 3, 4, and 5
- Numerous articles in the anthology are notable for their use of evidence. In this *Instructor's Manual*, the end of Chapter Guide 5 lists articles that use evidence effectively and other articles that clearly illustrate how writers' angles of vision dominate their selection and presentation of evidence.

Formal Writing Assignment

No formal writing assignment

Class Activities

- Group work on generating ***because*** clauses and brainstorming for a network of related issues
- Group work to help students use one another as questioning audiences
- Class discussion of the exercises in Chapter 5 asking students to examine the rhetorical effect of different presentations of data and to explore the idea of framing evidence
- Group and then class discussion on the effective use of evidence in various articles
- Group and class discussion of the student essay "'Half-Criminals or Urban Athletes? A Plea for Fair Treatment of Skateboarders" by David Langley (pages 141-43); students could examine this student writer's use of evidence and his personal investment in his claim. (See this *Instructor's Manual*, Chapter Guide 7, for discussion questions on this student essay.)

Possible Short or Informal Writing Assignments

- Responses to the exploratory tasks in Chapter 2; students could bring in university or college newspapers or regional newspapers to examine for issue questions of relevance to them
- An issue question and a working thesis statement (Writing Assignment, Chapter 3, pages 71-72) and/or A plan of an argument's details based on a working thesis statement (Writing Assignment, Chapter 4, pages 87-88)
- A microtheme (Writing Assignment, Chapter 5, pages 104-05)

Week 4: Constructing Whole Arguments

Objectives

- To help students move from analyzing arguments to writing their own arguments
- To help students understand the importance of thinking out the assumptions that their audience must accept in order to find their reasons persuasive
- To help students apply the concept that arguments are intensely rhetorical in that they grow out of specific occasions and are tailored to the needs, interests, and values of specific audiences

Copyright © 2010, Pearson Education, Inc., Publishing as Longman

- To help students analyze their audience, find audience-based reasons, and find strategies to build bridges to reach their audience
- To help students recognize the features of a strong argument

Readings

- Chapter 5 and Appendix 2
- A selected anthology unit

Formal Writing Assignment

Classical argument based on a claim and evidence drawn from personal experience (essay using experiential knowledge of a university/college issue, workplace issue, community issue; Writing Assignment, Chapter 7, page 140)

Class Activities

- Class work on the logical structure of argument with an emphasis on assumptions held by the audience; an introduction to Toulmin that mainly looks at enthymemes and then warrants as the assumptions that may or may not need to be explicitly supported in an argument
- Class work on finding audience-based reasons for students' claims
- Class work on selecting evidence for their arguments that meets the STAR criteria
- Class work on framing evidence rhetorically to shape a specific audience's response
- Group and then class discussion of the five essays in Appendix 2; group generation of criteria for strong arguments as a preparation for students writing their own arguments
- Work in groups or pairs responding to each other's classical arguments, perhaps as structured peer reviews

[Note: Although neither this classical argument assignment nor the next formal writing assignment is intended to become a researched argument, students often ask if they can consult a few sources to give authority to their evidence. Instructors might accept a small amount of research in specific cases, provided that this information truly deepens and enriches the argument (and is not merely superficial and extraneous) and that students document their sources accurately according to the conventions explained in Chapter 17: Using, Citing, and Documenting Sources.]

Weeks 5–6: Introduction to the Importance of Strong Appeals to Logos, Ethos, and Pathos in Reaching Audiences

Objectives

- To help students focus on the rhetorical situation of arguments by thinking about appeals to *ethos* and *pathos* as different ways to relate to audiences and to enhance the logical dimension of their arguments
- To give students practice with using concrete language, specific examples and illustration, narratives, and visual elements to involve their audiences
- To help students understand both the power and risk of metaphoric and connotative language
- To help students understand the uses of one-sided versus multi-sided arguments
- To give students practice with a variety of strategies for connecting with different kinds of resistant audiences, including knowing how to summarize opposing arguments fairly, when to concede points, and how to refute opposing positions
- To help students understand their options in terms of delaying their main claim or using Rogerian structure or possibly humor

Readings

- Chapters 6 and 7
- A number of articles in the anthology have effective, strong, or intriguing and problematic appeals to *ethos* and *pathos*. In this *Instructor's Manual*, see the section at the end of Chapter Guide 6 for suggestions (110-12) of particularly good articles to analyze.
- The end of Chapter Guide 7 lists articles that are particularly worth examining for their treatment of alternative views.

Copyright © 2010, Pearson Education, Inc., Publishing as Longman

Formal Writing Assignment

Dialogic Argument addressing a resistant audience (Writing Assignment, Chapters 7, page 140)

Class Activities

- Class and group work examining specific articles with a close look at the ways writers relate to their audiences and at successful and unsuccessful appeals to ethos and pathos
- Class and group work on visual arguments, particularly newspaper and magazine photos as a means to influence readers' responses to news events or contentious issues in the anthology unit, (see list of Visual Arguments, pages 126-28 in the IM) could provide material for a provocative discussion of the rhetorical effect of visual media.
- Class work on fair and unfair summaries
- Class could look at several short pieces employing humor to get an argument across

Possible Short or Informal Writing Assignments

- In preparation for the dialogic argument addressed to a resistant audience, students can do the audience analysis (Chapter 6, pages 119-20)
- Revision of arguments written earlier in the course (Writing Assignment, Chapter 6, page 123)

Weeks 7–8: Examining Visual Rhetoric and Creating Poster Arguments

[Note: For shorter courses, instructors may want to omit this two-week teaching unit and the poster argument assignment and instead do a few of the class activities within other teaching units throughout the course.]

Objectives

- To help students understand how visual and verbal elements can work together to produce rhetorical effects: supporting the logical core of an argument, enhancing the writer's credibility and authority, and stirring audiences' emotions and imagination
- To help students analyze and use the elements of visual design—type, layout, color, and image
- To help students think about displays of numerical data for rhetorical effect
- To help students understand that visual arguments, like all arguments, are products of specific historical, social, and cultural moments
- To help students apply their knowledge of arguments to analyzing and creating visual arguments

Readings

- Chapter 9
- In this *Instructor's Manual*, the end of the Chapter Guide 9 lists all the visual arguments in the anthology.
- The opening pages of the six major parts of this text include visual arguments: political cartoons, a poster argument, a historical photograph, and an advocacy ad.

Formal Writing Assignment

Poster argument (Writing Assignment, Chapter 9, page 198)

Class Activities

- Group or class work with the For Class Discussion exercises in Chapter 9.
- In groups, students could brainstorm for ideas for their poster arguments. Some suggestions are issues concerning university clubs or organizations, courses, programs, living accommodations; the availability of technology or food on campus; internships; volunteer work; and community problems or job problems.
- Students could bring newspaper or magazine articles that include graphic displays of numerical data to class and discuss how clear and useful these graphics are.
- Group or class work (perhaps as presentations) analyzing and contrasting ads for the military or "green" products that students find in a range of magazines. Students could look specifically at the ads' target audiences, their dominant impressions or appeals, the validity of their claims, the use of *logos*, *pathos*, and *ethos*. Students could analyze how these ads use visual elements and text to create visual arguments.
- Group or class work examining the effectiveness of visual arguments on different historical issues

Copyright © 2010, Pearson Education, Inc., Publishing as Longman

using section "Discussion Exercise Analyzing Visual Argument in American History" in this *Instructor's Manual* (92-94). This section offers ideas for instructor-led discussions and options for student presentations.

- There are many political cartoons in the text and anthology (refer to page 126-28 of the IM). Individually or in groups, students could examine these cartoons, develop criteria for effective political cartoons, and rate these cartoons according to how well they meet the criteria. Students could also bring political cartoons that they found particularly successful to class for discussion.
- Students could share the drafts of their poster arguments in peer review groups for audience feedback. Section "VIII. Samples of Student Writing for Discussion" includes student examples of drafts and revisions of poster arguments with For Class Discussion questions on them.

Possible Short or Informal Writing Assignments

- Any of the ideas for class activities can become class presentations or short written assignments; students could write a short analysis of an ad, an advocacy ad, a political cartoon, or a historical poster argument.

Weeks 9–11: Learning More Argumentative Moves and Using Criteria-Match Strategy in Definitional Arguments and Evaluation Arguments

[Note: Instructors can expand or reduce this unit of material by choosing to cover definitional arguments, and evaluation and ethical arguments, all of which use criteria-match strategy, or by focusing on just one of these claim types.]

Objectives

- To help students recognize different claim-type questions and the characteristic pattern of support for each claim type
- To help students understand the pattern of development for simple categorical arguments
- To help students understand criteria-match strategy
- To help students understand different kinds of definitions (Aristotelian and operational) and different approaches to generating definitional criteria (reportive and stipulative, and use of contrastive and borderline cases)
- To help students write definitional arguments that support both the criteria and the match
- To help students produce evaluation arguments by specifying the category that their X belongs to and by developing and weighing criteria for that category and its function
- To help students understand how to conduct principle-based and consequence-based ethical evaluations
- To help students construct evaluation arguments that support both the criteria and the match

Readings

- Chapters 10, 11 and/or 14
- In this *Instructor's Manual*, Chapter Guide 11 includes a list of anthology arguments with definitional claims. The following units have issues that foster definitional arguments: "Web 2.0 and Online Identity" and "Immigration in the Twentieth Century"
- Chapter Guide 14 lists specific articles in the anthology that have prominent evaluation claims. The network of issues in the following units tend to take the form of evaluation and ethical evaluation claims: "Video Games and Their Influence"; "The News Media: Responsible Production, Responsible Consumption"; "Women in Math and Science"; "Wal-Mart and the Public Good"; "Biotech Agriculture and the Ethics of Food Production."

Formal Writing Assignment

Definitional argument (or an evaluation or ethical argument) defending both the criteria and the match (Writing Assignment, Chapter 11, pages 25-28 or Writing Assignment, Chapter 14, pages 296-300)

Copyright © 2010, Pearson Education, Inc., Publishing as Longman

Class Activities

- Class work on different claim types in Chapter 10
- Collaborative writing in pairs, creating a simple categorical argument using exemplification to develop a claim
- Group and class work with the exercise "Using the Definitional Heuristic" in Chapter Guide 11
- Group and class work examining articles in the anthology as definitional arguments; a good place to start is with the student essay on obscenity and public art (Chapter 11, pages 134-35).
- Group and class work examining evaluation arguments, considering what criteria are implicitly or explicitly offered; a good place to start is with the student essay on women hip-hop artists (Chapter 14, pages 304-06)
- Peer reviewing of the students' simple categorical arguments, definitional arguments, and/or evaluation arguments leading to revisions
- This might be a good time in the course to show a short film that the class could then evaluate according to criteria that the students originate; classic films (old comedies, mysteries, westerns), art films, or documentaries are good material and tend to be shorter than contemporary feature films; another possibility is several episodes of a television series.

Possible Short or Informal Writing Assignments

- Collaborative work on constructing a frame for a definitional argument using contrastive and borderline cases to refine the criteria
- Revision of arguments written earlier in the course

Weeks 12–13: Writing Policy Proposal Arguments

Objectives

- To help students understand how to write policy proposals
- To give students practice with the "stock-issues strategy"
- To give students practice with using arguments of category, consequence, and resemblance to support a proposal argument
- To help students give presence to the problem they are seeking to solve
- To help students think about and weigh alternative solutions
- To help students develop research skills using library and Internet resources
- To help students use conventional documentation

Readings

- Chapters 15, 16, and 17
- In civic life, many arguments focus on social issues that need public attention and offer proposals to solve these real-world problems. These arguments are conducted across multiple argument genres, including, often, editorials. Chapter Guide 15 lists numerous articles that argue proposal claims.
- For an explanation of genres of argument and how genre shapes the form and content of arguments, students might consult Chapter 2, pages 32–35.

Formal Writing Assignment

Policy proposal as a guest editorial (Writing Assignment, Chapter 15, page 324)

Class Activities

- Group and class work focused on what makes an effective proposal argument, incorporating the specific challenges of editorials and the specific demands of proposal arguments
- Instructors may want to build in sessions with their institution's reference librarian early in this final unit to give students familiarity with their library's resources and layout.

Possible Short or Informal Writing Assignments

- Collaborative work on constructing an outline of an argument that would give a local or university problem presence, significance, and urgency

Copyright © 2010, Pearson Education, Inc., Publishing as Longman

Weeks 14–16: Writing Researched Policy Proposals

Objectives

- To give students more practice with the "stock-issues strategy"
- To give students more practice with using arguments of category, consequence, and resemblance to support a proposal argument
- To help students give presence to the problem they are seeking to solve
- To help students plan out their proposals to gain the attention of the intended audience, the people who have the power to change the situation (the decision-makers)
- To help students develop research skills using library and Internet resources
- To help students use conventional documentation

Readings

- Students will be reading for their own researched policy proposals.

Formal Writing Assignment

Researched policy proposal (using the number and kinds of sources specified by the instructor—say, 4–8 sources, including both popular and scholarly publications and no more than 2 Web sources; Writing Assignment, Chapter 15, page 324)

Class Activities

- Group and class work on evaluating Web sites to determine reliable and useful sources of information
- Review of appeals to *logos*, *ethos*, and *pathos*; students might want to work with the audience analysis questions in Chapter 6, pages 119-20, as well as the "stock-issues" strategy and invention using arguments of category, consequence, and resemblance.
- Group and class work at the invention and revising stages, to strengthen students' treatment of alternative solutions and their justification of their proposed solutions in their proposal arguments
- Peer reviewing of both the guest editorials and researched proposal arguments in preparation for revision
- A good way to end the course is to devote the last week of class to students' persuasive speeches on their proposal argument issues.

Copyright © 2010, Pearson Education, Inc., Publishing as Longman

SAMPLE SYLLABUS #2: EMPHASIS ON CLAIM TYPES

Course Design Decisions

- This course incorporates all the approaches to argumentation and includes a rigorous introduction to the concepts and language of argument.
- Students will write on common subject matter designated by the instructor for most of the course.
- This course will use readings to give students material for rhetorical analysis and to introduce students to controversial conversations that they will join with their own arguments.
- Writing process time is built into the course: for invention exercises, for peer reviews, and for revision exercises.
- Assignments will begin with generic argumentative skills and then move to a variety of claim types.

Scope of the Course

This rigorous course syllabus is intended to give students a strong and comprehensive introduction to argument. It is probably best suited for a second-semester first-year course in argument or for advanced students. The first part of the course provides a solid foundation in the concepts and vocabulary of argument, with concentration on the enthymeme, *logos*, *ethos*, and *pathos*, and the Toulmin schema as an invention tool to help writers find the most relevant and persuasive reasons for the intended audiences. Instructors may choose to apply the Toulmin schema in the second part of the course when students write arguments based on different claim types. This course includes ***seven*** formal writing assignments. The subject matter for most units of the course is a common network of issues that the instructor chooses. This syllabus provides suggestions of how to use units of arguments in the anthology. Instructors could also compose units based on readings in the rhetoric part of *Writing Arguments* or build their readings around local issues.

Formal Writing Assignments

1. Classical argument using evidence drawn from personal experience
   4–6 pages (Writing Assignment, Chapter 7, page 140)
2. Dialogic argument addressing a resistant audience
   3 pages (Writing Assignment, Chapters 7, page 140)
3. . Exploratory essay analyzing the sources of disagreement on the same issue
   3 pages (Chapter 2, page 50-51)
4. Definitional argument or evaluation argument defending both the criteria and the match
   4–6 pages (Writing Assignment, Chapter 11, pages 225-28 or Writing Assignment, Chapter 14, pages 296-300)
5. Causal argument or a resemblance argument
   2 pages (Writing Assignment, Chapter 12, pages 249-53 or Writing Assignment, Chapter 13, pages 271-73)
6. Proposal argument (either a policy proposal or a practical proposal)
   5–7 pages (Writing Assignment, Chapter 15, pages 323-27)
7. Advocacy advertisement
   1 page (Writing Assignment, Chapter 15, page 324)

Weeks 1–2: Introduction to the Core of Argument

Objectives

- To help students understand that the core of an argument is a claim with reasons
- To help students begin to see argument as a process of clarification and inquiry—searching for the best solutions to problems
- To introduce students to the rhetorical triangle

Copyright © 2010, Pearson Education, Inc., Publishing as Longman

- To help students distinguish between issue questions and information questions and between genuine argument and pseudo-argument
- To help students understand the enthymeme as a claim with a stated reason, often in a ***because*** clause
- To help students comprehend the way the Toulmin system provides the concepts of claim, reasons, warrants, grounds, backing, conditions of rebuttal, and qualifier as a means to construct an argument
- To help students understand the key concept of ***warrants*** as a means to check whether their particular audience will accept the soundness of their enthymemes
- To help students understand that arguments are intensely rhetorical in that they grow out of specific occasions, and through audience-based reasons must be tailored to the needs, interests, and values of specific audiences

Readings

- Chapters 1, 4, and 5

Formal Writing Assignment

No formal writing assignment

Class Activities

- Group discussion of Gordon Adam's petition; freewrite after groups' discussion; class discussion (Chapter 1)
- Class discussion and exercises distinguishing issue questions from information questions and genuine arguments from pseudo-arguments (Chapter 4)
- Group or pairs work generating ***because*** clauses for students' claims
- An introduction to the Toulmin system using or adapting the "IV. Suggestions for Teaching the Toulmin System" in this *Instructor's Manual*
- Group and class work on warrants in "IV. Suggestions for Teaching the Toulmin System"
- Class work using the "Quiz on Enthymemes and Toulmin Argument Frames" and the "Exercise: Practicing with Argument Cores" at the end of Chapter Guide 4

Possible Short or Informal Writing Assignments

- Collaborative work constructing (1) an argument frame for a claim and an audience that would not need support for the warrants and then (2) an argument frame for a claim and an audience that would need support for the warrants

Weeks 3–4: Developing Claims and Evidence

Objectives

- To equip students with a whole repertoire of strategies for generating claims that they will want to argue
- To help students think in terms of mustering the most rhetorically effective evidence for their claims and reasons
- To help students apply the STAR criteria (Sufficiency, Typicality, Accuracy, and Relevance) to the evidence they use to support their claims
- To help students understand the concept of angle of vision as the values, beliefs, and perspectives filtering writers' use of evidence
- To help students use evidence rhetorically by employing various strategies to frame their evidence to guide their audience's response

Readings

- Chapters 4, 5, and 7
- Numerous articles in the anthology are notable for their use of evidence. In this *Instructor's Manual*, the end of Chapter Guide 5 lists articles that are especially successful in their use of evidence, as well as other articles that illustrate clearly how writers' angles of vision dominate their selection and presentation of evidence.

Copyright © 2010, Pearson Education, Inc., Publishing as Longman

Formal Writing Assignment

Microtheme (Writing Assignment, Chapter 5, pages 104-05)

Classical argument (Writing Assignment, Chapter 7, page 140)

Class Activities

- Group work on generating ***because*** clauses and brainstorming for a network of related issues
- Group work sharing the results of students' responses to the Exploratory Tasks (pages 67–70)
- Group work to help students use each other as questioning audiences for their classical arguments
- Class discussion of the exercises in Chapter 5 asking students to examine the rhetorical effect of different presentations of data and to explore the idea of framing evidence
- Group and then class discussion of the effective use of evidence in various articles
- Group and class discussion of the student essay "'Half-Criminals or Urban Athletes? A Plea for Fair Treatment of Skateboarders" by David Langley (pages 141–43); students could examine this student writer's use of personal experience evidence to support his claim. (See this *Instructor's Manual*, Chapter Guide 7 for discussion questions.)
- Possible peer reviewing of students' microthemes
- Possible peer reviewing of students' classical arguments

Possible Short or Informal Writing Assignments

- Responses to the two sets of exploratory tasks in Chapter 2; students could bring in university or college newspapers or regional newspapers to examine for issue questions of relevance to them.
- An issue question and a working thesis statement (Writing Assignment, Chapter 3, pages 71-72; A plan of an argument's details (Writing Assignment, Chapter 4, pages 87-88)

Weeks 5–6: Focusing on the Importance of Audience in the Invention and Shaping of Arguments

Objectives

- To help students focus on the rhetorical situation of arguments by thinking about appeals to *ethos* and *pathos* as different ways to relate to audiences and to enhance the logical dimension of their arguments
- To help students understand that an effective argument speaks to the values, knowledge, and interests of the intended audience
- To give students practice with appeals to *pathos*, using concrete language, specific examples and illustrations, narratives, and visual elements to involve their audiences
- To help students understand the uses of one-sided versus multi-sided arguments
- To give students practice with a variety of strategies for connecting with different kinds of resistant audiences, including knowing how to summarize opposing arguments fairly, when to concede points, and how to refute opposing positions
- To help students understand their options in terms of delaying their main claim or using Rogerian structure or possibly humor

Readings

- Chapters 6 and 7
- A number of articles in the anthology have effective, strong, or intriguing and problematic appeals to *ethos* and *pathos*. In this *Instructor's Manual*, see the section at the end of Chapter Guide 6 for suggestions for particularly rich articles to analyze.
- The end of Chapter Guide 7 lists articles that are worth examining for their treatment of alternative views.
- For information on genres of arguments and their shaping of content and form, students could read Chapter 2, pages 32-35.

Formal Writing Assignment

Dialogic argument addressing a resistant audience (Writing Assignment, Chapters 7, page 140)

Class Activities

- Class and group work examining specific articles, with a close look at the ways writers relate to their audiences and at successful and unsuccessful appeals to *ethos* and *pathos*

Copyright © 2010, Pearson Education, Inc., Publishing as Longman

- The class could study op-ed pieces and editorials in the text and ones that students find on their own to see how writers handle opposing views, how explicitly they state their claims, and whether they place their claims up front or delay them.
- Class and group work on visual arguments, particularly newspaper and magazine photos or advocacy ads as a means to influence readers' responses to news events or products
- Class work on fair and unfair summaries
- The class could look at several short pieces employing humor to get an argument across.

Possible Short or Informal Writing Assignments

- Collaborative work on audience analysis using the audience analysis questions in Chapter 6, pages 119-20.

Week 7: Argument as Inquiry and Enriching Viewpoints

Objectives

- To help students see argument as a process of clarification, inquiry, and searching for the best possible answer to problems as well as an appeal to a particular audience
- To help students improve their ability to comprehend and interact with difficult reading material
- To help students listen to alternative viewpoints and expand their thinking by learning to summarize, agree with, and question arguments they read
- To help students recognize how genre shapes expectations about the form, depth, and complexity of arguments
- To help students cope with ambiguity and disagreement by identifying the points of disagreement as differences in interpretations of facts, values, or uses of analogies
- To help students explore these differences as a step toward asking their own questions about an issue

Readings

- Chapter 2
- Possible anthology articles to evaluate for disagreements in interpretations of facts, values, and assumptions are listed in this *Instructor's Manual* at the end of Chapter Guide 2; this list provides pairs of articles that talk to each other and clash over facts and values. The following units include particularly rich, multi-sided argumentative conversations: "Video Games and Their Influence"; "The News Media"; "Women in Math and Science"; "Finding Soldiers: The Volunteer Army, Recruitment, and the Draft"; "Wal-Mart and the Public Good"; "Biotech Agriculture and the Ethics of Food Production"

Formal Writing Assignment

A formal exploratory essay (Writing Assignment, Chapter 2, pages 50-51)

Class Activities

- Group and class discussion of the articles assigned; discussion of the articles' framing of the issue, interpretation of facts, and values and assumptions
- Discussion of summary writing with an examination of students' summaries
- Class discussion of a pair of articles in the anthology, examining sources of disagreement
- Peer reviewing of students' exploratory essays

Possible Short or Informal Writing Assignments

- Believing and doubting freewrites using articles supplied by the instructor
- A 250-word summary of one article

Week 8: An Overview of Types of Claims and Introduction to Finding, Selecting, Using, and Documenting Sources

Objectives

- To help students understand claim types (stasis theory) as a way to determine the point of disagreement between an arguer and audience and the point where an argument is created

Copyright © 2010, Pearson Education, Inc., Publishing as Longman

- To help students understand that different claim types have their own characteristic pattern of support
- To help students understand the range of sources available and to develop research skills
- To help students develop efficient habits of representing, incorporating, and documenting source material

Readings

- Chapter 10 and either all or parts of Chapters 16 and 17

[Note: Although this course design does not call for extensive student research, students may be locating and incorporating some source material into their arguments and should be developing good foundational research and documentation skills.]

Formal Writing Assignment

No formal writing assignment

Class Activities

- Group and class exercises practicing how to formulate different types of claims
- Group and class work discussing the quality of material gleaned from different sources (for example, general databases and the Web)
- A workshop on library resources conducted by a college/university reference librarian

Possible Short or Informal Writing Assignments

- Short evaluation of a Web site based on "Understanding the Rhetoric of Web Sites" (pages 363-67)

Weeks 9–10: Entering an Argumentative Conversation: Definitional Arguments and Evaluation Arguments

[Note: The emphasis for the second-half of this course is on students learning how to develop different types of claims and on entering a variety of argumentative conversations. The anthology provides a number of these lively conversations, but instructors could also assemble their own readings on an issue and also ask students to locate related reading,]

Objectives

- To help students understand the pattern of development for simple categorical arguments
- To help students understand criteria-match strategy
- To help students understand different kinds of definitions (Aristotelian and operational) and different approaches to generating definitional criteria (reportive and stipulative, and use of contrastive and borderline cases)
- To give students practice writing effective definitional arguments that support both the criteria and the match
- To help students produce evaluation arguments by specifying the category that their X belongs to and developing and weighing criteria for that category and its function
- To help students understand principle-based and consequence-based ethical evaluations
- To help students construct evaluation arguments that support both the criteria and the match

Readings

- Chapters 11 and 14
- In this *Instructor's Manual*, Chapter Guide 11 includes a list of anthology articles with definitional claims. The following units have issues that foster definitional arguments or claims: "Web 2.0 and Online Identity" and "Immigration in the Twenty-First Century"
- Chapter Guide 14 lists specific articles in the anthology that have prominent evaluation claims. The network of issues in the following units tend to take the form of evaluation and ethical evaluation claims: "Video Games and Their Influence"; "The News Media"; "Women in Math and Science"; "Wal-Mart and the Public Good"; "Biotech Agriculture and the Ethics of Food Production"

Copyright © 2010, Pearson Education, Inc., Publishing as Longman

Formal Writing Assignment

Definitional argument (or an evaluation or ethical argument) defending both the criteria and the match (Writing Assignment, Chapter 11, page 225-28 or Writing Assignment, Chapter 14, pages 296-300)

Class Activities

- Collaborative writing in pairs, creating a simple categorical argument using exemplification to develop a claim
- Group and class work with the exercise "Using the Definitional Heuristic" in Chapter Guide 11
- Group and class work examining articles in the anthology as definitional arguments.
- Group and class work examining evaluation arguments, considering what criteria are implicitly or explicitly offered; a good place to start is with the student essay on women hip-hop artists (Chapter 14, pages 304–06)
- Peer reviewing of the students' simple categorical arguments, definitional arguments, and/or evaluation arguments leading to revisions
- Class could see a short film and then evaluate it according to criteria that the students originate (classic westerns, mysteries, old comedies, art films, documentaries)

[Note: All students could be asked to address a specific definitional or evaluation issue or to formulate an issue question related to one of the anthology units studied by the class. For instance, the following issue questions are connected to the "Wal-Mart and the Public Good" unit: Is Wal-Mart a socially responsible corporation? Is social responsibility a major criterion from which to evaluate a business? Is providing affordable health care a good business practice?]

Possible Short or Informal Writing Assignments

- Continued work on summary writing: a summary of one of the readings or a reading of the students' own on the common topic
- Collaborative work on simple categorical arguments; pairs of students could construct a simple categorical argument using exemplification to develop a claim.
- Revision of arguments written earlier in the course

Week 11: Arguing for Causes or Consequences and Resemblance or Precedent

[Note: In a course that emphasizes stasis theory, covering causal and consequential reasoning and resemblance and precedent reasoning before proposal arguments can provide students with building blocks they will use in their proposal arguments later. In this last third of the course, students might connect several of the formal writing assignments by writing several arguments on the same issue:

- *Guest editorial and the researched proposal argument*
- *Researched proposal argument and the advocacy advertisement*
- *Practical proposal and the advocacy advertisement*

Objectives

- To help students understand the important methods of causal arguing
- To help students understand the benefits and pitfalls of arguing by analogy
- To give students practice with writing causal arguments and resemblance arguments
- To give students practice writing concise, pointed arguments as letters to the editor

Readings

- Chapters 12 and 13
- In this *Instructor's Manual*, Chapter Guides 12 and 13 list articles in the anthology that include causal and resemblance claims. The following anthology units employ prominent causal claims: "Web 2.0 and Online Identity"; "Video Games and Their Influence"; "Women in Math and Science"; "Finding Soldiers: The Volunteer Army, Recruitment, and the Draft"; "Wal-Mart and the Public Good"; "Biotech Agriculture and the Ethics of Food Production."
- Chapter Guide 13 lists articles that include resemblance, analogy, and precedent claims either as the main claim or as a line of reasoning in a larger argument.

Copyright © 2010, Pearson Education, Inc., Publishing as Longman

- For information on genres of arguments and their shaping of content and form, students could read Chapter 2, pages 32-35.

Formal Writing Assignment

A causal argument or a resemblance argument
(Writing Assignment, Chapter 12, pages 249-53 or Writing Assignment, Chapter 13, pages 271-73)

Class Activities

- Group and class work on the For Class Discussion exercises on causal methods of arguing
- Group and class work on the For Class Discussion exercise on writing analogies
- Class exercise in which parts of the class represent different positions in response to readings in Chapter 12 or Chapter 13; students might discuss op-ed pieces as public forums for expressing strong convictions and intense emotion.
- Students could find and bring to class letters to the editor that include causal reasoning or resemblance/analogy/precedent reasoning; students might discuss how the writers try to nutshell their arguments by using analogies and how well the analogies and these brief arguments work.
- Peer reviewing of students' letters to the editor as causal arguments and resemblance arguments

Weeks 12–14: Writing Proposal Arguments

[Note: Instructors might want to open up the issues for proposal argument to students' own interests and choices; students might choose an issue that has grown out of their earlier arguments.]

Objectives

- To help students understand how to write both policy and practical proposals
- To give students practice with the "stock issues" strategy
- To give students practice with using arguments of category, consequence, and resemblance to support a proposal argument
- To help students think about and weigh alternative solutions
- To help students give presence to the problem they are seeking to solve
- To help students plan out their proposals to gain the attention of the intended audience, the people who have the power to change the situation (decision-makers) or who need to think differently about this problem

Readings

- Chapter 15 and possibly review of parts of Chapters 16 and 17
- In this *Instructor's Manual*, Chapter Guide 15 lists numerous anthology articles that argue proposal claims.

Formal Writing Assignment

Proposal argument (either a practical proposal or a policy proposal; this essay may or may not be a researched argument with the minimum number of sources specified by the instructor; Writing Assignment, Chapter 15, pages 323-24)

Class Activities

- Review of appeals to *logos*, *ethos*, and *pathos*; students might want to enlist the audience analysis questions in Chapter 6, pages 119-20.
- Class work using the "stock-issues" strategy and the arguments of category, consequence, and resemblance as invention strategies to build students' proposal arguments
- Class and group work in which students share their presentation of their issues, their justification of their solutions, and their responses to their audiences' objections
- Class and group discussion of the strategies employed in several effective proposal arguments
- Peer reviewing of students' proposal arguments
- Students could deliver their proposal arguments as persuasive speeches.

Possible Short or Informal Writing Assignments

- Collaborative work on constructing an outline of an argument that would give a local or university problem presence, significance, and urgency

Copyright © 2010, Pearson Education, Inc., Publishing as Longman

Weeks 15–16: Examining Visual Rhetoric and Creating Advocacy Advertisements

[Note: For shorter courses, instructors may want to conclude with a proposal argument, omit this two-week teaching unit and the advocacy advertisement assignment, and instead do a few of these class activities within other teaching units throughout the course. For the advocacy advertisement, students could focus on an issue from their own experience (jobs, volunteer work, university organizations, etc.) or they could invent a fictional organization or advocacy group and role-play that they are representing it.]

Objectives

- To help students understand how visual and verbal elements can work together to produce rhetorical effects: supporting the logical core of an argument, enhancing the writer's credibility and authority, and stirring audiences' emotions and imaginations
- To help students analyze and use the elements of visual design—type, layout, color, and image
- To help students think about displays of numerical data for rhetorical effect
- To help students understand that visual arguments like all arguments are products of specific historical, social, and cultural moments
- To help students apply their cumulative knowledge of good argumentation to analyzing and producing visual arguments

Readings

- Chapter 9 and review of Chapter 15
- In this *Instructor's Manual*, the end of Chapter Guide 9 lists all the visual arguments in the anthology.

Formal Writing Assignment

Advocacy Advertisement (Writing Assignment, Chapter 15, page 324)

Class Activities

- Group or class work with visual arguments in Chapter 9.
- In groups, students could brainstorm for ideas for their advocacy advertisements. Some suggestions are issues concerning university clubs or organizations, courses, programs, living accommodations; availability of technology or food on campus; internships or volunteer work; or issues concerning community or job problems.
- Students could bring newspaper or magazine advocacy ads that include graphic displays of numerical data to class and discuss how clear and useful these graphics are.
- Group or class work (perhaps as presentations) analyzing advocacy ads in *Writing Arguments* or ones that students find on their own and bring to class.
- Group or class work examining the effectiveness of visual arguments on different historical issues using "Discussion Exercise Analyzing Visual Argument in American History" in this *Instructor's Manual* (pages 92-94). This section offers ideas for instructor-led discussions and options for student presentations.
- Students could share the drafts of their advocacy advertisements in peer review groups for audience feedback.

Possible Short or Informal Writing Assignments

- Any of the ideas for class activities could become class presentations or short written assignments; students could write a short analysis of an advocacy ad or a historical poster argument.
- Students could write the microtheme at the end of Chapter 9, Using a Quantitative Graphic (page 198) for practice working with numerical data and visual arguments.

Copyright © 2010, Pearson Education, Inc., Publishing as Longman

SAMPLE SYLLABUS #3: EMPHASIS ON GENRES OF ARGUMENT AND RESEARCH

Course Design Decisions

- This course can include all the approaches to argument.
- Students choose their own topics throughout the course.
- This course uses readings as material for rhetorical analysis and examination of argumentative strategies.
- Writing process time for invention exercises, peer reviewing, and revising is built into the course.
- The writing assignments progress from smaller incremental tasks to longer. A main focus is to give students the opportunity to produce several different genres of argument (among them, an op-ed piece, a speech, a longer magazine article, and a researched academic argument).
- Students do research on their issues of interest throughout the course.

Scope of the Course

This course, focusing on genres of argument, is most likely suitable for second-semester first-year students or for advanced students. The first third of the course gives students a strong common foundation in the concepts and strategies of argument. The second and third parts teach more advanced argumentative moves and give students practice with different forms that arguments can take for specific purposes, audiences, and contexts. The third part of the course also emphasizes truth-seeking and problem-solving through independent research and the production of several researched arguments, where students' choice of claim type arises out of their own sense of audience and purpose. Using this more open-ended approach, the instructor should tell students that each argument must be addressed to an actual audience and aimed at publication in a newspaper, magazine, employee bulletin, or newsletter. Since issues of definition, cause, analogy, evaluation, and proposal will naturally occur within students' sequence of arguments, Part Four of the text will be relevant to these assignments. This course has ***seven*** formal writing assignments.

Formal Writing Assignments

1. Op-ed piece or guest editorial (for university/college, local, or regional newspaper)
   500–1000 words
2. Advocacy advertisement
   1 page (Writing Assignment, adaptation of Chapter 15, page 324)
3. Evaluation argument as a magazine article for a public affairs or niche magazine
   4–6 pages (Writing Assignment, Chapter 14, pages 296-300)
4. Practical proposal
   4–6 pages (Writing Assignment, Chapter 15, pages 323-24)
5. Letter to the editor
   approximately 300 words
6. Policy proposal as a speech
   3–5 pages (Writing Assignment, Chapter 15, adaptation of Option 3, page 324)
7. Researched academic argument (students' choice of issue and claim type) or a white paper for a legislator (or an invented organization) on a political or civic issue
   6–10 pages

Copyright © 2010, Pearson Education, Inc., Publishing as Longman

Week 1: Introduction to Argument, the Rhetorical Triangle, and Discovering Arguable Issues and Claims

Objectives

- To help students understand that an argument must begin with an issue and must have as its core a claim with reasons
- To help students think of argument as a process of clarification, inquiry, and searching for the best solutions, as well as persuasion
- To introduce students to the rhetorical triangle
- To help students understand that a genuine argument must begin with an issue question (not an information question) and have a frame composed of a claim and reasons, often stated in ***because*** clauses
- To equip students with a whole repertoire of strategies for generating claims that they will want to argue

Readings

- Chapters 1, 2, and 3

Formal Writing Assignment

No formal writing assignment

Class Activities

- Group and class discussions of explicit and implicit arguments
- Group discussion of Gordon Adam's petition; freewrite after groups' discussion; class discussion (Chapter 1)
- Class discussion and exercises distinguishing issue questions from information questions and genuine arguments from pseudo-arguments (Chapter 3)
- Group and class work on generating ***because*** clauses and brainstorming for a network of related issues
- Group sharing of the results of students' responses to the "Exploratory Tasks" (pages @@–@@)

Possible Short or Informal Writing Assignments

- To gather a stock of interesting issues that students might draw on throughout the course, students could do both the sets of "Exploratory Tasks" in Chapter 2, (Set 1, pages 25-6, 29-30; Set 2, pages 30-31; Set 3, pages 45-6).

Week 2: Reading Arguments and Working with Sources as a Bridge toward Writing Arguments

[Note: Because students will be generating their own issue questions throughout the course and will be joining civic controversies as they write various argument genres, they might focus on developing some foundational research and documentation skills at the beginning of the course. A workshop or presentation by a reference librarian on the resources of the library and the Internet might be very useful at this point.]

Objectives

- To help students listen to alternative viewpoints and expand their thinking by learning to summarize, agree with, and question others' arguments
- To help students recognize how genre shapes expectations about the form, depth, and complexity of arguments
- To help students cope with ambiguity and disagreement by identifying the sources of disagreement in interpretations of facts, in values, or in uses of analogies
- To help students explore these differences as a step toward asking their own questions and taking their own stand on an issue
- To help students understand the range of sources available and to develop research skills using library and Internet resources
- To help students develop efficient habits of representing, incorporating, and documenting source material

Copyright © 2010, Pearson Education, Inc., Publishing as Longman

Readings

- Chapter 2 and either all or parts of Chapters 16 and 17
- Possible anthology articles to evaluate for disagreements in interpretations of facts, values, and assumptions are listed in this *Instructor's Manual* at the end of Chapter Guide 2; this list provides pairs of articles that talk to each other and clash over facts and values.
- Instructors could also focus on a local university or college issue or a regional issue that will give students experience with examining multiple perspectives on one issue.

Formal Writing Assignment

No formal writing assignment

Class Activities

- Group and class discussion of the articles assigned; discussion of the articles' framing of the issue, interpretation of facts, and values and assumptions
- Discussion of summary writing with an examination of students' summaries
- Class discussion of a pair of articles in the anthology, examining sources of disagreement
- Peer reviewing of students' exploratory essays analyzing sources of disagreement
- Group and class work discussing the quality of material gleaned from different sources (for example, general databases and the Web)
- A workshop on library resources conducted by a college/university reference librarian

Possible Short or Informal Writing Assignments

- Believing and doubting freewrites on an assertion provided by the instructor
- A 250-word summary of a reading
- Exploratory essay analyzing sources of disagreement between two articles chosen by each student or by groups of students interested in the same national, regional, community, or university/college issues (See example in Chapter 2, pages 50–51).
- Short evaluation of a Web site based on "Understanding the Rhetoric of Web Sites" (pages 363-67)

Weeks 3–4: Framing and Supporting an Argument

Objectives

- To help students comprehend the way the Toulmin system provides the concepts of claim, reasons, warrants, grounds, backing, conditions of rebuttal, and qualifier as a means to construct an argument
- To help students understand the key concept of *warrants* as a means to check whether their particular audience will accept the soundness of their enthymemes
- To help students understand that arguments are intensely rhetorical in that they grow out of specific occasions and through audience-based reasons must be tailored to the needs, interests, and values of specific audiences
- To help students understand the importance of thinking out the assumptions that their audiences must accept in order to find their reasons persuasive and thus to help students think about audience-based reasons
- To help students understand claim types (stasis theory) as a way to determine the point of disagreement between an arguer and audience and the point where an argument is created
- To help students understand that different claim types have their own characteristic pattern of support
- To help students think in terms of mustering the most rhetorically effective evidence for their claims and reasons
- To help students apply the STAR criteria (Sufficiency, Typicality, Accuracy, and Relevance) to the evidence they use to support their claims
- To help students understand the concept of angle of vision as the values, beliefs, and perspectives filtering writers' use of evidence

Copyright © 2010, Pearson Education, Inc., Publishing as Longman

- To help students use evidence rhetorically by employing various strategies to frame their evidence to guide their audience's response

Readings

- Chapters 4, 5, and 10
- Numerous articles in the anthology are notable for their use of evidence. In this *Instructor's Manual*, the end of Chapter Guide 5 (pages 106-07) lists articles that are especially successful in their use of evidence as well as other articles that illustrate clearly how writers' angles of vision dominate their selection and presentation of evidence.
- For information on genres of arguments and their shaping of content and form, students could read Chapter 2, pages 32-35.

Formal Writing Assignment

Op-ed piece or guest editorial (for university/college, local, or regional newspaper)

Class Activities

- An introduction to the Toulmin system using or adapting the "Suggestions for Teaching the Toulmin System" in this *Instructor's Manual*
- Group and class work on warrants in "Suggestions for Teaching the Toulmin System"
- Class work using the "Quiz on Enthymemes and Toulmin Argument Frames" and the "Exercise: Practicing with Argument Cores" at the end of Chapter Guide 4 in this *Instructor's Manual*
- As students become familiar with different claim types, they might find articles featuring a particular claim type to bring to class to share in groups.
- Class discussion of the exercises in Chapter 5 asking students to examine the rhetorical effect of different presentations of data and to explore the idea of framing evidence
- Group and class discussion of the effective use of evidence in various articles
- Group and class discussion of the student essay "'Half-Criminals or Urban Athletes? A Plea for Fair Treatment of Skateboarders" by David Langley (pages 141–43); students could examine this student writer's use of personal experience evidence to support his claim. (See this *Instructor's Manual*, Chapter Guide 7 for discussion questions.)
- Group work to help students use each other as questioning audiences for their op-ed pieces and editorials

Possible Short or Informal Writing Assignments

- Collaborative work constructing (1) an argument frame for a claim and an audience that would not need support for the warrants and then (2) an argument frame for a claim and an audience that would need support for the warrants

Weeks 5–6: Focusing on Logos, Pathos, and Visual Arguments

Objectives

- To help students focus on the rhetorical situation of arguments by thinking about appeals to *ethos* and *pathos* as different ways to relate to audiences and to enhance the logical dimension of their arguments
- To help students understand that an effective argument speaks to the values, knowledge, and interests of the intended audience
- To give students practice with appeals to *pathos* using concrete language, specific examples and illustrations, narratives, and visual elements to involve their audiences
- To help students understand how visual and verbal elements can work together to produce rhetorical effects: supporting the logical core of an argument, enhancing the writer's credibility and authority, and stirring audiences' emotions and imaginations
- To help students analyze and use the elements of visual design—type, layout, color, and image
- To help students think about displays of numerical data for rhetorical effect
- To help students understand that visual arguments like all arguments are products of specific historical, social, and cultural moments

Copyright © 2010, Pearson Education, Inc., Publishing as Longman

- To help students apply their cumulative knowledge of good argumentation to analyzing and creating visual arguments

Readings

- Chapters 6 and 9
- In this *Instructor's Manual*, the end of Chapter Guide 9 lists all the visual arguments in the anthology.
- The opening pages of the five major parts of this text include visual arguments: political cartoons, a poster argument, a historical photograph, and an advocacy ad.

Formal Writing Assignment

Advocacy Advertisement (Writing Assignment, Chapter 15, page 324)

Class Activities

- Group or class work with the visual argument in Chapter 9.
- In groups, students could brainstorm for ideas for their advocacy advertisements. Some suggestions are issues concerning university clubs or organizations, courses, programs, living accommodations; the availability of technology or food on campus; internships and volunteer work; or issues concerning community or job problems.
- Students could bring newspaper or magazine advocacy ads that include graphic displays of numerical data to class and discuss how clear and useful these graphics are.
- Group or class work (perhaps as presentations) analyzing advocacy ads in *Writing Arguments* or ones that students find on their own and bring to class
- Group or class work examining the effectiveness of visual arguments on different historical issues using "Discussion Exercise Analyzing Visual Argument in American History" in this *Instructor's Manual* (92-94). This section offers ideas for instructor-led discussions and options for student presentations.
- Students could share the drafts of their advocacy advertisements in peer review groups for audience feedback.

Possible Short or Informal Writing Assignments

- Any of the ideas for class activities could become class presentations or short written assignments; students could write a short analysis of an advocacy ad or a historical poster argument.
- Students could write the microtheme at the end of Chapter 9, Using a quantitative graphic (page 198) for practice working with numerical data and visual arguments.

Weeks 7–8: Accommodating Audiences and Making Evaluations

Objectives

- To help students understand the uses of one-sided and multi-sided arguments
- To give students practice with a variety of strategies for connecting with different kinds of resistant audiences, including knowing how to summarize opposing arguments fairly, when to concede points, and how to refute opposing positions
- To help students understand their options in terms of delaying their main claim or using Rogerian structure or possibly humor
- To help students understand criteria-match strategy
- To help students produce evaluation arguments by specifying the category that their X belongs to and developing and weighing criteria for that category and its function
- To help students understand principle-based and consequence-based ethical evaluations
- To help students construct evaluation arguments that support both the criteria and the match

Readings

- Chapters 7 and 14
- A number of articles in the anthology are particularly effective in addressing alternative views. In this *Instructor's Manual*, see the section at the end of Chapter Guide 8 for articles that merit special attention for their treatment of alternative views.

Copyright © 2010, Pearson Education, Inc., Publishing as Longman

- In this *Instructor's Manual*, Chapter Guide 14 lists specific articles in the anthology that have prominent evaluation claims. The network of issues in the following units tend to take the form of evaluation and ethical evaluation claims: "Web 2.0 and Online Identity"; "Video Games and Their Influence"; "The News Media"; "Women in Math and Science"; "Wal-Mart and the Public Good"; "Biotech Agriculture and the Ethics of Food Production"

Formal Writing Assignment

Evaluation or ethical argument written as a magazine article for a particular public affairs or niche magazine (Writing Assignment, Chapter 14, pages 296-300)

Class Activities

- Group and class work examining the way different articles and genres of argument handle alternative views
- Group and class work examining evaluation arguments, considering what criteria are implicitly or explicitly offered; a good place to start is with the student essay on women hip-hop artists (Chapter 14, pages 304-06)
- Group and class discussion to generate different sets of criteria for different evaluation arguments
- Class could see a short film and then evaluate it according to criteria that the students originate (classic westerns, mysteries, old comedies, art films, documentaries)
- Peer reviewing of the students' evaluation arguments leading to revisions

Possible Short or Informal Writing Assignments

- Revision of arguments written earlier in the course
- An audience analysis of the magazines that students are targeting for their evaluation arguments (Chapter 6, pages 119-20; Chapter 16, pages 357-63, for explanation of publications and political bias)

Weeks 9–10: Writing a Practical Proposal

Objectives

- To help students understand how to write practical proposals
- To give students practice with the "stock-issues strategy"
- To give students practice with using arguments of category, consequence, and resemblance to support a proposal argument
- To help students give presence to the problem they are seeking to solve
- To help students think about and weigh alternative solutions
- To help students plan out their proposals to gain the attention of the intended audience, the people who have the power to change the situation (decision-makers) or who need to think differently about this problem

Readings

- Chapter 15

Formal Writing Assignments

Practical proposal (Writing Assignment, Chapter 15, pages 323-24)

Class Activities

- Group exercise using the For Class Discussion exercises in Chapter 15.
- Review of appeals to *logos*, *ethos*, and *pathos*; students might want to enlist the audience analysis questions in Chapter 6, pages 119-20.
- Group exercises using the "stock- issues" strategy and arguments of category, consequence, and resemblance to support a proposal argument
- Class and group work in which students try out their approach to the practical problem they are trying to solve, their justifications of their solutions, and their response to objections or alternative solutions
- Peer reviewing of students' practical proposal arguments

Copyright © 2010, Pearson Education, Inc., Publishing as Longman

Possible Short or Informal Writing Assignments

- Collaborative work on constructing an outline of an argument that would give a local or university problem presence, significance, and urgency

Weeks 11–12: Joining a Conversation with a Letter to the Editor

Objectives

- To help students understand the important methods of causal arguing
- To help students understand the benefits and pitfalls of arguing by analogy
- To give students practice with writing causal arguments and resemblance arguments
- To give students practice writing concise, pointed letters to the editor

Readings

- Chapters 12 and 13
- In this *Instructor's Manual*, Chapter Guides 12 and 13 list articles in the anthology that include causal claims. The following anthology units employ prominent causal claims: "Web 2.0 and Online Identity"; "Video Games and Their Influence"; "Finding Soldiers: The Volunteer Army, Recruitment, and the Draft"; "Wal-Mart and the Public Good" "Biotech Agriculture and the Ethics of Food Production"
- Chapter Guide 13 lists articles that include resemblance, analogy, and precedent claims, either as the main claim or a line of reasoning in a larger argument.
- For information on genres of arguments and their shaping of content and form, students could read Chapter 2, pages 32–35.

Formal Writing Assignment

A causal argument or a resemblance argument
(Writing Assignment, Chapter 12, pages 249-53 or Writing Assignment, Chapter 13, pages 271-73)

Class Activities

- Group and class work on the For Class Discussion exercises on causal methods of arguing
- Class exercise in which parts of the class represent different positions in response to arguments in the chapter; students might discuss op-ed pieces as public forums for strong convictions and intense emotion.
- Group and class work on the For Class Discussion exercise on writing analogies
- Group and class work examining the articles in Chapter 13 and the articles in the anthology that use analogies;.
- Students could find and bring to class letters to the editor that include causal reasoning or resemblance/analogy/precedent reasoning; students might discuss how the writers try to nutshell their arguments by using analogies and how well the analogies and these brief arguments work.
- Peer reviewing of students' letters to the editor with causal or resemblance arguments

Weeks 13–14: Writing a Policy Proposal Speech

Objectives

- To help students write persuasive policy proposals
- To help students give presence to the problem they are seeking to solve
- To give students practice with the "stock-issues" strategy and with using arguments of category, consequence, and resemblance to support a proposal argument
- To help students think about and weigh alternative solutions
- To help students plan out their proposals to gain the attention of the intended audience, the people who have the power to change the situation (decision-makers) or who need to think differently about this problem
- To help students shape their policy proposals to reach their target audiences and to be comprehensible and compelling when presented as speeches

Copyright © 2010, Pearson Education, Inc., Publishing as Longman

Readings

- Chapter 15 and possibly review of parts of Chapters 16 and 17
- In this *Instructor's Manual*, Chapter Guide 15 lists numerous articles that argue proposal claims.

Formal Writing Assignment

Policy proposal speech (length in minutes to be set by the instructor; Writing Assignment, Chapter 15, adaptation of Option 3, page 324)

Class Activities

- Class and group work in which students share their presentation of the problems they are proposing to solve, their justification of their solutions, and their responses to objections and alternative views
- Review of appeals to *logos*, *ethos*, and *pathos*; students might want to enlist the audience analysis questions in Chapter 6, pages 119-20.
- Class and group discussion of the strategies of several effective proposal arguments
- Class and group discussion of the speeches throughout *Writing Arguments*
- Using publications such as *Vital Speeches*, students could find and bring to class examples of effective, memorable speeches that propose changes in policies.

Possible Short or Informal Writing Assignments

- Collaborative work on constructing an outline of an argument that would give a local or university problem presence, significance, and urgency

Weeks 15–16: Writing Researched Arguments

Objectives

- To help students approach argument as inquiry and problem-solving by posing complex, significant issue questions for which they do not yet have answers
- To give students practice using their research skills to "create" an answer to their research issue question through their own investigation, research, and critical thinking
- To give students a chance to synthesize their knowledge about writing arguments (including the rhetorical use of evidence) by writing a culminating piece as a researched academic argument or white paper
- To review effective means of incorporating material from sources and the conventions for documenting sources

Reading

- Students will be working on their own issues and their own research for the rest of the course.
- Instructors may direct the class to particular readings in the text to illustrate argumentative strategies and patterns of development for claim types.

Formal Writing Assignment

Researched academic argument (students' choice of issue and claim type) or a white paper on a political or civic issue (minimum number and kinds of sources specified by instructor)

Class Activities

- Collaborative work (pairs or groups) to serve as questioning audiences for each other
- Review of important ideas concerning incorporating, representing, and documenting sources
- Class discussion of particular special features of different claim-type arguments as a review
- Group sharing and peer reviewing of various stages of their researched academic arguments or white papers

Possible Short or Informal Writing Assignments

- Instructors may want students to bring the stages or segments of this project to class for incremental review, feedback, and discussion. For researched arguments in an academic format, students could share their core claims and reasons and their alternative views and rebuttals. They could also describe how they will convey a positive *ethos* and use appeals to *pathos*.
- For white papers, students could share their white paper scenarios (the letter they write in which they role-play that a real or fictional organization, employer, or advocacy group has

Copyright © 2010, Pearson Education, Inc., Publishing as Longman

commissioned this research in order to take an informed position on some issue); these scenarios can take the form of a letter to the student from the employer who is seeking to understand some issue better. Students could then share their executive summaries for their white papers (summaries of the background and current state of the issue under investigation). Students could also use peer review groups to get feedback on their core claims and reasons and their alternative views and rebuttals.

Copyright © 2010, Pearson Education, Inc., Publishing as Longman

SAMPLE SYLLABUS #4: EMPHASIS ON RHETORICAL ANALYSIS, RESEARCH AS DISCOVERY, AND CIVIC ARGUMENTATION

Course Design Decisions

- This course focuses on the analytical reading of written and visual arguments, presents and implements research as a means of discovery, and ends with civic and professional argumentation.
- Students choose most of their own topics for their arguments and research.
- This syllabus introduces students to academic research and also promotes field research about local problems/issues.
- Students will write on common subject matter designated by the instructor for the first assignment of the course, but the rest of the course demands that students research their own issues and problems and then use their writing to address civic issues in their communities.
- This course will initially use readings to provide material for rhetorical analysis and to introduce students to controversial conversations that they will join with their own arguments.
- Writing process time is built into the course: for invention exercises, for peer reviews, and for revision exercises.
- Assignments will begin with rhetorical reading skills, move to the I-Search essay, and ends with traditional claim types.

Scope of the Course

This rigorous course syllabus is intended to give students a strong and comprehensive introduction to rhetorical reading strategies and research-based writing and argumentation. It is probably best suited for a second-semester first-year course in argument or for advanced students. The first part of the course provides a solid foundation in the concepts and vocabulary of argument, with concentration on the enthymeme, *logos*, *ethos*, and *pathos*, and the Toulmin schema as an invention tool to help writers find the most relevant and persuasive reasons for the intended audiences. This course includes six formal writing assignments. The reading material for the initial unit in the course is provided by anthology selections. So all of the large writing assignments except for one (Rhetorical Analysis) are dependent on student research. Most of the course should be structured around local and/or global issues generated from students' interests and concerns.

Formal Writing Assignments

1. Rhetorical Analysis essay
   4 pages (pages 48-49 of the IM)
2. Analyzing Images essay (Rhetorical Analysis)
   4 pages (pages 51-52 of the IM)
3. Web Site Evaluation essay
   3 pages (pages 45-47 of the IM)
4. I-Search essay
   6-10 pages (pages 43-44 of the IM)
5. Proposal argument (either a policy proposal or a practical proposal), Civic Argument, or Civic Proposal
   7-10 pages (Writing Assignment, Chapter 15, pages 323-27; Civic Argument, pages 54-56 of the IM; Civic Proposal, pages 57-59 of the IM)
6. Advocacy advertisement
   1 page (Writing Assignment, Chapter 9, page 198; or Writing Assignment, Chapter 15, page 324)

Copyright © 2010, Pearson Education, Inc., Publishing as Longman

Weeks 1–3: Introduction to Argument and Analytical Reading

Objectives

- To help students understand that the core of an argument is a claim with reasons
- To help students begin to see argument as a process of clarification and inquiry—searching for the best solutions to problems
- To introduce students to the rhetorical triangle
- To help students distinguish between issue questions and information questions and between genuine argument and pseudo-argument
- To help students understand the enthymeme as a claim with a stated reason, often in a ***because*** clause
- To help students comprehend the way the Toulmin system provides the concepts of claim, reasons, warrants, grounds, backing, conditions of rebuttal, and qualifier as a means to construct an argument
- To help students understand the key concept of ***warrants*** as a means to check whether their particular audience will accept the soundness of their enthymemes
- To help students understand that arguments are intensely rhetorical in that they grow out of specific occasions, and through audience-based reasons must be tailored to the needs, interests, and values of specific audiences
- To provide students with opportunities to effectively summarize and analytically read various arguments

Readings

- Chapters 1, 2, 3, 4, and 5

Formal Writing Assignment

No formal writing assignment

Class Activities

- Group discussion of Gordon Adam's petition; freewrite after groups' discussion; class discussion (Chapter 1)
- Class discussion and exercises based on reading as a believer, reading as a doubter, and argument as inquiry (Chapter 2)
- Class discussion and exercises distinguishing issue questions from information questions and genuine arguments from pseudo-arguments (Chapter 4)
- Group or pairs work generating ***because*** clauses for students' claims
- An introduction to the Toulmin system using or adapting the "IV. Suggestions for Teaching the Toulmin System" in this *Instructor's Manual*
- Group and class work on warrants in "IV. Suggestions for Teaching the Toulmin System"
- Class work using the "Quiz on Enthymemes and Toulmin Argument Frames" and the "Exercise: Practicing with Argument Cores" at the end of Chapter Guide 4

Possible Short or Informal Writing Assignments

- Collaborative work constructing (1) an argument frame for a claim and an audience that would not need support for the warrants and then (2) an argument frame for a claim and an audience that would need support for the warrants
- In-class writing or formal journals that are argument summaries (Writing Assignment, Chapter 2, pages 50-51) in response to Chapter readings
- In-class writing or formal journals that showcase reading as believers and doubters (Exploratory Task, Chapter 2, pages 30-31)
- In-class writing or formal journals that showcase dialectical thinking (Exploratory Task, Chapter 2, pages 45-46)

Copyright © 2010, Pearson Education, Inc., Publishing as Longman

Weeks 4-5: How Writers Develop Claims and Evidence

Objectives

- To equip students with a whole repertoire of strategies for analyzing and generating claims
- To help students think in terms of mustering the most rhetorically effective evidence for their claims and reasons
- To help students apply the STAR criteria (Sufficiency, Typicality, Accuracy, and Relevance) to the evidence they use to support their claims
- To help students understand the concept of angle of vision as the values, beliefs, and perspectives filtering writers' use of evidence
- To help students analyze and use evidence rhetorically by observing various strategies to frame evidence to guide audience's responses
- To help students focus on the rhetorical situation of arguments by thinking about appeals to *ethos* and *pathos* as different ways to relate to audiences and to enhance the logical dimension of their arguments
- To help students understand that an effective argument speaks to the values, knowledge, and interests of the intended audience

Readings

- Chapters 6, 7, and 8
- Numerous articles in the anthology are notable for their use of evidence. In this *Instructor's Manual*, the end of Chapter Guide 5 lists articles that are especially successful in their use of evidence, as well as other articles that illustrate clearly how writers' angles of vision dominate their selection and presentation of evidence.
- In addition or in replace of articles listed in the IM for Chapter 5, the instructor can select a whole anthology for a reading assignment or arguments from various sections.

Formal Writing Assignment

Rhetorical Analysis essay (Writing Assignment, Chapter 8, pages 158-59 or pages 48-49 in the IM)

Class Activities

- Group work on generating ***because*** clauses and brainstorming for a network of related issues
- Group work sharing the results of students' responses to the Exploratory Tasks (pages 67–70)
- Group work to help students use each other as questioning audiences for their evaluations of arguments
- Group and then class discussion of the effective use of evidence in various articles
- Group and class discussion of the student essay "'Half-Criminals or Urban Athletes? A Plea for Fair Treatment of Skateboarders" by David Langley (pages 141–43); students could examine this student writer's use of personal experience evidence to support his claim. (See this *Instructor's Manual*, Chapter Guide 7 for discussion questions.)
- Possible peer reviewing of students' rhetorical analysis essays

Possible Short or Informal Writing Assignments

- An issue question and a working thesis statement (Writing Assignment, Chapter 3, pages 71-72)
- A plan of the details of the Rhetorical Analysis essay (modification of Writing Assignment, Chapter 4, pages 87-88)

Weeks 6-7: Focusing on Visual Arguments

Objectives

- To help students focus on the rhetorical situation of arguments by thinking about appeals to *ethos* and *pathos* as different ways to relate to audiences and to enhance the logical dimension of their arguments
- To help students understand that an effective argument speaks to the values, knowledge, and interests of the intended audience
- To give students practice with appeals to *pathos* using concrete language, specific examples and

Copyright © 2010, Pearson Education, Inc., Publishing as Longman

illustrations, narratives, and visual elements to involve their audiences

- To help students understand how visual and verbal elements can work together to produce rhetorical effects: supporting the logical core of an argument, enhancing the writer's credibility and authority, and stirring audiences' emotions and imaginations
- To help students analyze and use the elements of visual design—type, layout, color, and image
- To help students think about displays of numerical data for rhetorical effect
- To help students understand that visual arguments like all arguments are products of specific historical, social, and cultural moments
- To help students apply their cumulative knowledge of good argumentation to analyzing and creating visual arguments

Readings

- Chapters 9
- In this *Instructor's Manual*, the end of Chapter Guide 9 lists all the visual arguments in the anthology.
- The opening pages of the five major parts of this text include visual arguments: political cartoons, a poster argument, a historical photograph, and an advocacy ad.

Formal Writing Assignment

Rhetorical Analysis of a visual argument (Writing Assignment, Chapter 9, page 198) or Analyzing Images essay (pages 51-52 in the IM)

Class Activities

- Group or class work with the visual arguments in Chapter 9.
- Students could bring newspaper or magazine advocacy ads for discussion.
- Group or class work (perhaps as presentations) analyzing advocacy ads in *Writing Arguments* or ones that students find on their own and bring to class
- Group or class work examining the effectiveness of visual arguments on different historical issues using "Discussion Exercise Analyzing Visual Argument in American History" in this *Instructor's Manual* (92-94). This section offers ideas for instructor-led discussions and options for student presentations.
- Students could share the drafts of their rhetorical analysis of visual arguments in peer review groups for audience feedback.

Possible Short or Informal Writing Assignments

- Any of the ideas for class activities could become class presentations or short written assignments; students could write a short analysis of an advocacy ad or a historical poster argument.
- Students could write the microtheme at the end of Chapter 9, Using a quantitative graphic (page 198) for practice working with numerical data and visual arguments.

Week 8: Evaluating Web Sites

Objectives

- To help students see Web sites as highly rhetorical purveyors of information that frame the way viewers/readers take in information and receive arguments
- To help students improve their ability to comprehend and interact with Web site sources
- To help students cope with ambiguity and disagreement by identifying the points of disagreement as differences in interpretations of facts, values, or uses of analogies
- To help students explore these differences as a step toward asking their own questions about an issue

Readings

- Chapter 16

Formal Writing Assignment

Web Site Evaluation essay (pages 45-47 of the IM)

Copyright © 2010, Pearson Education, Inc., Publishing as Longman

Class Activities

- Presentation of Web sites in class and how to analyze them rhetorically
- Peer reviewing of students' Web Site Evaluation essays

Possible Short or Informal Writing Assignments

- A 250-word summary of a possible Web site for evaluation
- An issue question and a working thesis statement (Writing Assignment, Chapter 3, pages 71-72)
- A plan of the details of the Rhetorical Analysis essay (modification of Writing Assignment, Chapter 4, pages 87-88)

Week 9-11: Research as Discovery, the "I-Search" essay, and an Introduction to Finding, Selecting, Using, and Documenting Sources

Objectives

- To provide students the opportunity to research a topic or issue or problem they know little about
- To help students understand claim types (stasis theory) as a way to determine the point of disagreement between an arguer and audience and the point where an argument is created
- To help students understand that different claim types have their own characteristic pattern of support
- To help students understand the range of sources available and to develop research skills
- To help students develop efficient habits of representing, incorporating, and documenting source material

Readings

- Chapter 10 and either all or parts of Chapters 16 and 17

Formal Writing Assignment

The I-Search essay (pages 43-44 of the IM)

Class Activities

- Group and class exercises practicing how to formulate different types of claims
- Group and class work discussing the quality of material gleaned from different sources (for example, general databases and the Web)
- A workshop on library resources conducted by a college/university reference librarian
- Peer Review of I-Search essays

Possible Short or Informal Writing Assignments

- Abstract of the I-Search essay submitted early in this unit

Weeks 12–15: Writing Civic Arguments

[Note: If students have found issues or problems they care deeply about in their I-Search essays, their civic arguments can incorporate some of that source material to make arguments about the same topic. But the civic argument and civic proposal detailed in the IM (pages @@) foster the idea of students writing not only for the course but also for an outside reader to create dialogue and change.]

Objectives

- To help students understand how to write policy proposals, practical proposals, and civic arguments
- To have students write about issues they are passionate about
- To give students practice with the "stock issues" strategy
- To give students practice with using arguments of category, consequence, and resemblance to support a proposal argument
- To help students think about and weigh alternative solutions
- To help students give presence to the problem they are seeking to solve
- To help students plan out their proposals to gain the attention of the intended audience, the people who have the power to change the situation (decision-makers) or who need to think differently about this problem

Copyright © 2010, Pearson Education, Inc., Publishing as Longman

Readings

- Chapter 15 and possibly review Chapter 10 and review of parts of Chapters 16 and 17
- In this *Instructor's Manual*, Chapter Guide 15 lists numerous anthology articles that argue proposal claims.

Formal Writing Assignment

- Prospectus if students write either a Civic Argument or a Civic Proposal

Proposal argument (either a practical proposal or a policy proposal; this essay should be be a researched argument with the minimum number of sources specified by the instructor; Writing Assignment, Chapter 15, pages 323-24), Civic Argument (pages 54-56 of the IM), or Civic Proposal (pages 57-59 of the IM)

Class Activities

- Conferences with students to discuss each student's formal Prospectus
- Review of appeals to *logos*, *ethos*, and *pathos*; students might want to enlist the audience analysis questions in Chapter 6, pages 119-20.
- Class work using the "stock-issues" strategy and the arguments of category, consequence, and resemblance as invention strategies to build students' proposal arguments
- Class and group work in which students share their presentation of their issues, their justification of their solutions, and their responses to their audiences' objections
- Class and group discussion of the strategies employed in several effective proposal arguments
- Peer reviewing of students' proposal arguments
- Students could deliver their proposal arguments as persuasive speeches.

Possible Short or Informal Writing Assignments

- Collaborative work on constructing an outline of an argument that would give a local or university problem presence, significance, and urgency

Weeks 15–16: Examining Visual Rhetoric and Creating Advocacy Advertisements

[Note: For shorter courses, instructors may want to conclude with a civic argument, omit this two-week teaching unit and the advocacy advertisement assignment, and instead do a few of these class activities within other teaching units throughout the course. For the advocacy advertisement, students could focus on an issue from their own experience (jobs, volunteer work, university organizations, etc.) or they could invent a fictional organization or advocacy group and role-play that they are representing it.]

Objectives

- To help students understand how visual and verbal elements can work together to produce rhetorical effects: supporting the logical core of an argument, enhancing the writer's credibility and authority, and stirring audiences' emotions and imaginations
- To help students analyze and use the elements of visual design—type, layout, color, and image
- To help students think about displays of numerical data for rhetorical effect
- To help students understand that visual arguments like all arguments are products of specific historical, social, and cultural moments
- To help students apply their cumulative knowledge of good argumentation to analyzing and producing visual arguments

Readings

- Review of Chapter 9 and 15
- In this *Instructor's Manual*, the end of Chapter Guide 9 lists all the visual arguments in the anthology, in particular advocacy ads

Formal Writing Assignment

Advocacy Advertisement (Writing Assignment, Chapter 15, page 324)

Class Activities

- Group or class work with visual arguments in Chapter 9.
- In groups, students could brainstorm for ideas for their advocacy advertisements. Some suggestions are issues concerning university clubs or organizations, courses, programs, living

Copyright © 2010, Pearson Education, Inc., Publishing as Longman

accommodations; availability of technology or food on campus; internships or volunteer work; or issues concerning community or job problems.

- Students could bring newspaper or magazine advocacy ads that include graphic displays of numerical data to class and discuss how clear and useful these graphics are.
- Group or class work (perhaps as presentations) analyzing advocacy ads in *Writing Arguments* or ones that students find on their own and bring to class.
- Group or class work examining the effectiveness of visual arguments on different historical issues using "Discussion Exercise Analyzing Visual Argument in American History" in this *Instructor's Manual* (pages 92-94). This section offers ideas for instructor-led discussions and options for student presentations.
- Students could share the drafts of their advocacy advertisements in peer review groups for audience feedback.

Possible Short or Informal Writing Assignments

- Any of the ideas for class activities could become class presentations or short written assignments; students could write a short analysis of an advocacy ad or a historical poster argument.
- Students could write the microtheme at the end of Chapter 9, Using a Quantitative Graphic (page 198) for practice working with numerical data and visual arguments.

SAMPLE WRITING ASSIGNMENTS

The following pages provide nine sample writing assignments that can be adapted, modified, and used by instructors: I-Search Essay, Web Site Evaluation Essay, Rhetorical Analysis Essay, Synthesis Essay, Arguing about Images Essay (Rhetorical Analysis), Argument about Images Essay (Audience Analysis), Civic Argument Essay with Prospectus, Civic Proposal with Prospectus, and a Recommendation Report Case. These assignments are to serve as examples for instructors to create their own writing prompts.

All of these assignments have been used successfully in writing classrooms that focus on argumentation and research-based writing. And instructors could easily craft their own syllabus using assignments similar to these.

A brief description of each writing assignment is below:

The I-Search Essay

This assignment is adapted from Ken Macrorie's *The I-Search Paper*. The exploratory essay makes students see research as discovery rather than as drudgery. It's best to have students research an issue, problem, or concern about which they have little or no prior knowledge. The writing task fosters reflection about the research process and the topic itself while also challenging students to grapple with and synthesize various sources.

Web Site Evaluation Essay

Students have found this assignment instructive because they tend to look much more deeply at Web sites than they usually do. The assignment reinforces looking at a source's frame of vision, assumptions, and beliefs/values.

Copyright © 2010, Pearson Education, Inc., Publishing as Longman

Rhetorical Analysis Essay

As can be seen in two of the sample syllabi, the rhetorical analysis paper can serve as the linchpin for an argument-based composition course because its goal—an evaluation argument about an argument—combines argumentation and strong analytical reading. This academic essay in rhetorical criticism is especially productive if an instructor assigns sections from the anthology for reading and discussion.

Synthesis Essay

Similar to the textbook's writing assignment that makes a writer analyze sources of disagreement between two sources on the same topic, this writing assignment makes students synthesize four sources about an issue, argument, or controversy. This essay is very productive as a lead-in before student-writers write a researched argument. Student-writers can use the synthesis essay as a way to research a problem or issue that they plan to write about in a subsequent paper.

Analyzing Images Essay (Rhetorical Analysis)

This sample assignment is simply a visual argument rhetorical analysis as referenced in Chapter 9 of *Writing Arguments*.

Analyzing Images (Audience Analysis)

One way to modify the Arguing about Images assignment is to have students look at two different ads that sell the same type of products with different ads in different magazines (different audiences). Such a change in rhetorical purpose alters the essay to be a study both in audience analysis and rhetorical effectiveness.

Civic Argument Essay with Prospectus

This writing assignment has student-writers construct a classical argument, but it's an argument that can and should move beyond the classroom. Students write their arguments about a "local" issue, but they also craft cover letters that go along with the arguments. Writers can send their cover letters and arguments together to address a problem or issue that they see in their communities, their campuses, their hometowns, or their states. A formal prospectus before peer review of initial drafts ensures that student-writers have done substantial research prior to drafting and they've thought about how to construct their arguments. Many instructors conference with students after they submit their prospecti.

Part of one class day should be spent explaining and giving recommendations on how the cover letter for the argument should be constructed. In general, the first paragraph should address the outside reader's questions: Who are you? Why are you writing me? What is your argument/point? The second and third paragraphs should provide a synopsis of the author's argument. And the final paragraph of the cover letter should reinforce the writer's argument, offer good will, and relate some expectation for further contact.

Civic Proposal with Prospectus

This assignment is similar to the civic argument in that it fosters that idea that student-writers need to become critical citizens through their writing. But this assignment is somewhat different

Copyright © 2010, Pearson Education, Inc., Publishing as Longman

in that it is uses the genre of the professional practical or policy proposal. It's not an essay format. It's a proposal with single-spacing, headings, subheadings, and appendices. Like the civic argument it also requires a cover letter addressed to an outside reader.

Recommendation Report Case

This professional writing case format provides an example of how people craft arguments in the workplace. This example relies on the student-writer practicing rhetorical numeracy, meaning that the writer has to calculate and use numerical data for persuasive purposes. In this case, the two insurance plans—Logos Mutual and Alliance Federated—that the writer has to choose from provide slightly different costs for the company per month based on current staffing. An argument could be made for either plan because one writer could argue for Alliance Federated because it's cheaper per month, while another writer could argue for Logos Mutual because it's co-payments as a whole are better for employees although it's slightly more expensive for the company. The keys for a successful report are these: concise syntax and diction, reader-friendly design, a bottom-line (thesis) clearly stated in three different sections of the report, and well developed and argumentatively rich reasons for the writer's recommendation supported by accurate and persuasive data.

Copyright © 2010, Pearson Education, Inc., Publishing as Longman

The "I Search" Essay

Abstract due:
Peer Review:
Due:
Minimum page requirement: pages, Times New Roman—12

Writing Task
This paper is designed to teach the writer and the reader something valuable about a chosen topic and about the nature of searching and discovery. As opposed to the standard research paper where a writer usually assumes a detached and objective stance, the "I Search" paper allows you to relate your experience of hunting for facts and opinions firsthand, and to provide a step-by-step record of the search process. It's a research paper that is overtly reflective.

Topic
Choose a topic that truly interests you, a problem or concern you want to be more informed about. The topic, however, has to be argumentatively rich, meaning that there have to be many different viewpoints on the issue. It's up to you to choose a suitable topic, but there are some topics that cannot be researched.

The Abstract
After you have chosen a topic and checked to make sure research sources are available through resources at the library (the catalog, Lexis-Nexis, EbscoHost, Thomson-Gale, et al.), you will type up an abstract, no less than one page and not to exceed two pages (double-spaced) in length, in which you explain what your topic is, why you have chosen it, and how you intend to go about searching and writing. If you do not submit an abstract on [Date], 10 points will be deducted from the grade of your "I Search" essay each day that the abstract is late. You have to submit an abstract.

Format
The paper should have three distinct sections: 1) What I Know, Assume or Imagine; 2) The Search; and 3) What I Discovered. The three-part format of this paper can be organized explicitly—for example, set off with subheadings—or implicitly.

Part I: What I Know, Assume, or Imagine

Before conducting any formal research, write a section in which you explain to the reader what you think you know, what you assume, or what you imagine about your topic. For example, if you decide to investigate teenage alcoholism, you might want to offer some ideas about the causes of teenage alcoholism, provide an estimate of the severity of the problem, and create a portrait of a typical teenage drinker prior to conducting your search.

Part II: The Search

Test your knowledge, assumptions or conjectures by researching your topic thoroughly. Consult useful books, magazines newspapers, films, and library databases for information. When possible, interview people who are authorities or who are familiar with your topic. If you were pursuing a search on teenage alcoholism, you might want to check out a book on the subject, read several pertinent articles in a variety of current magazines, make an appointment to visit an

Copyright © 2010, Pearson Education, Inc., Publishing as Longman

alcohol rehabilitation center, attend a meeting of Alanon or Alcoholics Anonymous, and consult an alcoholism counselor. You might also ask a number of teenagers from different social and/or economic backgrounds what their first exposure to alcohol has been and whether they perceive any alcohol "problem" among their peers.

Write about your search in a narrative form (chronologically with specific details) to record the steps of the discovery process. Do not feel obligated to tell everything, but highlight the happenings and facts you uncovered that were crucial to your hunt and contributed to your understanding of the topic. Document sources of information using citations when appropriate and necessary.

Part III: What I Discovered

After concluding your search, compare what you thought you knew, assumed, or imagined with what you actually discovered and offer some personal commentary and/or draw some conclusions. For instance after completing your search on teenage alcoholism, you might learn that the problem is far more severe and often begins at an earlier age than you formerly believed. You may have assumed that parental neglect was a key factor in the incidence of teenage alcoholism, but now you have found that peer pressure is the prime-contributing factor. Consequently, you might want to propose that an alcoholism awareness and prevention program including peer counseling sessions be instituted in the public school system as early as sixth grade. This part of the paper will also contain citations indicating the information you learned from your sources.

Works Cited page and In-text Citations

Your essay should also use a minimum of 4 different sources either by quotation, paraphrase, or display of information documented in MLA or APA style (Chapter 17 of *Writing Arguments*). No long quotations are permitted. And "website" sources are not permitted, so you need to use Web search engines (EbscoHost, Infotrac, Lexis-Nexis, et al.). The essay requires a Works Cited page that follows MLA or APA specifications (Chapter 17 of *Writing Arguments*).

Audience

Address your paper to peer-scholars who might be interested in your subject and could be interested in your analysis and/or findings.

Copyright © 2010, Pearson Education, Inc., Publishing as Longman

Web Site Evaluation Essay

Peer Review:

Due:

minimum page requirement: pages, Times New Roman—12

Writing Task

The purpose of this paper is for you to provide your evaluation of a Web site. Think of the paper as a critique of the strengths and weaknesses of a certain Web site. As an evaluator you need to express the usefulness and limits of the site, and you can only analyze Web pages that end in .com (a business or corporate site) or .org (a nonprofit organization or advocacy group site).

This paper will obviously entail browsing the Web and finding an appropriate, rhetorically rich Web site. This is not a summary paper, but your essay should provide a concise summary of the Web site early on to orient your reader. Throughout the essay you will also need to acknowledge important aspects of the Web page through description, paraphrase, and a few direct quotations.

The heart of the essay should present and develop your own "take" about the Web site using appropriate criteria for evaluation (see "Criteria for Evaluating a Web Site"), and you must support that take with strong reflection, reasoning, and details. State your judgment clearly and support it with persuasive points that could influence your reader to your way of thinking or at least have your reader see your viewpoint clearly.

Here are some basic questions that will help you evaluate a Web site:

- Ethos—How credible or authoritative is the author or sponsor? Does the site seem fair-minded in that it permits alternative perspectives, or does the site only offer one frame of reference on issues or problems? Are different perspectives considered? Is the site one-sided? Is it biased in any way?
- Pathos—How does the site use emotional examples or visual images to persuade? Is this done ethically? How does the site appeal to certain values and beliefs of its target audience? Could those appeals distance some readers?
- Logos—How does the site use evidence? What is used to support the author or sponsor's rhetorical purpose: personal experience, field research, outside sources, statistics, hard evidence, anecdotes, real-life experiences, hypothetical experiences? Does the Web site use any specific argumentative modes like cause-effect reasoning, definitional claims, appeals to ethics/morals, resemblance arguments, proposals? Are these used effectively? Where are the flaws in reasoning or logic?

This essay involves working with a source, so you need to use quotation, paraphrase, or display of information using the MLA Style of referencing source material. The essay should also provide a separate Works Cited page that provides information about the article.

Audience

Address your paper to peer-scholars who might be interested in your subject and could be interested in your analysis and/or findings. But also imagine your audience as somewhat informed but undecided people who might take an opposing viewpoint from your own.

Copyright © 2010, Pearson Education, Inc., Publishing as Longman

Evaluation

Your essay needs to have a clear purpose with ample detail to support this purpose, and it should have a recognizable thesis/organizing idea by the end of third paragraph at the latest. The essay should have a beginning that generates interest, an ending that provides a sense of closure, and the parts in between should be arranged in a logical and rhetorically effective sequence. The essay should demonstrate stylistic maturity and mastery of editorial conventions (grammatical correctness).

Criteria for Evaluating a Web Site

The following criteria are taken from Ramage, Bean, and Johnson's *Writing Arguments*, 8th ed (365):

Criterion 1: Authority

- Is the author or sponsor of the Web site clearly identified?
- Does the site identify the occupation, position, education, experience, and credentials of the site's authors?
- Does the introductory material reveal the author's or sponsor's motivation for publishing this information on the Web?
- Does the site provide contact information for the author or sponsor such as an e-mail or organization address?

Criterion 2: Objectivity or Clear Disclosure of Advocacy

- Is the site's purpose (to inform, explain, or persuade) clear?
- Is the site explicit about declaring its author's or sponsor's point of view?
- Does the site indicate whether authors are affiliated with a specific organization, institution, or association?
- Does the site indicate whether it is directed toward a specific audience?

Criterion 3: Coverage

- Are the topics covered by the site clear?
- Does the site exhibit suitable depth and comprehensiveness for its purpose?
- Is sufficient evidence provided to support the ideas and opinions presented?

Criterion 4: Accuracy

- Are the sources of information stated? Can you tell whether this information is original or taken from someplace else?
- Does the information appear to be accurate? Can you verify this information by comparing this source with other sources in the field?

Copyright © 2010, Pearson Education, Inc., Publishing as Longman

Criterion 5: Currency

- Are dates included in the Web site?
- Do the dates apply to the material itself or to its placement on the Web? Is the site regularly revised and updated?
- Is the information current, or at least still relevant, for the site's purpose?

Helpful Analytical Tools for Analyzing Evidence

"Questions for Rhetorical Analysis" in *Writing Arguments*, 8th ed. (148-50)

From Richard Fulkerson's *Teaching the Argument in Writing*

STAR
S—*Sufficiency of grounds*: Is there *enough* evidence to warrant the claim drawn?
T—*Typicality*: Are the data *representative* of the group of data being argued about?
A—*Accuracy*: Is the information used as data *true*?
R—*Relevance*: Is the claim asserted *relevant* to the information about the sample?

GASCAP
G—Argument for a Generalization
A—Argument from Analogy
S—Argument from Sign
C—Causal Argument
A—Argument from Authority
P—Argument from Principle

Copyright © 2010, Pearson Education, Inc., Publishing as Longman

Rhetorical Analysis Essay

Peer Review:
Due:
minimum page requirement: pages, Times New Roman—12

Writing Task

Write an essay that responds to and evaluates a particular article we have read from this unit (see syllabus). This is not a summary paper, but your essay should provide a concise summary of the article early on to orient your reader. Throughout the essay you will also need to acknowledge important parts of the article through paraphrase, description, and a few direct quotations.

The overall purpose of this paper is to show your analysis and evaluation of the author's ideas. Think of the paper as a way to discuss the strong and weak points of a particular piece of writing by using concepts we have learned in this class—appeals to credibility/character (ethos), emotion (pathos), and logic (logos); the various types of assumptions (gascap); the Toulmin system; STAR; logical fallacies; and other essential concepts and analytical tools. The paper is a way to put your thoughts in dialogue with the author's to evaluate whether the author's argument is strong.

In short, this is an essay that analyzes/critiques the integrity of an argument, how effectively an author supports his/her argument, claims, and assertions.
This is not a summary paper. You are essentially judging whether the article provides a strong argument or not.

You should present and develop your own "take" on the article, and you should support that take with reflection and detail. State your judgment clearly and support your evaluation with persuasive points that could influence your reader to your way of thinking or at least have your reader see your viewpoint clearly.

This essay involves working with a source, so you should use quotation, paraphrase, or display of information from the selected article to MLA or APA specifications (see Chapter 17 of *Writing Arguments*). The essay should also provide a separate Works Cited page that provides accurate, properly formatted information about the article.

Audience

Address your paper to peer-scholars who might be interested in your subject and could be interested in your analysis and/or findings. But also imagine your audience as somewhat informed but undecided people who might take an opposing viewpoint from your own.

Evaluation

Your essay needs to have a clear purpose with ample detail to support this purpose, and it needs to have an assertive thesis at least by the end of the third paragraph. The essay should have a beginning that generates interest, an ending that provides a sense of closure, and the parts in between should be arranged in a logical and rhetorically effective sequence. The essay should demonstrate stylistic maturity and mastery of editorial conventions (grammatical correctness).

Copyright © 2010, Pearson Education, Inc., Publishing as Longman

A Successful Rhetorical Analysis Essay

- Provides a concise and accurate summary of the article early on to orient the reader
- Offers an assertive thesis that directs the action of the essay and reflects the whole essay
- Has a thesis that makes an evaluative judgment about the effectiveness of the author's argument
- Offers strong support for its thesis by using specific details and detailed analysis of how the author effectively or ineffectively supports his or her argument
- Uses analytical tools appropriate to the argument he or she is evaluating
- Paraphrases and integrates quotations from an article effectively, smoothly, and ethically through appropriate signal phrases and parenthetical citations in MLA Style
- Uses third person voice to analyze the article, not the first person or second person

Helpful Analytical Tools for Analyzing Evidence

"Questions for Rhetorical Analysis" in *Writing Arguments*, 8th ed. (148-50)

STAR

S—*Sufficiency of grounds*: Is there *enough* evidence to warrant the claim drawn?
T—*Typicality*: Are the data *representative* of the group of data being argued about?
A—*Accuracy*: Is the information used as data *true*?
R—*Relevance*: Is the claim asserted *relevant* to the information about the sample?

GASCAP

G—Argument for a Generalization
A—Argument from Analogy
S—Argument from Sign
C—Causal Argument
A—Argument from Authority
P—Argument from Principle

(from Richard Fulkerson's *Teaching the Argument in Writing*)

An Aristotelian and Toulmin influenced way of looking at looking at Argument:
An **enthymeme** is claim or assertion with reasons that has an unstated assumption.

An arguer makes a **Claim**

that has **Stated Reasons**, and

Grounds support the stated reasons by giving evidence to validate or verify them.

Many claims have unstated assumptions, which are called **Warrants**.

Backing needs to be provided, an argument to support the warrant.

Copyright © 2010, Pearson Education, Inc., Publishing as Longman

Synthesis Essay

Peer Review:

Due:

minimum page requirement: pages, Times New Roman—12

Writing Task

Write an essay that synthesizes at least four sources about a debatable issue, an issue that you may later write about for your [position or problem/solution] essay. The purpose of this paper is to show how different writers discuss and provide evidence for their viewpoints on a highly debated subject. You also need to think about each writer's reasons and assumptions in the debate. In sum, this paper's purpose is to inform the reader about the different sides/issues of a debate by identifying major points by each author and creating a balanced presentation about the issue.

Special Notes: Only one "website" source is permitted, but you can obviously use web search engines (examples—EbscoHost, Infotrac, Lexis-Nexis) to find published articles. And since this is a research-based paper, your essay has to provide a separate Works Cited page that has accurate information about the articles in MLA format (see Chapter 17 of *Writing Arguments*). In this paper, you will not be allowed to use 1st person point of view ("I" or "we") or 2nd person point of view ("you"). You have to use 3rd person point of view.

Audience

Address your paper to peer-scholars who might be interested in your subject and could be interested in your analysis and/or findings. Your audience needs to be informed about the issue through sound summary, paraphrase, and quotations (Chapter 17 of *Writing Arguments*). And you need to show how each writer supports his or her argument.

Evaluation

Your essay needs to have a clear purpose with ample detail to support this purpose, and it should have a recognizable thesis or organizing idea that is a summation of the perspectives on this issue by the end of the third paragraph. The essay should have a beginning that generates interest, an ending that provides a sense of closure, and the parts in between should be arranged in a logical and rhetorically effective sequence. The essay should demonstrate stylistic maturity and mastery of editorial conventions (grammatical correctness).

Copyright © 2010, Pearson Education, Inc., Publishing as Longman

Analyzing Images Essay (Rhetorical Analysis)

Peer Review:

Due:

minimum page requirement: pages; Times New Roman—12

Writing Task

Write an essay that analyzes one print advertisement. Describe the ad in detail so your reader can easily visualize it, but the main focus of the paper is analysis/critique. In addition to analyzing the rhetorical appeals made by the advertisement, you need to criticize the ad by commenting on what it conveys about our culture.

You can't assume that the reader can see the ad, so it's imperative that the essay has an effective lead-in to introduce the ad to the reader. You need to create a "hook" that transitions to the ad, you have to concisely describe it early on, and then the essay has to assert a thesis that is an argumentative conclusion about the ad. The essay has to have an identifiable position on what the ad does and means, and it has to support that position with detailed analysis.

Here are questions you have to consider:

- How does the ad appeal to its target audience? To what values does the ad appeal? And how is the ad constructed to appeal to those values? (use of color, copy, document design, layout, graphics, and images). What strategies does the advertiser use?
- What does this ad say about our culture? (issues of gender, race/ethnicity, body image, beauty, health, self esteem, sexuality, et al.) Are the explicit and implicit messages positive, negative, wholesome, troubling, realistic, infuriating, noble, pathetic?

Audience

Address your paper to peer-scholars who might be interested in your subject and could be interested in your analysis and/or findings. But also imagine your audience as somewhat informed but undecided people who might take an opposing viewpoint from your own.

Evaluation

Your essay needs to have a clear purpose with ample detail to support this purpose, and it needs to have an assertive thesis at least by the end of the second paragraph. The essay should have a beginning that generates interest, an ending that provides a sense of closure, and the parts in between should be arranged in a logical and rhetorically effective sequence. The essay should demonstrate stylistic maturity and mastery of editorial conventions (grammatical correctness).

Copyright © 2010, Pearson Education, Inc., Publishing as Longman

A Successful Analyzing Images Essay

- Provides a concise, accurate, and descriptive summary of the ad early on to orient the reader
- Offers an assertive thesis that directs the action of the essay and reflects the whole essay
- Has a thesis that makes an evaluative judgment about the effectiveness of the ad and how it reflects American culture
- Offers strong support for its thesis by using specific details and detailed analysis of how the ad attempts to persuade
- Uses the concepts of ethos (appeal to credibility, character), logos (appeal to logic, reason), and pathos (appeal to emotions, values, beliefs) appropriately with the ad he or she is evaluating
- Uses third person voice to analyze the article, not the first person or second person

Copyright © 2010, Pearson Education, Inc., Publishing as Longman

Analyzing Images Essay (Audience Analysis)

Peer Review:

Due:

minimum page requirement: 4 pages, Times New Roman—12

Writing Task

Write an essay that analyzes and critiques two print advertisements that sell the same kind of product but appeal to different audiences (for example, a car advertisement aimed at men and one aimed at women; a cigarette ad aimed at upper-middle-class consumers and one aimed at working-class consumers; a clothing ad from the *New Yorker* and one from *Maxim*).

You can't assume that the reader can see the ads, so it's imperative that the essay has an effective lead-in to introduce the ads to the reader. You need to create a "hook" that transitions to the ad, you have to concisely describe it early on, and then the essay has to assert a thesis that is an argumentative conclusion about the ad. The essay has to have an identifiable position on how effectively the ads connect to their target audiences and what they say about our culture, and the essay has to support that position with detailed analysis.

Here are questions you have to consider:

- How do the ads appeal to their target audiences? To what values do the ad appeals? And how are the ads constructed to appeal to those values? (use of color, copy, document design, layout, graphics, and images). What strategies does the advertiser use?
- What do these ads say about our culture and how we view those target audiences? (issues of gender, race/ethnicity, body image, beauty, health, self esteem, sexuality, et al.) Are the explicit and implicit messages positive, negative, wholesome, troubling, realistic, infuriating, noble, pathetic?

Audience

Address your paper to peer-scholars who might be interested in your subject and could be interested in your analysis and/or findings. But also imagine your audience as somewhat informed but undecided people who might take an opposing viewpoint from your own.

Evaluation

Your essay needs to have a clear purpose with ample detail to support this purpose, and it should have a recognizable thesis or organizing idea. It should have a beginning that generates interest, an ending that provides a sense of closure, and the parts in between should be arranged in a logical and rhetorically effective sequence. Essays should demonstrate stylistic maturity and mastery of editorial conventions (grammatical correctness).

Copyright © 2010, Pearson Education, Inc., Publishing as Longman

Civic Argument Essay

Peer Review:

Essay with cover letter due:

Format

Times New Roman—12 font

1 essay that articulates a problem you see and your position on that problem or issue (minimum of 6 pages, double-spaced), plus a Works Cited page

1 cover letter addressing a real audience (I will provide specifics on cover letter expectations)

Point total: __ point journal

Writing Task:

Write an essay that takes a stand on an arguable issue and supports its position through the use of strong description and evidence, real and/or likely examples, clear establishment of terms, acknowledgment and analysis of counterarguments, and careful reasoning. You need to analyze the issue and present your position by appealing to credibility/character (ethos), emotions/values (pathos), and logic (logos).

As for topics, you will have to identify a problem in your neighborhood, your city, the state of Illinois, or Eastern Illinois University and work with it. Keep in mind that you should pick a subject that you might be able to change, and also one about which you can address an outside audience. Here are the basic categories from which you should brainstorm a topic:

- An issue at [your university or college]
- An issue in the [town/city of the college]
- An issue in your neighborhood, city, or suburb
- An issue in the state of [your state]

This essay will have to be organized in an argumentative structure passed down from classical rhetoric. Here is the basic structure of classical argument:

- Introduction: background, context, review of conversation, why the reader should care.
- Thesis: statement of claim and reasons.
- Support of reasons and assumptions.
- Answers to possible objections (counterarguments).
- Conclusion: review of major points, the contribution of this argument, a call to action, possible solutions.

Your introduction should provide necessary background about the issue, interest your reader, establish your credibility, and clearly state your position (your thesis, which is an argumentative conclusion). The body of your argument will summarize and respond to opposing views as well as present reasons and evidence in support of your own position. You need to choose whether to summarize and refute opposing views before or after you have made your own case, or you can intermix the two components. The essay needs to avoid using first person singular ("I") and second person ("you"), but if you use personal experience or examples it's entirely appropriate to use "I" when relating that experience.

Copyright © 2010, Pearson Education, Inc., Publishing as Longman

Here are some subjects that are not permitted: abortion, capital punishment, euthanasia, affirmative action, cloning, gun control, medical marijuana, stem cells, the death penalty, drunk driving, the drinking age, seat belts, school uniforms, prayer in public schools, the conceal to carry law, smoking bans, constitutional bans on homosexual marriages, and the legalization of marijuana or other drugs. I reserve the right to veto topics. The prospectus works as a safety net.

Your essay should use a minimum of 4 different sources, either by quotation, paraphrase, or display of information. See these resources or me if you need assistance:

- Chapters 16 and 17 of *Writing Arguments*
- Purdue's OWL on Quoting, Paraphrasing, and Summarizing: http://owl.english.purdue.edu/owl/resource/557/01/

No long, block quotations are permitted. No Web site sources are permitted unless cleared by me, so you need to use web search engines to find appropriate sources and articles (EbscoHost, Infotrac, Lexis-Nexis, et al.).

And the essay will need to have a Works Cited page that follows MLA specifications.
See these resources or me if you need assistance:

- Chapter 17 of *Writing Arguments*
- Purdue's OWL on Works Cited pages: http://owl.english.purdue.edu/owl/resource/557/06/

In *Collision Course: Conflict, Negotiation, and Learning in College Composition*, Russel K. Durst effectively sums up the argument paper: "Written argument, to be effective, not only involves passion and enthusiasm. It also requires complexity of thought, preparation, and sustained attention. Such writing must be built systematically, conflicting positions examined, one's own developing views related to those of others, evidence generated and then sifted through, generalizations critiqued, audience taken into account, questions of essay structure considered" (108).

Your Role and Audience
You should write the essay from a position of power to readers who might take an opposing viewpoint from your own. You need to show that there is a problem and its effects. And then you need to have a plausible solution for that problem.

In addition to choosing a problem and proposing a solution for it, you can present your paper to one or more members of a group or to an outsider who might help solve the problem or address the issue. Your "paper" should include a cover letter that addresses your real audience and an argument essay. In the cover letter, you should briefly address why you are writing this person or group and provide an introduction to your argument paper. Besides submitting your paper to me, you can actually submit your work to your outside reader.

Copyright © 2010, Pearson Education, Inc., Publishing as Longman

Evaluation

Your essay needs to have a clear purpose with ample detail to support this purpose. It should have a beginning that generates interest, an ending that provides a sense of closure, and the parts in between should be arranged in a logical and rhetorically effective sequence. The essay should demonstrate stylistic maturity and mastery of editorial conventions (grammatical correctness).

Copyright © 2010, Pearson Education, Inc., Publishing as Longman

The Prospectus

Due: [a week or two prior to peer review]
minimum page requirement: 3 pages + working bibliography, Times New Roman
Point total: __ point journal

Writing Task
This pre-writing journal is designed to work as formal heuristic, a document that explores the subject you will write about in your argument/research paper. The focus is for you to reflect on your research and think about how you will construct your argument.

You should address these questions with a great deal of depth and development:
1. What research problem do you intend to address? Why is it problematic? Why is it important? Why should the reader care?
2. What are the many different sides (more than just two) to the issue? How do different people argue about this problem? What are the many possible solutions for this problem? Who are some possible outside readers?
3. What is your working thesis or organizing idea (your position) right now? What are your main points and what support (examples, evidence, likely stories, source material, and logical reasoning) will you provide and in what order? Provide specific details as to how you will support your position and also address counterarguments. How will people argue against your position? How can you concede, accommodate, and refute those counterarguments?
4. Attach a bibliography of sources you have read or intend to use. These must be provided in a separate Works Cited page with proper MLA documentation.

Special note: If you do not complete a prospectus and submit it by the due date, you forfeit your chance to write the essay.

Copyright © 2010, Pearson Education, Inc., Publishing as Longman

Civic Proposal

Peer Review:

Proposal with Cover Letter due:

Formats

The proposal should articulate a problem and argue for a specific solution.

Point total: ___ point writing assignment

The proposal should have these basics:

- a minimum of four pages of single-spaced writing, excluding the references or works cited page
- a report format with headings and effective use of white space
- source information cited either through the APA or MLA citation system
- a minimum of five outside sources used, one of which is peer-reviewed
- a references or works cited page

A cover letter must address an outside audience about your proposal.

Point total: __ point journal

Writing Task

Write a proposal that takes a stand and supports its position through the use of strong description and evidence, real or likely examples, clear establishment of terms, careful reasoning, and acknowledgment and analysis of counterarguments (how someone would argue against the problem or your solution).

You need to show that there is a problem that needs to be addressed (discussing causes and effects). You then need to sift through all the possible solutions and persuade your audience that your solution is the most effective strategy to help the problem.

As for topics, you will have to identify a "local" problem and work with it. Here are the basic categories from which you should brainstorm about an issue or problem:

- [College or University]
- Your workplace
- [Town-City/County]
- Your neighborhood, city, or suburb
- The state of [your state]

Keep in mind that you should pick a subject that you might be able to change, and also one about which you can address an outside reader. The proposal needs to avoid using first-person singular ("I") and second-person ("you"), but if you use personal experience or examples, it's entirely appropriate to use "I" when relating that experience.

In addition to choosing a problem and proposing a solution for it, you can present your paper to one or more members of a group or to an outsider who might help solve the problem or address the issue. This writing assignment should include a cover letter that addresses why you are writing this person or group and provides an introduction and summary of your proposal. Besides submitting your paper to me, you can actually submit your work to your outside reader.

Copyright © 2010, Pearson Education, Inc., Publishing as Longman

Your report should use a minimum of five different sources, either by quotation, paraphrase, or display of information. Long, block quotations are not permitted. If you need to use a website source, you must clear it with me, and Wikipedia is not a safe source. The proposal needs to have a References/Works Cited page that follows APA or MLA specifications.

In *Collision Course: Conflict, Negotiation, and Learning in College Composition*, Russel K. Durst effectively sums up the argument paper: "Written argument, to be effective, not only involves passion and enthusiasm. It also requires complexity of thought, preparation, and sustained attention. Such writing must be built systematically, conflicting positions examined, one's own developing views related to those of others, evidence generated and then sifted through, generalizations critiqued, audience taken into account, questions of essay structure considered" (108).

Here are some subjects that are not permitted: abortion, capital punishment, euthanasia, affirmative action, cloning, gun control, medical marijuana, stem cells, the death penalty, drunk driving, the drinking age, seat belts, school uniforms, prayer in public schools, the conceal to carry law, smoking bans, constitutional bans on homosexual marriages, and the legalization of marijuana or other drugs. I reserve the right to veto topics. The prospectus works as a safety net.

Your Role and Audience

You should write the proposal from a position of power to readers who might take an opposing viewpoint from your own. You need to show that there is a problem and its effects. And then you need to have a plausible solution for that problem.

Your proposal needs to have a clear purpose with ample detail to support this purpose. It should have a beginning that generates interest, an ending that provides a sense of closure, and the parts in between should be arranged in a logical and rhetorically effective sequence. The document should demonstrate stylistic maturity and mastery of editorial conventions (appropriate style/tone and grammatical correctness).

Format

This civic proposal should be organized in this manner and use headings and subheadings where appropriate:

- Title Page: provide a title and your name.
- Summary: present a concise one-paragraph summary of your proposal.
- Introduction: provide background information and key issues of the document while previewing the report's content and your bottom-line (your proposal).
- Problem/Opportunity: present an analysis of the problem that you are addressing with strong details and examples while contending with counterarguments.
- Solution: argue for your specific solution with cogent and sound argumentation while grappling with counterarguments.
- Conclusion: provide a summation of your civic proposal, but not in the same exact words as other sections.
- Back Matter: offer a properly formatted Works Cited or References page and appendices (tables, charts, diagrams) if they are not integrated into the text

Copyright © 2010, Pearson Education, Inc., Publishing as Longman

A Successful Civic Proposal

- Provides a concise summation of your proposal in the first section of report.
- Offers an introduction that provides context and background for the reader while briefly introducing your solution.
- Explains the problem by using appropriate, accurate, and logically sound assertions, examples, and details.
- Offers a solution section that persuades readers by making logical and ethical claims that show how your proposal will help solve the problem or address the opportunity through a solution that is ethical, just, and practical.
- Provides a concise conclusion section that connects to the bottom-line (your solution).
- Has focused and unified paragraphs that are appropriately developed.
- Is free of irrelevant details.
- Follows the proper format of a proposal by using headings and subheadings.
- Exhibits strong concision, cohesion, transitions, and sentence variety in length and type.
- Provides a medium level of tone and diction—not too formal but not too informal.
- Is free of mechanical and proofreading errors.

Copyright © 2010, Pearson Education, Inc., Publishing as Longman

The Prospectus

Due:

minimum page requirement: 3 pages (double-spaced) plus working bibliography, Times New Roman

Point total: __ point journal

Your task

This pre-writing journal is designed to work as formal heuristic, a document that explores the subject you will write about in your proposal. The focus is for you to reflect on your research and think about how you will construct your argument.

You should address these questions with a great deal of depth and development:

1. What problem do you intend to address? Why is it problematic? Why is it important? What are its causes and effects? Why should the reader care?
2. What are the many different sides (more than just two) to the issue? How do different people argue about this problem? What are the many possible solutions for this problem? Who are possibilities for your outside reader?
3. What is your working thesis or organizing idea right now—what do you think is the best solution and why? How do you intend to structure your argument specifically? What are your main points and what support (examples, evidence, likely stories, source material, and logical reasoning) will you provide in what order? Provide specific details as to how you will support your position and also address counterarguments and other solutions.
4. In regard to your tentative solution, how can it appeal to concerns about ethics, justice, and practicality? Germane to ethics, how can you argue from authority and principle? Germane to justice, how can you argue from analogy (precedent) and authority from law? Germane to practicality, how can you argue from analogies, from signs, and based from causality?
5. Attach a bibliography of sources you have read or intend to use. These must be provided in a separate Works Cited page with proper APA or MLA documentation.

Copyright © 2010, Pearson Education, Inc., Publishing as Longman

Recommendation Report Case

Peer Review:

Due:

What You Should Do First

Read everything on both sides of these sheets of paper before you begin drafting, composing, revising, and refining your report (your response to the case). Also remember that you are supposed to use your own prose when crafting this document.

Your Role and Position

You are the Associate Partner of Sweeney Brothers Consulting, a small firm based in St. Louis, Missouri. After you graduated from the University of Alabama with a Management and Marketing major and a minor in Professional Writing in 2000, you started with Sweeney Brothers and have steadily moved up the ranks of this prestigious and well-regarded international consulting firm. You began as an entry-level consultant, got promoted to Assistant Partner, and then moved to the position you have now. Within the organization of the company, you are third in charge since there are two Executive Partners who started the company in 1995. When the firm began, it consisted of those two gentlemen. Now in 2008 the original two are Executive Partners, there is one Associate Partner (you), there is one Assistant Partner, and the firm employs twelve Business and Organizational Consultants.

The Rhetorical Situation

The two Executive Partners, Stan and Frank Sweeney, have assigned you to research available insurance plans because health insurance costs for your company have risen steadily over the past few years. The firm is doing well financially, but health insurance costs have started to cut into profits. Both Stan and Frank are ready to drop the company's current insurance plan and move to a different one.

At present, Sweeney Brothers has tended to attract recent graduates from business programs across the country when they hire new people. Because of lucrative consultant contracts that you've won and negotiated over the past few years (one of the reasons why you're now Associate Partner), the firm has hired six new people over the past five years, and those new hires usually have been fresh out of college or a year or two out of college.

So of the company's twelve Business and Organizational Consultants, seven of them are single (one man, six women), two are married but don't have kids (one man, one woman), and three (two are men, one is a woman) are married and/or have kids. Of those three, two have been with the company for a long time—one since 1996, the other since 1998. Of those three employees, one ('96) is divorced and has two children (woman), one ('98) is married and has three children (man), and one is married and has five children (man). The Assistant Partner (male) is married and has two children. Stan is married and has three children. Frank, the black sheep of the Sweeney clan, is single. You are married and have two children.

After extensive research about insurance plans that are stronger than the company's current plan, you've selected two different plans that will work. But they're different in costs and co-payments.

Copyright © 2010, Pearson Education, Inc., Publishing as Longman

The first plan is from Logos Mutual. During your research, you jotted down notes of common medical procedures along with co-payments that employees will have to pay for (and their dependents). The typical medical procedures are as follows: emergency room, $110; routine physical, $45; diagnostics (x-rays, etc.), $75; outpatient mental health service, $50; pap smear, $45; prenatal checkup, $20; childbirth, $150. As for typical dental procedures, they are as follows: cleaning and checkups, $20; filling, $100; oral surgery, $200, orthodontics, pay 50%; orthodontic adjustments, $50.

You also calculated how much per month the company would have to pay per employee to buy into the Logos Mutual plan. The numbers are as follows: single person, $80; married couple, $150; each dependent, $100.

The competing plan is from Alliance Federated. The typical medical procedures are as follows: emergency room, $150; routine physical, $30; diagnostics (x-rays, etc.), $50; outpatient mental health service, $30; pap smear, $60; prenatal checkup, $40; childbirth, $300. As for typical dental procedures, they are as follows: cleaning and checkups, $40; filling, $80; oral surgery, $300, orthodontics, pay 30%; orthodontic adjustments, $75.

You also calculate how much per month the company will have to pay per employee to buy into the Alliance Federated plan. The numbers are as follows: single male, $65; single female, $70; married couple, $175; single person with dependent/s (not per dependent), $300; married couple with dependent/s (not per dependent), $400.

Both plans are stronger than the current insurance plan. For example, the company's current policy's numbers (by Dewey, Cheatham, and Howe) are as follows: single person, $110; married couple, $300; each dependent, $150.

The Executive Partners asked you to analyze two competing plans and give them the numbers in a recommendation report. The Sweeney brothers not only expect you to provide accurate numbers of the competing plans, but they also expect you to provide a recommendation for which plan the firm should select according to the current staff. And both brothers have told you that they plan to keep hiring young Business and Organizational Consultants in the future because their salaries aren't as costly as more experienced professionals. They may hire someone more experienced from time to time, but doing so simply would be an aberration.

Your Audience

You need to create a one to three page report for your bosses, Stan and Frank Sweeney. Headings and possibly sub-headings are expected. They will also expect a reasoned and substantial argument as to why Sweeney Brothers should select one insurance policy over the other. And they are big believers in concision. As Stan told you once, "When I read a memo or report, I want to know what you're talking about in important but concise details—no dilly-dallying, no fluff." Also keep in mind that this recommendation will affect lives of sixteen people (and more).

Copyright © 2010, Pearson Education, Inc., Publishing as Longman

Your Assignment for this Case

You need to craft a very important report for your company that will have a tremendous effect on the firm. Headings and possibly subheadings are expected. You have to analyze data in light of your staff's makeup and then make a cogent recommendation as to why Sweeney Brothers should adopt either Logos Mutual or Alliance Federated.

Also remember that you are supposed to use your own prose when crafting this document. You can use the facts and details from this case, but do your own writing. And make sure your numbers and calculations are accurate.

A Successful Recommendation Report

- Offers a concise introduction at the start of the report.
- Provides a clear and concise bottom-line (your recommendation) in a separate summary that follows the introduction.
- Details the benefits and drawbacks of both insurance plans in separate sections by using appropriate and accurate details about the competing insurance plans.
- Offers a recommendation section that persuades readers by making logical and ethical claims that show how your recommendation is cogent and sound.
- Provides a concise conclusion section that connects to the bottom-line (your recommendation).
- Has focused and unified paragraphs that are developed and connect to the bottom-line.
- Is free of irrelevant details.
- Follows the proper format of a professional report by using headings, subheadings, strong formatting, and appropriate use of white space.
- Exhibits strong concision, cohesion, transitions, and sentence variety in length and type.
- Provides a medium level of tone and diction—not too formal but not too informal.
- Is free of mechanical and proofreading errors

Copyright © 2010, Pearson Education, Inc., Publishing as Longman

III. GENERAL TEACHING STRATEGIES: SOME SUGGESTIONS

HOW THIS TEXT TREATS "INVENTION"

Much of this text focuses on the invention of arguments. The authors feel that the core of invention is the enthymeme, a concept that urges students to seek supporting reasons that are rooted in assumptions shared by the audience. Instructors are recommended to spend considerable class time with the collaborative tasks in Chapters 4–7 to help students understand ***because*** clauses as enthymemes with unstated assumptions. Using Toulmin's schema, students can detail their ***because*** clauses by seeking grounds that support the stated reasons and by seeking backing to support the often unstated warrants, all the while remaining aware of opposing views (conditions for rebuttal, qualifiers). The whole treatment of the Toulmin schema for the expansion of arguments is thus a part of invention. Additional approaches to invention, including use of the "stock issues" strategy and the "claim-type" strategy (arguing from category, from consequences, and from resemblance) are introduced to students in Part Three. Finally, "Set 2: Exploration and Rehearsal" (pages 70-71) uses freewriting and idea-mapping to encourage exploratory thinking about an argument prior to composing the first draft. It's recommended that students do the ten tasks in this sequence for each of their formal essays in the course.

USING "FOR CLASS DISCUSSION" EXERCISES AS COLLABORATIVE LEARNING TASKS

Although the For Class Discussion exercises work well as opportunities for conventional class discussions, they have been designed especially as collaborative tasks. Many instructors divide the class into small groups, asking each group to work independently on the tasks prior to a concluding plenary session in which groups' solutions are compared and debated. In the use of collaborative tasks, Kenneth Bruffee's work on collaborative learning, George Hillock's description of the "environmental mode" of teaching, and Harvey Wiener's discussion of assessment of collaborative learning have all influenced the text's underlying pedagogy (see bibliography at the end of this *Instructor's Manual*).

Design of Collaborative Tasks

Well-designed collaborative tasks should meet the following criteria: (1) Tasks should ask groups to *produce* something that the group recorder or leader presents to the whole class during the plenary session at the end. This "something" could be a thesis sentence, a brief paragraph, a tree diagram, an idea-map, and so forth. By making groups responsible for a product, the teacher insures that groups stay on task. Tasks that simply ask groups to "discuss" something often lead to diffuse, unproductive sessions. (2) Tasks should focus on learning objectives for the course, and students should be able to see the purpose of the task in terms of course design. (3) The task should be manageable within a set time period. Generally, tasks should take 15–30 minutes to accomplish so that students can shuttle back and forth between small group work and plenary work led by the instructor. (4) The task should be put in writing (often on an overhead projector)

Copyright © 2010, Pearson Education, Inc., Publishing as Longman

and should specify clearly what the students are to do. (5) A time limit should be placed on the board (for example, "Report in 20 minutes" or "Report at 1:50"). The For Class Discussion exercises in the text meet all these criteria except for the last: the teacher needs to determine how much class time to devote to the task before moving to the plenary sessions.

Dividing the Class into Collaborative Groups

Teachers often ask about ways to divide students into groups. Some teachers try to arrange groups to maximize diversity—good writers placed with weak writers, men placed with women, engineers placed with art majors, and so forth. Classroom experience suggests that randomly arranged groups work about as well as carefully designed groups and can save the instructor considerable time in setup. One trusted method is to divide a class randomly into groups of three to five students. It is preferable, however, to try to keep an even mix of men and women in each group if at all possible.

Forming Collaborative Groups That Can Also Meet Outside of Class as Study Groups or Revision Teams

Sometimes instructors want their collaborative groups to meet together outside of class—a constraint that can lead to scheduling headaches since random groups will invariably include people with conflicting class and work schedules. For a solution, try the following. Tell all people who have a free hour between 8:00 a.m. and 10:00 a.m. to meet in one corner of the room. Then in another corner assemble people who have a free hour between 10:00 and 12:00, then 12:00 to 2:00 and so forth throughout the day and evening. Finally, group those with a free hour on Saturdays or Sundays. Give the groups fifteen minutes to work out schedules among themselves. Tell them that there must be at least three people to a group and no more than five.

Should Groups Stay Together All Term or Should Groups Be Switched as the Term Progresses?

Like most difficult questions that trouble instructors, there is no right answer to this question. The advantages and disadvantages of each procedure balance out. Some instructors keep the same groups together all term unless there is a dysfunctional group, but other instructors prefer to consistently change group memberships to stimulate freshness and expose persons to as many different points of view as possible.

What about Non-Native Speakers?

Collaborative learning is an excellent teaching method for non-native speakers of English. Many instructors recommend that second-language students be mixed randomly within the collaborative groups. In fact, having a second-language learner in a group many times encourages groups to uncover perspectives and issues reflective of cross-cultural differences. For example, in response to the issue question—"Are arranged marriages more successful than

Copyright © 2010, Pearson Education, Inc., Publishing as Longman

romantic marriages?—a student from India might argue for the advantages of arranged marriages, thereby exposing American students to a perspective they would have scarcely respected or considered worthy of debate.

Instructor's Role During the Collaborative Task

There is much disagreement here. Ken Bruffee advises teachers to leave the room during the collaborative task and to return only for the plenary session. Other teachers like to move quietly from group to group listening in on the sessions and being available for clarification of the task or encouragement as needed. (Bruffee argues that a teacher "listening in" changes the dynamic of the group.) Still others like to join a group as a fellow discussant, encouraging students to regard the instructor as just another student. This method can work well if an instructor is able to overcome his or her privileged status. Using this method, the instructor joins a different group each time.

Instructor's Role During the Plenary Session

After collaborative tasks, when students have arrived at their own points of view and are emboldened by consensus of their groups, they can become passionate presenters of their positions. When disagreement occurs between groups, teachers can ask group recorders to debate the issue or can simply use the disagreement to initiate general class discussion.

The most sensitive moments occur when the class reaches a consensus solution different from the instructor's. The collaborative classroom posits a worldview in which the instructor is not the sole source of knowledge or authority. The instructor cannot therefore rely on "authority" to give a privileged status to his or her solution. Rather, the instructor must argue his or her case reasonably, just as the students must argue theirs, and hope that the reasonableness of the presentation wins the day. These moments can provide the ideal learning environment for a class devoted to argument.

USING COLLABORATIVE GROUPS FOR WRITING PROCESS WORKSHOPS

The For Class Discussion exercises are aimed primarily at helping collaborative groups become engaged with the subject matter of the text. As such, they are mainly content-centered exercises. However, collaborative groups can also be used successfully for workshops on rough drafts and on other phases of the writing process. Appendix Two gives numerous suggestions for using groups to help with writing. What follows are some further suggestions.

Using Collaborative Groups for Invention and Exploration

Early in the term, the collaborative tasks in Chapter 3 should be used to encourage students to participate in argumentative discussions. These tasks will help students discover issues that both interest them and engage controversy.

Copyright © 2010, Pearson Education, Inc., Publishing as Longman

Once writers have chosen an issue, groups are especially effective at encouraging exploration. Working either in groups of five or of three or two, students can be asked to share their issues and brainstorm reasons for and against another's preliminary claims.

Once writers have explored ideas through group work and through doing "Set 2–Exploration and Rehearsal" (pages 70-1), they can be placed in pairs and asked to interview each other about the planned argument. Each writer should "talk through" the argument with the listener, rehearsing ideas orally before writing a draft.

Using Collaborative Groups for Revision

Instructors should expect student-writers to bring legible copies of complete drafts to a rough draft workshop. There are several ways that rough draft workshops can be handled.

In Class Workshops

In class workshops can be effective in group sizes from pairs to five persons (although five people often don't have enough time to respond to each person's draft in a 50-minute period). Students can either exchange drafts in the group or between groups. (When drafts are exchanged between groups, group members can collaborate on responses without the writer's being present—a factor that often encourages more detailed and more frank criticism.) Asking students to follow a specific set of questions or "checksheet" in conjunction with the specific writing task is crucial. Sometimes instructors can ask critiquers to make paragraph-by-paragraph "says" and "does" statements for the writer's essay and/or a written summary of the writer's argument. If peer reviewers have trouble doing so, then the remainder of the session can focus on problems of clarity in the draft, with the reviewers explaining to the writer where the confusion occurs. Once the argument is reasonably clear, comments can focus on the rhetorical concerns reinforced in the review questions or checksheet.

At Home Critiques

Some instructors prefer having students critique each other's work outside of class. One way to do so is to have students make two copies of their drafts. In class, divide students into pairs who will work together as critiquing teams. Students A and B exchange drafts with students C and D. Outside of class, students A and B meet to critique C's and D's drafts while C and D meet to critique drafts from A and B. Each pair collaborates to write out a detailed critique of the two drafts. In class, the pairs meet to share their critiques of each other's drafts.

A variation on this procedure, which permits students more time to devote to the process (and subsequently to reflect on and learn from it), is to have students on the day that drafts are due bring to class enough copies of their drafts for all the members of their workshop group (plus one for the instructor), exchange their copies with those of the other members of their workshop group, and then perform the critiques of those drafts individually outside of class according to a checklist that the instructor provides. Students return the next class period to share their critiques with the writers in the context of their workshop group. This method also has the virtue of permitting a "dry run" of the review procedure, for on the day drafts are due, once the initial

Copyright © 2010, Pearson Education, Inc., Publishing as Longman

exchange of drafts has been accomplished, the instructor may spend the remaining class time leading students in an application of the checklist to a sample student or professional essay, thereby modeling for the students the procedure they are to follow in performing their own critiques. At the conclusion of the following class period, once students have had the opportunity to share their critiques with one another and once the instructor has had the opportunity to (at least) skim all of the drafts, the instructor may take a few moments both to solicit from the students the major problems they encountered in their peers' responses to the assignment and to point out any problems he or she noticed to be common to many of the drafts. The class may then be engaged in a discussion of possible solutions to those problems.

Reading Aloud, At Home Critique Hybrid Method

Another method that some instructors use is having select students (whether they volunteer or are selected randomly) read their drafts aloud for the whole class on designated peer review days. And for each peer review day throughout the semester, different writers present their work. Students read their papers with the essay shown by projection screen, thereby presenting their polished and complete drafts, and afterward they receive immediate feedback from their peers (an instructor should gauge 20-25 minutes per reading with feedback). Students listening and following the student papers should take notes, jotting down places where the writer can further develop, modify, or really re-see his/her paper. After each reading, the instructor gives the class some time to collect their thoughts on the paper (2-4 minutes roughly) and then directs students to provide substantive feedback about their peer's paper, with each reviewer providing 1-2 strengths of the paper and 1-2 areas of concern for the paper that are non-grammar related (examples: need for more detail, description, or examples; a need for addressing, accommodating, or refuting certain counterarguments; confusing or tangential passages; unnecessary points or details; organizational strategies) while offering suggestions on how to make the paper a stronger argument. Students should talk to the writer, not the instructor, and the instructor can also offer strengths and weaknesses also as long as his/her comments do not dominate the review.

During the read aloud critique period, reviewers can point out similar strengths as others have—validating those high points of the draft—and the same goes for areas of development as long as the reviewers articulate the draft's issues differently and offer varied suggestions on how to improve the argument. This method reinforces the professional practice of reading one's writing aloud to find troublesome areas. The critique period for each paper also reinforces fundamental concepts—audience awareness, clarity, cohesion, counterargumentation, level of detail, et al.—that writers must always keep in mind when writing an argument.

For the students who have not read their work aloud in class, those students will do peer review outside of the classroom. For example, if two people read their argument papers in class, all the other students would bring two copies of their papers to class, and then those students (the non-readers) select two different papers to review. The instructor must provide a peer review sheet with detailed questions and logistics on how (email or other methods) and when (designate a strict deadline) their comments will need to be sent to their peers. To check the quality of peer review, instructors must create some sort of "writing process" grade in their course point totals or signify that peer review is a significant portion of their "participation" or "citizenship" grades.

Copyright © 2010, Pearson Education, Inc., Publishing as Longman

Instructors can "grade" peer review comments from students in whatever method is compatible with their teaching philosophies (ranging from participation checkpoints to definite point totals).

Regardless of the peer review strategy instructors choose to use, instructors need to be aware of how students' drafts are progressing, whether by conferencing, by skimming/reviewing at least one set of the drafts written in response to each major assignment briefly, or by using various other coaching strategies. Such measures can help an instructor discover if a particular student or a whole class misconstrued the nature of an assignment in time to intervene during the writing process to provide more extensive explanations to the whole class. This informal assessment measure will facilitate stronger drafts in the long run.

Using Collaborative Groups for Editing

Pairs typically work best here. Students can bring late-stage drafts to class and exchange them in pairs. Students are responsible for helping each other edit for sentence errors. Sometimes teachers can hold the editor—as opposed to the writer—responsible for certain kinds of errors in the writer's draft, operating on the principle that it is often easier to spot errors in someone else's essay than in your own.

By using such editing activities, instructors can also introduce student-writers to methods that professional writers use: reading aloud, reading backwards (read the last sentence—scanning for grammatical/style issues; then on to the next to last sentence—scanning for grammatical/style issues; and so on backwards through the paper), and reading aloud and backwards (a hybrid of both methods).

Copyright © 2010, Pearson Education, Inc., Publishing as Longman

IV. SUGGESTIONS FOR TEACHING THE TOULMIN SYSTEM

Although Toulmin's system of argument analysis is widely discussed in the pedagogical literature and used regularly in argument textbooks, no two sources discuss it in exactly the same way, and most instructors, if honest, would admit to difficulties in teaching it. Moreover, teachers familiar with Toulmin's own work may be puzzled by the way *Writing Arguments* has superimposed the language of enthymemes (a claim with a stated reason and a missing premise) on Toulmin's language of grounds, warrants, and backing. For these reasons, instructors might find it useful to know why and how the authors have adapted Toulmin to their purposes as well as to see how they recommend teaching Toulmin to students in argument courses.

HOW AND WHY ENTHYMEMIC LANGUAGE IS ADDED TO TOULMIN'S SYSTEM

Instructors familiar with Toulmin's pioneering work *The Uses of Argument* [Cambridge: Cambridge UP, 1958] will recall that in Toulmin's system the arguer begins with a conviction about factual data, the "Grounds" that Toulmin calls "what we have to go on." The arguer moves directly from the Grounds to the Claim by means of the coordinate conjunction "so" or the conjunctive adverb "therefore." His seminal example concerns a certain Harry, born in Bermuda.

> Harry was born in Bermuda, so Harry is a British subject.

To analyze the underlying logic of this statement, Toulmin develops a complete system, which he diagrams as follows (*Uses of Argument*, page 105):

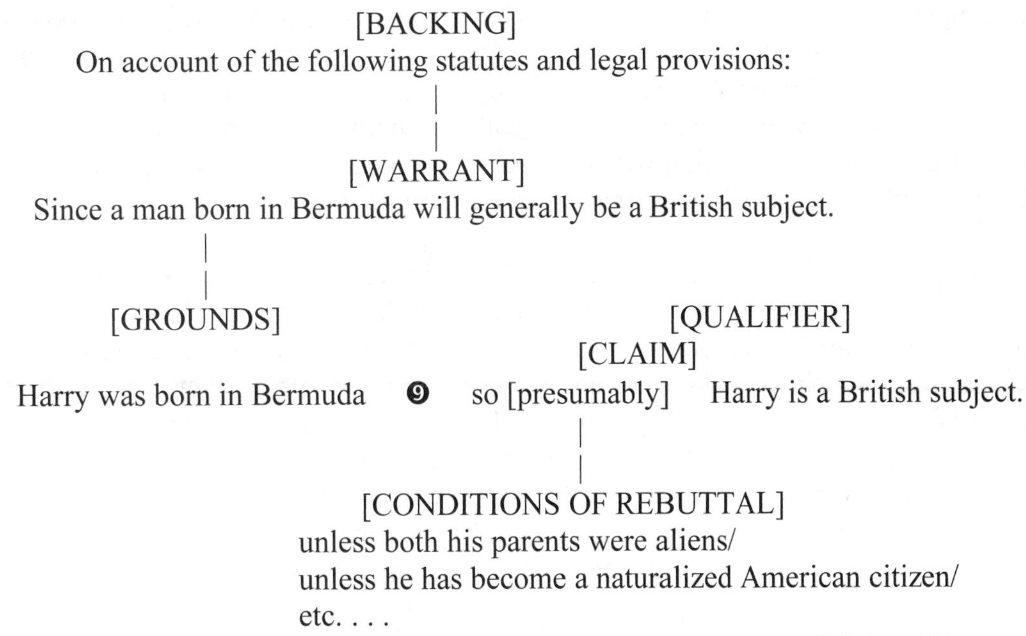

Toulmin's intention here is not to write a textbook on argument but to enter a philosophic discourse on the way humans establish conviction about their claims. His concern is to show the limits of formal logic for real language arguments—in his terms, to "reject as confused a

Copyright © 2010, Pearson Education, Inc., Publishing as Longman

conception of 'deductive inference,' which many recent philosophers have accepted without hesitation as impeccable" (Preface)—and to propose an alternative approach adapted from legal disputation. Despite the success and importance of his work, from the standpoint of teaching argument to college students, there are three difficulties with Toulmin's original system.

First, Toulmin's approach often seems curiously non-rhetorical. In the case of Harry from Bermuda, for example, we are supposed to presume that there is some sort of dispute about Harry's citizenship, but Toulmin never indicates who is disputing Harry's citizenship and under what circumstances, as if a question at issue is irrelevant. Without some larger question at issue, however, a rhetorician would be nonplussed about the contextual meaning of the grounds, which could support an infinite number of different claims:

> Harry was born in Bermuda, so he likes to scuba dive.
> Harry was born in Bermuda, so he should adapt to the Florida climate better than Yukon Bob.
> Harry was born in Bermuda, so you should interview him rather than Yukon Bob for your report on British colonialism.

It is clear that data by themselves are inert until they are related contextually to some meaning-creating assertion. In argumentation, these assertions arise out of different points of view related to a question at issue. By starting with the grounds rather than with the issue, Toulmin has no language for discussing the rhetorical conversation out of which disputes arise. This is no weakness for Toulmin himself, whose interests are epistemological rather than rhetorical, but it poses a substantial problem to teachers of argument.

Related to the first problem is a second one. Toulmin's system provides no slots for the common language terms "reason" and "because." These are such familiar, useful, and powerful terms (What is your *reason* for believing X? Well, *because* . . .) that the authors thought it unwise to adopt a system of argument analysis that had no place for them. Toulmin couldn't use these terms precisely because he starts with the data [Grounds] rather than with an issue and competing claims. By starting with data he is committed to a "Grounds, therefore Claim" structure rather than a "Claim because Reason" structure.

A third problem with Toulmin's system is Toulmin seems to have a positivist faith in the factualness of facts. His system has difficulty describing arguments in which the "facts of the case" are at issue. For Toulmin, Grounds are hard data, the indisputable facts ("what we have to go on") from which we make the inductive leap to a claim. If the facts are in dispute, then they aren't facts, and we have nothing to go on. But real world arguments often start in uncertainty about the facts, and real world arguers/writers need a system that allows them to examine uncertainties. Suppose, for example, that there is a real dispute about Harry's citizenship—that there are detectives working on a case that turns on Harry's citizenship. "Why do you think Harry is a British subject?" I ask you.

> "Because he was born in Bermuda," you reply.
> "Why do you think he was born in Bermuda?"
> "His mother told me so, and besides, I have seen his birth certificate."

Copyright © 2010, Pearson Education, Inc., Publishing as Longman

In this conversation, Toulmin's original hard datum (Harry was born in Bermuda) shifts its status from "fact" to proposition. It is now a new claim supported by a lower order of facts—his mother's testimony and a birth certificate. So when is a fact a fact?

As one looks through the examples in Toulmin's *Uses of Argument*, one senses his uneasiness with any argument in which the facts of the case are in doubt. Until you establish the facts, he explains, you have no grounds for argument. His belief that arguments can be grounded in correct facts leads to an unexamined inconsistency in his discussions of data throughout his book. Sometimes the grounds in his examples are indeed hard facts—physically verifiable data—but at other times his grounds are higher order claims summarizing the meaning he finds in the data, claims that seem to us very much like reasons. (Perhaps Toulmin doesn't distinguish between grounds and reason because he sees a generalization about the meaning of data as a non-problematic, correct summary of the facts rather than an interpretive claim.) Thus, "Harry was born in Bermuda" is certainly a plausible reason for believing Harry is a British subject, but it may or may not be a fact. Consider, then, the difference between Toulmin's original casting of Harry's case and our own casting of it as follows:

Issue: Is Harry a British subject?
Enthymeme: Harry is a British subject because he was born in Bermuda.
Claim: Harry is a British subject.
Stated reason: because he was born in Bermuda.
Grounds: evidence that he was born in Bermuda (mother's testimony, birth certificate, etc.)
Warrant: People born in Bermuda will generally be British subjects.
Backing: national and international laws and statutes
Qualifier: presumably, probably
Conditions of rebuttal: (attacking grounds and stated reason): unless his mother is lying and his birth records forged; (attacking warrant and backing): unless both his parents were aliens, unless he has renounced his citizenship and is a naturalized citizen elsewhere.

As can be seen, in adapting Toulmin the text begins with the enthymeme rather than with the grounds. The enthymeme, for the authors, is the single most powerful teaching tool in helping college students understand argument. Unlike inert data, the enthymeme is a contextual, rhetorical concept that depends on a question at issue (and hence an audience), a claim, a reason, and an unstated premise that necessitates attention to the audience's values. (An excellent introduction to the concept of enthymeme—one that has proven formative for us—is John T. Gage's "Teaching the Enthymeme: Invention and Arrangement" in *Rhetoric Review*, 2 [Sept. 1983], 38–50.) Moreover, the enthymeme can be quickly taught to students in familiar ordinary language as a claim supported by a reason expressed as a "because clause."

In the teaching of argument in the text, the concept of the enthymeme takes precedence over Toulmin. In fact, one can use *Writing Arguments* with only minimal attention to Toulmin, but the concept of the enthymeme (claim, reason, unstated assumption) is crucial. However, Toulmin's system meshes easily with the enthymeme—so easily, in fact, that the authors prefer

Copyright © 2010, Pearson Education, Inc., Publishing as Longman

to think of the marriage of the enthymeme and Toulmin's system as a refinement or improvement of Toulmin rather than a modification or departure. Toulmin's Grounds now become the facts and evidence used to support the Stated Reason in the enthymeme; the Warrant, as in Toulmin, is the unstated assumption linking the reason and grounds to the Claim; the Backing supports the Warrant, and the Conditions of Rebuttal expose the conditions under which the claim will not hold because either the facts of the case can be questioned or because the warrant can be questioned.

WHY USE TOULMIN?

Instructors will probably appreciate the value of Toulmin analysis if they know the reasons that the authors adopted it and particularly the kinds of writing problems that Toulmin's analysis helps instructors and writers solve.

The authors' approach to teaching composition changed substantially in the early 1980s when Professor Kenneth Bruffee of Brooklyn College gave a workshop at Montana State University where John Ramage and John Bean were then colleagues together. Bruffee, as the profession's chief proponent and apologist for collaborative learning, introduced them to the use of small groups in the classroom and inspired the emphasis on collaborative learning throughout *Writing Arguments*.

For several years at Montana State University, the Writing Program also adopted Bruffee's textbook *A Short Course in Writing*, which took a form-prescribed (some might say "by the numbers") approach to the teaching of argument through a sequence of three-paragraph essays:

Two Reasons:

paragraph 1: Introduction to issue followed by claim
paragraph 2: First supporting reason with development
paragraph 3: Second supporting reason with development

Copyright © 2010, Pearson Education, Inc., Publishing as Longman

Nestorian Order:

paragraph 1: Introduction to issue followed by claim
paragraph 2: Summary of several less important reasons
paragraph 3: Major supporting reason with development

Strawman:

paragraph 1: Introduction to issue followed by claim
paragraph 2: Summary of opposing view
paragraph 3: Refutation of opposing view

Concession:

paragraph 1: Introduction to issue followed by claim
paragraph 2: Summary of opposing view
paragraph 3: Concession to opposing view followed by own argument

Although Bruffee's assignments produced a stong argumentative focus in student writing and his assignment sequence influenced the text's use of microthemes and some of the For Class Discussion exercises, Ramage and Bean found student essays tended to be disappointingly thin. Bruffee's approach provided no consistent strategy for teaching students to generate and analyze arguments. Instructors tried to supplement Bruffee with instruction on informal fallacies and syllogistic logic, but they found that these approaches had almost no generative benefit and didn't produce the kinds of productive classroom discussion that led to more detailed and elaborated arguments.

The solution, then, became the integration of the enthymeme and Toulmin's system. In using this enthymeme/Toulminic system, they saw almost immediate improvement in the quality of our students' papers in terms of increased elaboration and development, heightened sense of audience, and willingness to examine underlying assumptions.

A CLASSROOM STRATEGY FOR INTRODUCING TOULMIN TO STUDENTS

All that remained for the authors was the development of an effective pedagogical strategy for introducing Toulmin to students in a way that makes them see Toulmin's power without intimidating them. The strategy to use is to begin with plenty of clear-cut, easy examples. The For Class Discussion exercises in Chapters 3 and 4 are particularly helpful in this regard.

The central feature of our pedagogy is to begin with the enthymeme rather than Toulmin and to get students used to the enthymemic concepts of issue, claim, stated reason, and unstated assumption before introducing Toulmin language. On the day that the authors assign students to read Chapters 3 and 4, they typically put such similar enthymemes on an overhead.

Copyright © 2010, Pearson Education, Inc., Publishing as Longman

Issue: What car should we buy?
Enthymeme 1: We should buy this Geo Metro because it is extremely economical.
Enthymeme 2: We should buy this used Volvo because it is very safe.
Enthymeme 3: We should buy this Ford Escort because it is red.

The hope is that students will find something humorously fishy about Enthymeme 3 as soon as they see it, even if they can't yet quite articulate what's wrong with it. Before getting specifically to Enthymeme 3, however, instructors can conduct a general class discussion about each of the enthymemes. Beginning to get students to articulate the unstated assumption behind each enthymeme is pivotal.

Assumption for Enthymeme 1: We should buy the car that is most economical.
(Economy is the major criterion we should use in selecting a car.)
Assumption for Enthymeme 2: We should buy the car that is most safe.
(Safety is the major criterion we should use in selecting a car.)
Assumption for Enthymeme 3: We should buy a car that is red.
(The color red is the major criterion we should use in selecting a car.)

An instructor can then enter a general discussion of Enthymemes 1 and 2 by talking about how to support them or try to refute them. One possibility is that some might agree with the criterion in Enthymemes 1 and 2 but disagree with the stated reason by arguing that the Geo Metro isn't as economical as another car or that the Volvo isn't as safe as another car. But another possibility is that some might disagree with the criterion in each case and argue that car buyers should base their decisions not on economy or safety but on performance or driving fun or cargo space or reliability. The key here is to have students see the difference between supporting or attacking the stated reason itself versus supporting or attacking the unstated assumption behind the reason.

Then switching to Enthymeme 3, an instructor can ask students why they thought something was fishy about that enthymeme, perhaps saying tongue in cheek that s/he sees nothing wrong with it. The instructor should assure students that the reason is really true—we can verify that the car is red through both the testimony of a survey of randomly chosen people (100 percent said the car was red) and through a special chemical spectroscopy test we ran on the paint. "No," they will say. "That's not what's at issue. We agree that the car's red, but we can't see what color has to do with buying the car." Then an instructor can reply, "Oh, you can't see how we get from the facts to the claim" (echoing Toulmin's phrase that the warrant is how you get from data to claim). Or, "So you think the claim is un*warrant*ed?" (trying to work in some Toulmin language naturally). "What we need, then, is some kind of argument to 'back up' this unstated assumption that redness is the major criterion we should choose."

Copyright © 2010, Pearson Education, Inc., Publishing as Longman

At this point, one can begin introducing Toulmin terminology to students. The unstated assumption behind each enthymeme can now be termed as the warrant. Together the claim, the stated reason, and the warrant constitute the frame or skeleton of the argument. These frame sentences can be stated in a single sentence each:

> **Claim:** We should buy this used Volvo.
> **Stated Reason:** It is very safe.
> **Warrant:** We should buy the car that is the safest.

It is important to explain that what fleshes out the argument—what gives it development and detail—are the grounds and/or the backing. The grounds are all the facts, data, examples, evidence, or chains of reasons the arguer uses to support the stated reason. The backing is all the facts, data, evidence, examples, or chains of reasons one can use to support the warrant. Whether concentrating on providing grounds, backing, or both depends on where an arguer can anticipate our audience's needs and objections.

An instructor now can return to discussing each enthymeme again, this time using Toulmin terminology. Taking the class through a series of questions like these is fruitful:

1. Imagine a situation in which a writer might need to provide extensive grounds for Enthymeme 1, but no backing. What would that situation be? What kinds of grounds might you use? [Possible answer: Writer and audience have already agreed that economy is the chief criterion for choosing the car; they are disagreeing on which of two cars is the most economical. The writer supporting the Geo Metro might provide grounds in the form of data about fuel economy, maintenance costs, taxes and licensing fees, and resale value.]

2. Imagine a situation in which a writer might need to provide backing for Enthymeme 2, but no grounds. What would that situation be? What kind of argument could be devised for backing? [Possible answer: Writer and audience agree that Volvos are very safe, but they disagree on whether safety should be the primary criterion. The writer might argue that this car is for a very safety-minded middle-class couple with young children. The husband of the couple lost a sister in an auto accident several years ago and is obsessed with safety. He could never enjoy driving or riding in a car that wasn't, in his mind, the safest car he could buy. The wife of the couple has similar concerns for safety.]

3. Now reverse the situation and imagine a scenario that requires no backing for Enthymeme 2, but plenty of grounds. [Here writer and audience have agreed that they will buy the safest car on the market, but there is disagreement over whether a used Volvo is the safest car. To argue for the Volvo's safety, the writer might provide grounds in the form of insurance claim data, crash test data, data about the actual construction of the car, and so forth.]

Finally, move to a discussion of Enthymeme 3. Ask why something seemed fishy about that enthymeme from the start. The answer, which can now be cast in Toulmin terms, is that the Warrant seems silly. Most people can readily see how economy or safety could be a criterion for

Copyright © 2010, Pearson Education, Inc., Publishing as Longman

buying a car, but not redness. In Toulmin's term, this enthymeme cries out for backing:

Claim: We should buy this Ford Escort.
Stated Reason: It is red.
Grounds: Direct observation; 100 percent consensus on informal survey that the car is red; statement "red" under "color" on sales form; scientific analysis of light spectrum as it is reflected from car's surface.
Warrant: If we find a car that's red, we should buy it.
Backing: ? ? ?

Then asking students either individually or in small groups, have them think of some kind of scenario in which one really might buy a car because it is red. In short, an instructor can ask them to think of a way to provide backing for the warrant. After students share some of their ideas, the following argument can be put on the overhead [which is based on a true case—John Bean's neighbor bought a little red Escort for his mother for exactly the reasons stated]:

> You must think it ludicrous that I think we should buy the Escort because it is red. But think for a minute about Grandma's situation. Grandpa died four months ago. Grandma has hardly left the house since then and needs to snap out of her depression. She likes to drive, even though Grandpa usually did all the driving in that clunky old Buick they owned. She never liked that car, and she won't drive it now—maybe because it reminds her of Grandpa. What Grandma needs is a sporty, new, little, easy-to-drive-and-park car. So, of course, redness isn't the only criteria we should think about. But there are dozens of sporty little cars on the market that fit our other criteria. What is most important, I think, is that the car be red. That has always been her favorite color. It is youthful and energetic. I think a little red car will help her snap out of her mourning and get her out of the house. And let's get it for her by next Monday, her birthday. Let's have her wake up and see her own little red car in the driveway. So I say, let's go get the Escort. It's available today, and it is just exactly the kind of red that will perk Grandma up.

These what-car-should-we-buy examples have proven effective for teaching students the difference between grounds and backing. Clearly, to provide grounds for Enthymeme 3 would be comically pointless. Nobody disputes the car's color in the way they might dispute the car's economy or safety. Just as clearly, it is essential to provide backing for Enthymeme 3 because no one will accept redness as a plausible criterion for buying a car the way they might accept economy or safety. The obvious difference between grounds and backing in Enthymeme 3 helps students see the distinction between grounds and backing in the other arguments also. Likewise,

Copyright © 2010, Pearson Education, Inc., Publishing as Longman

they see how Toulmin's system helps them make rhetorical decisions: Will my audience accept my stated reason? If not, I need substantial grounds. Will they accept my warrant? If not, I will need to make it explicit and provide backing.

This introductory lesson on Toulmin is on the following seven transparency masters for convenient use in the classroom. Instructors will most likely want to use this introduction to Toulmin in conjunction with teaching Chapters 3 and 4.

Copyright © 2010, Pearson Education, Inc., Publishing as Longman

Transparency #1

AN INTRODUCTION TO TOULMIN

Issue: What car should we buy?

Enthymeme #1: We should buy this Geo Metro because it is extremely economical.

Enthymeme #2: We should buy this used Volvo because it is very safe.

Enthymeme #3: We should buy this Ford Escort because it is red.

Does one of these arguments seem a little odd or off-base? Why?

Toulmin analysis will provide concepts and language to talk effectively about these enthymemes.

Copyright © 2010, Pearson Education, Inc., Publishing as Longman

AN INTRODUCTION TO TOULMIN: Transparency #2

Each of these enthymemes depends on an unstated assumption. If the audience is going to be swayed by the argument, the audience has to grant this unstated assumption. What is the unstated assumption behind each enthymeme?

Enthymeme #1: We should buy this Geo Metro because it is extremely economical.

Enthymeme #2: We should buy this used Volvo because it is very safe.

Enthymeme #3: We should buy this Ford Escort because it is red.

Assumption for enthymeme #1: We should buy the car that is most economical.
[Economy is the major criterion we should use in selecting a car.]

Assumption for enthymeme #2: We should buy the car that is most safe.
[Safety is the major criterion we should use in selecting a car.]

Assumption for enthymeme #3: We should buy a car that is red. [The color red is the major criterion we should use in selecting a car.]

Copyright © 2010, Pearson Education, Inc., Publishing as Longman

AN INTRODUCTION TO TOULMIN: Transparency #3

Here is how each of these enthymemes would be displayed using the Toulmin term "warrant" for the unstated assumption.

Enthymeme #1:
Claim: We should buy this Geo Metro.
Stated Reason: It is extremely economical.
Warrant: We should buy the car that is most economical.

Enthymeme #2:
Claim: We should buy this used Volvo.
Stated Reason: It is very safe.
Warrant: We should buy the car that is most safe.

Enthymeme #3:
Claim: We should buy this Ford Escort.
Stated Reason: It is red.
Warrant: We should buy a car that is red.

- We call these three statements (claim, stated reason, warrant) the "frame" or "skeleton" of a line of reasoning.

- This frame or skeleton needs to be fleshed out with "grounds" and/or "backing," depending on the rhetorical context.

- For each of the above enthymemes, imagine a scenario in which you would most have to defend the stated reason. Then imagine another scenario in which you would most have to support the warrant.

Copyright © 2010, Pearson Education, Inc., Publishing as Longman

TOULMIN SCHEME FOR ENTHYMEME #1

Claim: We should buy this Geo Metro.

Stated Reason: It is extremely economical.

Grounds: Evidence that the Geo Metro is extremely economical.
[Government statistics on gas mileage; projected repair costs; testimony from other Metro owners, etc.]

Warrant: We should buy the car that is most economical.

Backing: Arguments showing why economy is the most important criterion.
[Argument would be aimed at specific audience: We need to save money; we have a long commute and need to cut fuel costs; we can put the money saved into our dream vacation, better clothes, etc.]

Conditions of Rebuttal:
Questioning the stated reason and grounds: The Geo Metro isn't as economical as you think. [Granted it gets high gas mileage, but repair costs are high, resale value is low, etc.]
Questioning the warrant and backing: I'll grant you that the Geo Metro is economical, but economy shouldn't be our most important criterion. What about safety? Imagine that little Metro in a head-on collision with an SUV. Other arguments downgrading economy as the chief criterion.]

Qualifier: Perhaps the Geo Metro is the best choice for us.

Copyright © 2010, Pearson Education, Inc., Publishing as Longman

TOULMIN SCHEME FOR ENTHYMEME #2

Claim: We should buy this used Volvo.

Stated Reason: It is very safe.

Grounds: Evidence that the used Volvo is very safe.
[Crash and injury data on Volvos; insurance company figures on Volvo safety; government crash tests; other data demonstrating safety of this particular make of car.]

Warrant: We should buy the car that is most safe.

Backing: Argument for why safety is the most important criteria.
[Writer generates arguments aimed at particular audience: We have a young family; my sister died in an auto accident so I am uncomfortable in any car that isn't safe; lower insurance rates; we commute on a dangerous highway, etc.]

Conditions of Rebuttal:

Questioning the stated reason and grounds: Maybe the Volvo isn't as safe as you think. [Evidence suggesting that another kind of car would be more safe.]

Questioning the warrant and backing: While safety is important, other criteria are more important in our situation—economy, reliability, etc. [We'll spend a fortune keeping the Volvo running; other cars are nearly as safe so the difference is negligible; this used Toyota Camry will be cheaper to buy, gets much better mileage, and will have smaller repair costs.]

Qualifier: Let's put the Volvo high on our list of cars to consider.

Copyright © 2010, Pearson Education, Inc., Publishing as Longman

TOULMIN SCHEME FOR ENTHYMEME #3

Claim: We should buy this Ford Escort.

Stated Reason: It is red.

Grounds: Evidence that it is red.
[Humorous—nobody will dispute redness: testimony from others; scientific spectroscopy results; stated color on dealer's spec sheet for car.]

Warrant: We should buy a car that is red.

Backing: Argument that the color red should be the primary criterion for deciding what car to buy.
[Can you think of any situations in which a specific car color should be a primary criterion?]

[see next overhead]

Copyright © 2010, Pearson Education, Inc., Publishing as Longman

Possible Backing for Enthymeme #3

Warrant: We should buy a car that is red.

Backing: You must think it ludicrous that I think we should buy the Escort because it is red. But think for a minute about Grandma's situation. Grandpa died four months ago. Grandma has hardly left the house since then and needs to snap out of her depression. She likes to drive, even though Grandpa usually did all the driving in that clunky old Buick they owned. She never liked that car, and she won't drive it now—maybe because it reminds her of Grandpa. What Grandma needs is a sporty, new, little, easy-to-drive-and-park car. So, of course, redness isn't the only criterion we should think about. But there are dozens of sporty little cars on the market that fit our other criteria. What is most important, I think, is that the car be red. That has always been her favorite color. It is youthful and energetic. I think a little red car will help her snap out of her mourning and get her out of the house. And let's get it for her by next Monday, her birthday. Let's have her wake up and see her own little red car in the driveway. So I say, let's go get the Escort. It's available today, and it is just exactly the kind of red that will perk Grandma up.

Conditions of Rebuttal:

Questioning the reason and grounds: Nobody will deny the car is red.

Questioning the warrant and backing: I agree that red might perk Grandma up, but let's look at other criteria before we buy on impulse.

Qualifier: Maybe we should buy the Escort.

Copyright © 2010, Pearson Education, Inc., Publishing as Longman

HOW EXAMINATION OF THE SYLLOGISM MAY HELP MANY STUDENTS BETTER UNDERSTAND TOULMIN

In the first two editions of *Writing Arguments*, the authors included in their introduction to Toulmin a section headed "The Structure of Arguments: What We Can Learn Through Formal Logic." Following the advice of the majority of reviewers, they dropped this section beginning with the 3rd edition. However, some users of the text had found that material useful on the theory that students who have studied formal logic or who know something about syllogisms can benefit substantially from the conceptual clarity of the syllogism's three-term structure. For these instructors, this material has been included in the *Instructor's Manual* since the 5th edition of *Writing Arguments*. Instructors can reproduce the following pages explaining the syllogism if they find this approach helpful for their students.

Copyright © 2010, Pearson Education, Inc., Publishing as Longman

Handout: THE STRUCTURE OF ARGUMENTS: WHAT WE CAN LEARN THROUGH FORMAL LOGIC

What is a syllogism? As explained in Chapters 3 and 4, the core of an argument is an enthymeme, which we define as a claim with an attached ***because*** clause (the stated reason). For logical completeness this claim-with-reason depends on the audience's granting an unstated assumption. Consider the following enthymeme:

Women should be barred from military combat units because women lack the strength and endurance needed for combat duty.

As explained in Chapters 3 and 4, this enthymeme could be displayed as follows:

CLAIM: Women should be barred from military combat units.
STATED REASON: Because women lack the strength and endurance needed for combat duty.
UNSTATED ASSUMPTION: Persons who lack the strength and endurance needed for combat duty should be barred from combat units.

This same logical argument could be stated as a traditional syllogism, which is a three-part logical structure containing a major premise, a minor premise, and a claim (or conclusion). The syllogism links three terms, which can be labelled A, B, and C. The major premise, which is usually a general principle or rule, links together terms A and B. The minor premise, which is a specific kind of statement that is usually a fact or a statement verifiable by evidence, introduces a new term C and links it to A. The conclusion or claim then links B to C. Here are two examples.

A B
MAJOR PREMISE: All dogs are mammals.

C A
MINOR PREMISE: Bowser is a dog.

C B
CLAIM: Bowser is a mammal.

Copyright © 2010, Pearson Education, Inc., Publishing as Longman

Handout (continued)

MAJOR PREMISE: *Persons who lack the strength and endurance needed for combat duty* (A) should be *barred from combat units.* (B)

MINOR PREMISE: *Women* (C) are *persons who lack the strength and endurance needed for combat duty.* (A)

CLAIM: *Women* (C) should be *barred from combat units.* (B)

Syllogisms can often be rewritten as "if-then" structures, which are sometimes easier to formulate when you are composing your own arguments.

MAJOR PREMISE: If a *person lacks the strength and endurance needed for combat duty* (A), then that person should be *barred from combat units.* (B)

MINOR PREMISE: *Women* (C) are *persons who lack the strength and endurance needed for combat duty.* (A)

CLAIM: *Women* (C) should be *barred from combat units.* (B)

If you were to take a course in formal logic, you would study various kinds of syllogisms as well as valid and invalid ways of structuring them. In a writing course, however, the purpose of studying syllogisms is simply to see that a claim-with-reason depends for logical completeness on an unstated assumption—usually the major premise—that often needs to be supported in your argument. Formulating the major premise of each claim-with-reason is a way of reminding yourself of the assumptions your audience must grant if your argument is to be persuasive.

Another advantage of examining syllogisms is that doing so will help you appreciate the three-term structure of an enthymeme. Sometimes an arguer will formulate an enthymeme with logical gaps. Often such enthymemes will have four or five terms rather than three.

Copyright © 2010, Pearson Education, Inc., Publishing as Longman

Term 1 Term 2 Term 3
ILLOGICAL: *Women* should be *barred from combat units* because *the United States*
Term 4
needs a strong army.

In this example, the because clause introduces two new terms rather than repeating the first term from the claim. The connection between the reason and the claim is thus fuzzy and unarticulated. To make the enthymeme logical, the writer needs to repeat the term "women" as the subject of the because clause.

Term 1 Term 2 Term 1
LOGIC CLARIFIED: *Women* should be *barred from combat units* because *women* in
Term 3
combat units *will reduce the army's fighting strength.*

This enthymeme can be expressed as a syllogism.

A
MAJOR PREMISE: *Persons who will reduce the army's fighting strength* should be
B
barred from combat units.

C A
MINOR PREMISE: *Women* are *persons who will reduce the army's fighting strength.*

C B
CLAIM: *Women* should be *barred from combat units.*

Copyright © 2010, Pearson Education, Inc., Publishing as Longman

The Limitations of Formal Logic for Writers.

Although formal logic helps you appreciate the three-term structure of an enthymeme—and thus to formulate the missing major premise—formal logic deals only with the structure of an argument, not with the truth of its premises. Unless a properly structured argument also has true premises, we can conclude nothing about the truth of its claim. Consider the following arguments:

Any loan that can be paid back with funny money is a free gift.

Guaranteed Student Loans can be paid back with funny money.

Guaranteed Student Loans are free gifts.

The blood of insects can be used to lubricate lawn-mower engines.

Vampires are insects.

Therefore the blood of vampires can be used to lubricate lawn-mower engines.

Because their premises are untrue, these arguments are ludicrous; nevertheless, in a logic class they would be considered validly structured. The limitation of formal logic for writers, then, is that it deals solely with the validity of an argument's structure and not with the truth of its premises. Since the main concern of writers is to show the truth of the premises, formal logic is of limited value. For this reason, teachers of argument have looked for different ways of representing an argument's structure—ways that would more directly meet the needs of writers. Toulmin's system, based on a legal model of argumentation aimed at testing the truth of premises, is particularly suited for real-world argument.

Copyright © 2010, Pearson Education, Inc., Publishing as Longman

WHAT ABOUT MESSY STUDENT EXAMPLES OF ENTHYMEMES THAT DON'T "FIT" TOULMIN'S SCHEMA?

Of course, doing these exercises on textbook examples, where the enthymemes have been selected because the distinctions between stated reason and warrant and between grounds and backing are especially clear, won't mean that all enthymemes are equally easy to analyze. In arguments in a tangled rhetorical context, students often produce enthymemes that baffle us with their complexity. Sometimes the grammar is tangled; sometimes several lines of argument are conflated; sometimes important intermediate steps are omitted; sometimes the enthymeme seems like a hopeless *non sequitur*; sometimes the argument seems OK but one just can't quite unravel its parts in Toulmin's terms.

Therefore, after doing the For Class Discussion exercises in Chapters 3 and 4, all of which are analyzable using Toulmin's schema, giving students a taste of a non-textbook example enthymeme that is more like the ones they are apt to produce or encounter will help matters. A typical example is the following:

> We need to start a women's studies program at Clambake College because women are sick and tired of being treated as unequal.

Most students might think this is a good argument until one begins to analyze it in Toulmin's terms. Look first at the stated reason…

> Women are sick and tired of being treated as unequal.

and ask how might an arguer support it with grounds. Would he provide evidence that women are "sick and tired" (say, narratives of women faculty or students who are near points of exhaustion?) or evidence that women have been treated as unequals (data, say, about unequal pay or about the "glass ceiling")? When asking questions like these, students begin see that the reason has two parts that aren't clearly connected. The reason, as stated, doesn't help one know what kind of evidence to provide.

In more detailed analysis, students might encounter more confusion when they try to articulate the warrant. When asked to write out what they think is the warrant, many students will be unable to do so (this example doesn't click the way the textbook examples do). Those who try will disagree on how to word it. (One can puzzle over the warrant for this enthymeme and be left with an unsatisfactory if-then statement: "If something causes women to be sick and tired at being treated as unequal, then we should start a women's studies program" [?]) An instructor might make more progress by asking the simpler question, "What are some of the unstated assumptions behind this enthymeme?" It is easy to see some: It is bad to feel sick and tired; it is bad to be treated as unequal. But what do these bad things have to do with a women's studies program? Perhaps students will say, "A women's studies program will help end or eliminate these bad things"—an insightful answer that moves the argument forward.

Copyright © 2010, Pearson Education, Inc., Publishing as Longman

At this point, instructors can try to show that one problem with the original enthymeme is that it contains no term shared by both the claim and the stated reason. In other words, the stated reason doesn't repeat a key term from the claim. The claim is about starting a women's studies program, while the stated reason is about women's being sick and tired at being treated as unequals. Because the term "women's studies program" or "starting a women's studies program" doesn't appear in the stated reason, it is difficult to write a warrant that connects stated reason to claim. An instructor can easily ask students to revise the original enthymeme in order to repeat in the stated reason this key term from the claim.

> We should start a women's studies program because doing so [e.g. starting a women's studies program] will . . .
>
> We should start a women's studies program because it [e.g. a women's studies program] will . . .

Students can now break down the original bifurcated reason into its constituent parts:

> We should start a women's studies program because such a program will help promote equality of women and men in our society. [Develops the "treated as unequals" part of the original enthymeme]
>
> We should start a women's studies program here at Clambake College because doing so will help end the frustration and powerlessness felt by many women students and faculty who have spent years battling a patriarchal administration. [Develops the "women are sick and tired" part of the original enthymeme]

Once the enthymemes are worded this way, they become more readily analyzable in Toulmin's terms. Students agree that it is easier to see how to develop each of these enthymemes than was the case with the original enthymeme. This exercise helps students see that it can be worthwhile sometimes to examine their own enthymemes from a Toulmin perspective. Trying to analyze them in Toulmin's terms can help clarify the lines of reasoning to be developed. But it's important that students don't have to master Toulmin's schema. Like other heuristics, the Toulmin system is not an end in itself but only a means to better structured and more fully developed arguments. It is the quality of writing that instructors should be most interested in.

Copyright © 2010, Pearson Education, Inc., Publishing as Longman

V. SUGGESTIONS FOR TEACHING VISUAL ARGUMENT

In *Writing Arguments*, 8th edition, the text continues to emphasize the prevalence, importance, and power of visual argument. In particular, Chapter 9 focuses on genres of visual argument: advocacy advertisements, posters, product advertisements, political cartoons, fliers, Web sites, and graphical elements. It also explains the elements of visual design—type, layout, images, and color—and the way that arguers can strengthen their appeals to *logos*, *ethos*, and *pathos*. To show visual argument in action, the text has various examples of advertising, advocacy ads, political cartoons, and other forms of visual media. All these exemplify how arguments emerge from social rhetorical contexts and how verbal and visual elements can work in conjunction to achieve rhetorical goals.

DISCUSSION EXERCISE: ANALYZING VISUAL ARGUMENT IN AMERICAN HISTORY

In the following pages, a For Class Discussion exercise and sample notes are provided that instructors can use or adapt to lead a discussion to analyze political posters or important photographs from American History. This exercise is useful in activating students' interest in visual arguments and in providing an opportunity for them to analyze the way that images, like other arguments, are products of specific historical and rhetorical contexts. The goals for this exercise are to help our students analyze (1) how images encode powerful emotional and persuasive appeals; (2) how images draw on cultural symbolism and often create new symbols with political and social resonance; (3) how visual arguments focus arguments by zeroing-in on single issues, simplifying, clarifying, taking one powerful stand; and (4) how these visual arguments were effective at their historical moments.

One exercise that has proven fruitful is using posters created by the United States government to generate support and unify the country behind the war effort during World War II. On the National Archives Web site (http://www.archives.gov/index.html), there is a link to historical documents that teachers use quite extensively. Using this Web site or other related sites, instructors can foster students uncovering part of the past and the visual arguments that were important to that milieu. For example, by using the link of "Teaching with Documents" (http://www.archives.gov/education/lessons/), instructors can find interesting visual rhetoric to explore. In particular, the "Powers of Persuasion—Poster Art of World War II" exhibit can be quite helpful in showing how visual argument effectively uses color, layout/design, concise copy, and Aristotelian proofs (*ethos, logos,* and *pathos)*. The exhibit of war effort posters is accessible via this portal:
http://www.archives.gov/exhibits/powers_of_persuasion/powers_of_persuasion_intro.html.

Using this resource, instructors can show the immediacy and rhetorical force of visual arguments.

Copyright © 2010, Pearson Education, Inc., Publishing as Longman

In discussing visual argument in classrooms, it's also quite important that instructors demonstrate that because visual images are often historically rooted, readers may have to research the history of the issues to comprehend these images. Instructors may find it useful to consult a history text or use other appropriate resources at their disposal.

The handout that follows shows the kinds of questions used to guide the discussion, calling upon students' background in American history and fleshing out their understanding with the instructors' own notes and comments. After the handout, suggested answers are provided to the For Class Discussion questions, including background information.

Copyright © 2010, Pearson Education, Inc., Publishing as Longman

Handout: CLASS DISCUSSION EXERCISE ON WORLD WAR II WAR EFFORT POSTERS

Individually, in groups, or as an all-class discussion, use the following questions to analyze a historical war effort poster or posters. In analyzing these political posters, your instructor may provide some historical context, and you may also draw upon your own knowledge of the war effort during World War II. The following questions will help guide your critical thinking as you observe these posters, speculate about the issues they address, and analyze their historical effectiveness as visual arguments.

1. What historical information would be useful as background to help you analyze the significance of these war effort posters?

2. As you analyze each poster, consider the following questions:

A. What are the ***visual features*** of the poster?

Focus on and Analyze the poster's...

Layout, Organization, Framing
Foreground/Background
Placement of Copy (text)
Font of Copy
The Rhetorical Aim/Effect of the Copy
Use of Visual *Ethos, Pathos, and Logos*
Kairos
Tone

B. How does ***color*** function in the poster?

How do certain colors frame the poster, create an attention-getting quality, and what emotions do these colors evoke?

C. How does the poster connect with the ***cultural stakes*** and ***social problems*** surrounding the war effort during World War II?

To what value, beliefs, and assumptions does it appeal?
Can you provide any shared beliefs that this poster exemplifies?

D. What might have made the poster even ***more politically effective*** during its historical moment?

And if you were to create similar posters today, what would you do them on and why (purpose?), how (changes?), where (what target audience and occasion)?

Copyright © 2010, Pearson Education, Inc., Publishing as Longman

VI. CHAPTER GUIDES

CHAPTER 1 ARGUMENT: AN INTRODUCTION

For Class Discussion Exercises

(pages 6-7)
1. Students' answers will vary. You might ask students to discuss the advantages and disadvantages of these products along with the potential gains and risks of keeping phthalates in products. The photograph of the child obviously works on a strong emotional and values level whereas Sullivan's letter appeals to reason by citing studies to combat the implicit argument that we follow the "precautionary principle" like the EU. Sullivan argues that "facts" and scientific studies should trump possible negative outcomes.

2. Answers will vary, but below are some possible ones:

* Figure 1.3: A) "These Colors Don't Run" might refer to the idea that US forces need to stay in Iraq, not withdraw in a sustained fashion. B) The argument could be termed in this way: "Since America is a bold and strong nation, she should not leave Iraq because the war is unpopular. We should stay true to our commitment to bring democracy to Iraq and not be cowards in the face of a difficult situation. C) The Iraq war was misguided, and the US should pull out as soon as possible since most Iraqi don't want us there as an occupying force. Immediate withdrawal from Iraq is necessary to get our soldiers out of a war that never should have been started. D) The patriotic image of the tough looking bald eagle with a flag across its side appeals to patriotism, using two images that stir up positive and encouraging emotions about our nation.
* Figure 1.4: A) That flag cleverly takes the argument provided in Figure 1.3 and turns it on itself. The issue is the role of America in the world. B) America should not act as the world ruler and tell other countries and governments how they should run their countries. C) Some opposing views would be that America cannot be isolationist in the world. The spread of democracy and democratic principles is part of our county's destiny. D) The argument uses the flag in order to imply that we should care about our country first, but we don't want to involve ourselves in foreign conflicts that aren't absolutely necessary.
* Figure 1.5: A) The conversation implied in this piece is the controversy about physician-assisted suicide and whether doctors and family members have the right to let patients die because they are unable to live on their own without machines. B) The implied argument here is that physician-assisted suicide is justified because those who cannot live without machines do not live normal lives. Their quality of life and life in general is compromised. C) An alternative view would be that if we have the medical technology available we should keep patients alive because we might be able to save them in time. Also, God should be the one that takes a life, not humans. D) The comic uses the incongruity of the image of the patient contrasted by his wife's perspective on "natural" death.
* Figure 1.6: A) The conversation here is the argument about whether food sources should be used as source of fuel, in particular corn-based ethanol. B) This argument makes the causal claim that America's use of ethanol is directly affecting the amount of food that

Copyright © 2010, Pearson Education, Inc., Publishing as Longman

the poor in developing nations have. C) An opponent of this cartoon could argue that our use of ethanol is not directly affecting the poor abroad since local conditions in those nations really are the factors that affect starving children. In fact, some argue that the food we export for humanitarian purposes never reaches the people it needs to reach. D) The cartoon uses the contrast between a malnourished child with an empty bowl in his hand and an older, wealthy gentleman in a suit taking corn away from the child. The image paints Americans who use ethanol as cold and heartless.

* Figure 1.7: A) The comic joins the conversation about airlines limiting the amount of carry-on luggage that people can bring onto an airplane. B) The claim is whatever penalties or limits that airlines might try to enforce, people will find inventive ways to get around them. C) Opposing arguments might be that the policies about carry-on bags are wise because people bringing on too much luggage slows down departures and arrivals. D) The strip provides the image of the classic American family driving themselves to ridiculous lengths to not have to check in bags and possibly have them lost by the airlines. The comic uses humor to persuade people about the way humans are.

This exercise anticipates Chapters 9, which discuss the use of images and visual elements to shape rhetorical effects. In preparation for more in-depth discussion of implicit argument and visual elements, students might want to begin collecting comic strips, editorial cartoons, print advertisements, and news photos that they find particularly powerful, memorable, disturbing, or persuasive.

(pages 17-8)
The purpose of this exercise is to stimulate class discussion and reveal to students the complexity of issues that turn on differences of values and belief. The instructor can either lead a general class discussion on the value conflicts in these newspaper stories or conduct simulation games as suggested in the task itself. The easiest way to run the simulation game is first to assign students from small groups, with each group assigned to one of the roles. Ask the groups to brainstorm all the arguments the assigned "role" is apt to make. Then each group can select a spokesperson to play the role in the actual simulation. Here are the kinds of arguments that should emerge from the "college athletics" and "homeless" simulations:

Case 1: This case works on many different levels. First many of the people in this simulated meeting would argue for a very broad definition of freedom of speech since they believe that citizens should have the ability to place whatever they choose to on social-networking sites. And limiting that freedom would be considered unconstitutional and un-American. An adult should have the individual freedom to post how they want as protected by the first amendment, some would argue. Others might take a cautionary approach since they want student-athletes to have the same activities as other students. Some of these stakeholders would argue that using those sites is fine, but student-athletes need to be careful about how they present themselves since they agree to codes of conduct that they should follow. If postings conflict with certain codes of conduct such as drinking, student-athletes should be held responsible for that content since they are responsible adults who should know better. Some would argue that freedom of speech only goes so far, especially when slanderous material on a site can spread quickly across campus. So while a person might have a right to post whatever they want on his or her site, that person has to be held liable for unfounded assertions. Others will also bring a public relations outlook to the

Copyright © 2010, Pearson Education, Inc., Publishing as Longman

conversation since students, whether they like or not, represent the institution, and codes of conduct and legal principles cover all students/citizens.

Case 2: This case pits the rights of homeless people to use public property against the rights of shoppers and business people to have a clean and pleasant downtown city. Supporters of the homeless should argue that sitting is not a crime, that the economy doesn't provide adequate housing, jobs, or medical care for poor people, that no public restrooms are available, and that asking for money is legal. Someone might question the difference between a homeless person asking for money and a Salvation Army volunteer ringing a bell at Christmas. Supporters of a vibrant downtown could argue that panhandlers hurt business, that the foul smell of urine and feces drives away shoppers, that the deterioration of downtown businesses harms the city's economy, making it impossible to provide the services that homeless people need, that enforcement of these laws will force at least some of the homeless to seek treatment for chemical dependency or help them turn their lives around, and so forth.

(pages 22-3)
In some classes the majority of students vote not to approve Gordon Adams' petition, thus not waiving his math requirement, and in others the class is fairly divided. The text takes up the Gordon Adams' case again in Chapter 5 in the section on audience-based reasons. For the present exercise, it is useful for the instructor to help students see the issue from a faculty member's perspective and look at how Adams' presents his argument. Would faculty accept Adams' basic assumption that career utility is the prime consideration for requiring a core course? Would granting Gordon's petition set a precedent for waiving any core course that is irrelevant to a student's chosen career, and how fair would that be to other students who are required to fulfill the math requirement? Are those statements and data gathered from lawyers helpful? In addition, how logical/sensible is Adams' statement that he's "more than willing to substitute another course or two in its place"? For this exercise, instructors can also help students observe their own decision-making processes. Ask for examples of how students' ideas evolved during the discussion. It's important to praise students who admit changing their position as a result of listening to good arguments from fellow students because that validates that argument and critical thinking is an evolving process that leads to the best answers or solution for the greater good of all.

Copyright © 2010, Pearson Education, Inc., Publishing as Longman

CHAPTER 2: ARGUMENT AS INQUIRY: READING AND EXPLORING

For Class Discussion Exercises

(page 27)
Answers will vary, but here are some typical responses:
Figure 2.1: 1) Employers who use illegal immigrants should be held responsible for unlawful activity. 2) The protester assumes that Americans are well aware that many employers willfully use illegal immigrants because they can pay them less and don't have to provide benefits to them. 3) Issues involved include the degree to which employers know that employees are "legal," the degree of culpability that employers should have if they do employ illegal immigrants, and how the legal system should or should not respond to this important wrinkle in the debate about immigration and illegal immigrants. 4) Answers will vary. because of tougher border security. 4) Answers will vary.
Figure 2.2: 1) Integration of illegal immigrants is an easier and more humane way of addressing illegal immigration. 2) The protesters assume that Americans believe that integration is a better path than sending immigrants back to their home countries. In addition, "comprehensive" is a vague word that can be interpreted quite differently by diverse viewers of the problem. 3) Issues involved include America's traditional role as a nation of immigrants, what constitutes "earning" citizenship, and how integration is defined. 4) Answers will vary.
Figure 2.3: 1) Americans really don't want to stop undocumented workers because they depend too heavily on them to do laborer jobs. 2) The assumed background information is that many undocumented migrants work at various less-skilled and skilled jobs in the American economy. 3) Issues involved are the border fence, the effect of limiting undocumented migrants from working, and the effect on Mexico
Figure 2.4: 1) If Americans really want to restrict the migrant work force, a number of jobs, such as housekeepers, will go unfilled since "regular" Americans are unwilling to take those jobs. 2) This cartoon assumes that the reader knows that many housekeepers are recent immigrants and that machines have replaced many jobs in American industries. 3) Issues involved include the low-paying jobs that immigrants tend to get when they come to America and the mechanization of American industry. 4) Answers will vary.

(page 31)
Answers will vary, but the main point is for students to get a taste of different viewpoints than they might take and how one might reason or rationalize those positions. Here are some possible responses, however.

A) *Reasons for Believing*: Cheating is unethical, students have an ethical responsibility to report wrongdoing, cheating creates an unlevel playing field academically, people shouldn't be rewarded for unethical behavior. *Reasons for Doubting*: It's not the students responsibility to act as a disciplinarian, instructors should be responsible for detecting these problems, everyone does it
B) *Reasons for Believing*: Women are equal to men, they can operate machinery just as effectively as men, women are strong in group problem-solving and thus could be assets to the military. *Reasons for Doubting*: Women are physically and intellectually weaker, women are too emotional for combat missions, having women in combat goes against tradition.

Copyright © 2010, Pearson Education, Inc., Publishing as Longman

C) *Reasons for Believing*: Taking steroids and human growth hormones is fine as long as a doctor supervises the doses, in many sports steroid and HGH don't provide competitive advantages, athletes should be able to use whatever advantages they can find. *Reasons for Doubting*: Unprofessional physicians will prescribe both for simply monetary reasons, steroid and HGH provide unfair competitive advantages, steroids and HGH constitute cheating.
D) *Reasons for Believing*: Illegal immigrants already living here have already established themselves and put down roots in this country, disrupting families because of a parent's decision to work illegally is wrong, they are working here now and are productive. *Reasons for Doubting*: These people should be held responsible for their bad decisions, those who are here illegally shouldn't be given preferential treatment over those who are legally trying to immigrate, granting amnesty will only attract more illegal immigrants.

(pages 42-3)
Following the examples provided in the text, individual students or small groups should create does and says statements, raising doubts, and dialectic thinking. Answers and comments will vary according to individuals' and groups' frames of vision on the topic. What follows are "does statements" and "says statements" for the remaining paragraphs of Kavanaugh's article.

Paragraph (P) 7: *Does*: Contrasts those opposing views to other opposing views that depict illegal immigrants as criminals. *Says*: People with such close-minded views are misguided and not compassionate.
P8: *Does*: Further contrasts the bluster of these people with other notions of compassion. *Says*: We need to think of these illegal immigrants as fellow human beings, and we should care about their welfare and safety.
P9: *Does*: Establishes precedents and examples of how people have argued through Christian ethical frameworks. *Says*: We should question the laws on the book rather than simply reverting to the idea that illegal immigrants are not following the law.
P10: *Does*: Articulates reasons why border security and broader political issues are important to consider in this debate. *Says*: Americans need to look at the more complex causes of this issue/problem, namely that there are major economic causes that drive people to immigrate illegally.
P11: *Does*: Argues that a workable solution needs to be struck. *Says*: If citizens are contributing to "our common good," "amnesty" or some type of legal status is an appropriate response to a complex situation.
P 12: *Does*: Provides a soft proposal that could be enacted. *Says*: Using "citizen panels" is a workable solution to addressing whether illegal immigrants should stay in the country or be deported.
P 13: *Does*: Appeals to Judeo-Christian values of charity and compassion to make readers consider the situation. *Says*: Instead of portraying illegal immigrants in a negative light, it's important to see them as individuals and offer an open view of how current laws only make the situation problematic.

Copyright © 2010, Pearson Education, Inc., Publishing as Longman

Examining Sources of Disagreement: Arguments for Analysis

A number of the arguments in the anthology present clashing or intersecting arguments that would give students good practice in analyzing disagreements in interpretations of fact, in values, and assumptions. The following is a list of pairs of articles that are particularly good for comparative analysis:

Web 2.0 and Online Identity

- Bronwyn T. Williams, "'Tomorrow Will Not Be Like Today': Literacy and Identity in a World of Multiliteracies" (429-34)
- Alice Mathias, "The Facebook Generation" (438-39)

- Alice Mathias, "The Facebook Generation" (438-39)
- Dana L. Fleming, "Youthful Indiscretions: Should Colleges Protect Social Network User from Themselves and Others?" (440-43)

Video Games and Their Influence

- Iowa State University News Service, "ISU Psychologists Publish Three New Studies on Violent Video Game Effects on Youth" (449-50)
- Henry Jenkins, "Reality Bytes: Eight Myths About Video Games Debunked" (450-54)

The News Media: Responsible Production, Responsible Consumption

- William Powers, "The Massless Media" (467-72)
- Dan Kennedy, "Plugged In, Tuned Out: Young Americans are Embracing New Media but Failing to Develop an Appetite for News" (473-79)

- Chris Shaw, "Should Killers Be Given Air Time?" (479-80)
- Daryl Cagle, "Those Terrible Virginia Tech Cartoons" (480-82)

Immigration in the Twenty-First Century: Accommodation and Change

- Maileen Hamto, "My Turn: Being American" (494-95)
- Jay Nordlinger, "Bassackwards: Construction Spanish and Other Signs of the Times" (500-03)

Women in Math and Science

- Linda Chavez, "Harvard Prez's Admission: Men and Women are Different" (507-08)
- Brian McFadden, "Amazing Facts About the Fairer, Yet Equal, Sex" (509)

- Nature Neuroscience, "Separating Science from Stereotype" (510-11)
- Deborah Blum, "Solving for X" (512-13)

- Stephen Pinker, "The Science of Sex Difference: Sex Ed" (514-17)
- Ben A. Barres, "Does Gender Matter?" (517-25)

Copyright © 2010, Pearson Education, Inc., Publishing as Longman

Finding Soldiers: The Volunteer Army, Recruitment, and the Draft:

* Phillp Carter and Paul Gastris, "The Case for the Draft" (530-40)
* Lawrence J. Korb and Sean E. Duggan, "An All-Volunteer Army? Recruitment and Its Problems" (541-49)

Wal-Mart and the Public Good

* Arindrajit Dube, T. William Lester, and Barry Eidlin, "A Downward Push: The Impact of Wal-Mart Stores on Retail Wages and Benefits" (558-65)
* Steve Maich, "Why Wal-Mart is Good" (568-74)

* Robert B. Reich, "Don't Blame Wal-Mart" (566-68)
* Dan Piraro, "Greeter Gone Wild" (566)

Sustainability: The Search for Clean Energy

* Nicholas Kristof, "Our Gas Guzzlers, Their Lives" (579-80)
* Charles Krauthammer, "Save the Planet, Let Someone Else Drill" (584-85)

Biotech Agriculture and the Ethics of Food Production

* Jonathan Rauch, "Will Frankenfoods Save the Planet?" (599-606)
* Miguel A. Altieri and Peter Rosset, "Ten Reasons Why Biotechnology Will Not Ensure Food Security, Protect the Environment, and Reduce Poverty in the Developing World" (608-15)

* Gregory A. Jaffe, "Lessen the Fear of Genetically Engineered Crops" (615-16)
* Froma Harrop, "Food Industry Should Modify Its Stance on Altered Food" (617-18)

Student Responses to Assignments. For an example of a student essay analyzing sources of disagreement in two articles, see "VII. Samples of Student Writing for Discussion." Student Adrian Walther analyzed two articles from the anthology unit "The United States as Sole Superpower" from the 6th edition of *Writing Arguments*. His paper is "An Analysis of the Sources of Disagreement between Jeff Guntzel and Mona Charen" and begins on page 169 of the *Instructor's Manual.*

Copyright © 2010, Pearson Education, Inc., Publishing as Longman

Handout: ANALYZING SOURCES OF DISAGREEMENT

Use the following questions as a guide to help you analyze your two articles for sources of disagreement.

1. In your own words, summarize the core of each writer's argument.

2. What is the key issue for each writer? How does each frame that issue? How has the genre of each article shaped its argument?

3. Where do the writers disagree over interpretations of facts?

4. Where do the writers disagree over values, assumptions, or analogies?

5. What questions would you like to ask each writer? Where do you see gaps, fuzziness or confusion in the argument?

6. What further information would you like to have about the issue?

Copyright © 2010, Pearson Education, Inc., Publishing as Longman

CHAPTER 3: THE CORE OF AN ARGUMENT: A CLAIM WITH REASONS

For Class Discussion Exercises

(page 65)
1. This question is most likely an issue question with the concept "failing" open for interpretation and definition. If the arguer and audience had previously agreed on a straightforward definition of what it means for a school to fail and a research instrument to gain numerical data, then this question could become an information question. 2. Issue question. 3. This question is most likely an issue question because it is positing a strong, single cause-effect relationship that is debatable. If any definitive research studies could come up with clear evidence or if a number of studies agreed, then this would be an information question. If studies disagreed or if an audience found flaws in a study's research design, then the question would become controversial and hence an issue question. 4. This question certainly could be an issue or information question. As for information, a student could easily consult various authorities—the FDA, a well-known bioethicist, a biologist, etc.—and perhaps get a straight yes or no answer. However, this is certainly an issue question. It is hotly debated by arguers who could raise serious questions about each researchers' claims, grounds, warrants, backing, statistical data, and casual projections. 5. Again, this is an issue question so long as medical controversies are incorrect, poorly correlated, or illogical.

(page 67)
1. Reasonable arguments. Disputants will argue about the criteria for "good" and about whether the Star Wars series meets the criteria. 2. Reasonable arguments. Disputants will need to establish criteria for "beautiful," as well as define features for "postmodern architecture." 3. Reasonable arguments. Writer could establish consequences of subsidizing the professional sports venues and argue that the positive consequences do or do not outweigh the negative ones. Disputants might argue about the proper domain of public funds and profit companies. 4. Although controversy here is apt to degenerate into pseudo-argument, it is possible to establish rational criteria for "true art" and then to argue that a monkey's painting does or does not meet the criteria. 5. Pseudo-argument. There is probably no way to argue for shared criteria for "attractive," because such trends as jewelry, hairstyles, and clothing styles are highly subjective.

(page 70)
This is an important collaborative exercise because it gives students practice composing "because clauses" for their own claims and because it encourages students to see the power of alternative and opposing views.

Copyright © 2010, Pearson Education, Inc., Publishing as Longman

CHAPTER 4: THE LOGICAL STRUCTURE OF ARGUMENTS

For Class Discussion Exercises

(page 76)
1. Bossy people don't make good leaders. 2. Legalization of drugs would automatically make more people use druges. 3. Stopping terrorists is the proper role of airport screeners, and racial profiling is effective in identifying terrorists. 4. Civil rights are an important consideration in our society. 5. Genetic diversity is something important to keep intact. 6. Damage to the economy should be avoided, and the act damages the economy.

(page 80)
2. Claim: Drugs should not be legalized. Stated reason: because legalization would greatly increase the number of drug addicts. Grounds: Evidence of how legalization of other substances creates addiction, examples of people who have become addicts after substances were legalized, anecdotes from experts on drug policy and addiction. Conditions of Rebuttal for the Reasons and Grounds: Questioning of the causal relationship between legalization and addiction, examples of where legalization of substances has decreased addiction, expert testimony about the psychological factors of legality tied to addiction. Warrant: We should not pass legislation that increases the number of drug addicts. (Increasing the number of drug addicts is bad.) Backing: Examples of how drug addiction has destroyed relationships and damaged other people, drug addiction is unhealthy and damages people mentally and physically. Conditions of Rebuttal for the Warrant and Backing: Being able to identify and help addicts because of legalization will facilitate help more quickly, individuals have the right to be addicted to drugs if they want to be, the government shouldn't tell citizens what to do with their own bodies.
3. Claim: Airport screeners should use racial profiling. Stated reason: because doing so will increase the odds of stopping terrorism. Grounds: Facts about what screening systems can catch, examples of how screeners have caught terrorists attempting to board planes, appeals to emotion about how screening will help stop atrocities like those on Septmenber 11th. Conditions of Rebuttal for the Grounds: Screeners have definite limits on what they can detect, examples and studies that show the fallibility of screening systems, experts who argue that airport screeners are simply "feel good" measures that simply slow down the boarding process. Warrant: Anything that helps to stop terrorism is good and should be pursued. Backing: Examples of how terrorists acts affect the American population, points about how terrorist acts are detrimental to the American economy, anecdotes about how terrorist acts create a guarded and xenophobic populace. Conditions of Rebuttal for the Warrant and Backing: Terrorism is a part of world, Americans need to confront the fact that terrorism will happen again, unnecessary invasion of personal property isn't pragmatic, terrorists can take over or blow up a plane without bringing something onto it.
4. Claim: Racial profiling should not be used by airport screeners. Stated reason: because it violates a person's civil rights. Grounds: Civil rights should never be violated, racial profiling is a violation of civil rights, terrorist don't look the same. Conditions of Rebuttal for the Reasons and Grounds: Racial profiling is not a civil right violation—it's smart policing, most terrorists fit a certain profile, people have to give up certain civil rights in response to global terrorism. Warrant: Policies and actions that violate people's civil rights are bad should not be pursued. Backing: Examples of how civil right violations led to unrest, government has a responsibility to

Copyright © 2010, Pearson Education, Inc., Publishing as Longman

protect our civil rights, anecdotes about how loss of civil rights leads to other concessions on the part of the citizenry. Conditions of Rebuttal for the Warrant and Backing: People who have nothing to hide have nothing to worry about, the government's first goal is to protect its citizens, airport security is much different than freedom of speech and other rights.

5. Claim: We should strengthen the Endangered Species Act. Stated reason: because doing so will preserve genetic diversity on the planet. Grounds: Examples of how genetic diversity is crucial for sustainable and adaptable ecosystems, anecdotes about how many beneficial drugs come from diverse plants from across the globe, humans should be caretakers of the earth and protect its diversity. Conditions of Rebuttal for the Reasons and Grounds: Genetic diversity is not as important as economic vitality, examples of how the ESA kept industry from flourishing, belief that humans can do with the planet whatever they choose to since they're the "higher" mammal. Warrant: Preserving genetic diversity on the planet is good. Backing: Experts who agree that genetic diversity is a noble and important goal, anecdotes about how genetic diversity creates ecosystems that are less likely to crash under stress, beliefs that stewardship is part of human's role on earth. Conditions of Rebuttal for the Warrant and Backing: Idea that because we have the most power we should be able to do whatever we wish to environments, examples of how the ESA put insects and animals before human's values and economic interests.

6. Claim: The Endangered Species Act is too stringent. Stated reason: because it severely damages the economy. Grounds: Examples of how ESA rulings have restricted logging, mining, and other business ventures, experts in business who agree with the idea that the ESA restricts economic growth, anecdotes about how businesses are severely limited in what they can do in their operations. Warrant: The economy is the most important factor in considering what to do with natural environments. Backing: The anecdote that America's business "is to do business," money matters more than genetic diversity and natural beauty, examples of how communities have been decimated by the ESA. Conditions of Rebuttal for the Warrant and Backing: Argument that economy doesn't trump all other factors, examples of how the ESA brings in tourism dollars without destroying the natural environment, economic experts who agree that the ESA does no harm to local economies.

(page 84)

1.a. To show the annoyance of sales taxes, the writer could provide personal experiences about carrying around pocketfuls of change, of having dresser drawers full of pennies, of never being able to figure out the price of something quickly, of forgetting to include sales tax in consideration of big ticket expenses, and so forth. 1.b. Writer could quote lyrics from rap songs that denigrate women; writer could mention rap singers' disrespectful and negative attitudes toward women; writer could do a survey of teens who listen to rap music and find out how they refer to women. 1.c. For example, last Tuesday afternoon Professor X spent two hours with Theresa and then went over to her house in the evening to talk personally with her parents. The week before, Professor X had helped Sam look for a job and excused Sally from an exam because of Sally's concern for her grandmother's illness.

2.a. Annoying taxes cause resentment against government, and they encourage cheating. 2.b. Writer could show how disrespect for women can lead to poor relationships, discrimination, and violence. 2.c. Teachers need to be role models for their students, and it is rare indeed for a student to see caring, altruistic behavior from a teacher. Such a teacher instructs students in lifelong values—a benefit that may exceed mere book learning.

Copyright © 2010, Pearson Education, Inc., Publishing as Longman

3.a. Unless the benefits of a sales tax—such as not needing a state income tax—outweigh the annoyance. 3.b. Unless rap music does not have any effect on listeners; unless some rap music lyrics are not as hard on women as some people think; unless rap music empowers women. 3.c. Unless counseling students is outside the bound of instructor responsibilities and student expectations; unless the educational institution provides other services that are especially designed to help students with personal problems; unless Professor X's counseling of students is a misuse of time; unless this time would be better used to help students with their academic skills and many students are in need of this academic guidance.

(page 86)
1a. Warrant: The educational system should prepare students for a competitive, cut-throat business environment. 1b. Warrant: The education system should be adapted to individual learning styles and make students find their own inner excellence. Audience Analysis: The audience would side with 1b since 1a contrasts with the beliefs and assumptions of that audience. An audience who is against competition will likely reject the first warrant because it accepts the idea of competition. This audience might be reached by the concept of developing individuals' potential.
2a. Warrant: Lowering cholesterol levels is an important factor when deciding on a diet. Warrant: Animals should not suffer. Audience Analysis: Since young people ages fifteen to twenty-five are quite diverse in political views and ideas about health, the enthymemes are persuasive according to the subset of that larger group. But unless young people have a history of serious heart problems in their families (family members died young of heart attacks), they are likely to be more moved by appeals to reduce the suffering of animals than long-term health consequences.
3a. Warrant: Public acceptance of homosexuality should be avoided. Warrant: gay people have the same right to establish long-term relationships. Audience Analysis: The audience would likely side with 1a since "family values" in the conservative circles is equated with only a man and woman being married, not same-sex partners.

Student Responses to Assignments. For an example of a student essay analyzing sources of disagreement in two articles, see "VII. Samples of Student Writing for Discussion." For this assignment, student Adrian Walther analyzed two articles in the anthology unit "The United States as Sole Superpower" from the 6th edition of *Writing Arguments*. His paper is "An Analysis of the Sources of Disagreement between Jeff Guntzel and Mona Charen" (page 169 of the IM).

Copyright © 2010, Pearson Education, Inc., Publishing as Longman

(Chapter 4)

Quiz: ENTHYMEMES AND TOULMIN ARGUMENT FRAMES

Part I: Write out the warrant for each of the following enthymemes.

1. Transracial adoption should be encouraged because transracial adoption especially removes children who might not be adopted from the foster care system and provides them with loving adoptive homes.

2. Vaccines for children should be required by law because vaccines have virtually eliminated dreaded childhood diseases such as diphtheria, measles, mumps, whooping cough, polio, rubella, tetanus, and hepatitis B.

3. Globalization is ethically wrong because it does not improve the quality of life for people in poor, developing countries.

4. MTV is good television programming for teen viewers because it raises teens' social and political awareness.

5. Smart guns (guns that can be activated only with the owner's fingerprint or by pressing buttons in a sequence) should be required by law because they will prevent the gun use among youths that has resulted in suicides, accidents, and school violence.

Part II: Now choose **one** of the enthymemes above and sketch out a complete Toulmin argument frame, including claim, reason, grounds, warrant, backing, conditions of rebuttal, and qualifier for that argument.

Copyright © 2010, Pearson Education, Inc., Publishing as Longman

(Chapter 4)

Exercise: PRACTICING WITH ARGUMENT CORES

Directions: For each of the three argument cores below, use your own knowledge of the issue to generate the missing parts according to the Toulmin schema. Consider the audience specified for each issue question.

ISSUE QUESTION #1: SHOULD WE ESTABLISH ONE UNIVERSAL RATING SYSTEM AND RATING BOARD FOR MOVIES, TELEVISION, AND VIDEO GAMES?

Audience: Parents of young children and teens

Claim: A universal rating system for movies, television shows, and video games should be established.

Reason 1: because the current rating systems are vastly different and therefore hard to understand

> **Grounds**: A Mature-rated video game can get a teen rating just by taking out the blood; a Mature-rated game can contain topless nudity; examples of the different labeling that the three media use; surveys to indicate how few parents understand the ratings
> **Warrant**:____
> ____
>
> **Backing**:____
> ____

Reason 2: because the current rating systems are easy for producers and video game manufacturers to get around

> **Grounds**: Give examples of the way the movie industry has claimed "art" as an excuse for nudity and violence.
> **Warrant**:____
> ____
>
> **Backing:**____
> ____

Reason 3: because a universal rating system would provide parents with a reliable guide to age-suitable movies, TV programs, and video games

> **Grounds**: An age-suitable numbering system would work better than confusing letters such as R (restricted), M (mature), and E (for everyone); with one standard.
>
> **Warrant:**____
> ____
>
> **Backing:**____
> ____

Copyright © 2010, Pearson Education, Inc., Publishing as Longman

Exercise (continued)

Conditions of Rebuttal for Reasons 1, 2, and 3: There are too many differences between movies, television shows, and video games for one rating system: with movies and television shows, the viewer is a spectator whereas with video games, the viewer is an active participant; a universal rating system might bring the government into regulating ratings; people's idea of what is violent or unsuitable varies

Qualifier: With specified guidelines, a universal rating system should be established for movies, television shows, and video games.

ISSUE QUESTION #2: SHOULD IT BE LEGAL FOR DRIVERS TO TALK ON CELL PHONES WHILE DRIVING?

Audience: Your state political representatives

Claim: Cell phones should be illegal to use while driving.

Reason 1: because holding a cell phone in one hand diminishes drivers' capacity to control their cars physically

Grounds: Find statistics showing how many drivers have had trouble making turns or staying in their lanes when talking on a cell phone; statistics of number of accidents caused by cell phone users

Warrant: Anything that interferes with drivers' ability to handle their cars is bad.

Backing:____

____

Reason 2:

Grounds:____

____

Warrant:____

____

Backing:____

____

Conditions of Rebuttal for Reason 1: Cell phones have been shown to be valuable in road emergencies; many business people need cell phones to make contact with clients and need to save time by talking while they are driving; drivers use their hands to do a lot of other equally or more distracting things while driving, such as drinking coffee, reading, fiddling with CDs and tapes, shaving, putting on make-up; should all these activities be banned too?

Conditions of Rebuttal for Reason 2:____

____

Qualifier: Except with a headset or speaker-phone, cell phones should be illegal to use while driving.

Copyright © 2010, Pearson Education, Inc., Publishing as Longman

Exercise (continued)

ISSUE QUESTION #3: IS REGULAR HOMEWORK OF TWO OR MORE HOURS A NIGHT A GOOD EDUCATIONAL POLICY FOR ELEMENTARY SCHOOL CHILDREN?

Audience: Teachers and prospective teachers

Claim: Assigning regular homework of two or more hours a night is a bad educational policy for elementary school children.

Reason 1: because it jeopardizes children's sleep and health when they have to stay up too late regularly doing homework

Grounds: Most children need about ten hours of sleep a night;____________________________

____

____

Warrant: Any educational practice that jeopardizes children's sleep and health is bad.
Backing:____

____

Reason 2:____

____

Grounds:____

____

Warrant:____

____

Backing:____

____

Conditions of Rebuttal for Reasons 1 and 2:_______________________________________

____

Qualifier: Except in the case of occasional special projects, regular homework of two or more hours a night is not a good educational policy for elementary school children.

Copyright © 2010, Pearson Education, Inc., Publishing as Longman

CHAPTER 5: USING EVIDENCE EFFECTIVELY

For Class Discussion Exercises

(page 95)
Students will undoubtedly pick Fig. 5.1 for the blog post that's for crowd surfing, and Fig 5.2 would be perfect for a blog post coming out against crowd surfing. The pictures are a study in contrast. 5.1 exudes security and help and community while 5.2 is violent, chaotic, and menacing. In addition, 5.1 looks as the pit from afar with a serene and relaxed crowd, whereas 5.2 provide negative energy and an image of violent activity.

(pages 96-7)
Answers will vary. Students could write the two speeches in groups and then choose two members of the group to deliver the speeches to the class.
1. The speech supporting the proposed city ordinance to ban mosh pits should focus on building a case for how dangerous mosh pits are. It should include the data describing the various unpleasant incidents (woman who was groped), accidents, injuries, and deaths that occur. While it would be wise to acknowledge the alternative view, including the popularity of festival seating and mosh pits, this speech should convey the hazards and unpredictability of crowd surfing and the physical contact that occurs when a crowd of people are bumping against one another and moving to the music. The speech opposing the proposed city ordinance to ban mosh pits should emphasize how important festival seating, mosh pits, and crowd surfing are to a large number of concert goers. It should mention that many bands favor mosh pits and find this kind of audience response energizing. It should include the survey of students who go to rock concerts and who believe mosh pits should be allowed, as well as the passionate and enthusiastic quotations praising the experience and claiming that festival seating, crowd surfing, and mosh pits substantially contribute to the atmosphere of rock concerts. Although this speech should minimize the dangers, to show that proponents are informed, it should admit that accidents have occurred. It might propose greater emphasis on signs saying that concert-goers enter mosh pits at their own risk.
2. Answers will vary. Students might discuss how and where they chose to mention opposing views. How did the speakers convey that they were knowledgeable, informed, and fair, while shifting the attention to the position they were advocating?
3. Answers will vary. Before composing arguments representing their own views, students might want to do a little research on this subject on their own, by interviewing their own friends or dorm residents. They might want to investigate their own city's approach to this issue, as well as statistics about concert accidents. They also might want to draw on their own experiences or those of friends. After creating their own arguments, students might discuss their dominant claims and their reasoning behind their selection and framing of evidence.

(page 101)
This exercise alerts students to the various ways the same set of numbers can be employed and manipulated to support entirely different claims. Those opposed to the proposed ballpark would probably cite the last three statements, which seem to emphasize the considerable cost of the construction, while those in favor would probably cite the first three, which essentially minimize that cost. Connecting this exercise to the text's "Special Strategies from Framing Statistical

Copyright © 2010, Pearson Education, Inc., Publishing as Longman

Evidence" bullet points will also help students dig more deeply about how each data item is framed appropriately or inappropriately. Instructors should guide students to see the qualifiers within the statements that offer these statistics—"during a twenty year period," "per person per year," "about the price of a movie ticket," "building a new home," and "Seattle area."

Using Evidence: Anthology Arguments for Analysis

The following arguments in the anthology create powerful rhetorical effects by their use of evidence. These arguments use personal experience evidence, facts and examples, or numerical data to support their claims. These articles are recommended for group and class discussion:

- Bronwyn T. Williams, "'Tomorrow Will Not Be Like Today': Literacy and Identity in a World of Multiliteracies" (429-34)
- Dana L. Fleming, "Youthful Indiscretions: Should Colleges Protect Social Network Users from Themselves and Others?" (440--43)
- Henry Jenkins, "Reality Bytes: Eight Myths about Video Games Debunked" (450-54)
- William Lugo, "Violent Video Games Recruit American Youth" (460-65)
- William Powers, "The Massless Media" (467-72)
- Dan Kennedy, "Plugged In, Tuned Out: Young Americans Are Embracing New Media but Failing to Develop an Appetite for News" (473-79)
- Francisco X. Gaytan, Avary Carhill, and Carola Suarez-Orozco, "Understanding and Responding to the Need of Newcomer Immigrant Youth and Families" (486-93)
- Nature Neuroscience, "Separating Science from Stereotype" (510-11)
- Steven Pinker, "The Science of Sex Difference: Sex Ed" (514-17)
- Ben A. Barres, "Does Gender Matter?" (517-5)
- Phillip Carter and Paul Gastris, "The Case for the Draft" (530-40)
- Arindrajit Dub, T. William Lester, and Barry Eidlin, "A Downward Push: The Impact of Wal-Mart Stores on Retail Wages and Benefits" (558-65)
- Steve Maich, "Why Wal-Mart is Good" (568-74)
- Gwyneth Cravens, "Better Energy" (582-84)
- David Tilman and Jason Hill, "Fuel For Thought: All Biofuels Are Not Created Equal" (586-89)
- Jonathon Rauch, "Will Frankenfood Save the Planet?" (599-606)
- Miguel A. Altieri and Peter Rosset, "Ten Reasons Why Biotechnology Will Not Ensure Food Secruity, Protect the Environment, and Reduce Poverty in the Developing World" (608-15)
- Martin Luther King, Jr., "Letter from Birmingham Jail" (623-35
- Garret Hardin, "Lifeboat Ethics: The Case Against Aid that Does Harm" (635-42)

The following arguments in the anthology use evidence problematically in support of their claims. Students might explore whether this evidence meets the STAR criteria (Sufficiency, Typicality, Accuracy, Relevance) and how the writers' angle of vision dictates what evidence is excluded. In addition, students might discuss how audience and genre contribute to the writers' use of evidence.

Copyright © 2010, Pearson Education, Inc., Publishing as Longman

* Iowa State University New Service, "ISU Psychologists Publish Three New Studies on Violent Video Game Effects on Youths" (449--50)
* Fatemah Fakhraie, "Scarfing It Down" (498-99)
* Donald Rumsfeld, "New Model Army" (528-30)
* Lawrence J. Korb and Sean E. Duggan, "An All-Volunteer Army? Recruitment and Its Problems" (541-49)
* John Tierney, "Shopping for a Nobel" (574-75)
* Charles Krauthammer, "Save the Planet, Let Someone Else Drill" (584-85)

Copyright © 2010, Pearson Education, Inc., Publishing as Longman

Handout: ANALYZING THE USE OF EVIDENCE IN ARGUMENTS

Use the following questions to analyze how the use of evidence in an argument supports the claim and adds rhetorical power to the argument.

1. What kinds of evidence (personal experience narratives or data, examples, details, or statistical data) does the writer use to develop his/her claim? Give a few examples. If the writer uses evidence from personal experience, how does he/she give it authority and validity?

2. Considering the original audience, occasion, and purpose of this argument, how well do you think this evidence meets the STAR criteria (Sufficiency, Typicality, Accuracy, and Relevance)? How well does the evidence fit this rhetorical context?

3. What would you say is the writer's angle of vision guiding the selection and framing of evidence? What strategies has the writer used to frame his/her evidence in this argument? (Strategies include choosing what to emphasize and what to exclude; choosing kinds of evidence; presenting context and interpretation of evidence; treating contrary evidence; using labels, names, and images; and revealing the writer's value system.)

4. If the writer uses statistical data, how does he/she make it clear, comprehensible, and meaningful? How has this statistical data been framed for rhetorical effect?

5. What do you find rhetorically effective or ineffective about this evidence?

Copyright © 2010, Pearson Education, Inc., Publishing as Longman

CHAPTER 6: MOVING YOUR AUDIENCE: *ETHOS*, *PATHOS*, and *KAIROS*

For Class Discussion Exercises

(page 115)
This exercise is fruitful in that it provides student-writers with an opportunity to revise an argument in order to give more of a presence. Students should use this in-class exercise as an opportunity to showcase how they can appeal to credibility and appeal to the audience's emotions, values, and beliefs.

(page 116)
1. Answers will vary. But many students will probably comment on the buildings that are more like "shacks" than homes. They will also comment on the amount of refuse around the living environment and contrast that with how someone like the person has to get by washing clothes, eating, and keeping sanitary.
2. Answers will vary. But the image provides an "everyday" look at poverty—the garbage, the dire living conditions, the close quarters. The focus, instead of being on the human face of the human body, is on the surroundings—the environment in which people in poverty have to live.

(page 122)
1. Appeals to *Ethos*: Expression of wanting to protect innocent people, relation of other indicators other than race are taken into account, show of respect for Islam, expressed support of affirmative action. Appeals to *Pathos*: Acknowledgement that some racial profiling is "despicable," agreement with audience that racial profiling in other cases is not justified. Appeals to *Logos*: Point about increasing efficiency of searches, sub-argument that airline safety is more important than civil liberties, efficiency of screeners' time is important, causal claim that profiling would increase odds of finding terrorists, definitional claim that airline security than police practices.
Answers with vary in response to 2a, b, and c. But below are possible answers:
2a. Possible Problems: Audience's belief that video games cause violent behavior in children; argument that even though a rating system is available, it's difficult for companies to police children; argument that creation of video games is not free speech. Possible Solutions: Experts and studies that indicate that video games do not cause violent behavior; rating systems are all that companies can do, and parents should be held responsible for their children's activities; video games are free speech just like other software programs and expressions via the Internet are.
2b. Possible Problems: Belief that GPAs will drop and hurt graduates' chances at jobs versus graduates from other colleges; argument that students will get penalized in they enroll in honors courses or happen to be in sections that have many exceptional students, the idea that limiting the number of As and Bs given restricts the academic freedom of professors. Possible Solutions: This policy will become well known and enhance the quality of a degree from the college, thus giving graduates a better chance in applicant pools; fewer As and Bs given will create more competition and motivate students to become better students; precedents at other prestigious colleges where grade inflation has been addressed by similar measures; many professors give As and Bs in fear of getting poor evaluations at the end of the course—this mandate will get rid of this fear.

Copyright © 2010, Pearson Education, Inc., Publishing as Longman

2c. Possible Problems: Argument that cocaine is a destructive drug that destroys people's lives; belief that the state should legislate in order to keep a check on morality; assumption that drugs are bad. Possible Solutions: Argument that uses studies that show legalization of drugs in other countries has helped drop levels of addiction; appeal to the libertarian streak of conservatism by calling on the belief that citizens have the right to do whatever they want in their personal lives; examples of how legalizing drugs has created tremendous revenue from taxes and has helped fund various clinics to address reduced addiction.

Critiquing "Fancy a Breath of Fresh Air?" by Toyota

Answers will vary. But here a possible answers about the rhetorical appeals.

Logos: Logical appeals reside mostly in the copy of the Prius ad. Toyota references the high m.p.g. of the Prius (61.4) and alludes to a causal claim that buying the Prius will provide "optimum performance and efficiency at all times." The ad then follows up the appeal to values of efficiency and performance by extending a hypothetical claim of "If everyone drove a Prius, we all be able to breathe little easier." The advertiser links the negative effects of car usage with the fact that cars with high m.p.g. produce fewer emissions than traditional gas-only vehicles.

Ethos: The copy at the top right corner alludes to Toyota's stature as a car company. Toyota is one of the carmakers "in front" because it is one of the sales leaders of cars worldwide. And "in front" also alludes to its reputation as a company that has been innovative in creating cars that are environmentally friendly, from subcompacts decades ago to gas-electric hybrids now. The copy at the bottom of the ad reinforces the character of Toyota by stating that the Prius is "the first mass production car to combine a petrol engine and an electric motor." The Prius and image symbolize a shift in car-making where environmental consciousness is a significant factor for building and buying vehicles.

Pathos: The image of the young woman evokes a negative image of environmental problems but uses that image to build its ethos because of the green background and the leaf as a mask. When air is polluted, people sometimes use masks to breathe much easier, and Toyota has artfully presented that image in a manner that makes Toyota look as though they are doing something for the environment. The Prius produces less air pollution, and the evocative leaf mask presents a car as being "green." Instead of using a car that has a traditional engine, Toyota attempts to persuade people to invest in a cleaner vehicle as the young woman stares directly at the viewer with the question, "Fancy a breath of fresh air?" The connotation is that the Prius is not only an environmentally friendly vehicle, but also it represents a new direction in manufacturing cars.

Kairos: Capitalizing on the consumers' desire for car options that reduce health problems and addresses other environmental concerns, namely global warming, Toyota has crafted an ad that presents the Prius as the best option for people to still use a car in a sustainable manner.

Moving an Audience via *Ethos* and *Pathos* While Considering *Kairos*: Anthology Arguments for Analysis

A number of the arguments in the anthology achieve their power through the writer's emphasis on *ethos* and *pathos*. A useful class exercise is to have students examine how a writer's creation of a knowledgeable, trustworthy *ethos* contributes to an argument's persuasiveness and how appeals to *pathos* influence the argument's power. The handout, "Examining *Ethos* and *Pathos*" can be used to guide students' analysis of arguments. The following articles in the anthology

Copyright © 2010, Pearson Education, Inc., Publishing as Longman

rely heavily on the *ethos* of the writer and *pathos*, the emotional and imaginative involvement of the reader:

* Jeff Chu, "You Wanna Take This Online?" (434-36)
* John Seigenthaler, Sr., "A False Wikipedia 'Biography'" (436-37)
* Sydney H. Schanberg, "Not a Pretty Picture" (482-84)
* Francisco X. Gaytan, Avary Carhill, and Carola Suarez-Orozco, "Understanding and Responding to the Need of Newcomer Immigrant Youth and Families" (486-93)
* Matali Perkins, "A Note to Young Immigrants" (493-94)
* Fatemah Fakhraie, "Scarfing It Down" (498-99)
* Jay Nordlinger, "Bassackwards: Construction Spanish and Other Signs of the Times" (500-03)
* Steven Pinker, "The Science of Sex Difference: Sex Ed" (514-17)
* Ben A. Barres, "Does Gender Matter?" (517-25)
* Philip Carter and Paul Gastris, "The Case for the Draft" (530-40)
* Louis Caldera, "Military Service" (550-52)
* (Army)Wife, "Stop-Loss" (552-54)
* Steve Maich, "Why Wal-Mart is Good" (568-74)
* Nicholas Kristof, "Our Gas Guzzlers, Their Lives" (579-80)
* Al Gore, "Nobel Lecture" (592-97)
* "Monsantoland" (615)
* Sustainusa.org, "What Is the FDA Trying to Feed Us?" (618)
* Gerald D. Coleman, "Is Genetic Engineering the Answer to Hunger?" (619-21)
* Martin Luther King, Jr., "Letter from Birmingham Jail" (623-35)
* Rachel Carson, "The Obligation to Endure" (644-48)

The following articles have problematic appeals to *ethos* and *pathos*:

* Alice Mathias, "The Facebook Generation" (438-39)
* "A Message from the Creators" (445-46)
* William Lugo, "Violent Video Games Recruit American Youth" (460-65)
* Daryl Cagle, "Those Terrible Virginia Tech Cartoons" (480-82)
* Linda Chavez, "Harvard Prez's Admission: Men and Women are Different" (507-08)
* Brian McFadden, "Amazing Facts About the Fairer, Yet Equal Sex" (509)
* Dan Piraro, "Bizarro, Greeter Gone Wild" (566)
* Steve Maich, "Why Wal-Mart is Good" (568-74)
* John Tierney, "Shopping for a Nobel" (574-75)
* Charles Krauthammer, "Save the Planet, Let Someone Else Drill" (584-85)
* Iain Murray, "Time to Recycle Recycling?" (591-92)
* Froma Harrop, "Food Industry Should Modify Its Stance on Altered Food" (617-18)
* Garret Hardin, "Lifeboat Ethics: The Case Against Aid that Does Harm" (635-42)

The following articles strongly exemplify arguments presented at a specific historical opportunity, arguments that consider the timeliness of a certain rhetorical situation (*kairos)*:

* The Whole "Women and Science" Section
* Selective Service System, "How the Draft Has Changed" (541)

Copyright © 2010, Pearson Education, Inc., Publishing as Longman

* (Army)Wife, “Stop-Loss” (552-54)
* John Tierney, “Shopping for a Nobel” (574-75)
* Nicholas Kristof, “Our Gas Guzzlers, Their Lives” (579-80)
* Andrew C. Revkin, “Carbon-Neutral Is Hip, but Is It Green?” (580-82)
* Gwyneth Cravens, “Better Energy” (582-84)
* Charles Krauthammer, “Save the Planet, Let Someone Else Drill” (584-85)
* David Tillman and Jason Hill, “Fuel for Thought: All Biofuels Are Not Created Equal” (586-89)
* Al Gore, “Nobel Lecture” (592-97)
* Gerald D. Coleman, “Is Genetic Engineering the Answer to Hunger?” (619-21)
* Martin Luther King, Jr., “Letter from Birmingham Jail” (623-35)

Student Responses to Assignments. For a class discussion exercise giving students practice thinking about how writers use introductions to establish a positive *ethos* and give their arguments presence through appeals to *pathos*, see “Discussion Exercise Examining Students’ Introductions for Appeals to *Ethos* and *Pathos* in “VII. Samples of Student Writing for Discussion.” This exercise uses introductions by three student writers for analysis.

Copyright © 2010, Pearson Education, Inc., Publishing as Longman

Handout: EXAMINING APPEALS TO ETHOS AND PATHOS

Use the following questions to guide your analysis of the writer's appeals to ethos and pathos.

1. What image does the writer project of himself or herself in this argument? What is the writer's investment in the issue?

2. How does the writer convey that he or she is knowledgeable about the issue?

3. Where does the writer acknowledge alternative views? What makes you think the writer is fair in his/her summary or recognition of these views?

4. Which of the strategies for engaging the audience's emotions and imagination does the writer use: concrete language, specific examples, narratives, and connotative and metaphoric language?

5. How are the writer's appeals to ethos and pathos tailored to the argument's original audience and site of publication?

6. For you, the reader, how important are the ethos of the writer and the emotional and imaginative appeals in winning your consideration of this argument?

Copyright © 2010, Pearson Education, Inc., Publishing as Longman

Handout: ANALYZING YOUR AUDIENCE

Use the following questions to explore what you know about your intended audience for your argument.

1. Who is your audience?

2. How much does your audience know or care about your issue?

3. What is your audience's current attitude toward your issue?

4. What will be your audience's likely objections to your argument?

5. What values, beliefs, or assumptions about the world do you and your audience share?

6. What argumentative strategies are you considering to reach this audience?

Copyright © 2010, Pearson Education, Inc., Publishing as Longman

CHAPTER 7: RESPONDING TO OBJECTIONS AND ALTERNATE VIEWS

For Class Discussion Exercises

(page 129)
Answers will vary. It is useful here to have the students read their summaries aloud (or prepare them in working groups on transparencies for sharing on an overhead projector), and then identify the features that make each version either loaded or fair.

(page 134)
1a. Opposing reason #1: First Place School is too expensive; it costs taxpayers more dollars per child than a mainstream school (paragraph 1). Opposing reason #2: First Place School should spend all of its funding on educational needs rather than on providing social services for students and their families (paragraph 2). Opposing reason #3: Critics say that First Place School doesn't help students in the long run because they are only there a short time (paragraph 3). Opposing reason #4: Critics say that removing students from regular classrooms highlights these children's differences from mainstream children.
1b. Refutation for opposing reason #1: First Place School actually saves taxpayers' dollars by working to reduce the need for expenditure on crime, welfare, and drug rehabilitation programs (refutes the grounds). Refutation for opposing reason #2: Spending money to help families in crisis does help the education of children by improving the families' chances to get out of poverty and by helping to prevent abuse of children. In showing that this money is well-spent, Marybeth supports the reason with evidence that these social services are needed and also supports her own warrant that the well-being of families is connected to the education of the children, that the social health of the family contributes to the child's ability to become educated; thus, schools should think of education in these broader terms (refutes reason and warrant, a limited view of education). Refutation for opposing reason #3: Even a short stay at First Place School builds children's self-esteem and often helps them to move up several grade levels in their skills. It also provides a safe extended day care environment: all these results have long-term consequences (refutes the reason with counter-examples). Refutation of opposing reason #4: Removing children from regular classrooms helps rather than alienates children because being with other children like them provides a nurturing environment so they learn better (refutes the reason).
1c. Answers will vary. Refutations #1 and #2 make monetary appeals to city residents, explaining the financial gain of supporting First Place School. City residents most interested in how much children are learning and how they gain emotionally from First Place School would favor refutation reasons #3 and #4. Students might note how Marybeth successfully argues many points related to her issue.

2a. Answers will vary, but these examples should provide some ways in which such claims can be refuted.
Stated Reason: because reducing greenhouse emissions would seriously harm the American economy. Methods of Rebuttal: Calling into question how "seriously" the Kyoto pledge would damage the economy if at all, the warrant; Offering studies/data from other countries that have adopted Kyoto parameters that shows that reducing emissions actually created more efficiency and greater productivity; Questioning the warrant that the economy is the most important

Copyright © 2010, Pearson Education, Inc., Publishing as Longman

criterion to consider in this debate (what about environmental effects, human health issues, long-term flooding, higher insurance rates because of global warming, etc.?); Showing examples of cities in the US that have pledged to uphold the treaty and their economies weren't damaged whatsoever; Questioning the evidence provided/causal argument that Kyoto will hurt economies. Et al.

2b. Stated Reason: because engineers make more money than musicians. Methods of Rebuttal: Questioning the warrant that future income is the most important determining factor in selecting a major; Providing examples of students who graduated with engineering degrees and then changed careers because the profession didn't utilize their creativity; Offering examples of professional musicians/composers and music professors and providing average salaries of a wide-ranging sample; Providing a research study that indicates some engineers are losing well-paying jobs to outsourcing to Asia. Et al.

2c. Stated Reason: because doing so is the only way to maintain a large enough military to preserve freedom in trouble spots in the world. Methods of Rebuttal: Questioning whether a large military force is able to "defend American interests" in the long term; Questioning whether the military is even preserving freedom in these various trouble spots; Questioning the assumption that the American military should be used as the "world's police officer" and whether that's financially feasible; Providing persuasive data that a leaner military force with less personnel and more technical "know how" is able to respond to worldwide threats with agility; Offering a reasoned sequence of ideas that shows, in contrast, that the US should help strengthen the efficacy of UN Peace Keeping forces around the globe. Et al.

2d. Stated Reason: because nuclear reactors will provide substantial electrical energy without emitting greenhouse gases. Methods of Rebuttal: Questioning whether greenhouse gas emissions are a suitable important criterion for US energy policy; Offering examples and studies about the insecurity of nuclear power facilities, thereby relating how more nuclear reactors equals more sites for terrorism; Providing historical examples of how nuclear power plants are unsafe—Chernobyl, Three Mile Island, etc.; Offering insider reports or various experts' opinions on how radioactive waste is extremely hazardous to human and environmental health; Showing vivid examples of how nuclear waste sites have been linked to cancer. Et al.

2e. Stated Reason: because owning handguns helps them protect their homes against potentially violent intruders. Conditions of Rebuttal: Questioning the effectiveness of handguns as a way to protect one's home; Questioning whether a homeowner would be able to use a handgun in time to protect one's home; Offering statistics showing that handguns are one of the leading causes of accidental deaths in the US; Describing a plausible or real scenario where children or young adults have accidentally killed themselves by playing with a parent's handgun; Showing data connecting handgun ownership with spousal abuse and murder; Questioning data presented by a NRA study that shows handguns make America "safer"; Questioning whether Americans have a true right to own a handgun because of the historical context of the 2nd amendment ("for a well regulated militia"). Et al.

A Sample Critique of "'Half-Criminals' or Urban Athletes? A Plea for Fair Treatment of Skateboarders" by David Langley

This student essay is a good example of how students can develop a strong argument using their personal interests and knowledge. The questions and answers that follow suggest ways that instructors could initiate discussion of this essay.

Copyright © 2010, Pearson Education, Inc., Publishing as Longman

1. *What are student writer David Langley's main claims and supporting reasons?*

Claim: Cities need to change their unfair treatment of skateboarders

Reasons: (1) because skateboarders are urban athletes, not antisocial misfits as popularly conceived; (2) because the laws regulating skateboarding are ambiguous; (3) because skateboarders are not given enough legitimate space to practice their sport.

2. *What are the warrants in this argument?*

(1) Urban athletes merit fair treatment by cities
(2) Ambiguous laws are bad and should be changed
(3) Cities should provide public space for urban sports

3. *What evidence does Langley use to support his reasons?*

Reason #1 (paragraph 6): Skateboarders are not delinquents or misfits but urban athletes and users of a reasonable means of transportation in cities.

Chain of reasons and personal experience examples: Sports develop in response to an environment; just as snowshoes and skis developed to move over snow and surfboards and boats were invented to move over water, so skateboards were invented to move over the flat panels of cement and cement stairs and curbs; because skateboarders are responding naturally, gracefully, cleanly to their city environment (without pollution), they should be respected.

Reason #2 (paragraph 7): The laws regulating skateboarding are unfair; they are too restrictive and are ambiguous.

Examples: Langley's experience with his friends of being stopped, frisked, ticketed by a police officer at UCSD for skateboarding when the sign permitted it on holidays; mention of unposted areas in the state of Washington; mention of the confusion over what is safe and what is reckless; conversation with a police officer at Seattle East Precinct; police officer's acknowledgment that officers sometimes interpret the laws harshly.

4. *How does Langley handle alternative views?*

He brings them in before his third reason and uses his third reason as a rebuttal point. He then adds a second paragraph including alternative views and responds to those with his own examples.

Alternative View #1 (paragraph 8): Cities have tried to create skateboard parks to accommodate skateboarders; rebuttal points: (1) skateboard parks are poorly designed so they are dangerous to skateboarders; (2) skateboard parks tend to be too crowded so they are dangerous; (3) in one skateboard park in Redmond, Washington, skateboarders are thrown in with graffiti artists who create noxious fumes

Alternative View #2 (paragraph 9): Some people don't think that skateboarders deserve to be treated fairly. Alternative View #3 (paragraph 9): Skateboarders destroy public and private property by leaving marks and chips on the cement and granite; Langley concedes that skateboarding does do some damage to concrete sidewalks, curbs, benches, stairs; rebuttal points: (1) skateboarders help the environment by not littering (2) skateboarders don't pollute the air.

Copyright © 2010, Pearson Education, Inc., Publishing as Longman

5. *What argument moves does Langley make in his conclusion?*

He uses a proposal conclusion to sketch the changes he thinks would correct the unfair treatment of skateboarders. He includes better and clearer rules and laws and more convenient, safer skateboard parks, designed by knowledgeable people. He ends by affirming the positive and natural characteristics of skateboarding.

6. *It is particularly effective about Langley's use of evidence from his personal experience? What pieces of evidence persuade you the most?*

Langley's classical argument grew out of a class discussion about the negative image of some sports and the tendency for older adults to misjudge newer sports such as skateboarding and snowboarding and to misjudge those who do these sports. Students might mention Langley's narrative introduction that sets up the problem and gives his most memorable, specific example. Langley's numerous other examples throughout the essay give his argument credibility and show his awareness of hostile views. His calm, rational tone and his persistent effort to change the negative image of skateboarders and the unfair treatment they experience make his readers seriously consider his perspective.

7. *How would a neutral or resistant reader respond to this argument?*

Although Langley's argument has obvious strengths, some may question some of his assumptions and support. Here are few that might be instructive to point out to students. Here are some possible questions a more skeptical reader might pose to the author: How are skateboards exactly "natural"? Are they really a viable means of transportation? Is skateboarding, by definition, a true sport? Do his personal experiences seem typical? How exactly do skateboarders "help the environment" since many probably skateboard for recreation and not true transportation? In the greater scheme of where tax dollars go, how high of a priority are skate parks?

Addressing Resistant Audiences: Anthology Arguments for Analysis

Many real-world arguments seek mainly to reinforce or deepen positions already held by their audiences. However, some arguments take on the tougher task of trying to win the hearing of readers hostile to their perspective. These arguments are particularly interesting for the way they summarize alternative views, refute and concede points, and enlist abundant evidence in favor of their claims. Many arguments in the anthology merit close analysis of their strategies for treating alternative views and for seeking to win the consideration of resistant audiences. Students can be asked (1) to identify the argumentative strategies; (2) to explain why they think these strategies would or would not work for the intended audience; and (3) to explain what they found arresting, thought provoking, and persuasive. The following anthology articles are examples of appeals to resistant audiences:

- Dana L. Fleming, "Youthful Indiscretions: Should Colleges Protect Social Network Users from Themselves and Others?" (440-43)
- Henry Jenkins, "Reality Bytes: Eight Myths about Video Games Debunked" (450-54)
- Malcolm Gladwell, "Brain Candy" (454-57)
- Dan Kennedy, "Plugged In, Tuned Out: Young Americans Are Embracing New Media but Failing to Develop an Appetite for News" (473-79)

Copyright © 2010, Pearson Education, Inc., Publishing as Longman

- Scarf Ace, "Miss or Diss?" (496-98)
- Deborah Blum, "Solving for X" (512-13)
- Steven Pinker, "The Science of Sex Difference: Sex Ed" (514-17)
- Ben A. Barres, "Does Gender Matter?" (517-25)
- Phillip Carter and Paul Gastris, "The Case for the Draft" (530-40)
- (Army)Wife, "Stop-Loss" (552-54)
- Robert B. Reich, "Don't Blame Wal-Mart" (566-68)
- Gwyneth Cravens, "Better Energy" (582-84)
- Al Gore, "Nobel Lecture" (592-97)
- Jonathan Rauch, "Will Frankenfoods Save the Planet?" (599-606)
- Miguel A. Altieri and Petter Rosset, "Ten Reasons Why Biotechnology Will Not Ensure Food Security, Protect the Environment, and Reduce Poverty in the Developing World" (608-15)
- Gerald D. Coleman, "Is Genetic Engineering the Answer to Hunger?" (619-21)
- Martin Luther King, Jr., "Letter from Birmingham Jail" (623-35)

The following articles are problematic in their treatment of alternative views—in the assumptions they make about them, in way they summarize them, or in the way they respond to them:

- John Seigenthaler, Sr., "A False Wikipedia 'Biography'" (436-37)
- William Lugo, "Violent Video Games Recruit American Youth" (460-65)
- Maileen Hamto, "My Turn: Being American" (494-95)
- Linda Chavez, "Harvard Prez's Admission: Men and Women are Different" (507-08)
- Brian McFadden, "Amazing Facts About the Fairer, Yet Equal Sex" (509)
- Steve Maich, "Why Wal-Mart is Good" (568-74)
- John Tierney, "Shopping for a Nobel" (574-75)
- Iain Murray, "Time to Recycle Recycling?" (591-92)
- Garret Hardin, "Lifeboat Ethics: The Case Against Aid that Does Harm" (635-42)
- Rachel Carson, "The Obligation to Endure" (644-48)

Student Responses to Assignments. For an exercise giving students practice analyzing how writers acknowledge and respond to opposing views, see "Discussion Exercise on Accommodating Opposing Views" in "VII. Samples of Student Writing for Discussion." This exercise asks students to analyze the alternative views and rebuttal section of student writer Patty Gillispie's researched proposal argument in favor of parents taking an active role in teaching their children responsible attitudes toward alcohol.

Copyright © 2010, Pearson Education, Inc., Publishing as Longman

CHAPTER 8: ANALYZING ARGUMENTS RHETORICALLY

For Class Discussion Exercises

(pages 147-48)
1. Rev. Ball's overall strategy is to use his writing style—emotional discourse that gives the problem "presence"—as a method for persuasion. He connects scriptural exegesis to the rhetorical concept of *kairos*. His use of repetition is similar to a homily from the pulpit, and diction, such "now is the time," "No more," and "deliverance," provides an emotional coloring to his discourse. The Sierra Club, on the other hand, attempts to persuade purely by *logos* by showing how the problem of global warming can be addressed and in turn help create a green economy and energy infrastructure while helping consumers and businesses adapt to a changing energy future. The blurb from the website relies on causal claims.
2. Rev. Ball's adapts his message to an audience that relies on belief and conviction more so than Sierra Club members who might value *logos* more than *pathos*.
3. Answers will vary. But some students might point out that Rev. Ball may need to provide examples and scientific proof even to a religious audience. And some might also say that the Sierra Club needs to provide more specifics on its proposal.
4. Answers will vary. However, one could argue that if both passages were meshed together—a collaborative writing by both Rev. Ball and the Sierra Club—the document would be quite persuasive.

(page 154)
1. Lopez makes logical appeals through the use of examples and statements from doctors, college students, and other data. Specifically, the detail of the donor process is used to provide the details of how intensive the process is (paragraph 3), and Lopez also makes causal claims about the possible effects of egg donation (4). Lopez uses examples of how much eggs cost (5-6) and then provides an example of college "girl" who donated eggs (7). The author also shows the statistical increase of IVF programs (8). Lopez uses a number of experts in the field that show the positive view of the procedure along with ending with more negative views of egg donation later in the argument. The last two examples provide non-typical ones to sway the audience in how those who choose IVF procedures are not fit to be parents.
2. The essay has a number of appeals to *pathos* that connect to a mostly conservative readership. The initial description and example of the clinic provides a foreboding mood to the argument and is reminiscent to descriptions that people use about abortion clinics. Lopez also uses the data of 15% to shock readers in that so many people use help in getting pregnant, although it's not clear what percent of 15% is actually IVF. There are word choices that resonate with a conservative readership too: "macabre version of adoption," "eugenics issue," "the frontierswomen of feminism," "reproductive prostitution," "intrusion of children in their lives," and "mother is being reduced to a good leisure-time activity." This diction paints those who use IVF to get pregnant as somehow tainted or just "feminists" who put careers over motherhood.
3. Lopez is slanted against egg donation although word choice and presentation of support later in the essay tends to be more overtly anti-egg donation in the latter part of the argument. The writer invites the reader into this phenomenon (sounding mostly objective) and the disregard for egg donation intensifies as the argument progresses. Even when she quotes people who favor egg donation, those statements are slanted toward her view too in that they depict egg donation as

Copyright © 2010, Pearson Education, Inc., Publishing as Longman

making money and selective reproduction. Examples of couples using IVF to simply have children is not presented in a respectful manner. The non-typical examples of infertile couples at the end of the essay show Lopez's bias.
4. Answers will vary according to the questions selected.
5. Answers will vary according the frame of vision of each student.

(page @160-61)
1. Goodman's main claim could be summarized as this: The use of surrogate mothers from abroad is unethical because the market-based approach to reproduction relies on mostly poor people as surrogates, and the practice comes close to enslaving oneself and selling a natural part of one's body. Human reproduction should not be seen a commodity to be sold.
2. The emotional appeal that would strike many Americans is the idea of outsourcing, a word that has extremely negative connotations in our country. Goodman's relation about how poor women are being used by rich couples is another. And the resemblance claims to slavery and selling children appeal to values of the traditional procreation. These appeals function to set the mood of the reader to be repulsed by reproductive outsourcing.
3. Answers will vary according to the questions selected.
4. Answers will vary according the frame of vision of each student.

Copyright © 2010, Pearson Education, Inc., Publishing as Longman

CHAPTER 9: ANALYZING VISUAL ARGUMENTS

For Class Discussion Exercises

(pages 169-71)
1. *Core argument of "What We Know About Ecstasy" ad*: In making policies and laws to control drugs (in this case, Ecstasy), we need to focus on being knowledgeable and rational because the dangers may not be as great as they are trumped up to be; because the real dangers are different from what people think, for example, adulterating the drug; because dangers and problems come from criminalizing drugs and where they are used (raves, in this case), thus driving the drug and users underground, away from responsible controls. This ad voices a middle-of-the-road position, not condoning the use of Ecstasy, but not completely condemning it either. It seeks to give voters and users and potential users maximum information in order to make wise choices. In general, Common Sense for Drug Policy believes that criminalizing drugs has bad effects. While both this ad and the ad in 9.2 recognize the dangers of Ecstasy, this ad leans toward minimizing the dangers—claiming that they can be counteracted or have been exaggerated—while the ad in 9.2 dwells entirely on the unpredictability and the dangers of Ecstasy. The Common Sense for Drug Policy ad gives historical information on the drug, supplies its medical name, MDMA, and draws evidence from documented sources. In contrast, the Drug Enforcement Administration ad focuses on a simple cautionary message: Ecstasy is more harmful than you think.

2. The ad in 9.2 is eye-catching, visually intriguing, and memorable in its use of type and design. The ad in 9.3 uses type styles and layout to present a substantial amount of text and lots of information on one page. It uses a main heading and three subheads in bold sans serif type to set up main points. A statement, also in bold sans serif type, three-quarters of the way down the page comes closest to stating the claim of the ad. The body text that presents the bulk of the information in the ad, which is actually the reasons and evidence, is in serif type for easy reading. The contact information, in small but readable type, is centered. The documentation of sources appears in the smallest type at the bottom of the page–there to contribute to the authoritative *ethos*, but not be obtrusive. The whole effect of the type and layout is to make this ad functional, professional, matter-of-fact, and highly informative. In contrast, the type and the layout of the ad in 9.2 are playful, creative, more emotional, and more disturbing. Clearly, each ad has used type and layout very purposefully to create a dominant effect.

3. The type, layout, and spacing choices in 9.3 are serious and businesslike to give a dry and rational impression, intended to counteract the "hysteria" that the ad says dominates discussions of policies and laws about drugs. In effect, the ad is saying, "Let us tell you the facts, and let's all use common sense." The more intellectual and knowledgeable this ad can appear, the more it will drive home its message. In fact, in the guise of being mostly informative, it actually presents a fairly strong argument: the dangers of Ecstasy have been over-emphasized. Real problems have to do with adulteration of the drug, criminalizing the drug, and irresponsible use.

4. The decorative type and artistic layout in 9.2 are designed to catch the attention of casual readers reading for pleasure and light information. This ad visually appeals to both young people and adults. It lures readers in and carries them along, leaving them thinking about one main point: that Ecstasy is actually more harmful than people may have heard. Assuming that readers are skimming for pleasure, it offers little evidence for its claims but plants and suggests a course of action. In contrast, the ad in 9.3 catches readers' attention with the word "Ecstasy" because

Copyright © 2010, Pearson Education, Inc., Publishing as Longman

that drug is currently much discussed; however, the more intellectual appeal of this ad counts on a readership already committed to exploring serious social and political issues. Aimed at a more intellectual audience, who most likely have seen ads by this group before and know the group's basic opposition to criminalizing drugs, this ad gives evidence to influence neutral or assenting audiences. Ultimately, it seeks to influence voters by giving them a new way to think about Ecstasy.

(pages 179-83)
1. Fig 9.7 President Reagan: a) The most noticeable features are Reagan atop his horse and President's gaze looking forward with optimism coupled with smile. The implicit argument is that this person will lead the country in the right direction. He's a visionary who is ready to lead America. b) Reagan is centered, and the angle of the photographer is below the figures in order to make them look larger. The backdrop creates a bucolic setting of a ranch, which further the Westerner or "cowboy" image. c) The dominant image is that this main is someone who takes charge of things—he's a modern day Westerner who's vibrant and optimistic. The image attempts to create a positive persona of Reagan as someone who is a leader and a good guy (on a white horse, of course).
Fig. 9.8 Senator Kerry: a) The most noticeable feature is the wind surfboard and Kerry leaning back to ride the wind. The dominant impression is that he's relaxed and fun-loving, but to others the dominant impression was that Kerry is a well-to-do person since most people don't wind surf. b) Kerry and the wind surfboard are the main focus, which blocks viewers from perhaps seeing other people wind surfing. Kerry is alone because of the way the photo is framed. c) The image attempts to make Kerry look athletic and vibrant. d) (1) The intended effect of the picture was to present Kerry as out of touch and rich. (2) The image backfired because it created a powerful symbol that cohered with the argument Kerry was a "flip-flopper." The visual image presents Kerry as someone who simply moves with the wind, buffeted by public opinion—not good reasons.
Fig. 9.9 President Clinton: a) Clinton's smile along with him bending down on his knees to talk to child are the main features of the photo. The implicit argument could be that Clinton cares about the future and he wants to connect to every American. He looks toward the future and is a likeable fellow who loves children. b) The close-up focuses the viewer just on the young child and Clinton's open expression of joy and understanding. c) This photo attempts to portray Clinton as a leader who is able to speak to anyone, regardless of age, and someone who looks toward the future.
Fig. 9.10 Barack Obama: a) The dominant image is the flag and the connection of Obama to the flag and the United States. b) The photo, shot from below Obama, shows him only above the chest as he's talking. The shot frames Obama as being connected to the flag and patriotism and the ideals of the United States. c) The image makes two main implicit claims. First, the connection of the flag and Obama is important because the candidate at that time was trying to show himself as someone who exemplifies America. Obama is a product of a racially mixed marriage who had the fortitude and strength to improve himself through education. In some ways, he represents Emersonian "self-reliance," a very American concept. The framing of the flag and Obama also assures voters that he is one of "them," someone who cares about America and wants to see it succeed. Second, Obama's gesture is significant because he's pointing. The gesture symbolizes a leader who provides direction for a country, that some people feel, is in dire straits.

Copyright © 2010, Pearson Education, Inc., Publishing as Longman

3a. The movie poster plays with images of films from the 50s and 60s, so that huge monster colors one's view about the company. Ordinary Americans are running from the monster while cars, people, and money are held in the monster's hands. The smiley face has a menacing look while donning a corporate looking suit.
3b. Wal-Mart is a company that is presented as an entity good for families; however, the company actually destroys middle class America. This is a resemblance argument in that the creator equates Wal-Mart with a destructive smiley-faced monster who only says it helps people get lower prices.
3c. The intertextual images are crucial. The Wal-Mart logo is colored by money, symbolizing greed and all that the company cares about. And the large figure presents a smiley face with intense eyebrows with a monstrous body and multiple arms. Playing on the horror films with plots that involve gigantic people or animals or insects along with the imagery of Godzilla films, the giant smiley-faced corporate man is presented as a destructive force that wreaks havoc in middle class America. Wal-Mart in this presentation represents what's wrong with the economy of America. The smiley face is distinctly different by the eyebrows—they're intense, and the monster is focused on destroying the middle class through the hokum of "Everyday Low Prices."

4a. The screen captures convey a sense of direct combat that a soldier would experience, but the player is also detached from the scenes. In Figure 9.12, the player is to the side and watching the combat take place; the soldiers are shooting beyond the player's perspective. In Figure 9.13, the player is closer to a soldier, but to the side and once again not directly involved in the action. These screen captures make it seem like the player is almost like an embedded journalist. In both these images though, the player does not clearly see against whom the soldiers are firing; the enemy is hidden and non-descript.
4b. The compositional qualities of the screen captures the attempt to portray a realistic setting for a player—the drab, earth tone cityscape in 9.12, the village's dwellings in 9.13, the skeletal cover used in 9.12, the vivid firing of the rifles in both. Figure 9.13 does have some romantic quality to it, indicated by the sky's vivid reddish-purple tinge. That coloring complements the up-close depiction of the soldier and accentuates the firing of the rifle.
4c. In 9.12 the soldiers seem as though they're on a regular patrol of some sort, a typical "day in the life" of soldiers in the larger cities of Iraq. The four soldiers provide a sense of teamwork and unified purpose—all are concerted in their actions. Both screen shots reinforce the idea that soldiers must be vigilant and wary while de-emphasizing the psychological and physical tolls soldiers might incur.
4d. The game has probably created a heated discussion because in previous military conflicts Americans haven't had video games overtly created and used for recruitment purposes in this manner. Video games have been used for training purposes for years, but to have the military produce its own game for recruiting is unparalleled in our history. To some, the idea of having young adults kill fictional characters in a video game about an ongoing war is reproachable and insensitive to military personnel, their families, and Iraqis. Critics would say that such a game desensitizes young adults from the reality of war—killing is just a thrill that has little psychological costs—and manipulates a receptive audience for tacitly supporting the Iraq War. By analogy, some Vietnam veterans have criticized the gaming industry on similar grounds for games that depict the Vietnam experience. From their perspectives, the idea of people playing out horrific wartime experiences doesn't do justice to what that war was really like and its social milieu. From that perspective, if you were in Vietnam, you surely don't want to relive it or be

Copyright © 2010, Pearson Education, Inc., Publishing as Longman

reminded about your time there. Answers will vary on the how effective the game is. In light of dropping enlistments for military service, some students may relate that the games could be "fun," but the idea of actually putting themselves in danger is not an option.

(pages 186-7)

1. Answers will vary. The readers' eyes are drawn immediately to the images of the lizards, Goldilocks, and the table in the top two-thirds of the ad. The bright yellows, greens, purples, and browns in this ad are visually stimulating and memorable. The bold black type that comments on the image is the next part of the ad that readers notice: "IT'S JUST NOT THE SAME WITHOUT BEARS." Readers also notice the smaller bold black type at the bottom of the ad that expresses the main claim of the ad: "HELP KEEP BEARS IN THE PICTURE" and the logo of the advocacy organization, Earthjustice. Next, readers notice the white type displayed on the table that represents a passage from the revised fairytale. Finally, readers intrigued by the image and the novelty of the concept behind the ad, turn to the smaller paragraphs of type that present the argument in greater detail, supplying reasons and some evidence. This ad does a good job of creating hierarchies of information and of indicating relationships among parts of the ad with the size, color, and style of the type. While the image and the use of color create strong appeals to *pathos*, the professional, balanced layout of this ad and the clear contact information construct a positive *ethos*.
2. *Core of the argument*: We should protect grizzly bears more because their numbers have been drastically reduced in the lower forty-eight states; because they are part of an interdependent wilderness ecosystem; because they are an important part of our history and culture; and because special interests are working to remove Yellowstone grizzlies from the endangered species list so that these interests can increase their own economic opportunities and profits, which are destructive of wild lands near Yellowstone.
3. Earthjustice captures readers' interest with a familiar children's story. Most people, even as adults, love stories, and picture books conjure up powerful childhood memories. The low-angle perspective of the frightening, intimidating lizards also resembles the exciting scariness of many children's stories. Some of our students commented that this image has an apocalyptic feel: giant reptiles have taken over a world that has gotten out of control. Lizards are slimy, scaly, and more frightening to most people than bears; in this picture, the lizards conjure up monsters and creatures like Godzilla, especially the Mama Lizard, whose forked tongue is snaking out toward the startled Goldilocks. Grizzly bears are majestic, magnificent, awesome, but they are not cuddly or friendly to humans; in fact, they can be very dangerous. Earthjustice chooses to avoid the idea of grizzlies as dangerous predators, instead suggesting that bears are an important part of our culture and history. This advocacy ad works associatively, emotionally, imaginatively; most people would probably say that the bears usually depicted in versions of Goldilocks are brown or black bears, not grizzlies. Still, this ad effectively grabs readers' attention, draws them in, and asks them to ponder for themselves the question, What will we lose if grizzly bears are extinct in all but the remotest parts of the United States (parts of Alaska)? It also asks readers to weigh profit-driven economic interests against societal and environmental interests.
4. Answers will vary. This question asks students to consider the problem of enlisting readers' support for protecting a creature that is not endearing, cuddly, cute, or sweet. Most people do not want a close encounter with a grizzly bear while hiking, camping, or visiting a national park, although they might be thrilled to see one in the distance. Even pictures of mother grizzlies with

Copyright © 2010, Pearson Education, Inc., Publishing as Longman

babies are problematic because most people do know that mothers fiercely defend their cubs and can be extremely dangerous. Wrestling with the choice of visuals will help students develop more appreciation for Earthjustice's strategy in this advocacy ad.

(pages 180-81)
1. Mini-narrative of Figure 1.6: The story that this cartoonist is providing is one of an either-or situation. The incongruity of the two people—a rich Westerner in a suit contrasted with a starving person from a developing country—uses exagerration and distortion about the use of ethanol by Western countries and how that affects the distribution of food worldwide. The cartoon paints with very broad strokes by providing an either-or fallacy, a supposed decision between feeding the starving and using corn for ethanol.
Mini-narrative of Figures 2.3 & 2.4: Both cartoons depict the labor issue connected to migrant workers and illegal immigrants. Both cartoons present Mexican-Americans as only representing a work force who take only low-paying jobs and implicitly indicting Americans as not willing to do manual labor anymore. Migrant workers and illegal aliens are seen as only machines, not as humans.
2. Because of the satirical nature of political cartoons, this will likely be an entertaining exercise. Students can present their cartoons to the whole class and generate ideas and interpretations about the cartoon during class, which will reinforce core concepts of visual and written rhetoric working together, the use of contrasts, and application of exaggeration for humorous yet serious intent.

See also another sample exercise, "Discussion Exercise Analyzing Visual Argument In American History" (pages 70-72 of the *Instructor's Manual*) for another activity that will open up discussion of effective visual arguments that capture the *kairotic* moment of the war effort during World War II.

(page 191)
Students will be originating their own work for this exercise, which is connected to the Writing Assignment: Option 1 at the end of this chapter.

Examining Visual Arguments

The part openers, figures not in this chapter, and visual arguments in the anthology can be used to extend students' practice with the concepts in Chapter 9:

Political Cartoons

- Figure 1.5: "Assisted Suicide Isn't 'Natural'" (8)
- Figure 1.6: "Ethanol Versus Food" (9)
- Figure 1.7: "Air Plane Baggage Dilemma" (9)
- Figure 2.3: "Imagine: A Border Barrier Truly Impenetrable to Undocumented Migrants" (28)
- Figure 2.4: "Anti-Immigration Nation" (28)
- Matt Davies, "Pump & Circumstance" (264)
- Clay Bennett, "Just Emancipated" (275)
- Mike Luckovich, "The Military's Raising Enlistment Age…" (307)

Copyright © 2010, Pearson Education, Inc., Publishing as Longman

* Part Six Opener: Kirk Anderson, "Please Remove Any Remaining…" (423)
* Paul Noth, "I Can't Wait" (439-40)
* Yasuhide Fumoto, "The Thinker, Reimagined" (446)
* Daryl Cagle, "Those Terrible Virginia Tech Cartoons" (481)
* Brian McFadden, "Amazing Facts About the Fairer, Yet Equal Sex" (509)
* Peter Kuper, "Soldier as Atlas" (535)
* Matt Carmody, "I Need You" (555)
* Dan Piraro, "Bizarro, Greeter Gone Wild" (566)
* David Horsey, "A New World to Conquer" (576)

Advocacy Ads

* Figure 1.1: "Protect Our Kids" (4)
* "Think You Can be a Meat-Eating Environmentalist?" (145)
* Part 4 Opener: "I Need a Liver" (199)
* Adbusters, "Big Mac Attack" (244)
* Figure 15.1: "What Is Left for Teenagers to Do…" (317)
* Protect.Choice.org, "When Your Right to an Abortion…" (322)
* Council for Biotechnology Information, "Would You Be Surprised to Know that Growing Soybeans Can Help the Environment" (606-07)
* Monsantoland" (615)

Product Advertisements

* Toyota, "Fancy a Breath of Fresh Air?" (117)
* GM, "Creatures of the Evergreen Forest" (178)
* *Wal-Mart: The High Cost of Low Price* (181)
* ConocoPhillips, "Tomorrow Begins Today" (210)
* *A Day Without a Mexican* (284)
* Sustainable Forestry Initiative, "Two Ways to Show You Care About Our Forests" (590)

Posters

* "Early Warning Signs of Fascism" (215)
* Sustainusa.org, "What Is the FDA Trying to Feed Us? (618)

Photographs/Illustrations/Screen Shots

* Part One Opener*: Under the Same Moon* (1)
* Figure 1.2: "Trouble in Toyland" (5)
* Figure 1.3: "These Colors Don't Run" (7)
* Figure 1.4: "These Colors Don't Run the World" (7)
* Figure 2.1: "It's Illegal to Hire Illegals" (27)
* Figure 2.2: "Legalize My Parents" (27)
* Part Two Opener: *Tomb Raider* (59)
* Figure 6.1: La Saline, a slum in Port-au-Prince, Haiti (116)
* "Push.PickensPlan.com" (310)
* Part Five Opener: "Smart Car versus Hummer" (343)

Copyright © 2010, Pearson Education, Inc., Publishing as Longman

- ICED (I Can End Deportation) (457-58)
- Yahoo! Home Page (472-73)
- Student Advocates for Immigration Reform (499-500)
- Selective Service System, “How the Draft Has Changed Since Vietnam” (541)
- U.S. Department of Defense, “Heroes” (549-50)

Video Game Images

- Tomb Raider (59)
- America’s Army, “Urban Assault” (182)
- America’s Army, “Village scene” (182)

Student Responses to Assignments. For examples of students’ poster arguments, see “Discussion Exercise Examining Students’ Poster Arguments” in “VII. Samples of Student Writing for Discussion.” In that section, we show two students’ poster arguments in draft and revised form and offer questions for discussing these student pieces.

Copyright © 2010, Pearson Education, Inc., Publishing as Longman

CHAPTER 10: AN INTRODUCTION TO THE TYPES OF CLAIMS

For Class Discussion Exercises

(page 202)
Instructors might have students rephrase these questions as claims and note how different wording can shape the type of the claim.
1. This is proposal claim. Instructors should call attention to use of "should," in that many times the use of *ought, must, or should* entails some type of deliberation on action to (not) be taken. 2. This question exemplifies a hybrid. First, there is an argument that asserts or disputes whether that drug actually increases one's concentration (causal), a definitional argument about what constitutes cheating and whether taking drugs is "cheating" (definitional) or if "cheating" is well-defined a categorical argument, and possible resemblance claims about how that drug is similar to steroids, etc. 3. Causal claim: This question is asking whether gas taxes will *cause* a reduction in traffic. 4. Hybrid claim: While the question is evaluative (based on the criteria of learned behavior), an argument for or against this claim will also involve causal arguments and definition of terms. 5. Resemblance claim. 6. Causal claim, especially because of the word "how." Causality is assumed. 7. Evaluation claim: however, the claim could also be considered categorical because the arguers must agree on what "quackery" and "real medicine" mean. 8. This could be a complex hybrid argument because it involves a philosophical proposal (Should we or shouldn't we?), could involves strong casual arguing (the benefits and drawbacks of public funding), and perhaps evaluative claims involving criteria about what's best for one's city. 9. Definitional claim, setting up a particular interpretation of "sweatshop" and showing how Mattels's factories fit that interpretation. 10. This is a causal claim that merely tries to look for reasons/causes for the greater rate of divorce.

(pages 206-7)
1. Each class and each educational institution will be drawn to different issues, but here is a hypothetical illustration based on a controversy from the authors' own campus, a Jesuit university with a strong Catholic identity. A group of students representing "peer educators" petitioned the student government to make free condoms available on campus. The issue involved the use of university funds. After lively debate, the student government approved the petition, but it was vetoed by the university administration, again after lively debate. Here are various claim-type issues that arose within the two forums.

<u>Claim-Type Analysis: Student Government as Audience</u>

Simple categorical argument: Does this proposal have wide student support? Is it difficult to obtain condoms near campus? Is student sexual activity widespread? Is it frequent?
Definitional argument: Is distributing condoms in the dorms a "legitimate use" of student body funds? Is recreational sex a "meaningless game" (as charged by a professor writing a letter to the editor in the student newspaper)? Is passing out condoms a violation of Catholic teachings about sexuality and social justice?
Causal argument: Will distribution of condoms encourage safe sex? Will it lead to more sex?
Resemblance argument: Is distributing free condoms in the dorms analogous to providing free antidepressants at the health center? Is it like providing clean rooms and healthy food? Is not providing free condoms like not teaching evolution in science (as charged by one student writing

Copyright © 2010, Pearson Education, Inc., Publishing as Longman

to the school paper)? Since my high school provided free condoms, so should the university, many students claimed—thus making a precedence argument.
Evaluation argument: Is premarital sex moral or immoral? Would passing out condoms benefit or harm persons living in the dorms?
Proposal argument: Should student body officers approve a proposal to use student government funds to provide free condoms in the dorms?

Claim-Type Analysis: University Administrators as Audience

Simple categorical argument: Are the main student leaders behind this proposal highly respected students or fringe persons? Are they likely to bring national attention to this issue? Is the issue of high interest to faculty? Is unsafe sex a serious, widespread campus problem? Is this primarily a symbolic issue or a legitimate campus problem?
Definitional argument: Is passing out free condoms primarily a health issue or a moral issue? Would failure to approve the use of student body funds for condoms be considered "legislation of morality"? Would failure to approve this initiative be a "violation of our commitment to diversity"? Does use of student body funds automatically mean "university approval or endorsement"?
Causal argument: What effect would approving this proposal have on alumni giving? On our relationship with the Catholic diocese? On the administration's relationship to the faculty? On our relationship with student government? On our Catholic identity? Will distributing free condoms lead to an increase in sexual activity? Will it decrease disease?
Resemblance argument: Have any other Catholic universities allowed the free distribution of condoms? Is allowing student government to distribute free condoms analogous to granting free speech to the student newspaper?
Evaluation argument: Do the bad consequences of unsafe sex outweigh the positive consequences of being true to Catholic principles of sexual morality? If unsafe sex is a widespread problem, is passing out free condoms the best solution?
Proposal argument: Should the university administration approve or disapprove the student body proposal to distribute free condoms in the dorms?

2. The brief's table of contents offers a host of evaluative, definitional, and causal claims. "Real-world harm" seems to be the rhetorical linchpin of the brief. The overarching claim is evaluative in that, based on the importance of "real-world harm" (criteria), violent video games are not dangerous. Section I is primarily evaluative but would have to establish "real-world harm." Section II offers a causal argument in Section A and an evaluative argument in Section B. Section III entails a definitional argument about "fantasy violence" and a causal/evaluative argument about it being "good."

Copyright © 2010, Pearson Education, Inc., Publishing as Longman

CHAPTER 11: DEFINITIONAL ARGUMENTS: IN WHAT CATEGORY DOES THIS THING BELONG?

For Class Discussion Exercises

(pages 212-13)
1. Definitions will vary, but it's plausible that "companion" or "friend" or "nuisance" might be part of students' definitions. Students' criteria for defining a pet might include the following: a pet sheds fur, hair, or feathers and therefore can be messy and cause allergic reactions in people; a pet makes noise that could be disruptive to neighbors; a pet is mobile and could get out of a cage or apartment and bother neighbors. By this criteria, the only "pet" that would be allowed in this apartment would be a tank of fish. All the other animals have the potential to be messy or noisy and to escape from the confines of cages or apartments. 2. Answers will vary according to their definitions.

(page 214)
1. "Sport-utility vehicles" and "environmentally unfriendly" would have to be clearly defined and agree upon. To support the claim, writers would have to show exactly what entails being environmentally unfriendly, which would usually be based on miles-per-gallon since that is the typical determinant of the amount of pollution (CO_2) a vehicle emits. An suv getting 18 mpg could be a simple example, but someone could easily rebut that claim with examples of hybrid suvs that get very good gas mileage. 2. Using Nelly's lyrics to show how he fits the category of "gangsta" (which would have to be defined) is crucial. The arguer would have to establish the mores and characteristics of gangsta rappers and then show through Nelly's attitudes, actions, and lyrics how he exemplifies a gangsta rapper. 3. This categorical claim calls for examples that show Americans' preoccupation with appearance. Examples might include numerical figures about the amount of money Americans spend on diet and beauty products, on clothes, on anti-aging products, on hair care and athletic clubs, and on cosmetic surgery. Challenges to this claim might focus on showing that "obsession" is not an accurate description of American attitudes. Resistant readers might employ numerical figures to show that Americans today spend no more money proportionately on their appearance than did Americans fifty or one hundred years ago or that Europeans spend comparable amounts of money on their appearance. Challenges might also put the money Americans spend on appearance in relation to money they spend in other categories: recreation, education, basic necessities. 4. To support this claim, writers could use numerous examples of the salaries of college football coaches like Rich Rodriguez (Michigan), Nick Saban (Alabama), Jim Tressel (Ohio State), Urban Meyer (Florida), among others. They could then compare the salary figures (using average salaries would be wise) to the salaries in a number of other professions or even other coaches in Division I college sports. To counter this claim and justify the high salaries of college football coaches, writers would need to show that these coaches have comparatively short careers where they coach because if they don't produce they get fired, show how much revenue college football programs bring into Division I athletic departments (thus, they subsidize other collegiate sports since football usually creates a great deal of revenue, explain how winning football programs unify a campus and enhance the "brand name" of the school to help with recruitment of students, and describe the fact that college football provides millions of people stimulating entertainment during fall weekends—creating a lucrative market that creates high salaries. 5. Authors would

Copyright © 2010, Pearson Education, Inc., Publishing as Longman

need to fully define what "physically risky" means and show real-world examples of high school and college cheerleading teams' rate and types of injuries incurred during practice and competitions.

(page 218)
Answers will vary on some of the problems. 1. Presence of gills is a necessary criterion (all fish have gills) but not a sufficient criterion for an animal to be a fish (tadpoles have gills also). 2. Profane and obscene language is a sufficient criterion for a film to be R-rated, but not all R-rated films have profane and obscene language; therefore, this language is not a necessary criterion for a movie to be R-rated. 3. Having rhyming line endings is neither a necessary criterion for a piece of writing to be a poem (many poems don't rhyme) nor a sufficient one (many language constructs that rhyme aren't true poems). 4. Spanking a child for discipline can be either an accidental criterion for child abuse or no criterion. Some might argue that spanking used exclusively for discipline is not at all related to child abuse. 5. Eating no meat, ever, is a sufficient criterion for being a vegetarian, but many people would argue it is not a necessary one (since some vegetarians eat some, for example, fish). 6. Killing another human being is a necessary criterion for being a murderer but not a sufficient one. 7. Most people would agree that a good sex life is not a sufficient criterion for a happy marriage (other factors are important too); it is probably arguable whether or not a good sex life is a necessary criterion.

(page 224)
This is an important exploration activity for students writing a definitional argument in response to the assignment on page 225. (A full discussion of this activity is found in the following NCTE research booklet: Johannessen, Larry R., Elizabeth A. Kahn, and Carolyn Calhoun Walter, *Designing and Sequencing Prewriting Activities*, Urbana, IL: NCTE, 1982.) This activity is adapted from the booklet.
1. and 2. Student answers, of course, will vary. Most groups, however, arrive at similar conclusions. Here is a typical conclusion. For an act to be courageous it must meet the following criteria: (1) it must involve risk of something of value (usually one's life, but occasionally one's reputation); (2) it must be done consciously, with the doer being aware of the danger; (3) it must be done reasonably, with some hope of success (ruling out the case of the foolhardy parent in case d.); (4) it must be done for a noble purpose (ruling out the teenager saving the memento in case c). Most groups believe that the fireman in case b. is courageous but not as courageous as the neighbor in case a. since the neighbor faces greater risk of harm. This is a difference of degree rather than kind. 3. Answers will vary.

Critiquing Exercises for the Chapter's Readings

Critiquing "Protecting Our Homes Can Lead to Animal Cruelty" by Jenefer Domingo
1. Domingo's definition of animal cruelty is if people "intentionally inflict unnecessary pain for an unjust reason or unworthy purpose. She argues that killing the starling is a "worthy purpose" because, like rats and mice, they are invading the family's home and are deemed as a nuisance by many people. She argues against some classmates, saying that although starlings cannot go everywhere in a person's house, they can damage the attic and enact psychological damage on the family by keeping them up instead of sleeping regularly. She concedes that starlings are not like mice, but she attempts to show that the birds are damaging in their own way. Her main

Copyright © 2010, Pearson Education, Inc., Publishing as Longman

rebuttal to opposing views is that killing the starling is not unjust, but the manner in which they were killed is the real issue to her. Instead of starving the baby birds as the family did, she argues that the humane way to take care of this pest problem is to exterminate them in "the most painless way." She thinks the birds should have been killed quickly instead of slowly dying from starvation. The deaths were just, but the method was unjust, in her view.

2. Answers will vary. But the "pest" definition is one that some would argue with. One could argue just because people on the internet have various ways of killing starlings and that starlings are invasive species do not justify the deaths of the baby birds.

3. All of these cases could be seen as "cruelty to animals" because basing the definition on the idea that "inflicting pain" to "sentient beings" is "cruelty" and also the idea that animals living in their natural habitats is "normal" or "natural." However, some sample arguments are provided: (1) Keeping animals in zoos is "cruelty" because the animals are not in their native habitats, and they live in confinement facilities that are not natural, which restrict their freedom, exact psychological damage (depression), and change their habits and demeanor to a state counter to they way they would act in their native habitats. (2) Catch-and-release fishing is "cruelty to animals" because fish are sentient being who feel pain. To inflict pain through hooking a fish through its lip, dragging it to a boat or shore, and then taking it out of the water is cruel treatment. (3) Bullfighting signifies "cruelty to animals" because the bulls are slaughtered in a manner that is prolonged and preys on their natural instincts. The animals are exhausted and die slowly from losing blood and being teased/tricked into their deaths. (4) Factory-farmed cattle and chickens represents "cruelty to animals" because these animals are kept in psychologically damaging conditions and not given the chance to stretch their legs, graze, and move as they are meant to be. In particular, chickens have to have their beaks snipped off so that they do not peck their neighbors in pens since they are quartered so closely. Although both animals are raised for meat, cattle and chickens deserve to live in a tranquil but domesticated habitat. (5) Medical research using animals represents "cruelty to animals" because researchers methods inflict undue harm to animals, inflicting pain repeatedly.

Critiquing "Oncore, Obscenity, and the Liquor Control Board" by Kathy Sullivan

1. *Reportive approach*: From *Black's Law Dictionary*, Sullivan derives three criteria for photographs to be obscene:

> (1) The dominant theme of the photographs, when judged by the average person applying "contemporary community standards," must appeal to prurient interest.
> (2) The material must be pornographic in a hard core sense or at least go beyond customary limits in candor and representation.
> (3) The photographs must be utterly without redeeming social purpose.

From Pember's *Mass Media Laws*, she derives a fourth criterion: A work is obscene if it has a tendency to corrupt the minds of children.

2. *Sullivan's argumentative strategies*: (1) She begins by arguing that relevant community standards should be those of the homosexual community, not the general community, since this bar is patronized predominantly by gays. (2) Instead of catering to "prurient interest," she contends that these photographs depict homosexual affection, which is appropriate and normal subject matter for its intended audience, the gays who come to this bar. (3) Further, she argues

Copyright © 2010, Pearson Education, Inc., Publishing as Longman

that because the photographs do not depict sexual acts, but simply show male nudity, they are not pornographic. (4) She maintains that the location of the photographs in a gay bar means that children will not see them. (5) Her final, climactic point, is that these photographs serve an important, constructive social purpose: to promote the prevention of AIDS through safe sex.

3. Answers will vary.
(a) *Persuasive*: Sullivan is effective in emphasizing the importance of the audience and context for these photographs
(b) *Ineffective*: Without a description of the photographs, it is difficult to tell how nudity portrays the theme of safe sex. One larger issue that Sullivan's argument touches on but does not pursue is, Is it just for society to be permissive about female nudity but not male nudity, or to endorse heterosexual eros (in advertising, say) but not homosexual eros?
(c) *Shaping for audience*: Sullivan is saying to a general, heterosexual audience, "You don't have to see these pictures so you don't have to be offended by them." Because parents are concerned about their children's exposure to sexual material, she argues that children will not see these photographs. They are not being displayed in general public areas like McDonald's or Red Robin.
(d) *A lawyer's response*: A lawyer from the liquor control board might argue that there is no legal precedent for Sullivan's narrowing of community standards. Should standards vary by state, city, side of the street? Such narrowing might lead to anarchic splintering of large communities into sub-communities. Should the standards for a working class bar on the waterfront differ from those of an upscale bar in the banking district? Should art with homosexual themes get restricted to homosexual establishments and therefore banned from places where heterosexuals gather? Sullivan seems to take this position.

Critiquing "What Defines a Sport?" by David Andriesen
1. He ends the article with the idea that no one will ever agree on what constitutes a sport, but he provides specific criteria that are important to consider: ball-like objects involved, a race emphasis, competition is emphasized, objective scoring, and a physical nature.
2. Answers will vary, but having accepted criteria would help, say, in the Olympics where that competition seems to acquire more sports all the time. Insurance companies might like a definition of sport to classify coverage status.
3. Answers will vary, but students the criteria showcased in the article (see answer to 1 above). With those criteria in mind, synchronized swimming is not a sport because it doesn't rely on objective scoring, poker is not a sport because it doesn't involve a strong level of physical effort, video game playing doesn't usually involve a strong level of physical effort, and NASCAR is not a sport because it doesn't rely on a simple machine.

Anthology Arguments Related by Claim Type: Definitional Claims

The following articles in the anthology use categorical or definitional claims either as their major claim or as one of their primary lines of argument in support of the main claim:

- Alice Mathias, "The Facebook Generation" (438-39)
- "A Message from the Creators" (445-46)
- Sydney H. Schanberg, "Not a Pretty Picture" (482-84)
- Matali Perkins, "A Note to Young Immigrants" (493-94)

Copyright © 2010, Pearson Education, Inc., Publishing as Longman

* Maileen Hamto, "My Turn: Being American" (494-95)
* Selective Service System, "How the Draft Has Changed Since Vietnam" (541)
* U.S. Department of Defense, "Heroes" (549-50)
* Sustainable Forestry Initiative, "Two Ways to Show You Care about Our Forests" (590)

The following articles in the anthology use definitional claims as important stases for the argument:

* Jeff Chu, "You Wanna Take This Online?" (434-36)
* Malcolm Gladwell, "Brain Candy" (454-57)
* Daryl Cagle, "Those Terrible Virginia Tech Cartoons" (480-82)
* Scarf Ace, "Miss or Diss?" (496-98)
* Fatemah Fakhraie, "Scarfing It Down" (498-99)
* (Army)Wife, "Stop-Loss" (552-54)
* Steve Maich, "Why Wal-Mart Is Good" (568-74)
* David Tilman and Jason Hill, "Fuel for Thought: All Biofuels Are Not Created Equal" (586-89)

Copyright © 2010, Pearson Education, Inc., Publishing as Longman

Handout: USING THE DEFINITIONAL HEURISTIC: CRUELTY TO ANIMALS

Scenario: The Starling Case

A bunch of starlings build nests in the attic of a family's house, gaining access to the attic through a torn vent screen. Soon the eggs hatch, and every morning at sunrise the family is awakened by the sounds of birds squawking and wings beating against rafters as the starlings fly in and out of the house to feed the hatchlings. After regularly losing early morning sleep, the family repairs the screen. Unable to get in and out, the parent birds are unable to feed their young. The birds die within a day.

1. Working as a group and using the scenario of the family's treatment of the starlings, try the definitional heuristic on the topic "cruelty to animals." Make three lists.

   a. obvious examples of cruelty to animals

   b. contrastive examples—that is, behaviors that are not cruel to animals (Try to vary a few features of each entry under "a" above, so that the example switches from cruelty to noncruelty.)

   c. borderline cases

2. Once you have created your list of cases, create a one-sentence definition of "cruelty to animals" following the pattern described earlier for police brutality. Your definition should include each of the criteria that you established. Do not discuss the starling case directly when you create your definition.

3. Apply your definition to the starling case. Does the starling case fit or not fit the criteria in your definition?

Copyright © 2010, Pearson Education, Inc., Publishing as Longman

Possible Answers for the Exercise Using the Definitional Heuristic

1. a. Obvious examples of cruelty to animals: torturing an animal for the fun of it; going out of your way to hit an animal while driving your car; starving your pet gerbils through neglect. b. Contrastive examples: causing suffering to animals for a significant human reason (medical research); accidentally hitting an animal while driving your car; discovering a gerbil starved to death in your drawer when you didn't know where the gerbil was. c. Borderline cases: Causing animals to suffer for scientific research of questionable value (development of lipsticks or hair shampoo); squirrel hunting; catch-and-release fishing; stepping on ants; branding cattle; drowning newborn kittens.
2. Through conversation, students will generally discover that at least four criteria are involved in a definition of cruelty to animals: (1) intention—intentionally harming an animal versus accidentally harming an animal; (2) adequate human need or purpose—killing for food, medical research, protection of property versus killing or maiming for the fun of it or for inadequate purpose; (3) limiting suffering to absolute minimum—killing a deer quickly and cleanly versus letting it suffer, using anesthetics in medical research versus absence of anesthetics; and (4) relative "worth" of the animal—killing a gopher in your yard versus killing a squirrel in your yard, killing starlings versus killing robins, killing squawfish versus killing trout (this last criterion always raises troubling issues of human-centrism).

Typical theses statements:
"Although the father in the Starling Case intentionally killed the birds, his act is not cruelty to animals because the psychological harm to the family justified their getting rid of the starlings, because starlings are damage-causing pests, and because no other means of solving the problem, short of killing the birds in this way, was possible."
[or]
"The Starling Case involves cruelty to the animals because the father intentionally killed the birds without adequate justification, because he caused needless suffering in doing so, and because, despite the claim of some classmates, starlings are as deserving of life as robins or kittens."

Copyright © 2010, Pearson Education, Inc., Publishing as Longman

CHAPTER 12: CAUSAL ARGUMENTS

For Class Discussion Exercises

(pages 242-43)
Answers will vary. Here are some possibilities: 1a. The high price of oil made it more expensive for people to use their cars to commute to work, to the extent that commuters' monthly expenditures on gas for their vehicles more than doubled. People wanted to quit using their vehicles for commuting, so they initially used buses more often. Then they demanded light-rail systems using the existing interstates, freeways, and main roads, which in turn made urban and suburban developers redesign more walker-friendly communities located near public transportation. 1b. Invention of the automobile creates opportunities for teenagers to get away from adult chaperones by driving to a remote place; automobile becomes a transportable "bedroom." 1c. The invention of the telephone makes it possible to keep in touch with people over a distance. For the first time you could talk with your friends when they were not present. Consequently, people had less emotional need to know their neighbors since friendship networks were now different from neighborhood networks. Talking to your friends via telephone reduced your need to develop a sense of community in your neighborhood. 1d. Minority cultures create art forms as distinctive self-expression and also as rebellion against oppression; rap grows out of an urban black street culture affected by poverty and minimal economic and social opportunities for advance. A generation of black youth, many from inner cities, embrace rap as an expression of their experiences. Rap artists and their music gain popularity and become successful, earning them money and glamorous notoriety. White middle-class youth learn of rap and are attracted to its rebellious, in-your-face style and its racial "otherness." They adopt rap as an expression of their youthful rebellion. 1e. The development of a way to prevent rejections in transplant operations led to a rapid increase in the number of transplants being performed, which led, in turn, to a greater need for donors of organs. Because of the scarcity of transplantable organs left intact from fatal accidents, social pressure mounted to use organs from people who desired death by euthanasia. This social pressure led to enactment of more liberal euthanasia laws.

2a. Answer in text. 2b. The invention of the automobile led to changes in sexual mores because the automobile became a transportable bedroom that allowed couples privacy away from chaperones. 2c. The invention of the telephone damaged a sense of community in neighborhoods because the telephone enabled people to maintain networks of friends at a distance, thus lessening people's dependence on neighborhoods. 2d. The origination of rap in the black urban music scene led to its acceptance as the dominant musical expression of black youth and to its popularity among white middle-class youth because rap expressed a rebellion against the harsh social, political, and economic realities of young urban blacks, and its offensiveness, rebellion, and racial "otherness" attracted white middle-class youth who sought ways to rebel and challenge authority and the older generation's cultural tastes. 2e. The development of a way to prevent rejections in transplant operations led to liberalization of euthanasia laws because the increased demand for transplant operations increased the demand for organ donors.

Copyright © 2010, Pearson Education, Inc., Publishing as Longman

(page 247)
a. Perhaps daily meditation causes a reduction in stress, but perhaps the kind of person who enjoys daily meditation is already someone with low stress levels so that there is no causal connection at all between the correlated phenomena. b. A white female teenager is likely to see glamorous magazine ads promoting female smoking and linking it to slimness; this teenager is likely to have spending money to buy cigarettes, and might see smoking as a cool, easily accessible avenue of rebellion. c. Living in a house with two bathrooms suggests a certain middle-class economic level and families that would have middle-class values. These families are more likely to be able to afford to have books in the home and to value reading and attending cultural events. Wide reading and cultural experiences build vocabulary, reading and verbal skills, and critical thinking. This knowledge, in addition to these skills, leads to higher SAT scores. Or homes that have two bathrooms are likely to be in neighborhoods that have well-equipped and funded schools, which, in turn, can provide students with better academic skills that show up in higher SAT scores. d. A person who buys many ashtrays is likely to be a smoker or at least be close to someone who smokes heavily. Because such a person probably smokes heavily or is a constant recipient of passive smoke (both probable causes of lung disease) the person is likely to develop lung cancer. There is a high correlation between NRA membership and support of the death penalty. Unlike most "hobby organizations" such as gardening clubs, the National Rifle Association has become a major political force lobbying against gun control legislation. Its members see gun control as government intrusion on individual rights. NRA members believe that the need is not for gun control (don't take guns away from the good citizens or make it harder for good citizens to buy guns) but rather for capital punishment for those people (criminals) who use guns to commit crimes (take the bad guys away from the guns and for that matter this world).

(page 249
1. Answers will vary. 2. Answers will also vary. But here are some possibilities:
a. Why women's fashion and beauty magazines are the most frequently purchased magazines in college bookstores: A remote cause might be that many young women in college have come from families that have been able to afford beauty products, fashionable clothing, and attention to physical appearance, and these magazines are channels of information on these subjects. An immediate cause might be that young college women are in the prime dating period of their lives and want to look their best; they also feel peer pressure to keep up with fashions. A contributing cause could be the whole cultural and social emphasis on female beauty that is promoted in advertising, films, and mass media. A precipitating cause might be young college women's desire to look their most attractive for a date or some social event on campus. At college, women are on their own so the constraints that parents may have put on them have lifted, and they can follow their own tastes, which might be influenced by these magazines.
b. Why American students consistently score below Asian and European students in academic achievement: Remote causes could be the decreasing emphasis on education in the United States and the movement away from rote learning and high standards and toward building self-esteem in students. An immediate cause could be a change toward a less rigorous curriculum. Contributing causes could be the amount of television that students watch and the number of hours they spend working at jobs after school. A precipitating cause could be de-emphasis on test-taking and more emphasis on long-term projects that involve parents and creativity but don't build testable skills. Constraints that might be removed are graduation requirements.

Copyright © 2010, Pearson Education, Inc., Publishing as Longman

c. Why the number of babies born out of wedlock has increased dramatically in the last thirty years: Remote causes could include the breakdown of older sexual values, troubles at home, loss of religious influences on behavior, movies and advertisements glamorizing sex. Contributing causes could be lack of happiness at home, the increased number of friends who are active sexually, peer pressure to lose virginity, the belief that "I won't get pregnant this time," and perhaps the unacknowledged desire to get pregnant as a way of getting back at parents or forcing boyfriend into marriage. A precipitating cause for a particular case could be a teenage girl has fight with mother, causing her to rebel sexually. An immediate cause could be that a girl goes to her boyfriend for comfort; sympathy turns to passion. Things go too far, and they aren't using birth control. Constraints could include fear of pregnancy, parental disapproval, desire to make sex meaningful, lack of birth control, lack of appropriate place.

Critiquing Exercises for the Chapter's Readings

Critiquing "Why Lawrence Summers Was Wrong" by Julee Christianson

1. Christianson uses a counterargument/argument structure in her essay. She first summarizes her opponents arguments and then uses other authors who agree with her thesis—an editorial from *Nature Neuroscience*, Deborah L. Rhode, a study by Melissa W. Chearfield and Naree M. Nelson, and Ben A. Barres. The points about differences in test scores among various countries, stereotypical gender roles, and the examples of different ways in which males and females are socialized are all strong forms of evidence to support her position. The anecdotal evidence from Barres and Hopkins could be persuasive also.
2. Summers and Pinker's variability argument is a strong one because the population that they are talking about are high-powered research scientists at prestigious universities. Christianson and others tend to imply that Summers meant all women are not able to do as well as men. His argument is that, if you look simply at the numbers, there's a larger field to pull from in regard to men. Christianson does a fine job of summarizing opponents' arguments, but the structure of the argument sets up her opponents to look bad.
3. Answers will vary. Christianson's *ethos* is well-mannered and objective-sounding. The author provides a calm and appreciative tone that indicates she's willing to listen to various viewpoints. Since much of the article is an analysis and response to others' arguments, there are few emotional appeals. However, she does provide some loaded language and appeals in the final paragraph, stating, "we should not accept Lawrence Summers' hypothesis…" and "Blaming biology for the lack of women in these fields and refusing to fault our culture is taking the easy way out. Our culture can change." In regard to *logos*, Christianson pits other's arguments against themselves. She brings up the point about socialization with some strong, realistic examples but doesn't comprehensively refute the variability argument.

Critiquing "Different but (Probably) Equal" by Olivia Judson

1. Judson's position draws support from her biological study of significant (or lack thereof) differences correlated to sex among various animals. Taking all the evidence before her—from elephants to jackdaws—she argues that there are probably some small intellectual differences between human males and females, but the differences are so small they're hard to draw any conclusions from. Although she offers this claim, she's willing—in contrast to knee-jerk, over simplistic reactions from various commentators on the left and right—to pursue scientific

Copyright © 2010, Pearson Education, Inc., Publishing as Longman

methods to see if the "slight" differences are significant or insignificant for the human species. Her position sides with "nurture" over "nature."

2. Support for the nurture view: Judson's concise discussion of the historical context about why Summers' comments were seen as politically incorrect (paragraph 6), the fact that in "blind" peer reviews grant applications from women are more likely to be approved (7), her information about how "[s]ex differences never arise in isolation" and how genes are in both females and males (8-11), the example of jackdaws and green spoon worms (12, 13). Support for the nature view: The various examples of extreme differences between males and females in different species—elephants, peacocks, et al (however, how do those differences relate to intelligence or certain styles of reasoning?), her questioning attitude and accommodation of the viewpoint that maybe science can show us some significant differences (14 and the final paragraph).

3. Analogies between humans and other species: The green spoon worm and the jackdaw analogies are important in that they show how sexual differences don't evolve in isolation; both sexes contribute to the natural selection and variation within the species. Her relation that genes "spend equal time in each sex" along with her assertion that "the bigger the advantage in one sex, the more detrimental those genes are in the other" shows that the two sexes have an evolutionary interest in being helpful to each another for the mutual benefit of propagating the species. She states that the most interesting questions resound from "intrinsic difference" and "variation" because her angle of vision is one of a scientist who sees the possibility (although a slight possibility in her mind) of sexual differences affecting "particular sorts of thinking." If one sex is poor at science because they tend to either brilliant or weak in that subject (perhaps implying the reason behind the paucity of women scientists?) and the other sex is ignobly average (perhaps males?), she's open to that viewpoint as long as the subject is well researched.

4. Judson's ethos: Her strong credibility is brought out by her sound analysis, playfulness, and respect for different views. She's fair-minded and doesn't attack her opponents; rather, she accommodates their viewpoints and shows sympathy for them in saying, "it seems a shame if we can't even voice the question." The last paragraph, in particular, shows her open-mindedness to views going against her own feeling that the intellectual differences, if any, between men and women are "slight." Rather than providing an argument that is "war-like," hers exemplifies truth-seeking and persuasion. The fact that readers know she's a woman could be important to readers. In contrast to, say, a male suggesting that we should explore if there are true intellectual differences between the sexes, her gender strengthens her ethos because some readers may think, "If a respected woman scientist is willing to consider this perspective, maybe we should also at least consider it?"

Critiquing "The Credit Card Company Made Me Do It!"—The Credit Card Industry's Role is Causing Student Debt" by Carlos Macias

1. Effectiveness of the argument: Many students will probably identify and concur with Macias' argument that credit card companies "exploit" or "hook" college students because they can identify with his opening Gap store example and because of they probably carry a balance on a credit cards or various cards. Macias' Appeals to Logos: The author does a strong job of relating a typical example of how college student can easily obtain a credit card. Macias also realistically depicts the credit companies' advertising campaigns, which provide images of "emergency uses" for using credit cards while offering the cards as a way to purchase items that reflect the lifestyles they desire in the future (Bernthal's article). The main strengths of his argument—relevant information that many may be unaware of—are how he describes and informs the reader

Copyright © 2010, Pearson Education, Inc., Publishing as Longman

about the parameters of credit scoring based on "outstanding debts and payment history" and the complicated means by which credit card companies mask their fees and raise interest rates based on various factors. He uses varied sources in his argument: personal experience, realistic anecdotes, a peer-reviewed journal article, and relevant monographs on the subject. The statistical information and data are persuasive and lend credence to his argument that there is a "system" or marketing "game" at work. Macias'Appeals to Pathos: In using his personal experience, he attempts to connect with fellow college students or other adults who have been in similar situations, where cards are offered to consumers having very little income to speak of. His data even might provoke an emotional reaction from readers, who may be surprised at how extensively many college students go into debt through credit card spending sprees. While those statistics could provide such emotional coloring, it could also work against his argument by provoking reactions from some readers such as, "Why aren't they responsible with their money!?" Macias' argument, in addition, falters in his use of loaded language that may distance some skeptical readers. Word choices such as "exploiting," "hooking," "predatory," and "vicious monster," et al. highlight that he needed to consider how some readers might question his depiction of college students as victims. The Author's Ethos: As stated, Macias provides varied types of sources; however, these sources all seem to veer toward his frame of vision about credit cards. To further strengthen the credibility of his argument, Macias would need to provide more comprehensive work with counterargumentation, such as respectfully considering perspectives from the business world and more extensively developing his concession in paragraph three, where he relates that "individual responsibility" is a serious factor. By contending with how skeptical readers might question and rebut his grounds, warrant, and backing, he would provide a more balanced presentation of his causal argument. Although he provides substantial detail for his claims, his argument would have more credibility by grappling with various conditions of rebuttal.

2. Places of Rebuttal for Macias' Argument: Answers will vary. Here are some possibilities: College students simply spend beyond their means; many times they use credit cards for non-essential items (beer, cds, concert tickets, clothing that is overpriced and trendy, etc.); they buy highly esteemed items when a less expensive item would be fine (Banana Republic prices vs. Old Navy prices); college students are adults, and most know that credit cards will "gouge" the consumer if they don't make their payments; if college students go into debt, that is merely a life lesson they need to remember, et al. An arguer could construct a case against Macias' argument by proceeding point by point and providing substantial and well-detailed counterarguments for each separate supporting point that he provides. Including industry perspectives and data showing college students' debt levels are not all that statistically different than older adults when age computes into the equation would certainly help an oppositional viewpoint. Some solid examples of college students who use credit cards responsibly would help also.

Anthology Arguments Related by Claim Type: Causal Claims

The following articles in the anthology use causal claims as either their major claim or as one of their primary lines of argument in support of their major claim:

- Bronwyn T. Williams, "'Tomorrow Will Not Be Like Today': Literacy and Identity in a World of Multiliteracies" (429-34)
- Jeff Chu, "You Wanna Take This Online?" (434-36)
- Paul Noth, "I Can't Wait" (439-40)

Copyright © 2010, Pearson Education, Inc., Publishing as Longman

- Dana L. Fleming, "Youthful Indiscretions: Should Colleges Protect Social Network Users from Themselves and Others?" (440-43)
- Yasuhide Fumoto, "The Thinker, Reimagined" (446)
- Iowa State University New Service, "ISU Psychologists Publish Three New Studies on Violent Video Game Effects on Youths" (449-50)
- Henry Jenkins, "Reality Bytes: Eight Myths about Video Games Debunked" (450-54)
- Michael Humphrey, "For a Virtual Dose of Reality, a Different Kind of Video Game" (458-60)
- William Lugo, "Violent Video Games Recruit American Youth" (460-65)
- Dan Kennedy, "Plugged In, Tuned Out: Young Americans Are Embracing New Media but Failing to Develop an Appetite for News" (473-79)
- Chris Shaw, "Should Killers Be Given Air Time" (479-80)
- Daryl Cagle, "Those Terrible Virginia Tech Cartoons" (480-82)
- Francisco X. Gaytan, Avary Carhill, and Carola Suarez-Orozco, "Understanding and Responding to the Need of Newcomer Immigrant Youth and Families" (486-93)
- Matali Perkins, "A Note to Young Immigrants" (493-94)
- Steven Pinker, "The Science of Sex Difference: Sex Ed" (514-17)
- Ben A. Barres, "Does Gender Matter?" (517-25)
- David Malakoff, "Girls = Boys at Math" (525-26)
- Phillip Carter and Paul Gastris, "The Case for the Draft" (530-40)
- Arindrajit Dub, T. William Lester, and Barry Eidlin, "A Downward Push: The Impact of Wal-Mart Stores on Retail Wages and Benefits" (558-65)
- Dan Piraro, "Bizarro, Greeter Gone Wild" (566)
- John Tierney, "Shopping for a Nobel" (574-75)
- Nicholas Kristof, "Our Gas Guzzlers, Their Lives" (579-80)
- Charles Krauthammer, "Save the Planet, Let Someone Else Drill" (584-85)
- David Tilman and Jason Hill, "Fuel For Thought: All Biofuels Are Not Created Equal" (586-89)
- Rachel Carson, "The Obligation to Endure" (644-48)
- Stanley Milgram, "The Perils of Obedience" (649-58)

Copyright © 2010, Pearson Education, Inc., Publishing as Longman

CHAPTER 13: RESEMBLANCE ARGUMENTS

For Class Discussion Exercises

(pages 268-69)
Answers will vary. Here are some possibilities: 1. Spanking a child to teach obedience is like blackmailing a mate into fidelity: it uses coercion and makes people act out of fear rather than love. 2. Using racial profiling for airport security is like giving tickets to everyone driving a red car: it uses a piece of evidence that has some validity and yet generalizes wildly, deprives people of their rights, and punishes people based on categorical rather than individual traits. 3. The use of steroids by college athletes is like putting herbicide on a dandelion: it makes it grow vigorously for a short time and then kills it. 4. Paying college athletes is like giving hefty tax cuts to wealthy people: it is unnecessary; expensive to others (the country or the universities), and it gives more money to those who already have privileges. 5. Eating at fast-food restaurants is like cleaning your room by throwing all your things in your closet: it is convenient and efficient in the short run, but in the long run it may have unpleasant consequences (to your room and your things or to your health).

(page 271)
1.a. To what extent should the United States follow precedents set by other Western countries? Are there differences in the social structure of the US and other Western countries that should make US military policy on gays different from policies of other countries? Are there differences in demands made on the military in the US? Have there been any problems with gays in the military in other Western countries? 1.b.. Supporters would draw analogies between Hitler and Saddam Hussein, both of whom were tyrants, and how Germany and Japan are flourishing democratic governments now. Both supporters and skeptics could ask, Is Iraq in the early 21st century in a comparatively similar historical context as Japan and Germany post WWII? Skeptics could ask, Is the culture of Iraq conducive to democratic practices as compared to Germany and Japan at that time period? Aren't the military conflicts (WWII and the Iraq War) wars that the US went into for very different reasons? Skeptics could point out historical examples of countries in which the US has waged war and hasn't helped build democracies.
2. How is the Netherlands' euthanasia law worded? Does the law refer to passive or active euthanasia (letting someone die by withholding treatment versus taking action to kill a patient)? How many people (the patient, family, several doctors) are involved in the decision to use euthanasia? How many people choose euthanasia every year? What economic and psychological consequences has euthanasia had in this country?

Copyright © 2010, Pearson Education, Inc., Publishing as Longman

Critiquing Exercises for the Chapter's Readings

Critiquing "Whales Need Silence" by Megan Matthews

1. Analogy in this piece: Humans' use of blasting, low-frequency active sonar, and other sonar systems destroys the quiet of the ocean that marine mammals need in order to communicate and maintain communities in the same way that forcing humans to live next to constantly noisy freeways would add physical and emotional stress and interfere with communication for humans.
2. Effectiveness of this analogy: Although the analogy probably does not fully do justice to the suffering and harm inflicted on marine mammals by manmade underwater noise, especially by sonar, it does effectively convey the idea of inescapable, destructive noise. While humans understand the noise of a freeway because it is produced by humans, whales and dolphins may be confused as well as harmed by sounds made by humans. However, the analogy works well because everyone has some familiarity with freeway noise, with the roar of engines, tire sounds, and sirens, and all readers can imagine how difficult life would be if these sounds dominated their lives.
3. Main point in letter to the editor: We need to stop Congress' funding of low-frequency active sonar to protect marine mammals.

Summary of longer argument: Megan actually summarizes her longer argument in paragraphs 2–5. Paragraph 2 presents the problem; paragraph 3 further specifies the issue; paragraph 4 summarizes the dangers that navy sonar poses to marine mammals, and paragraph 5 presents her claim and implies that "environmental security" should be considered as important as military defense.

Points from Megan's researched argument: In her longer argument, Megan rebuts the Navy's argument that adequate testing has been done on the effect of sonar systems on whales and other marine mammals. She might have plunged into this argument in her letter to the editor. In the longer argument, she also argues that because nations compete in their build-up of defense systems, the US's. use of LFA could likely lead to other countries' use of similar equipment, greatly increasing the underwater noise and making its regulation and mammal protection much more difficult. She might have addressed the idea of an arms race and its impact on marine mammals. A third rebuttal point that she argues in her researched argument is that cargo ships with terrorist bombs pose a greater threat to national security than submarines and therefore LFA is not as needed as the Navy suggests. A final point she makes is the importance of ocean health. Each of these points could become a smaller argument; however, Megan recognized that a letter to the editor needs to zero in on one key idea and boldly, yet specifically, sketch that argument. The focus she chose for her letter to the editor is actually the most interesting and suitable for a short discussion, and it succeeds in vividly bringing the issue to the attention of readers.

Critiquing "Just Emancipated" by Clay Bennett and "Toon Offensive" by Beth Reis

1. Bennett's cartoon equates the inability of same-sex couples to marry to enslavement. The implicit argument that California's law is a historic moment in our nation's history, an act that has effectively scored a civil rights victory on behalf of same-sex couples.
2. Reis' letter calls Bennett on painting the ruling with a very broad brush, that in essence it's demeaning and disingenuous to compare the freedom of enslaved African Americans to same sex couples' being able to legally marry in California.
3. The analogies are that both groups of marriages have had to withstand widespread and well-documented discrimination and prejudice for years. At one time, inter-racial marriages were rare

Copyright © 2010, Pearson Education, Inc., Publishing as Longman

and looked down up by many people in American society. To a certain extent, same-sex marriages have endured and still endure the same challenges. However, race could be seen quite differently from sex. Racial differences, as many argue, are cultural constructs, whereas male and female are biologically and anatomically different. To some people's view, same-sex marriage is entirely different because same-sex couple cannot procreate and have children, which to some is a defining aspect of marriage.

4. Reis establishes her *ethos* in the first paragraph by identifying herself as a plaintiff in another same-sex marriage lawsuit, and she threads it throughout by dictions and concessions such as "I feel a little more equal," "Yes, it matters that some people are now first-class citizens," and "I am proud to be gay." Employing *pathos*, she uses emotionally-loaded diction to show her disgust and disapproval for the cartoon such as "brutality, forced labor, and families being separated and sold," "offensive," and "But, please." In regard to *logos*, Reis effectively questions the equating of same-sex marriage to the freeing of slaves, an analogy that contrasts two very different issues and historical time periods in American history.

Critiquing "Football Coach Salaries" by the American Association of University Professors

1. To some, the Harley-Davidson comparison will ring true because the comparison of motorcycles to producing graduates makes sense. To others, they may find it to be a forced analogy, one that equates higher education to a production or "market"

2. The author rebuts this analogy by showing that professional sports and movie stars work under a profit system whereas higher education, for the most part, works under a non-profit status. The rebuttal is persuasive if one believes that only priority of higher education is the classroom experience/academic programs and doesn't remember the Harley-Davidson analogy. The rebuttal is not persuasive if the reader sees collegiate football programs serving different roles: to offer non-academic diversions in an academic climate, to bind the campus community around a common interest, and to generate a strong brand identification with a school for recruiting purposes.

Critiquing the Passage from *Against Our Will: Men, Women, and Rape* by Susan Brownmiller

1. Summary: Recent trends (freedom of speech/sexual revolution) have taken steps to protect porn but have failed to recognize the damage it does to women. Porn does not foster sexual freedom/expression. Instead, it is a form of "anti-female propaganda" similar to anti-Semitic caricatures or racial jokes. Because women are not realistically portrayed, they cannot relate to or enjoy porn. Further, it is likely that the abuse of women in porn films leads to overly-aggressive male behavior, like rape.

2. Humiliation and degradation of women: Porn is not at all geared toward female interest. It is focused on entertaining men and boosting the "masculine ego" by (1) making female sex activities "dirty" (e.g., lesbianism); (2) exposing and shaming women's naked bodies; and (3) portraying women as powerless, anonymous, playthings to be "used, abused, broken, and discarded" (paragraph 6).

3. Possible disanalogies (dissimilarities between the two terms or two circumstances): (1) In intention: While the intention of porn is simply to entertain, and any negative feelings toward women are side effects of that entertainment, the intention of Nazi propaganda was to turn people against the Jews. (2) Breadth: While porn reaches a select group within a population (white middle-class married men) and involves some choice on the part of the viewers,

Copyright © 2010, Pearson Education, Inc., Publishing as Longman

successful propaganda reaches and influences the majority of a population and is publicly disseminated. (3) Method of broadcast: Because porn is a private, secret activity, it could be considered fairly self-contained. Propaganda's goal, however, is to infiltrate people's daily lives and alter their way of thinking. (4). Choice: People choose to watch porn, which means that they may already have negative/aggressive feelings about women/sex. However, people influenced by propaganda have little control over their exposure to its messages. (5) Students will generally mention that pornographic films are made by paid performers, both women and men, who voluntarily choose this work and who—Linda Lovelace's protestations notwithstanding—often profess to enjoy their work and who see themselves as liberating people from Victorian taboos. There seem to be no parallel cases of Jewish or black actors who voluntarily produce Nazi-like racist propaganda.

4. <u>Brownmiller's contributions</u>: In our effort to protect freedom of speech and the sexual revolution, we're forgetting to make distinctions between things that take us forward and things (like porn) that set us back. (1) She makes us question our "good intentions." She argues forcefully that pornography is not about sexual liberation, certainly not liberation for women. (2) She shows that porn does do a significant amount of damage to women. (3) She questions our foundations of knowledge (scientific evidence) as a prerequisite for taking action. (4) She points out our inconsistency (limiting TV violence but not porn violence). (5) She suggests that we systematically support negative images of women's sexuality.

Anthology Arguments Related by Claim Type: Resemblance Claims

The following articles in the anthology have prominent resemblance claims or lines of argument:

- Michael Humphrey, "For a Virtual Dose of Reality, a Different Kind of Video Game" (458-60
- William Powers, "The Massless Media" (467-72)
- Brian McFadden, "Amazing Facts About the Fairer, Yet Equal Sex" (509)
- Steven Pinker, "The Science of Sex Difference: Sex Ed" (514-17)
- Sustainable Forestry Initiative, "Two Ways to Show You Care About Our Forests" (590)
- Al Gore, "Nobel Lecture" (592-97)
- "Monsantoland" (615)
- Garret Hardin, "Lifeboat Ethics: The Case Against Aid that Does Harm" (635-42)

These articles employ important analogies or reasoning from precedents at key points in their arguments:

- Dana L. Fleming, "Youthful Indiscretions: Should Colleges Protect Social Network Users from Themselves and Others?" (440-43)
- Chris Shaw, "Should Killers Be Given Air Time" (479-80)
- Matali Perkins, "A Note to Young Immigrants" (493-94)
- Maileen Hamto, "My Turn: Being American" (494-95)
- Ben A. Barres, "Does Gender Matter?" (517-25)
- Donald Rumsfeld, "New Model Army" (528-30)
- (Army)Wife, "Stop-Loss" (552-54)
- Andrew C. Revkin, "Carbon-Neutral Is Hip, but Is It Green?" (580-82)

Copyright © 2010, Pearson Education, Inc., Publishing as Longman

CHAPTER 14: EVALUATION AND ETHICAL ARGUMENTS

For Class Discussion Exercises

(pages 290-91)
Answers will vary.

(page 295)
Answers will vary, but here are possibilities:
1. For: Humans have eaten meat for millennia (precedent), and our status as a higher animal gives us the right to eat them (principles). We should eat what tastes good, and meat tastes good (principles). Diets that don't include meat are dangerous because they lack protein. Against: Eating meat is unethical because most of the meat comes from factory farms that use procedures that create undue stress on animals and don't allow them to roam freely (consequences). The procedures don't respect the animals and recognize their status as sentient beings (principles). In addition, meat production and distribution are two of the main factors that contribute to global climate change, so not eating meat will reduce carbon dioxide and methane levels (consequences).
2. For: Using a hybrid vehicle will reduce the amount of carbon dioxide in the atmosphere, which will in turn stop destroying God's creation (principles and consequences). Since consumers should be ethical, they should support products that are environmentally friendly (principles). Against: We shouldn't buy a hybrid car because it still uses gas, which creates pollution and global warming (principles). Instead, we should use electric cars and more sustainable forms of transportation (principles). Hybrid cars don't significantly reduce the amount of greenhouse gases, so using one is mostly a feel-good measure (consequences).
3. For: Terminally ill patients do enjoy a strong quality of life and cannot live naturally, so legally assisted suicide is ethical as long as the patient has agreed to it before he or she got into a terminally ill, vegetative state (principles and consequences). In addition, this form of suicide will lessen the burden from patients' families both psychologically and economically (principles and consequences). Against: God is the only entity who should take a person's life, and humans shouldn't intervene (principles). Because some terminally patients have recovered, legally assisted suicide denies that chance for change (consequences).
4. For: Selling organs is good because it helps other people who are sick or who are close to dying (consequences). If a person wants to sell his or her organs, that is fine because they are their bodies, and the state should not intervene to restrict what people do with their bodies (principles). Against: Selling organs is unethical because it creates a market for human life, and market-based principles should not frame the standards of human life (principles). The selling of organs could create a market that preys on poor people and people in developing countries (consequences).
5. For: Lotteries provide needed revenue for state governments to more fully fund education and other entities (consequences). People have the right to do what they want with their money, and lotteries and games of chances are simply outlets for that right (principles). Against: Lotteries are a counter-productive means of generating revenue since they simply take money away from parts of the economy that produce good-paying jobs (consequences). Many people could play lotteries instead of using that money toward essential needs (consequences). Lotteries are gambling, and gambling is sinful (principles).

Copyright © 2010, Pearson Education, Inc., Publishing as Longman

Critiquing Exercises for the Chapter's Readings

Critiquing "The 'News Team' from *The Daily Show*"

Answers will vary. The image parodies the typical presentation of its journalists—walking tough with serious looks on their faces, the head anchor out in front with a steel gaze looking forward. They all look professional and ready to take on the news in an aggressive manner.

Critiquing "Would Legalization of Gay Marriage Be Good for the Gay Community?" by Sam Isaacson

1. Audience: the gay community
2. Liberationist arguments: (1) Gay marriage would reinforce social values and pressures about monogamous marriage. (It is the only right way to live.); it would lead to greater marginalization of non-married people; and gays must be sensitive to the "tyranny of the majority" (paragraph 3); (2) Gay marriage would lead to the loss of a distinctive gay culture with its creative relationships and equality and communication.
Issacson's responses: (1) He agrees with the arguments but says that the potential benefits outweigh these losses. (2) He claims the "voice" of the gay community will not be lost. (3) This "voice" will not be heard unless mainstream society accepts gays (i.e. lets them get married 3.
Isaacson's criteria: (1) Marriage is good and (in some form) necessary for society. It is necessary for children because children need a stable environment; people are happiest in long-term relationships; everyone benefits from marriage. (2) The gay community needs to obtain equal rights with straight people: tax benefits, job benefits, inheritance rights, rights to make medical and funeral decisions. (3) Marriage is socially symbolic and the denial of marriage to gays says that gay love and relationships are not respected.
4. Persuasiveness of Isaacson's argument: (1) He combines his claim (marriage is good for everyone) with his counter-argument (the gay "voice" will not be lost). (2) His criteria are easily accepted. (3) He presents marriage as both commonplace and ideal.
Lack of persuasiveness: It lacks empirical or specific data.

Critiquing "A Woman's View of Hip-Hop" by Tiffany Anderson

1. Moving the discussion of hip-hop to the public arena and reasoned discussion: Tiffany succeeds at providing specific reasons why she does not like most male hip-hop and even some female hip-hop. By giving reasons and explanations, she moves readers beyond emotional and gut rejections of hip-hop and prods others to think about specific features they like about hip-hop. Audience: Tiffany's audience is people who dislike hip-hop, who don't know much about it, and who think all hip-hop is alike. These people could be middle-aged adults as well as college students, her peers.
2. Criteria for great female hip-hop artists: Tiffany offers three main criteria: these artists give female listeners a sense of self-empowerment and awareness of identity; they give a woman's perspective on issues; and they offer hopeful messages, unlike the negative ones of male rap, that help African-American females and all females. Answers will vary. These criteria seem reasonable and valuable for women. Other possible criteria: offer messages of female success and offer messages of social protest. Students may have their own ideas based on their knowledge of current music. Students might know of other female hip-hop artists that don't fit Tiffany's criteria.

Copyright © 2010, Pearson Education, Inc., Publishing as Longman

3. Other possible categories for female rappers: Students' answers will vary according to their knowledge of female hip-hop artists. Students might say that female rappers could be categorized according to their styles within hip-hop. They could be put in categories according to how much money they have made off their music, in categories based on fame or image (most outrageous and edgy to most tame), or in a category with other "hot" female musicians.
4. Addressing alternative views: The main alternative view that Tiffany addresses is that rap has to be negative because it is conveying important social and political messages about the social realities of urban and racial struggle. She acknowledges that rap often speaks of racial profiling, police brutality, guns and violence, poverty, self-hatred, lack of education, and cycles of drugs and despair. Some people would say that these realities must be proclaimed if any change is to come about and that artists need to sing about their harsh experiences. Tiffany acknowledges these realities and needs, but comments that this bleak music does nothing to help people break cycles of despair or help themselves to a stronger, healthier sense of self. 5. Effectiveness of the argument: Students' answers will vary. Most readers probably agree that this evaluation argument is well-focused, well-structured, and packed with lively, interesting evidence that supports the match part of the argument. Tiffany explains why her criteria are significant to her and offers persuasive explanations why this hip-hop music is beneficial to women as opposed to much male hip-hop that devalues women. The most memorable features of this argument are Tiffany's personal voice and investment and the quality and vividness of her examples. All these features contribute to this essay's success as an evaluation argument.

Critiquing "The Military's Raising the Enlistment Age" political cartoon

1. Claim and implied supporting argument: The background is that the Iraq War is going poorly, and the military is having a difficult time finding new recruits. The basic claim is that young men and women don't want to fight in Iraq for various reasons, and because of this the military is severely relaxing its standards for enlistment to make its recruiting and troop quotas. An implied argument could be that the military is more like a faceless corporation driven merely by profits than an entity whose purpose is to protect the American people. Like Wal-Mart, the cartoonist implies, the military will provide someone with a hellish and/or thankless job with poor pay and a dangerous safety net.
2. Features of the old soldier: The cartoonist uses the old soldier as a prop to catch the viewer's attention. The use of verbal humor (the well-worn corporate phrase of "Hi, welcome to Wal-Mart") and visual incongruity (a senior citizen soldier) implies that the military is not meeting its troop goals because of the war in Iraq. And perhaps the cartoon also questions the "real" motivation for going into Iraq.
3. Wal-Mart background info: Wal-Mart is notoriously known for caring most about the bottom-line by both its supporters and detractors, and the cartoon draws from the audience's probable knowledge that this corporation is typically depicted as being "heartless" and willing to hire senior citizens and young adults at very low wages, without "good" benefits.
4. Implied criteria for "good soldiers": The implied criteria for a good soldier is someone who is young, strong, and perhaps not just fighting because they have to for economic reasons.

Critiquing "Human Organs for Sale?" by David Holcberg

1. Princples and Consequences: Holcberg offers these principles from which he supports the sale of human organs: freedom to make choices about one's body (paragraphs 7 and 8), Americans' ideal of individualism and autonomy (7 and 10), the belief in the efficacy of the "free market"

Copyright © 2010, Pearson Education, Inc., Publishing as Longman

(10). And he provides support about consequences through these means: 6,000 dying every year (1), families reaping a financial windfall (3), the limited risks of donation (5), and the gift of life (10).

2. Addressing Opposing Views: Holcberg addresses a counterargument in paragraph seven by relating that people who oppose him claim that poor people "are incapable of making rational choices." This depiction of his opposition seems a bit extreme, bordering on Holcberg creating a strawman of sorts, bringing class issues into the debate when such assertions may not be at the heart of the argument. In that paragraph he quickly moves to the principle of "freedom" to sell an organ, an assumption that many would question. For example, there are many laws that are instituted to "protect people from themselves." Later on (9) he counters the oppositional view that people would murder others for their organs in a minimalist fashion. He needs greater support for asserting that such crimes would be "difficult-to-execute" in light that there are various "black markets" throughout the world. Finally, in the subsequent paragraph Holcberg grapples with the counterargument that only the rich can afford donated organs. He makes a sweeping claim that the poor in need of organs would still be able to "rely on charity" when organ donation is a "free market" set to acquire the highest price attainable and even more dependent on demand. How can "charity" even be a viable option in such a free market scenario? And how exactly would a free market "enhance" non-profit organizations' abilities to acquire organs? Holcberg offers no plausible causal reasoning for these assertions—he relies upon belief in the free market rather than providing "seeable examples" and realistic hypothetical examples.

3. Reflection of the Sponsoring Organization: Holcberg's argument exemplifies the belief in the free market and the individualistic inclinations of those who subscribe to Ayn Rand's philosophy. The argument's ethos could be seen as believing that people acting purely out of self-interest will make the world better and more equitable.

4. Pathos and Persuasiveness: The author employs word choices and emotional examples throughout that make the argument vivid, and he evokes beliefs that might be dear to many readers: raw numbers that relate the people who could be helped (1), a hypothetical example of father and child (6), "human beings (poor or rich) do have the capacity to reason, and should be free to exercise it" (7), a direct question pointed toward the reader (11), 87,000 Americans "spared hideous suffering and an early death" (13). Holcberg's use of scientific information from the Mayo Clinic and the *New England Journal of Medicine* lends validity to his argument, and those who believe in strong individualism and the free market might heartily support his argument. To some readers, however, his almost sophistic use of *pathos* and unfair treatment of oppositional views would make them pause. Assertions that imply that we don't have to make laws to protect people from themselves and that purchasing "an organ is part of your right to life" would seem logically and/or ethically inconsistent with others' frames of vision on the subject.

Anthology Arguments Related by Claim Type: Evaluation Claims

The following anthology arguments have prominent evaluation claims as either their main claims or as one of their lines of argument:

- John Seigenthaler, Sr., "A False Wikipedia 'Biography'" (436-37)
- Henry Jenkins, "Reality Bytes: Eight Myths about Video Games Debunked" (450-54)
- Malcolm Gladwell, "Brain Candy" (454-57)

Copyright © 2010, Pearson Education, Inc., Publishing as Longman

* William Lugo, "Violent Video Games Recruit American Youth" (460-65)
* William Powers, "The Massless Media" (467-72)
* Sydney H. Schanberg, "Not a Pretty Picture" (482-84)
* Nature Neuroscience, "Separating Science from Stereotype" (510-11)
* Deborah Blum, "Solving for X" (512-13)
* Steven Pinker, "The Science of Sex Difference: Sex Ed" (514-17)
* Ben A. Barres, "Does Gender Matter?" (517-25)
* Louis Caldera, "Military Service" (550-52)
* Robert Reich, "Don't Blame Wal-Mart" (566-68)
* Steve Maich, "Why Wal-Mart is Good" (568-74)
* John Tierney, "Shopping for a Nobel" (574-75)
* Andrew C. Revkin, "Carbon-Neutral Is Hip, but Is It Green?" (580-82)
* David Tilman and Jason Hill, "Fuel For Thought: All Biofuels Are Not Created Equal" (586-89)
* Iain Murray, "Time to Recycle Recycling?" (591-92)
* Jonathan Rauch, "Will Frankenfood Save the Planet?" (599-606)
* Miguel A. Altieri and Peter Rosset, "Ten Reasons Why Biotechnology Will Not Ensure Food Security, Protect the Environment, and Reduce Poverty in the Developing World" (608-15)
* Martin Luther King, Jr., "Letter from Birmingham Jail" (623-35)
* Stanley Milgram, "The Perils of Obedience" (648-58)

Copyright © 2010, Pearson Education, Inc., Publishing as Longman

CHAPTER 15: PROPOSAL ARGUMENTS

For Class Discussion Exercises

(page 320)
Answers will vary, but the following illustrative responses will be useful for generating discussion.

1.a. Marijuana should be legalized because marijuana is a natural, organic substance; because possessing marijuana is a victimless "crime"; because people who want to smoke marijuana are primarily law-abiding, responsible citizens (principle/definition); because legalizing marijuana will have these good consequences: increased tax revenues, decriminalization of many people's recreational activities, and the growth of a new profitable agricultural industry (cause/consequence); because prohibiting marijuana is as futile as was prohibiting alcohol; because drinking alcohol is legal and yet is demonstrably more harmful than smoking marijuana (resemblance).

1.b. Division I college athletes should receive salaries because they perform the same function for their schools as professional athletes do for their organizations; because they deserve just compensation for their talent, skills, and the degree of commitment that college athletics requires them to have to their sport (principle/definition); because receiving a salary might enable them to provide their families with the financial support that their absence from home otherwise deprives their families of; because receiving a salary as a college athlete might encourage more college athletes to stay in school and to graduate (cause/consequence); because paying college athletes for services rendered is like paying anyone else for a particular skill or expertise, or like paying any other entertainer (resemblance).

1.c. High schools should pass out free contraceptives because contraceptives are preventative medicine (reason from category); because these contraceptives will reduce the spread of STD's and AIDS and will decrease the illegitimate pregnancies and the number of teen abortions (cause/consequence); because providing contraceptives is a public health measure like the city providing free vaccinations for contagious diseases (resemblance).

1.d. Violent video games should be made illegal because they are a waste of time; because they are the products of irresponsible businesses (category/definition); because they addict children to graphic violence and gore; because they promote anti-social behavior; because they endanger emotionally imbalanced children (cause/consequence); because playing violent video games is like the training that the military does to prepare soldiers for combat and real killing; because playing violent video games is like needing stronger and stronger drugs in greater amounts to get the same emotional high (resemblance).

1e. Parents should be heavily taxed for having more than two children because having large families is selfish; because large families are unfair to the rest of society (category); because large families contribute to the overpopulation problem; because large families drain the world's resources; because parents only have time to do a good job of parenting two children and neglected children are burdens on society; because penalizing parents for having more than two children will encourage responsibility (cause/consequence); because the government's current policy of offering tax breaks for large families is like publicly rewarding greediness (resemblance).

2. Reverse the arguments. Answers will vary. Instructors can count this exercise successful if they sense that students are producing more lines of reasoning than they might otherwise

Copyright © 2010, Pearson Education, Inc., Publishing as Longman

produce. Students shouldn't worry whether a particular reason exactly fits one of the three slots. Stress that the purpose of this exercise is suggestive only; it prods writers to explore several different avenues into an argument. Here is one example:

> Marijuana should not be legalized because marijuana is more dangerous than many people realize; because the desire of some people to smoke marijuana doesn't outweigh society's general interest in preventing public acceptance of another dangerous drug (principle/definition); because legalizing marijuana would have these bad consequences: increased use of marijuana throughout the country, greater temptation to use even more dangerous drugs, glamorization of a drug-dependent way of life, increased health risks from the known dangers of marijuana (cause/consequence); because legalizing marijuana will set a precedent for legalizing cocaine and heroin (resemblance).

(pages 322-23)
Answers will vary. This exercise is extremely useful for helping students construct a practical proposal aimed at a specific audience of decision makers. It also helps students work out a justification for a solution that is tailored to this audience. Students will most likely have occasion to write a practical proposal during their careers. For that reason, proposal writing assignments often assume a reality for students and elicit a commitment from them that no other kind of writing assignment ever does. If students do indeed invest seriously in this assignment, they often produce arguments that demonstrate a remarkably clear conception of, and sensitive response to, the demands of a particular rhetorical situation. This exercise gives students a strong start toward achieving this rhetorical awareness and effectiveness in their proposal arguments. For this group exercise, students might want to write the outline of their proposal on overhead transparencies for presentation to the class.

Critiquing Exercises for the Chapter's Readings

Critiquing "A Proposal to Provide Tips for Hosts at Stone's End" Laurel Wilson

1. Summary of the problem, the solution, and the justification: Students' wording will vary. Wilson argues that hosts at Stone's End restaurant, who must wear dressy clothes and who make the first impression on customers, are underpaid for the amount and importance of the work they do and in comparison to the hourly wage plus tips that servers get. Her solution is that servers should give one percent of their tips to the host. Her justification is that hosts work very hard and often assume extra duties to help the servers; their job is very stressful and vital to the smooth running of the restaurant; they often work longer shifts than servers but make far less money; the manager and the servers at her restaurant thought that hosts should get more money; hosts at other comparable restaurants are better paid with a percentage of the servers' tips and even get a clothing allowance.

2. Addressing her audience: Wilson addresses the CEO of Stone's End restaurants because he has the power to change policies, and because this restaurant is part of a chain, policies would be uniform for the whole chain. The manager and servers at Wilson's restaurant may sympathize with hosts, but they cannot change the treatment of hosts. Audience-based reasons: Wilson's audience-based reasons focus on the good of the restaurant chain and its reputation, on maintaining customer satisfaction, and on maintaining a good work environment by having happy employees. All these reasons connect with the CEO's concern for the reputation and success of the restaurant. Response to objections: Laurel admits that the owners must have a

Copyright © 2010, Pearson Education, Inc., Publishing as Longman

reason behind their current policy, yet she argues that her reasons merit consideration and may outweigh the corporate reasons. She acknowledges that servers work very hard and deserve their tips and that hosts have a higher hourly wage and work longer shifts than servers. She answers this objection by offering figures to show that servers make a lot more money than hosts. Confronting these objections and answering them with evidence is an effective argumentative strategy.

3. Establishing a positive ethos: Wilson speaks calmly and matter-of-factly from her experience working as a host at this restaurant. The details of the hosts' job that she describes and her careful explanation of servers' and hosts' shifts and earnings show that she knows what she is talking about. Basically, she provides an "in the trenches" perspective that the owners probably have not thought through before. She comes across as a good employee that the restaurant must have been sorry to lose.

4. Effectiveness of the proposal: Wilson constructs a logical, well-organized case and provides enough evidence to make her proposed change sound reasonable, doable, and appealing.

Critiquing "Why the United States Should Adopt Nuclear Power" by Juan Vazquez

1. Vazquez's major reasons are that nuclear energy is substantially cleaner that coal-fired plants, it would offer a great deal of power for the electrical grid once plants are established, nuclear power is safer than it used to be, it offers a larger "wedge" for addressing reduction of carbon dioxide and providing substantial power, and other countries have used the technology successfully.

2. Some objections that the author fails to address as much as he could have are the life span of radioactive waste, where more waste will be stored in the future, safety issues with transporting the waste, other experts who argue that nuclear energy is still not a good option, other views that alternative energy can provide much more power than he suggests, people who argue that efficiency and conservation is the first step to take, and finally the contingency that a cap and trade system might not be implemented.

3. Vazquez does a fine job of summarizing opponent's viewpoints, but one could argue that he doesn't address the safety issue in as much detail as he could have. Also, he relies heavily on an article by Sweet in *Discover* magazine, which is a specialized magazine about Science, but not a peer-reviewed academic journal. The experts he uses side with him, so it would have helped to hear other experts with different viewpoints. In addition, he doesn't address how long it takes to build a nuclear plant especially in light of his argument that nuclear power "produces the quickest, surest, and most dramatic reduction of the world's footprint."

4. Vazquez does a good job of opening his argument with a dire call for action on climate change, which is a value and argument that many of those who dislike nuclear energy would agree with. He connects to the reader in that way, and he establishes his *ethos* by thoughtfully summarizing counter-arguments and then responding to them. He also concedes that nuclear is not the only option too, which might please a reader who isn't pro-nuclear energy. The *pathos* of the argument comes through in the opening paragraph and when he discusses the negative consequences of using coal-fired energy. As for *logos*, Vazquez makes solid points throughout, but more development on France and Sweden might have helped. His use of Pacala and Socolow's study on energy wedges provides a strong point of comparison to show how nuclear energy can address American needs.

Copyright © 2010, Pearson Education, Inc., Publishing as Longman

Critiquing the "Advocacy Ad from the Center for Children's Health and the Environment"

1a. Problem addressed by this proposal: Currently, parts of the chemical industry (not related to medicine) are bypassing the regulatory system for pre-market testing of products, chemicals linked to health problems are being allowed in household and outdoor products, and toxic chemicals are present in America's air, water, and food. The ad argues that citizens need to hold elected officials and the chemical companies accountable for their inaction or actions. 1b. Giving presence to the problem: This ad begins with a carefully phrased statement ("appear linked to rising rates…") of the problem and relation of shocking trend: more and more children are being diagnosed with cancer, a disease normally associated with adults.

2. Strategies of visual argument: The boldface statement and one word question in display type at the top of this ad immediately grab the reader's attention. That statement—"More kids are getting brain cancer"—and the big one-word question "Why?" give presence to the problem and sound an alarm. The photograph at the top right-hand corner shows a nurse or family member embracing a newborn. The emotional clutch of the woman creates emotional, primal stirrings in the audience, and the newborn looks both healthy yet vulnerable. The text below the photographic image juxtaposes this image of endearment and protection with the simple declarative statement of "More kids are getting brain cancer." The word choice of "brain cancer" connects to the bald head of the newborn by providing a stark and shocking visual/textual connection. Because this ad needs to transmit a complex argument and a substantial amount of information for a one-page ad, it counts on its headline and photograph to disturb and engage readers so that they will hopefully read all of the copy. Headings in boldface type help to organize the argument so that it progresses from an introduction about the horrible problem to "What We Know" and then finally to a call to action in "What We Can Do."

3. Effectiveness of the verbal argument of this ad: The heading in boldface that presents the main claim of the ad ("Toxic chemicals appear linked to rates of some cancers") sets up the argument that the ad makes in the first column of text. The copy of the ad provides concise support for why kids are more susceptible than adults to the effects of toxic chemicals in the environment and offers specifics about the dangerous aspects of being a farmer or a child regularly exposed to garden and home pesticides. 4. Proposed solution: In the third column, the ad instructs parents on what to avoid exposing their children to and directs them to the organization's Web site for more information. In the final paragraph, the ad calls for public action against toxic chemicals and in favor of a better system of regulation for testing products.

5. Overall effectiveness of this advocacy ad: Answers will vary. This ad is highly successful at grabbing readers' attention, disturbing them through the image of newborn, and providing concise details about how exposure to toxic chemicals has been linked to cancer. The second paragraph does a solid job of introducing products that may be at fault, and it then follows up on that general statement in "What We Know" by describing the products that are likely culprits (paints, pesticides, hair dyes, air/water pollution, food, herbicides, and cigarettes). Unfortunately, readers might be left with some questions: What companies are the culprits? How can we phase out these toxic chemicals? How can we institute a better regulatory system? How exactly can we create change? Will our leaders actually do anything?

Copyright © 2010, Pearson Education, Inc., Publishing as Longman

Critiquing "Gone Parkin'" by Donald Shoup

1. Shoup argues that curb parking is too low, and as a consequence people cruising for spots create congestion and pollution.

2. His proposal is to enact performance-based prices for curbside parking. He's arguing that price will affect demand for these spaces.

3. Shoup relates the amount of gas wasted and the amount of greenhouse gases emitted in just one 15-block district in LA as an example of how large of a problem this is. Additionally he connects with the reader in regard to their frustration with congestion. He uses a resemblance claim that offers that parking is like rent-controlled apartments and offers causal claims about how adjusting for a 85 percent occupancy rate will reduce congestion. The specific example to support his position is Redwood City, which did what he proposed and generated a million dollars in revenue.

4. Answers will vary, but asking this question will reveal the principle of supply and demand. Would a higher price for curbside parking make citizens park more in parking garages?

5. Answers will vary. But one could argue that drivers need to have other options than just curbside parking. It's also not clear how adjusting for time of the day will create change. Crucial to his proposal is that there are other options than just curbside parking. It's also not clear exactly how this proposal will reduce congestion. He relates later in the argument that Redwood City generated substantial revenue, but there's no mention about the reduction of congestion.

6. For *logos*, refer to answers in 3 and 5, but some readers might mention that his proposal rest mostly on conjecture and is based on one example of where is seems to have worked. Skeptical readers would probably want more examples to be thoroughly persuaded. In regard to *ethos*, Shoup has a conversational but objective sounding tone in the article. He establishes commonality with the audience by relating that many people hate congestion. He appeals to emotions, values, and assumptions early on too through the relation of facts about how much gas is wasted and how much carbon dioxide is emitted in one large district in LA. His humorous use of a quotation from the character George Constanza also would probably connect with the audience in that Americans are well known for wanting goods or services that are cheap or free. His proposal effectively goes against the cheapskate mindset.

Critiquing "When Your Right to an Abortion…" by Planned Parenthood

Answers will vary. But in general the policy proposal of this ad is that citizens should support and fight for reproductive choice or the "pro-choice" position because the consequences of not doing so would create a host of problems that America has encountered in the past. The consequence, of course, is the spectre of coat-hanger abortions. The coat-hanger/question mark appeal provides a succinct reason for supporting a woman's right to an abortion while also playing on the emotions of the audience. The visual image of the coat-hanger is shocking and simple. For its audience (in liberal leaning magazines), the ad does a fine job because it appeals to their assumptions and beliefs effectively—choice, dire consequences. Opponents of the ad, however, might point out that Planned Parenthood is using a scare tactic and that the probability of people going to back-alley or coat-hanger abortions is very slim.

Copyright © 2010, Pearson Education, Inc., Publishing as Longman

Anthology Arguments Related by Claim Type: Proposal Claims

The following arguments develop proposal claims:

- Bronwyn T. Williams, "'Tomorrow Will Not Be Like Today': Literacy and Identity in a World of Multiliteracies" (429-34)
- Dana L. Fleming, "Youthful Indiscretions: Should Colleges Protect Social Network Users from Themselves and Others?" (440-43)
- Daryl Cagle, "Those Terrible Virginia Tech Cartoons" (480-82)
- Francisco X. Gaytan, Avary Carhill, and Carola Suarez-Orozco, "Understanding and Responding to the Need of Newcomer Immigrant Youth and Families" (486-93)
- Ben A. Barres, "Does Gender Matter?" (517-25)
- Donald Rumsfeld, "New Model Army" (528-30)
- Phillip Carter and Paul Gastris, "The Case for the Draft" (530-40)
- Selective Service System, "How the Draft Has Changed" (541)
- Lawrence J. Korb and Sean E. Duggan, "An All-Volunteer Army? Recruitment and Its Problems" (540-49)
- Louis Caldera, "Military Service" (550-52)
- Gwyneth Cravens, "Better Energy" (582-84)
- Charles Krauthammer, "Save the Planet, Let Someone Else Drill" (584-85)
- David Tilman and Jason Hill, "Fuel For Thought: All Biofuels Are Not Created Equal" (586-89)
- Al Gore, "Nobel Lecture" (592-97)
- Jonathan Rauch, "Will Frankenfood Save the Planet?" (599-606)
- Gregory A. Jaffe, "Lessen the Fear of Genetically Engineered Crops" (615-16)
- Sustainusa.org, "What Is the FDA Trying to Feed Us?" (618)
- Gerald D. Coleman, "Is Genetic Engineering the Answer to Hunger?" (619-21)
- Martin Luther King, Jr., "Letter from Birmingham Jail" (623-35)
- Garret Hardin, "Lifeboat Ethics: The Case Against Aid that Does Harm" (635-42)
- Rachel Carson, "The Obligation to Endure" (644-48)

Copyright © 2010, Pearson Education, Inc., Publishing as Longman

Handout: USING THE "STOCK ISSUE" STRATEGY TO DEVELOP A PROPOSAL ARGUMENT

1. Stock issue 1: Is there really a problem here that needs to be solved?

2. Stock issue 2: Will the proposed solution really solve this problem?

3. Stock issue 3: Can the problem be solved more simply without disturbing the status quo?

4. Stock issue 4: Is the proposed solution really practical? Does it stand a chance of actually being enacted?

5. Stock issue 5: What will be the unforeseen positive and negative consequences of the proposal?

Copyright © 2010, Pearson Education, Inc., Publishing as Longman

Handout: USING THE CLAIM-TYPE STRATEGY TO DEVELOP A PROPOSAL ARGUMENT

1. Argument from category: This proposal should (should not) be enacted because the proposed action is____.

[Fill the blank with a noun, adjective, or phrase that appeals in some way to your audience's values. Your purpose is to show that your proposed action fits into a category or fulfills a principle that your audience adheres to.]

2. Argument from consequence: This proposal should (should not) be enacted because this proposed action will lead to the following good (or bad) consequences:

- ____
- ____
- ____
- ____

(List as many good or bad consequences as you can think of.)

3. Argument from resemblance: This proposal should (should not) be enacted because the proposed action is like (similar to)

____

[Fill the blank with an analogy or precedent that will have a favorable (or unfavorable) impact on your audience. Your purpose is to transfer your audience's favorable (or unfavorable) attitude to the precedent or analogy back to your proposed action.]

Copyright © 2010, Pearson Education, Inc., Publishing as Longman

CHAPTER 16: FINDING AND EVALUATING SOURCES

For Class Discussion Exercises

(page 351)
Answers will vary. For another version of this assignment, ask students to bring two very different kinds of sources with information on the same issue or topic to class. For instance, students might bring an issue of *Sports Illustrated* and an academic sociology journal that both contain articles on the psychological challenges of playing professional sports. Or students might bring a trade book and a scholarly book on extreme sports. Students might bring a medical journal and a popular niche magazine with articles on the dangers of fad diets. In groups, students could examine these materials (covers, Tables of Contents, advertising, layout and appearance of articles, use of photographs, documentation) and make a list of the most salient differences.

(pages 355-56)
1.The results list for a search using a licensed database such as EBSCOHost provides more information about sources and much clearer information than the "hits" list for keywords on the Web. Licensed databases give the title of articles, and these usually give researchers a good lead on the focus of the articles and the quality of the information. The dates of publication are clear; the length of articles is clear; most researchers readily recognize a number of the publications (for example, *Time*, the *New York Times*, *Christian Science Monitor*). In many cases, the complete article is available on the database so researchers can read or print out the article immediately. If the full text of the article isn't available, the results list indicates if that particular library takes the publication. In contrast, the "hits" for keyword searches on the Web yield information that is much more vague, haphazard in its relevance and quality, and inclusive. The Yahoo! "hits" list includes some newspaper and associated press sites, some advocacy sites, and some sites that list too little information to be clear. Often researchers have to check out sites and follow the links to determine if the information has any value for a particular project. The challenge of searches on the Web is to wade through the huge amount of extra information and material that is not the caliber that you need. The other problem of Web site "hits" lists is that the information about the sites is not regularized. Consequently, searching for information on the Web can be very time consuming.
2. Orca Network, from its name and its use of the word choice "Blast" in the article's title, appears to be an advocacy group with a strong environmentalist and animal protectionist bias.
3. Answers will vary, but many students will probably say that *Science Now* simply sounds like a general magazine about science. Many may not know or be able to see the left-leaning bias of *Mother Jones* from the title of an article, but having students actually look at a magazines table of contents in a single issue or statement of purpose could show how to get a grasp of certain magazine's angle of vision. A "scavenger hunt" activity looking for bias in magazines or articles might be an appropriate activity to have students delve into angle of vision and degree of advocacy by looking at specific magazines.

Copyright © 2010, Pearson Education, Inc., Publishing as Longman

CHAPTER 17: USING, CITING, AND DOCUMENTING SOURCES

For Class Discussion Exercises

(page 370)

1. Writer 1 incorporates a few ideas from the source that are related to his/her main issue, which is arguing for a new way to treat alcoholism. This writer is broadening and deepening the central argument by mentioning what studies about vegetarianism contribute to the discussion. Writer 2 is using the studies about vegetarianism as a main source to argue in favor of vegetarianism and thus uses more ideas from the article and emphasizes the many health benefits of vegetarianism. Writer 3 is challenging vegetarianism and therefore has chosen to emphasize the uncertainties in the article, the weaker correlations, and the possibility of alternative explanations.
2. Answers will vary. All three writers are using the article fairly and accurately. None falsifies or slants the information or takes it out of context. They differ in which ideas are incorporated and highlighted and how much they focus on the article.
3. <u>Summary of the article</u>: This article posted on the Web site of the American Council on Science and Health states that while vegetarianism is widely believed to promote good health, how it affects health is more complex than people think. The Council suggests that some vegetarians are healthy for non-dietary reasons such as not smoking, exercising regularly, controlling weight, and being generally health conscious. In addition, vegetarians tend to be more wealthy than non-vegetarians and therefore have good living conditions and consistent medical care. The American Council on Science and Health does claim that studies have shown there are some quite definite health benefits of vegetarianism, such as lower risk of alcoholism, obesity, constipation, and lung cancer. In addition, vegetarianism likely lowers the risk of adult-onset diabetes mellitus, coronary artery disease, hypertension, and gallstones. These studies yield only weak evidence that vegetarianism lowers the risk of various kinds of cancers, osteoporosis, and other health problems. Basically, the Council wants to convey that "Diet is but one of many risk factors for most chronic diseases" (385). <u>Explanation of summary</u>: This summary aims to cover the entire article, to follow the order of its ideas, and to do justice to its purpose and tone. Readers encountering this distillation of the article would have a good idea of its content.

(page 375)

Answers will vary. Students should be able to see that the purpose of Writer 3 is to create an original argument. Ideas from the article are incorporated into this argument to serve Writer 3's purpose–to challenge vegetarianism's direct health benefits. Writer 3 has also written in his own voice. Writer 4, however, has written a fairly long passage that does not seem to be supporting an independent argument or any point in it. Instead this paper borrows a huge hunk of the original article, uses many of its words and phrases exactly without using quotation marks, and follows the article's progression of ideas. Writer 4 does not write in his own voice. He is simply copying, which is stealing, and has failed to create his own argument and thus has failed to do the assignment.

Copyright © 2010, Pearson Education, Inc., Publishing as Longman

APPENDIX 1: INFORMAL FALLACIES

For Class Discussion Exercises

(page 408)
1. False Dilemma/Either-Or. There may be other choices that the arguer doesn't consider, and this statement tries to make the audience choose between two stark options without considering the other ways to decrease criminal activity. This also smacks a bit of being a Non Sequitir too because the arguer links marijuana use with lawbreaking; there's a large gap in the chain of reasoning. 2. Confusing Correlation for Cause/Post Hoc, Ergo Propter Hoc. Although this statement seems very plausible, the arguer must provide persuasive support for the assertion. The arguer must show exactly how smoking is linked to lung cancer through substantial proof. 3. Hasty Generalization. The arguer makes a sweeping generalization from one single bit of evidence. There is insufficient support. 4. Circular argument. Here the reason is merely a restatement of the claim in different language. 5. Hasty Generalization. Although this statement appeals to a commonly held belief in American society, the assertion is based from insufficient support—the observation of two renters in a single neighborhood. 6. Appeal to False Authority and Hasty Generalization. This statement is an interesting hybrid of both a fallacy of ethos and logos. With "false authority," the statement could be seriously questioned because "hundreds of scientists" is a vague word choice. How reputable are the "hundreds" of scientists (pars pro toto) among the thousands upon thousands of scientists who do not recognize Intelligent Design as a theory based in conventional science? 7. Slippery Slope. This statement stirs fear within certain audiences by making a claim that implies a convoluted chain of events: a) mandatory *registration* of *handguns* > b > c > d > e > f > g) "confiscation of hunting rifles." 8. Strawman. The arguer simplifies gun control advocates' views to an extreme and unfair position. 9. Bandwagon appeal. The fact that other nations have adopted socialized medicine does not mean that it is the best form of health care or that it is appropriate for the US. This could also be a faulty analogy in that conditions that make socialized medicine work in other countries might not exist in the United States. (On the other hand, this could also be a very persuasive analogy, suggesting how hard it is to tell when a good argument slips into a fallacious one.) 10. Appeal to the Person/Ad Hominem. The author of this assertion calls into question Dr. Smith's credibility because of his profession. The writer assumes that Dr. Smith is naturally prejudiced toward federally funded health care and links doctors in general with wanting to preserve the status quo of the health care system. Although this statement could be fallacious, the arguer may have a persuasive point because doctors may lose income if universal health care is instituted and may be prejudiced toward such a system.

Copyright © 2010, Pearson Education, Inc., Publishing as Longman

APPENDIX 2: SMALL GROUP STRATEGIES FOR PRACTING ARGUMENT SKILLS

For Class Discussion Exercises

(pages 414-15)
A Several Days' Group Project: Defining "Good Argumentative Writing." This group task is explained in detail in the text. Instructors might like to know, however, what instructors in our own programs have said about the four essays. Our evaluations, of course, should not be regarded as "correct answers."

"Bloody Ice"

This essay inevitably falls into the "B" range in many staff norming sessions. Most instructors praise it for its vivid opening and its relatively clear sense of structure, as well as for its transitions between paragraphs. People tend to fault it for the awkwardness of its language (e.g. "a tradition for survival" is a phrase that makes little sense), the abruptness of its transitions between sentences, and its logic. It is unclear just how the quotas set by the US Seal Protection Act add up. Moreover, the writer suggests that "the seals are being killed off at an almost greater rate than they can remultiply," which would seem to be a level of zero population growth, not diminishment. (The confusion apparently hinges on the fact that the other factors mentioned combined with the seal killing result in declining populations.) Moreover, the student's second reason for opposing seal killing–that it's "inhumane"–needs considerable development by way of a definitional argument. Why is kicking a seal in the head less humane than clubbing? Moreover, the student's concluding proposal appears to skirt much of the ethical issue raised in the opening. Would a vivid description of domestic seal "harvesting" be any less repugnant to us?

"RSS Should Not Provide Dorm Room Carpets"

In its present state, this essay gets a "C" or "C-" from teachers in our programs, but its potential is much higher. The student writer herself was pleased with this draft because, as she reported, "it changed the minds of students in my group." The loss of opportunity to paint and decorate one's own room, the increased possibility of damage from spills, and the likelihood of higher room fees and forfeited damage deposits proved to be effective audience-based reasons opposing the installation of university-provided carpets.

But the draft is confusingly organized and underdeveloped. The end of the first paragraph predicts three parallel reasons (but note that the lack of parallel structure in the last three sentences of the introduction confuses the writer's intention). The body of the essay, however, maps two reasons (reason three, as predicted in the introduction, gets collapsed into reason two). Most readers get confused in the transition from Tricia's blueberry pie to the carpet issue and get more confused when Tricia returns in paragraph two. Paragraph two is especially confusing because it opens by summarizing and refuting opposing views when the mapping and transitions led the reader to anticipate development of the first reason. Despite the length of the paragraph, the writer provides few grounds to support the reason "many students don't want carpets." Similarly, reason two could be strengthened with more financial data. Readers aren't quite sure

Copyright © 2010, Pearson Education, Inc., Publishing as Longman

how to interpret $300 per room. How many total rooms would be carpeted? What is the total figure for carpeting? How large a figure is that comparatively, in terms of the total budget for maintenance or capital improvement? Where would that money come from? Would student room rates really skyrocket? In short, by clarifying the organization of the essay and by providing more factual grounds, this writer could improve the argument dramatically.

"The Sterling Hall Dorm Food"

Most composition teachers have encountered a few "bad dorm food" snoozers, but this one seems worse than usual. We give it an "F." The dominant problem is that the writer has invented his grounds–the hypothetical case of Johnny, who pays too much for lousy food and finds a hair in his burrito to boot. An attack on dorm food, we tell students, is serious business. Managers and cooks and food buyers make their living running cafeterias and stand to lose their livelihoods if the charges against them are well grounded. We remind students that it is dishonest to make up data. Additionally, the essay is organized chronologically rather than hierarchically. Instead of reasons supported by evidence, we get the narrative of Johnny as he progresses through the cafeteria. Nor are the narrative details consistent. Sometimes Johnny is a struggling poor student trying to make ends meet, yet he still has a Giorgio wallet. The writer needs to start over.

"ROTC Courses Should Not Get College Credit"

Students almost always cite this essay as the best of the group. So do we. We give it an "A" as an example of good first-year college writing. The writer's three reasons are clearly stated and differentiated from each other: (1) ROTC courses do not stress inquiry and true questioning. (2) ROTC courses are not academically strenuous and thus inflate the GPA's of ROTC students. (3) ROTC classes keep students from taking more valuable liberal arts courses. One of the strengths of this essay—one certainly worth pointing out to students—is the way it emphasizes both grounds and warrants. Note, for example, the copious grounds provided for reason number one—the need of officers to follow orders, the difference between ROTC and other courses in frequency of in-class debates, the testimony of the writer's uncle from Vietnam days, and the similarity of the uncle's experience with the writer's own during the Kuwait crisis. But as he cites these grounds, he simultaneously focuses the reader's attention on the warrant—the value of critical thinking and open questioning as emphasized in his other courses. Another strength of this essay is its proposal conclusion. Rather than arguing for the abolition of ROTC—the writer clearly values being a cadet–the writer proposes that ROTC training be considered an extra-curricular activity like athletics.

Supporters of ROTC as an academic field might raise numerous objections to this paper. At the level of grounds, they might claim that ROTC provides more room for intellectual debate than the writer acknowledges or that the writer doesn't provide hard data on grade distribution in ROTC courses. Similarly, they might object to some of his examples as biased and unrepresentative. Or they might question the writer's warrants: Should ROTC be an inquiry and debate course–like literature or political science, say–or is it more like a science and engineering course, where, presumably, great policy debates are also infrequent? There is plenty to praise here, but clearly only one side of the issue is represented.

Copyright © 2010, Pearson Education, Inc., Publishing as Longman

"Legalization of Prostitution?"

This is a tricky one. Our students tend to like this essay. Sometimes, in fact, they rate it second behind the ROTC argument. Most instructors rate it low, although occasionally some will give it high marks. Clearly there are strengths in this essay intermixed with glaring weaknesses. The authors of this text give it a "D." The overriding weakness we find in the paper is the writer's lack of control over organization, leading to a circular repetition of generalizations and an almost total absence of grounds. The second paragraph ends with a clear enough claim, accompanied by four parallel ***because*** clauses as reasons. This claim, however, doesn't emerge coherently from an introduction that raises the issue question and sets the parameters of the debate. She could begin, for example, with a review of the controversy over legalization of prostitution or, alternatively, with an exposition of the problem that she proposes to solve. But it is not clear that she is doing either of these. When the writer states (in paragraph 2) that "crime rates are soaring, diseases are spreading wildly, and the environment on the streets is rapidly decaying," it is not clear whether she is talking about crime and disease among prostitutes, among the people who associate with prostitutes, or among the population in general. Nor is it clear what she means by "environment." The reader isn't quite sure whether the writer is concerned with the plight of prostitutes or the plight of society.

The organization of the paper is confusing because the writer sets up expectations that aren't met. The body of the paper seems to follow the chronological order of objections made by opponents rather than the order predicted in the thesis. The thesis predicts the following order: legalization of prostitution would (1) reduce the wave of epidemics, (2) decrease high crime rates, (3) provide revenue, and (4) get the girls off the streets where sexual crimes often occur (although it isn't clear how the last reason differs from the second reason). The actual order of paragraphs is quite different: (1) reduction of epidemics; (2) increase of business revenues; and (3) discussion of the morality of the issue. In none of these paragraphs, however, does the writer bring data to bear on a reason–e.g., data about epidemics, facts and figures about prostitution as a business, and so forth. This writing suggests a lack of research and/or problems in seeing how to use data.

Part of the writer's problem seems to be a kind of psychological preoccupation with her readers' moral objections. She imagines her reader saying, "But if you legalize prostitution aren't you saying that it is morally OK?" To which she replies: "It exists; it is the oldest profession; it is a reality; if we say it is the root of all evil, it still won't go away; who's to say whether it is right or wrong?" and so forth. She needs to consolidate her discussion of the moral issue into one section–perhaps the introduction or conclusion–and use the rest of the space to develop her cost/benefit analysis with research data. The plan presented in her thesis and 'because' clauses seems workable. For a rewrite, she might be encouraged to stick to that plan, fleshing out each section with grounds.

Copyright © 2010, Pearson Education, Inc., Publishing as Longman

VII. SAMPLES OF STUDENT WRITING FOR DISCUSSION

In this section, we provide examples of students' writing produced in response to the assignments in *Writing Arguments*, 6th edition. The handouts in the following pages show this student writing and offer questions to guide group or class discussion of these student pieces.

DISCUSSION EXERCISE EXAMINING AN ESSAY THAT ANALYZES SOURCES OF DISAGREEMENT

In the following two-page handout, we present an analysis by student writer Adrian Walther, written for the Writing Assignments for Chapters 1–3, Option 2, page 70. Adrian's class read and discussed the readings in the anthology unit "The United States as Superpower" from the **6th ed.** of *Writing Arguments*, and students chose a pair of readings to analyze closely for disagreements in facts, interpretations of facts, assumptions, and values.

Adrian's analysis could be used in class when students are reading Chapters 2 and 3 in *Writing Arguments*. Even if students have not read the two articles that Adrian analyzes, the discussion questions here can help them examine how Adrian has focused, structured, and developed his analysis of these articles.

Copyright © 2010, Pearson Education, Inc., Publishing as Longman

Handout: FOR CLASS DISCUSSION: EXAMINING AN ANALYSIS OF DISAGREEMENT

In the following analysis, student writer Adrian Walter explores points of disagreement in two articles on United States foreign policy. These questions can guide your examination of Adrian's analysis:

1. How has Adrian structured his analysis? What main points does he emphasize?
2. In your own words, briefly state the focus of each paragraph of this analysis.
3. How does Adrian's analysis demonstrate reading strategies for arguers such as believing and doubting and using disagreement to lead to further investigation?

An Analysis of the Sources of Disagreement between Jeff Guntzel and Mona Charen

Adrian Walther (student)

Two articles that represent divergent views on President Bush's post 9/11 foreign policy are Jeff Guntzel's Web site advocacy piece, "Briefing #2: Preemptive Strikes and International Law" and Mona Charen's op-ed piece, "The Moral Authority of the UN." Guntzel and Charen disagree on most of the facts concerning the functioning of the United Nations. These writers' political perspectives and values also lead them to argue for different approaches to the United Nations and to the United States' superpower status.

Although Guntzel and Charen agree on the facts about the UN's purpose, they disagree about how well the UN has achieved that purpose. They both believe the UN's primary purpose is to promote and seek to maintain peace. Jeff Guntzel asserts that the United Nations exists "to help in the settlement of international disputes by peaceful means" (790). Mona Charen, too, states that the UN "embodies the hope that the nations of the world can cooperate to eliminate scourges. . .and settle their differences over polished conference tables rather than with machetes and M16s" (792). However, she believes that this peacekeeping role has always been unfeasible. Guntzel and Charen really differ over their view of the historical effectiveness of the UN. While Guntzel praises the UN and its role as an international peacekeeping organization, Charen says the UN's "record on peace and reconciliation is abysmal" (792). She cites examples of the Egypt-Israel crisis in 1967 and the Croatian-Serbian crisis in 1991 when she claims the UN troops failed at peacekeeping.

Guntzel's and Charen's interpretation of the facts of the UN's record influences their views of the level of respect, if any, the US should give the UN. In "Briefing #2," Guntzel quotes political analysts and praises the body of international law developed by the UN. He states that the UN is an institution that has proven worthy of respect and that countries of the world, especially the US with its superpower status, should follow the international law established by the UN Charter as the best path to a stable and peaceful world. Questioning the UN's moral authority, Charen argues that the US does not need to adhere to the UN's international laws. She claims that the UN's membership is full of "corruption, bias, indolence and waste" (792). Charen wonders why American presidents ever feel the need to seek out approval of their foreign policy from such a corrupt institution.

Copyright © 2010, Pearson Education, Inc., Publishing as Longman

Handout (continued)

Guntzel and Charen also have different political priorities, underlying values, and assumptions about international relations among countries, influencing their view of the UN and leading them to recommend different policies for the US. Guntzel is affiliated with Voices in the Wilderness, an anti-war advocacy organization, and the Iraq Peace Team, a humanitarian organization concerned about economic suffering in Iraq after the 1990s Gulf War. Believing that the best way to solve conflicts between countries is through peaceful means, Guntzel finds flaws in President Bush's new preemptive strike plan, specifically in regard to Iraq. He argues that this plan directly violates the UN Charter's prohibition of aggressive, as opposed to defensive, military efforts. Guntzel warns that if the US ". . . does not recognize the UN Charter and international law as the foundation of global society, how can we expect others to do so?" (791). He cautions that by continuing to pursue our bent toward a unilateral course and elevating our superpower status, we're increasing hostility towards the US throughout the world, cutting ourselves off from our country's allies, and jeopardizing our future national security.

In contrast, Charen's op-ed piece advocates that we abandon the UN and the methods it uses to pursue peace. A well-known conservative journalist writing for the *Jewish World Review*, Charen's pro-Israel views and her commitment to self-defense fuel her harsh criticism of the UN. She believes that because of the power of our country, the US doesn't need permission from any organization to pursue its goals. She concludes by stating that the US should use its power to the full extent because "[p]eace is maintained today as it always was, by armed force and balance of power" (793). She believes that we should take advantage of our supreme economic and military might and use those assets to maintain peace.

Both of these brief arguments leave many of their assertions unsupported, and both raise questions that they don't answer. Charen's pessimistic claim that "the world does not and probably never will run on cooperation, peaceful dispute resolution, and friendship" (793) makes readers wonder how abandoning peaceful means and promoting the US's continuous drive to be the biggest, toughest nation in the world will further world peace? Guntzel's blend of optimism and respect for the global community could be a useful tack for the Pentagon, yet he doesn't answer the Charen's criticisms of the UN or explain how the UN can become a more effective player in promoting world peace.

Works Cited

Charen, Mona. "The Moral Authority of the UN." *Jewish World Review* 20 Sept. 2002. Rpt. in *Writing Arguments: A Rhetoric with Readings*. John D. Ramage, John C. Bean, and June Johnson. 6th edition. New York: Longman, 2004. 791-93. Print.

Guntzel, Jeff. "IPT Briefing #2: Preemptive Strikes and International Law." *Iraq Peace Team.* Voices in the Wilderness, 27 August 2002. Rpt. In *Writing Arguments: A Rhetoric with Readings.* John D. Ramage, John C. Bean, and June Johnson. 6th edition. New York: Longman, 2004. 790-91. Print.

Copyright © 2010, Pearson Education, Inc., Publishing as Longman

DISCUSSION EXERCISE EXAMINING STUDENTS' INTRODUCTIONS FOR APPEALS TO *ETHOS* AND *PATHOS*

The student writing in the exercise in the following two-page handout is connected to Chapter 7, particularly the For Class Discussion exercise in *Writing Arguments* on pages 135–36. Here, we show examples of the introductions to three students' proposal arguments directed at parents and older teens. These students are working on setting up their claims as responses to problematic issues, on creating effective appeals to *ethos* and *pathos*, and on giving presence to their arguments.

Copyright © 2010, Pearson Education, Inc., Publishing as Longman

Handout: FOR CLASS DISCUSSION: INTRODUCTIONS CREATING PRESENCE WITH APPEALS TO ETHOS *AND* PATHOS

In their introductions to their proposal arguments, shown in this exercise, the student writers try to establish their claims as answers to problematic, significant issue questions, to connect with their audiences, and to give presence to their arguments. Their arguments are directed toward parents of pre-teens and teens and toward older teens who have younger siblings. After reading these introductions by Michael Quiroz, Darby Moeller, and Patty Gillispie, use the following questions to guide group or class discussion of them.

1. What is the claim of each writer's argument? How has the writer made the issue seem problematic and significant?
2. What strategies (concrete language, specific examples, narratives, metaphors, analogies, and connotative words) do these writers use to give their arguments presence? How do they appeal to *pathos*?
3. How do these writers try to establish an effective *ethos* in these opening paragraphs of their arguments?
4. Which features of each introduction would work well for the intended audience? Which features do you find effective?

Photo-Realistic Graphics—Too Real for Comfort

Michael Quiroz (student)

As the camera slowly pulls around the armed cop, you can see the sweat on his forehead, and each strand of hair is clearly visible. His eyes squint as he sees a group of armed men approaching and pointing their weapons at him. The camera cuts to the cop, showing the smirk on his face. A hail of gun fire begins to fill the warehouse. The cop dodges behind some crates. He pulls out two handguns, his weapon of choice, and blazes away. As the bullets hit the men, their arms flail in the air while blood squirts out of the wounds. The cop runs out of ammo with one enemy left. He chases down the culprit and grabs him from behind. The camera is now focused on the two men's faces. The once-confident criminal is sweating profusely and breathing heavily. As the cop snaps the criminal's neck, the body drops, and the camera pulls out to show the viewer the destruction left in the cop's path. Bodies are strewn on the floor; pieces of broken crates lie everywhere, on the ground, in pools of blood, and on top of bodies. As the camera pulls out farther, music comes over the speakers, an orchestrated piece like Hollywood movie music. This scene you have witnessed was not a movie. Outside the television screen where it was enacted sits a young boy whose heart rate, adrenaline, and excitement are at a fever pitch. Little Timmy just killed seven men in a photo-realistic cyber world, beating the level of the game, but what are the effects in the real world on Timmy and countless other gamers?

While photo-realistic graphics are not yet on the market, they will be shortly within five to ten years, possibly less. Games will no longer have the polygonal look they have adapted over the past decade and instead will look and feel like movies: they will be an exact replica of our real world. What effect will photo-realistic violence controlled by the gamer have on gamers, particularly those at risk for emotional imbalance and aggression? What should we do to minimize the possible negative effects? Parents, the video game industry, and retailers need to work together to reduce the risky effects that photo-realistic graphics could have on some gamers.

Copyright © 2010, Pearson Education, Inc., Publishing as Longman

MTV Rocks!
Darby Moeller (student)

When I was little, I wasn't allowed to watch TV except on the weekends, and then I could watch whatever I wanted, except for MTV. Since junior high I've been an avid MTV viewer, and when I do watch TV, it is almost one hundred percent guaranteed that MTV is what I'll be watching. It's also almost guaranteed that if I enter my college dorm's lounge MTV will be on. Still, I know that a lot of people have mixed feelings about the network. In an informal survey I conducted in the Campion Dorm, eight out of ten students watched MTV on a regular basis, and nine out of ten thought it had a bad influence on teenagers. One person said that it glorifies celebrity and manipulates the public into buying products and watching these celebrities' movies. When asked if they thought other TV channels or magazines such as *Cosmopolitan* or *Maxim* were equally bad or worse, eight out of ten students simply stated that MTV was worse. However, I feel the need to defend MTV because few others will and there are shows and programs that I think are extremely worthwhile. I believe MTV has a positive influence on its viewers by raising political and social awareness, as well as by giving a teen perspective on issues of morality and justice. Shows such as *Flipped*, *True Life*, and *Fight For Your Rights*, as well as programs in the community such as Choose or Lose: Rock The Vote and Fight For Your Rights have an enormous, constructive impact on viewers.

[Note: Darby's argument was written in response to the Writing Assignment for Chapters 7 and 8 on page 164—arguing in favor of a popular cultural form to a resistant audience.]

Unlocking the Mystery: Parents Hold the Key
Patty Gillispie (student)

The color is gone from her face, replaced by a sickly white hue. She glances weakly at me, anticipating what will inevitably follow, with a look of complete dread. My blank expression is meant to look sympathetic as I brace myself for what is to come. She bends over the trash can, with me at her side, gently patting her back, as she heaves and eventually regurgitates her dinner. The smell is debilitating, so I open a window before asking her if she would like a glass of water or a tissue to wipe her mouth. Only a few hours earlier, my friend was carefree and at ease, unoccupied by any of the stresses of her daily life. Now the alcohol has caught up to her and what began as a night of fun quickly transforms into sleepless hours spent hunched over the side of the bed. Despite this unpleasant experience, my friend will, for a variety of reasons, most likely abuse alcohol again. Whether it is to have fun, loosen up, or feel like part of the group, she will probably overlook her episode of frequent vomiting, highlighting the good memories of the night, and continue to drink when the opportunity appears. The truth is my friend is like many teenagers in this respect. She and many of her drinking peers did not discuss alcohol at home, and she rarely saw either of her parents in an environment where drinking was prevalent. The growing number of underage binge drinkers stems, at least in part, from this lack of communication between parents and their children about the serious, relevant issue of alcohol use. Parents should have an open relationship with their children about alcohol because it is the best way to prevent them from relying on other sources, such as the media or their peers, to answer their questions; it helps eliminate the curiosity they have about the substance and the need to discover it for themselves, and it enables their first encounter with alcohol to be in a controlled environment under adult supervision.

Copyright © 2010, Pearson Education, Inc., Publishing as Longman

DISCUSSION EXERCISE ON ACCOMMODATING OPPOSING VIEWS

In the exercise in the following two-page handout, we show the alternative views and rebuttal section of student writer Patty Gillispie's researched proposal argument in favor of parents' taking an active role in teaching their children about responsible attitudes toward alcohol. (The introduction to Patty's argument is shown in the preceding exercise.)

Copyright © 2010, Pearson Education, Inc., Publishing as Longman

Handout: FOR CLASS DISCUSSION: HANDLING OPPOSING VIEWS

Individually or in groups, read the alternative views and rebuttal section from student writer Patty Gillispie's proposal argument. Use the following questions to guide your examination of this paper.

1. Summarize each of the opposing reasons that Patty anticipates from her audience.
2. Which of the strategies for treating alternative views (summarizing them, conceding to them, rebutting them, and so forth) does Patty use? How does she refute opposing points?
3. How does Patty use material from her research to support her position?
4. Which of her counter-reasons do you think is her strongest? How do you think her target audience of parents would respond to her rebuttal argument?

from **Unlocking the Mystery: Parents Hold the Key** (Alternative Views Section)
Patty Gillispie (student)

One major concern voiced by the opposition is that some parents are unable to draw a line between educating their children about alcohol and serving as their suppliers and party chaperones. According to Ferris Morrison, project manager for the North Carolina Initiative to Reduce Underage Drinking, "A lot of the problem is that parents just don't see alcohol as a problem" (Gardner I). While this is truly a legitimate objection, my intent is not to suggest that parents should encourage their children to drink and provide them with a safe environment in which to do so. Instead, I recommend that parents make the effort to have serious, regular discussions with their children about the dangers of alcohol and the importance of drinking responsibly to address any questions young people have surrounding the issue of alcohol use. Assuming that all teenagers will drink, no matter what efforts are made on the part of the parent, is erroneous. In fact, a 1998 study "indicate[d] that parents continue to have significant influence on their children, even into late adolescence" (Booth-Butterfield and Sidelinger 295). Ongoing, dynamic communication about alcohol between teens and parents, therefore, is both imperative and worthwhile.

Another hotly contested aspect of this argument is the amount of time involved before significant results are seen among the country's adolescent population. Making alcohol a more openly discussed topic within families, I must admit, would be a gradual process and would probably take years to have great impact on the drinking habits of America's youth. Nevertheless, the best solution to a complex problem is usually not the easiest, or the fastest. In order for this strategy to have an effect on society, it would have to happen slowly. My proposal involves cultural change, not passing laws or changing a national policy. It is making a decision to alter the entire nation's view of an issue. Gone are the vain attempts to protect our young people from a substance they see everyday—in the media, followed by trying to prevent them from satisfying their curiosity about it. Rather, teens will receive honest, true information about alcohol from people they can trust: their parents. This approach will, in turn, foster better relationships between parents and children and could have considerable advantages in areas unrelated to drinking. The benefits—namely a decline in the rate of teenage drinking and

Copyright © 2010, Pearson Education, Inc., Publishing as Longman

associated problems—of making our country more open about alcohol, starting in the home, will outweigh the time involved to implement it.

Still others have problems even accepting this idea and propose a solution from the other end of the continuum. This group feels that instead of making teenage alcohol consumption a more commonly discussed issue, current laws should be more stringently enforced and new legislation should be passed to minimize and, if possible, eliminate adolescent exposure to alcohol. They point out that many of these laws seek punishment for adults who supply teenagers with alcohol. One of these is the Zero Adult Providers (ZAP) law, passed in Minnesota, which says that "those convicted...can be jailed, fined, or sued for damages" (Gardner I). These kinds of laws are important in holding adults accountable for their contributions to the problem of underage drinking. However, zero tolerance policies, such as the legislation passed in Texas in 1997 that could mean serving six months in jail for a third offense, have been ineffective among young people, according to Andrew Stuttaford, a writer for the *National Review*: "Elevating [alcohol] to the status of forbidden fruit is counterproductive. Adult disapproval magically transforms [it] from a simple pleasure into an especially thrilling act of rebellion" (32). Teenage interest in alcohol will not be curbed by attempting to shield them from it altogether since it is impossible to prevent adolescents from hearing about alcohol from friends, peers, and especially the media. Attempts to do so only create curiosity and fuel desire to learn more about the substance.

Works Cited

Booth-Butterfield, Melanie and Robert Sidelinger. "The Influence of Family Communication on the College-Aged Child: Openness, Attitudes, and Actions about Sex and Alcohol." *Communication Quarterly* 46.3 (Summer 1998): 295-308. *Proquest.* Web. 5 March 2003.

Gardner, Marilyn. "When Teens Drink, Parents May Pay." *Christian Science Monitor* 6 Sept. 2000: I. *Academic Search Elite.* Web. 5 March 2003.

Stuttaford, Andrew. "De-Demonizing Rum." *National Review* 25 June 2001: 32+. *Academic Search Elite.* Web. 5 March 2003.

Copyright © 2010, Pearson Education, Inc., Publishing as Longman

DISCUSSION EXERCISE EXAMINING STUDENTS' POSTER ARGUMENTS

In the exercise that follows (in a five-page handout), we offer examples of two of our students' poster arguments created for the assignment, Option 1, in Chapter 9, page 196 in *Writing Arguments*. To help students generate ideas for their own poster arguments and to help them revise their posters for greater rhetorical effect, we provide discussion questions and show each of our students' poster arguments in two forms, as drafts and as the revised versions.

The first set of posters by Jenna Kedziorski calls for student support for a better meal plan at Seattle University. Although reproduced here in black and white, Jenna used color in both her first draft and final version. She used smoky blue letters for "WHERE has your money GONE??" for the first words of each of her bulleted items, and for her call to action at the bottom of the poster. The rest of the verbal text used black type. The illustrations were gray, black, and blue.

The second set of posters by Kasey Zimmer-Stucky encourages college students to participate in mentoring programs for young kids. Kasey's original posters also used color—black, white, and red type, with red and yellow highlighting the heading, "BECOME A MENTOR," the phrase under the photo, and the final line.

For instructors who might use these student examples in a class discussion, we include both the questions that could be used in a peer review exercise (in the following handout) and the actual comments that Jenna's and Kasey's peer review groups made about their poster arguments that led to their revisions (below).

Peer Review Comments on Jenna's Draft of Her Poster Argument:

- The image of the money going down the toilet is not entirely clear. The toilet image also takes up a lot of space for the amount of meaning that it conveys. What is the connection to the food service on campus, (Bon Appetit)?
- Could Jenna include some image that would make it immediately clear to readers that she is talking about wasting money on campus food?
- Could she streamline the wording of the ad, particularly in the bulleted phrases?

Peer Review Response to Jenna's Revised Poster Argument: Jenna's peer review group praised her revised version for its use of images. The addition of the image of the money bag on the plate, particularly clarified her argument. The group also preferred the tighter wording in the final version.

Peer Review Comments on Kasey's Draft of Her Poster Argument

- There is a lot of text in this poster argument. How could Kasey condense and sharpen the message of her verbal text?
- What are the differences in the various bulleted reasons that she gives for becoming a mentor? How could she clarify and simplify these reasons?
- The photo of Kasey with the two little girls conveys the warm relationship between them. Could she make this photo more prominent?

Copyright © 2010, Pearson Education, Inc., Publishing as Longman

- Readers get a little confused by the contact information at the end of the poster. How could she clarify and simplify this information?
- She uses numerous font styles and sizes in this poster. How could she make her use of type less busy and easier on readers' eyes while preserving the decorative element?

Peer Review Response to Kasey's Revised Poster Argument: Kasey's group praised the final version of her poster for its clarity, unity and focus, and for its visual harmony.

Copyright © 2010, Pearson Education, Inc., Publishing as Longman

Handout: FOR CLASS DISCUSSION:
DRAFTS AND REVISIONS OF TWO STUDENTS' POSTER ARGUMENTS

Working individually or in groups, use the following questions to guide your discussion of Jenna's and Kasey's drafts of their poster arguments:

1. What is the main claim in this poster argument? What are the reasons?
2. What images has the writer used? Are they visually attractive and clearly relevant to the poster's argument? What would make the images more effective for the writer's argument?
3. How does the verbal text in this argument work? How could the writer clarify, simplify, streamline, or emphasize the verbal text more to support the argument?
4. How does the layout of this poster contribute to the argument? What other options for use of space might the writer consider?
5. If you were designing this poster, what colors would you use?

After examining and discussing the drafts of Jenna's and Kasey's poster arguments, look at their revised versions and answer these questions:

1. How well has the writer revised her poster argument to solve the problems that appear in the draft versions?
2. What is strong and effective about the revised version of the poster argument? What features, if any, could use additional work?

Copyright © 2010, Pearson Education, Inc., Publishing as Longman

Where

Has Your Money Gone??

» College *Should* Be All About Independence And Responsibility....But Is It?? «

- ***Have control*** **over your own expenses**
- **Spend Cautiously and *get the most* out of your money**
- ***Stop wasting*** **money on overly priced food**

Call Seattle University's Food Service, Bon Appetit, To Protest Mandatory Meal Plans!

Jenna Kedziorski, Draft of Poster Argument

Copyright © 2010, Pearson Education, Inc., Publishing as Longman

WHERE has your money **GONE**??

College *Should* Be All About Independence And Responsibility....But Is It?

- ***Have control*** **over your own expenses**
- ***Get the most*** **out of your money by spending cautiously**
- ***Stop wasting*** **money on over-priced food**

Call Seattle University's Food Service, Bon Appetit, To Protest Mandatory Meal Plans!

Jenna Kedziorski, Revised Poster Argument

Copyright © 2010, Pearson Education, Inc., Publishing as Longman

Wanna be the next HANNAH MONTANA or one of the JONAS BROTHERS?!?

Ok, so maybe you don't look, sing, or dance like Hannah or Kevin, Joe, or Nick, but you can be looked up to as much as they are. Like it or not, young girls look up to Hannah Montana and young boys want to be just like one of the Jonas Brothers. They imitate everything they do from the way they dress, to lip-syncing to their sexy songs. Why? Because they think that's "cool." YOU can be "cool" too! How?

BECOME A MENTOR!

Why Mentor?

***To be a POSITIVE role model!**
***To help a child SUCCEED!**
***To be IDOLIZED in a positive way!**
***To make a DIFFFERENCE!**
***Just 1 hour a week makes a child's life happy!**
***BECAUSE IT'S FUN!**

Studies have shown that children who have mentors are less likely to skip school, have higher self esteem, are less likely to use drugs and alcohol, and get along better with their parents, teachers, and peers.

BEING A MENTOR IS ABOUT BEING A FRIEND! BE A FRIEND AND CHANGE A LIFE OR TWO WHILE YOU'RE AT IT

The Big Brothers/Big Sisters mentoring program is one of many programs nationwide designed to give underprivileged children the chance to succeed that they otherwise might not have gotten. To learn more, visit the Big Brother/Big Sister Web site at www.bigbrobigsis.org. If you would like to learn more about other programs, go to your local elementary, middle, or high school and speak with a counselor or perform a local on-line search.

YOU MIGHT NOT GET TO BE FAMOUS TO THE WORLD, BUT YOU'LL BE A STAR IN A CHILD'S EYES!

Kasey Zimmer-Stucky, Draft of Poster Argument

Copyright © 2010, Pearson Education, Inc., Publishing as Longman

Wanna be the next HANNAH MONTANA or one of the JONAS BROTHERS?!?

Ok, so maybe you don't look, sing, or dance like Hannah or Kevin, Joe, or Nick, but you can be looked up to as much as they are. Like it or not, young girls look up to Hannah Montana and young boys want to be just like one of the Jonas Brothers. They imitate everything they do from the way they dress, to lip-syncing to their sexy songs. Why? Because they think that's "cool." YOU can be "cool" too! How?

BECOME A MENTOR!

***To be a POSITIVE role model!**
***To have FUN while you are helping make a child happier!**
***To help a child SUCCEED!**

Studies have shown that children who have mentors have higher self esteem, are less likely to skip school, are less likely to use drugs and alcohol, and get along better with their parents, teachers, and peers.

Just 1 hour a week can make a difference in a child's life. Be a mentor, be a friend, change a life!

To learn more:

1. **Visit the Big Brother/Big Sister Web site at www.bigbrobigsis.org. (The Big Brothers/Big Sisters mentoring program is one of many programs nationwide designed to give underprivileged children the chance to succeed.)**
2. **Perform a local on-line search for information about other programs.**
3. **Visit a local elementary, middle, or high school and speak with a counselor.**

YOU MIGHT NOT GET TO BE FAMOUS TO THE WORLD, BUT YOU'LL BE A STAR IN A CHILD'S EYES!

Kasey Zimmer-Stucky, Revised Poster Argument

Copyright © 2010, Pearson Education, Inc., Publishing as Longman

VIII. PEER REVIEW GUIDELINES FOR CLAIM-TYPE ASSIGNMENTS

In this section of the *Instructor's Manual*, peer review guidelines geared toward the claim-type assignments are provided in Part Four. First, here are some aspects of each claim-type argument that students may find challenging and a few suggestions for helping students. There are peer review guidelines on handouts that students can use when giving feedback to one another on their claim-type arguments.

CHALLENGING POINTS OF EACH CLAIM-TYPE ARGUMENT

Definitional Arguments (Chapter 11)

In constructing and revising definitional arguments, students need to think particularly about rhetorical context and audience and about crafting a definition for their Y term by applying good critical thinking. While the "match" portion of a "criteria-match" definitional argument may be pretty straightforward, the development of criteria is much trickier. Forming criteria forces students to examine relationships among concepts and to fashion subtle distinctions. At several points during the writing process, students might want to review Chapter 11 to refine their understanding of how to generate definitions by using Aristotelian categorizing and operational, reportive, and stipulative strategies. In creating their own definitions, students should give special attention to coming up with boundary cases that really test the adequacy of their criteria.

Causal Arguments (Chapter 12)

We are bombarded by causal arguments, and yet these causal arguments are often irresponsibly and deceptively manipulative. Too often in the public realm, writers claim that some X is the sole cause of some Y, when in fact it is only a contributing or partial cause. Indeed, these writers argue that if X is not the sole cause, then it can't be any part of the cause: for example, someone might argue that if sex shown in television programs is not *the* cause of teen promiscuity, then it doesn't affect teen promiscuity at all. When students write causal arguments, they can avoid this fallacious thinking by qualifying their claims and arguing that X is a contributing cause of Y and not *the* cause. In addition, because causal arguments are often built on what might happen, it is difficult to make them persuasive. Therefore, students need to provide solid evidence that will be convincing to the chosen audience at every point in their causal chains.

Resemblance Arguments (Chapter 13)

Because resemblance arguments are difficult to sustain as full arguments, they often function as pieces of longer arguments or form the basis of shorter arguments such as letters to the editor, a genre that particularly benefits from striking, thought-provoking and often emotionally stirring comparisons. Really successful arguments by analogy or precedent are difficult to construct; arguing by resemblance can be powerfully persuasive, but it is also risky because skeptical readers are often quick to take resemblance arguments apart. Still, knowing the strategies for creating resemblance arguments can be an important part of an arguer's

Copyright © 2010, Pearson Education, Inc., Publishing as Longman

repertoire, and students should try their hand at creating short resemblance arguments that could become part of their longer arguments.

Categorical Evaluation Arguments (Chapter 14)

One challenge of evaluation arguments is to move beyond subjective values to assess an item from the point of view of its purpose and function. Students need to discover criteria for their X that writers and readers are likely to share; therefore, the rhetorical context of evaluation arguments is particularly important, and students should think about the stakes in the evaluation argument. Awareness of this context will also help writers determine how to weigh criteria and how much they need to support their criteria. (Although ethical evaluations are a subcategory of evaluation arguments, for convenience a separate set of peer review questions for ethical arguments is provided.)

Evaluation Arguments (Chapter 14)

Ethical evaluations are a subcategory of evaluation arguments, but instead of determining whether an X is good (or bad) in its category, ethical evaluations ask students to argue the right or wrong of an X. Writing ethical arguments can be both intellectually daunting and emotionally strenuous for many students; "the Good," as opposed to "a good X," is a complex notion. In addition, ethical arguments often ask arguers to submit some of their most deeply held beliefs for rational scrutiny. We have found that a brief introduction to principle-based versus consequence-based ethical theories gives students a good start toward a more thoughtful analysis of their own ethical decisions. With ethical evaluations, students should think about the assumptions and values that they share with their audience and build on those.

Proposal Arguments (Chapter 15)

Proposal arguments, especially policy proposals, are a common type of argument for students to write. While often enlisting other claim types as lines of support, proposal arguments also challenge students to convince readers that a problem truly exists, to create a workable solution to the problem, to generate persuasive reasons to act on the proposal, and to justify the cost of the proposal, as well as refute objections and alternative solutions to the problem. Students might want to work in class with the various strategies for generating ideas for proposal arguments and at the invention and drafting stages to role-play for one another an audience of decision-makers who needs to be moved to action.

Preparation for Peer Review Sessions

Students generally benefit from preparation for peer review sessions. Instructors might ask students to write down questions, points, or problems on which they would particularly like feedback from their peer reviewers. For instance, a student might ask her reviewers for feedback on enlivening her introduction or clarifying her claim, or a student might tell his reviewers that he has been puzzling over the order he should use to present his evaluation criteria or the amount of evidence he needs to support one of his reasons. These questions can increase both writers' and reviewers' investment in reading and responding to drafts and can ensure that writers get individual, specific comments that help to motivate them to revise.

Copyright © 2010, Pearson Education, Inc., Publishing as Longman

Handout: PEER REVIEW GUIDELINES FOR DEFINITIONAL ARGUMENTS

Directions to Peer Reviewers: Some of the following questions are descriptive, helping you closely examine what this argument is about and play back to the writer what you see as you read the argument. Some questions are more analytical, leading you to give the writer feedback on how well this argument works for readers. Question 8 asks you to respond to the specific questions or concerns on which the writer has asked for help with his/her argument. In order to give the writer comments to reflect on later, you might write your responses to these questions on the other side of this paper.

Reviewer's Name__________________________ Writer's Name____________________

1. What is the definitional issue in this argument? What is the X term in the argument and what is the Y term? What criteria does this writer use to say that this X is (or is not) a Y?

2. What audience do you think the writer has in mind? Who is disputing this definition and who are the stakeholders in this controversy? In other words, why is defining the X term important to people? How could the writer's main definitional claim be presented more effectively for this audience?

3. How could the writer make the criteria for something to qualify as a "Y" more logically sound according to the strategies for developing definitional criteria (reportive, stipulative, and so forth)?

4. If the criteria are at stake, how could the writer make the criteria clearer and more effective for this audience?

5. What evidence does the writer give to show that the term at issue (the X) matches up with these criteria? How could the writer strengthen the match part of the argument more? What evidence would be helpful for the audience?

6. How does the writer acknowledge counterarguments and refute them? What might improve the effectiveness of this part of the argument?

7. How could the writer strengthen the argument's appeals to *ethos* and *pathos*? How could the writer set up the issue at stake more powerfully in the introduction to the argument?

8. What are your responses to the writer's specific questions about his/her definitional argument?

<u>Summary</u>: List what you see as the strengths and weaknesses of this definitional argument.

Copyright © 2010, Pearson Education, Inc., Publishing as Longman

Handout: PEER REVIEW GUIDELINES FOR CAUSAL ARGUMENTS

Directions to Peer Reviewers: Some of the following questions are descriptive, helping you closely examine what this argument is about and play back to the writer what you see as you read the argument. Some questions are more analytical, leading you to give the writer feedback on how well this argument works for readers. Question 7 asks you to respond to the specific questions or concerns on which the writer has asked for help with his/her argument. In order to give the writer comments to reflect on later, you might write your responses to these questions on the other side of this paper.

Reviewer's Name__________________________ Writer's Name_____________________

1. What audience do you think the writer has in mind? What is at issue in this controversy? What are the stakes involved?

2. What is the writer's main causal claim? How could it be presented more effectively for this audience?

3. Does the causal argument presented deal with a specific, one-time-only event or phenomenon or does it deal with a recurrent event or phenomenon? If the argument deals with a one-time occurrence, how does the writer establish a clear causal chain? How does the writer explain the causal mechanism? How could the writer make these causal relationships more compelling for this audience?

4. How does the writer explain the causes or consequences of his or her phenomenon? What could the writer do to build a stronger case? How might the writer improve the argument through strategies such as explaining the causal chain more directly, using informal induction, referring to scientific experiments, establishing correlations, or using analogies?

5. How has the writer addressed and responded to alternative explanations or causal chains? What causal factors might be more important than the one(s) focused on by the writer? Can you think of any exceptions to the posited causal chain, any unnamed factors, problems with correlations, data, or disanalogies, or examples of oversimplification?

6. How could the writer strengthen this argument's appeals to *ethos* and *pathos*? How could the writer set up the issue at stake more powerfully in the introduction to the argument?

7. What are your responses to the writer's specific questions about his/her causal argument?

<u>Summary</u>: List what you see as the strengths and weaknesses of this causal argument.

Copyright © 2010, Pearson Education, Inc., Publishing as Longman

Handout: PEER REVIEW GUIDELINES FOR RESEMBLANCE ARGUMENTS

Directions to Peer Reviewers: Some of the following questions are descriptive, helping you closely examine what this argument is about and play back to the writer what you see as you read the argument. Some questions are more analytical, leading you to give the writer feedback on how well this argument works for readers. Question 8 asks you to respond to the specific questions or concerns on which the writer has asked for help with his/her argument. In order to give the writer comments to reflect on later, you might write your responses to these questions on the other side of this paper.

Reviewer's Name__________________________ Writer's Name____________________

1. What audience do you think the writer has in mind? Whom is the writer trying to persuade with this analogy or precedent?

2. What is the writer's purpose? What does the writer hope to clarify or make the audience understand through this analogy or precedent?

3. What is the writer's resemblance claim? How could it be presented more effectively for this audience?

4. What is being compared to what? List all pertinent points of comparison that the writer has made in the argument. What points would make the comparison more relevant or effective for this audience?

5. What evidence does the writer supply to develop the comparison? How could the writer improve the support for this comparison or qualify it so that it is more supportable?

6. How has the writer addressed and responded to objections and alternative views? What major dissimilarities ("disanalogies") between the two terms or the two circumstances (in a precedent argument) can you think of?

7. How could the writer make appeals to *ethos* and *pathos* more effective in this argument? If the writer is using a resemblance to shock an audience into some sort of recognition about the term at issue, how could the resemblance work as a more effective appeal to *pathos*?

8. What are your responses to the writer's specific questions about his/her resemblance argument?

<u>Summary</u>: List what you see as the strengths and weaknesses of this resemblance argument.

Copyright © 2010, Pearson Education, Inc., Publishing as Longman

Handout: PEER REVIEW GUIDELINES FOR EVALUATION ARGUMENTS

Directions to Peer Reviewers: Some of the following questions are descriptive, helping you closely examine what this argument is about and play back to the writer what you see as you read the argument. Some questions are more analytical, leading you to give the writer feedback on how well this argument works for readers. Question 8 asks you to respond to the specific questions or concerns on which the writer has asked for help with his/her argument. In order to give the writer comments to reflect on later, you might write your responses to these questions on the other side of this paper.

Reviewer's Name_________________________ Writer's Name____________________

1. What audience is the writer addressing? Who has a stake in this evaluation? Why is this evaluation important?

2. What is the writer evaluating (What is the X term)? What category does the writer place X in (What is the Y term)? What is the function of this category? Is the evaluation issue clear, sensible, and meaningful for this audience? How could the writer make the evaluation claim more effective?

3. What criteria does the writer establish for evaluating X? How could the writer make these criteria clearer, more fitting, or more logically weighted for this audience?

4. How much are the criteria in dispute and what is the writer's strategy for defending them? How could the writer make this criteria part of the argument more effective?

5. What evidence does the writer present that X meets (or does not meet) the established criteria? How could the writer strengthen the match part of the argument?

6. How does the writer handle alternative views and counterarguments? What approach might make this part of the argument more effective?

7. How could the writer enhance this argument's appeals to *ethos* and *pathos*? How could the writer set up the issue at stake more powerfully in the introduction to the argument?

8. What are your responses to the writer's specific questions about his/her evaluation argument?

Summary: List what you see as the strengths and weaknesses of this evaluation argument.

Copyright © 2010, Pearson Education, Inc., Publishing as Longman

Handout: PEER REVIEW GUIDELINES FOR EVALUATION ARGUMENTS

Directions to Peer Reviewers: Some of the following questions are descriptive, helping you closely examine what this argument is about and play back to the writer what you see as you read the argument. Some questions are more analytical, leading you to give the writer feedback on how well this argument works for readers. Question 7 asks you to respond to the specific questions or concerns on which the writer has asked for help with his/her argument. In order to give the writer comments to reflect on later, you might write your responses to these questions on the other side of this paper.

Reviewer's Name__________________________ Writer's Name_____________________

1. What audience is the writer addressing? Who has a stake in this ethical evaluation? Why is this ethical evaluation important?

2. Is the argument that X is wrong (or right) based on some enduring principle, on the consequences of the ethical choice, or on some combination? How could the writer make the principle or consequence base of the evaluation more in tune with the audience?

3. What evidence, reasoning, and explanation does the writer use to support the argument that the X follows (or violates) a given principle or will lead (or not lead) to certain consequences? What additional evidence or reasoning would positively influence the audience?

4. How does the writer handle alternative views and counterarguments? What approach might make this part of the argument more effective?

5. Where might a resistant audience challenge the relationship between the claim and the principle or suggest that negative consequences will follow from the decision based on principle? Where might a resistant audience challenge the anticipated consequences or suggest that the benefits of the consequences do not outweigh the costs?

6. How could the writer build up this argument's appeals to *ethos* and *pathos*? How could the writer set up the issue at stake more powerfully in the introduction to the argument?

7. What are your responses to the writer's specific questions about his/her ethical evaluation argument?

Summary: List what you see as the strengths and weaknesses of this ethical evaluation argument.

Copyright © 2010, Pearson Education, Inc., Publishing as Longman

Handout: PEER REVIEW GUIDELINES FOR PROPOSAL ARGUMENTS

Directions to Peer Reviewers: Some of the following questions are descriptive, helping you closely examine what this argument is about and play back to the writer what you see as you read the argument. Some questions are more analytical, leading you to give the writer feedback on how well this argument works for readers. Question 7 asks you to respond to the specific questions or concerns on which the writer has asked for help with his/her argument. In order to give the writer comments to reflect on later, you might write your responses to these questions on the other side of this paper.

Reviewer's Name________________________ Writer's Name____________________

1. What audience is the writer addressing with this proposal? Who are the stakeholders and who are the decision-makers?

2. What is the problem that needs to be addressed? How does the writer give "presence" to the problem and show why it is a significant? How could the writer be more effective in establishing the problem and making it real to the audience?

3. What reasons does the writer use to support the proposal claim? Could additional or better reasons be developed using the strategies of principle/category, consequence, or resemblance?

4. What evidence does the writer use to support each of the reasons? What could the writer do to clarify how the proposal will solve the problem, how the benefits of enacting it outweigh any negative consequences, and how it will be paid for? How could this evidence be more attuned to the needs/interests of the audience being addressed by the proposal?

5. How does the writer answer objections to the proposal and answer alternative proposals that offer better/cheaper solutions? How could the writer improve the response to objections and alternative views?

6. How could the writer enhance this argument's appeals to *ethos* and *pathos*? How could the writer set up the issue at stake more powerfully in the introduction to the argument?

7. What are your responses to the writer's specific questions about his/her proposal argument?

Summary: List what you see as the strengths and weaknesses of this proposal argument.

Copyright © 2010, Pearson Education, Inc., Publishing as Longman

IX. ANALYSIS OF READINGS IN PART SIX: AN ANTHOLOGY OF ARGUMENTS

USING THE ANTHOLOGY

The *Instructor's Manual* provides suggestions for ways to incorporate readings, specifically readings from the anthology, into courses on argument. In this part of the *Instructor's Manual*, each analysis systematically applies the principles and concepts from the rhetoric part of the text to the readings in the anthology. These analyses demonstrate how a grasp of such concepts as appeals to *ethos*, *pathos*, *logos*, *kairos*, and claim types, among others, can give students necessary analytical tools to understand the way real-world arguments support their claims and how awareness of genre and of the writer's angle of vision can clarify the form and limitations of the argument. This kind of wrestling with the way writers have constructed their arguments and tailored them to reach particular audiences will, in turn, empower students to understand the demands placed on arguers, as well as help them to appreciate the options available to them.

The key descriptor of the readings in the anthology is "real-world arguments" because the readings for *Writing Arguments* exemplify the highly contextual, complicated, compound, and imperfect nature of arguments that surround us. Although some arguments in these readings are brilliantly crafted and gracefully expressed, most are not. They range in approach and tone from aggressive and defensive to exploratory and reflective. However, they all have one thing in common: they are the products of highly motivated writers, writers who want to change people's thinking or move them to action. The goal in this part of the *Instructor's Manual*, then, is this: to help students become better critical readers of the arguments they encounter in all parts of their lives—on the op-ed page of their local newspaper, in university or college newspapers, in magazines, in marketing materials and advertising, in their academic disciplines, in course readings, in corporation newsletters, and elsewhere. The second goal is to help students apply this practical knowledge of the strengths and weaknesses of real-world arguments. Learning to distinguish between substantiated and unsupported claims, between responsible and irresponsible uses of evidence, and between powerful and alarmist appeals to emotion, and to recognize how audience and context affect these judgments can lead students to be more successful writers of arguments.

Instructors can incorporate the anthology readings into their courses in a number of ways: (1) for rhetorical analysis (How is this argument put together?); (2) for models of argumentative moves and strategies (What is worth emulating?); and (3) for introducing students to current national and global controversial conversations they may want to enter. The analyses of the readings are designed to facilitate all these uses of the anthology.

Because students tend to read better, more closely and more thoughtfully, when they are asked to produce something in writing, the following approaches to deepen students' engagement with the readings are recommended. To help students understand and appreciate the strengths and weaknesses of these arguments, instructors might ask students to apply the reading strategies explained in Chapter 2: read as a believer, read as a doubter, explore how the rhetorical

Copyright © 2010, Pearson Education, Inc., Publishing as Longman

context and genre are shaping the argument, consider alternative views and analyze sources of disagreement, and use disagreement productively to prompt further investigation. Instructors might use the introductions to each unit as discussion starters—to provide context, the major stakeholders, the ways they frame their claims, and a sense of the network of issue questions inherent in the dialogue of ideas.

Instructors also might assign the questions in the For Class Discussion exercise at the end of each topic unit that focus on the specific issues in those readings. Often, these questions suggest ways to compare and contrast different writers' interpretations of facts and expression of values. Instructors might also ask students to analyze and discuss the readings using the three lists of questions in the "Guide Questions for the Analysis and Evaluation of Arguments" that prefaces the anthology (453-55) or to apply the appropriate supplemental checklist provided for each of the various kinds of arguments in Section VI of this *Instructor's Manual*. As an alternative, instructors may want to create their own questions for analysis. Still another idea is to give students an opportunity to practice adopting a perspective—not necessarily their own—on an issue by asking them to analyze one writer's argument from the point of view of another writer on that same topic. Finally, instructors can encourage students to extend the argumentative conversations in each subject grouping by asking students to find their own articles on that subject that offer a different perspective on the issues.

How the Analyses Are Structured

This section of the *Instructor's Manual* is intended to provide quick-reference analyses of the readings in the anthology, not definitive or exhaustive interpretations of these readings. Each analysis of reading selection includes these components:

- Core of the argument: identification of how the writer frames the issue, including the writer's stated or implied claims and reasons
- Major stasis or stases: identification of major or prominent stases in each argument and often in the lines of support
- Use of evidence and argumentative strategies: discussion of the kinds and quality of evidence and any noteworthy argumentative strategies (such as use of analogies, defense of warrants, rebuttal strategies)
- Weaknesses of the argument: objections to parts or points of the argument that resisting readers might raise
- Appeals to ethos and pathos: discussion of how the writer establishes an ethos and appeals to the audience's values, imagination, and sympathies
- Genre of the argument: reflections on how the genre of the argument (for example, op-ed piece, scholarly article, white paper, speech) and its rhetorical context (targeted audience and specific purpose) have shaped the argument.

Copyright © 2010, Pearson Education, Inc., Publishing as Longman

How Stasis Theory Informs the Reading of Arguments

Throughout *Writing Arguments* the text primarily presents stasis theory, or the theory of claim types, as an inventional tool. Knowledge of claim types can help a writer focus the argument on a point of crucial disagreement with a particular audience. The writer can then enlist the characteristic pattern of support for that claim type as an aid to invention and development.

In this section of the *Instructor's Manual*, stasis theory also shows that it has explanatory power in analyzing arguments; however, here are two provisos: (1) ***most arguments are hybrids of several stases*** and (2) ***readers may differ in their perceptions of major stases***. Even so, the interpretive practice of determining the major stasis or stases of an argument can help readers identify pivotal claims in an argument. Also, the critical thinking required by this exercise can force a deeper grappling with the interrelationship of lines of argument, with the structure of the argument, and with the patterns of support. Sometimes readers' confusion over the stases of an argument occasionally signals the writer's muddy reasoning or insufficient development of a point. Further, sometimes claims are implicit rather than overtly stated. When readers reconstruct and articulate these implicit claims, they may cast these claims as different stases depending on which aspect of the claim they emphasize.

For instance, evaluation arguments are often just one word away from becoming proposal arguments: X is good (implied: therefore we should do it). Or, evaluation arguments are enmeshed in causal arguments: X is bad (implied: it has negative consequences). In short, although stasis theory can be a means of coming to terms with arguments, determining the stasis of an argument should not be a reductive end in itself. Examining the stasis or stases of an argument should open up discussion, not close it off with rigid categories. Discussion of stases should illuminate how many arguments consist of a compound of claim types and how these claim types work together.

With these views of stasis theory in mind, the *Instructor's Manual* offers interpretations of the major stases in each argument in the anthology, but you and your students may see the major claims in these arguments in a different light.

Note: Quotations from readings are cited by the paragraph number in the analyses.

Copyright © 2010, Pearson Education, Inc., Publishing as Longman

WEB 2.0 AND ONLINE IDENTITY

Bronwyn T. Williams, "'Tomorrow Will Not Be Like Today': Literacy and Identity in a World of Multiliteracies"

- ✷ Core of the argument: Students reading and writing almost exclusively via computers and online along with their use of various emerging technologies has made them very different media consumers but adept rhetoricians in regard to negotiating their identities online. Therefore, educators should take advantage of students' methods of using technology and reach out to them in order to make classrooms more relevant to our computer-based, multitasking population of learners.
- ✷ Major stases: Williams uses causal reasoning to show how students use technology and how that affects their literacy practices and then transitions into a soft proposal argument.
- ✷ Use of evidence and argumentative strategies: The author employs a causal argument early on to show readers how their students navigate the Web and use social networking sites. After her claim that "the change communication technologies that seems to happen almost daily is both real and dramatic in the ways it is changing how young people read and write with words and images" (paragraph 1), she uses a detailed example from an adolescent girl's use of technology when doing her homework (2). Using various sources to support her claims that multitasking and online communication has made young adults very savvy presenters of identity, Williams asserts that students are indeed having learning experiences about rhetoric counter to traditional perceptions that students working online are isolated on their computers (7). At the mid-point of the column, Williams concedes what some critics might bring up about their use of computers—they focus mostly on pop culture—but counters that argument by discussing how students present themselves via Facebook, MySpace, et al. represents intricate rhetorical acts focused on *ethos* and identity. The way they design their sites and write in certain ways to express and validate their characters, in a sense, is the argument. So the author proposes is that educators need to "find out from them what rhetorical and literacy practices they have learned when reading and writing in diverse online settings from one day to the next" (11). Learning from students' online practices, she avers, will enrich classrooms, expand our notions of literacy, and reveal "our common humanity" (17).
- ✷ Weaknesses of the argument: Williams marshals forth a number of sources to back her contentions that literacy practices are being altered by computer technologies, but some assertions don't seem to be sufficiently supported. She assumes the reader will agree with her statements that "young people" are "reading and writing far more than they were 20 years or even a decade ago" (2), that students' literacy experiences "are far more complex than previous generations" (6), and that young people "think and feel about literacy and communication in fundamentally different ways than I do" (15). Some readers would want more direct proof and backing of those assertions because they seem to be based more on belief than cognitive studies. Likewise, while Williams may not have been given enough space to grapple with substantial counterarguments since it's a column, some critics of various computer technologies have argued that the mere speed by which we use the technologies and the newer literacy practices associated with social networking sites or other venues cater to superficiality rather than in-depth, analytical thinking. While it may be true that young adults know how to present themselves online in multiple ways,

Copyright © 2010, Pearson Education, Inc., Publishing as Longman

what about the depth of thought and the time to reflect? If these systems are instantaneous, where is the time for deep thought and reflection? And there are cognitive studies that show, whether one is a young adult or just an adult, that multitasking is counterproductive, hurts retention of material, and makes readers focus on superficiality over substance. In regard to her soft proposal about reaching out to students directly about their online literacy practices, some arguers may contend that we need to focus on more traditional reading and writing because the workplace and citizenship still requires those literacies.

- Appeals to ethos and pathos: Williams establishes here *ethos* right away in the first sentence when she references her tenure writing the column. Also, she refers to herself as an older person throughout the piece, which lends itself to showing that she's open-minded to how young adults use these technologies and she's willing to work with them halfway. For her audience, who are educators, she ends with emotionally-laden language that connects to their missions as educators—"[r]eading and writing offer distinct opportunities for connecting our minds and hearts to those around us. As we teach reading and writing to young people we can help them understand the potential for connection and how, even as it raises our awareness of what divides us, it reveals our hope in our common humanity" (17). Her tone is one of connection and openness, which would probably work well with her audience.
- Genre of the argument: This is a different sort of column than students might be used to reading because it's in a specialized, peer-reviewed journal devoted to education, which explains Williams' extensive use of sources.

Jeff Chu, "You Wanna Take This Online?"

- Core of the argument: Instant messaging, blogs, and text messaging are changing the culture of young adults by creating a different form of bullying and opening them up to being taken advantage of by dangerous individuals.
- Major stases: Chu portrays the negative consequences that new technologies have had on youth culture.
- Use of evidence and argumentative strategies: Chu utilizes three main bases of support for his argument that cyberspace is creating a hostile and scary environment for young adults: the experiences of Taylor Hern (paragraphs 2, 4) and Courtney Katasak (5), data and conclusions from a comprehensive study about cyberbullying by researchers at Clemson University (3-4, 7), and the use of revealing statements and from Parry Aftab (6, 8, 10) and Brittany Bacon (9) of WiredSafety.org along with important statements by a psychologist (7), a counselor (10), and Taylor Hern's mother (11). All levels of support point toward effects of this new media: teens use this technology to bully people, and it's done disproportionately by girls; young adults are open prey to negative and possibly dangerous influences; and bullying via technology has made it more public, which could be a sign of "emotional and psychological problems" (7). In addition, the lack of knowledge about computers by parents makes the situation worse, Chu argues, and parents need to pay close attention to what their teens are doing with these technologies.
- Weaknesses of the argument: The author offers the interesting conclusion of the Clemson study that girls are more likely to cyberbully than boys, but Chu never extrapolates or discovers exactly why this is. Other than offering the clichéd example of male

Copyright © 2010, Pearson Education, Inc., Publishing as Longman

playground bullies, he draws no logical conclusions as why girls bully through this medium more often. Through Bacon, Chu offers a soft proposal, that "teens need to learn boundaries and manners in cyberspace" (9), but how is that possible if parents aren't typically as knowledgeable about cyberspace as their teens are?

* Appeals to ethos and pathos: Chu's article has an informational tone to it, and he provides some plausible effects how advancing technologies have taken bullying to a more public venue. The vivid examples of the Kennesaw, GA teens' experiences with the "List of Hos" is demeaning yet typical, but the frightening examples of Katasak's experience and the thirteen year old in New Jersey, whose hobby was "death threats," would emote a great deal of fear in readers and perhaps even create some paranoia for reflective parents. Those chilling examples might move readers to take Bacon and Agatston's advice in paragraphs nine and ten.
* Genre of the argument: Typical of the general newsmagazine, *Time*, Chu offers a short informational causal argument that plays to its readership, mainly older readers who could be parents.

John Seigenthaler, Sr., "A False Wikipedia 'Biography'"

* Core of the argument: Wikipedia is not a trustworthy source of information because volunteer editors are amateurs and because the wiki system itself, abetted by federal laws that protect online corporations from lawsuits, cannot be held responsible for incorrect content.
* Major stases: Based on his personal experience, Seigenthaler makes an evaluative argument about the validity of content on Wikipedia.
* Use of evidence and argumentative strategies: The author uses one example to make his case for the fallibility of Wikipedia. He uses direct quotations from entries while providing statements from the corporation's founder to show the distinct difference between what people might perceive about the site and its reality. The fact that online corporations are protected from lawsuits shows that there is no legal recourse available for such entries, which hurts the credibility of Wikipedia. What is implicit in the piece is that we should expect the criteria of truth or responsibility for reference sources.
* Weaknesses of the argument: Seigenthaler's argument rests solely on his extreme personal experience, which exemplifies how fallible the site can be, but he fails to address counterarguments whatsoever. Some could argue, using comparisons of Wikipedia entries on subjects compared to other prestigious print encyclopedias like Britannica, that the site is quite accurate and informational without the help of professional editors.
* Appeals to ethos and pathos: The gist of the argument is based on credibility and emotions. The author attempts to shock the reader by showing this extreme example and then uses this example as a pathway to attack the *ethos* of Wikipedia. His tone of frustration colors his diction throughout the piece, which could move some readers but distance others.
* Genre of the argument: As in many op-eds, the author uses one example or a few examples to give the readers an interesting take on a phenomenon or issue. The tone is conversational and condemnatory.

Copyright © 2010, Pearson Education, Inc., Publishing as Longman

Alice Mathias, "The Facebook Generation"

- Core of the argument: While some see social networking sites like Facebook as online arenas for "human connectivity," the site is really just an arena for humor and entertainment among friends who usually know one another already.
- Major stases: Mathias's column is a light-hearted definitional argument that makes the case that Facebook is mostly about entertainment rather than altruistic aims.
- Use of evidence and argumentative strategies: Mathias supports her argument from personal experience and observation of people in her age range, and she uses broad generalizations about what the site provides: "it's entertaining to watch…" (paragraph 4), it's "online community theater" (5), "[i]t's all comedy" (6), and anecdotes and references to fake profiles and online hijinks. In essence, she argues that the site is more about voyeurism and "yet another form of escapism" (14) for college students rather than a serious site for connections and to be used as a "legitimate social reference" guide (15). She supports these points based on the assumption that her generation is "bizarrely comfortable" with being self-obsessed (10). She does, however, confront that using the site has made her generation "wary of real human connection," which caters to some people's arguments that social networking sites induce people to create alternate personas to their real personalities since, as Mathias asserts, "[d]welling online is a cowardly and utterly enjoyable alternative to real interaction" (12).
- Weaknesses of the argument: Apropos of a column meant to entertain, Mathias uses broad generalizations about her generation that some might argue against, such as they're "me-focused" or closetly voyeuristic. Some could argue that creating these multiple personas or partaking in this online entertainment/discussion are rhetorical acts that are quite complex—ones worthy of discussion and analysis, not ridicule. She only uses anecdotes to support her assertions, so the reader has to trust her opinion, which is problematic.
- Appeals to ethos and pathos: The snarky tone of the piece presents an author who attempts to make herself sound smart by being sarcastic. Mathais' sense of humor provides a degree of *pathos* by warming up the reader to her angle of vision about Facebook.
- Genre of the argument: The op-ed piece offers a conversational tone for a wide audience that provides a distinct viewpoint about the world. The tone of Mathias—sarcastic, jovial, at times silly, represents a "person on the street" (or perhaps "person online") quality to the column.

Paul Noth, "I Can't Wait"

- Core of the argument: Online forums make people act and communicate differently than they would if they were involved in face-to-face communication.
- Major stases: This is a causal claim.
- Use of evidence and argumentative strategies: Noth uses an iconic image of young man and women walking hand-in-hand along the ocean to juxtapose how they might act to one another in an online discussion forum or a social networking site. The implied argument is that we have a different persona when hiding behind the computer screen, a persona that is exaggerated for effect.

Copyright © 2010, Pearson Education, Inc., Publishing as Longman

* Weaknesses of the argument: One could argue that many people act just as they normally would face-to-face in an online environment. In fact, some might argue that online environments give people with shy personalities or people who prefer writing over speaking to show their real feelings and thoughts because they're comfortable using the computer as a medium for communication. The cartoon might imply that people lie about themselves online, while in reality people might actually be more truthful through Web sites.
* Appeals to ethos and pathos: The cartoon presents a picture of a good relationship through that iconic image of a couple walking on the beach to contrast the possible character of an online relationship. The framing of the relationship in the cartoon creates good connotations to contrast what one might speculate as to how the couple would act like in online fora.
* Genre of the argument: Typical of cartoon, the message seems simple and clear (online conversations are fictional or somehow degraded), but the image and copy make readers think about the validity of that argument.

Dana L. Fleming, "Youthful Indiscretions: Should Colleges Protect Social Network Users from Themselves and Others?"

* Core of the argument: The use of social networking sites by college students has created issues with public safety, personal privacy, and student conduct, so institutions should implement some policy that reviews these sites when needed and warranted.
* Major stases: The argument uses a number of causal claims to show how the use of social networking sites has created problems for young adults, and the author proposes that institutions create review procedures to monitor online postings when necessary.
* Use of evidence and argumentative strategies: Fleming begins his article with a broad overview of the popularity of social networking sites and how easy it is to become a "friend" or be "friended" (paragraphs 1-4) while also relating that very few users employ the sites' privacy settings (5). In paragraphs 6-9, he offers a host of examples of how young adults foolishly used their sites and either got in trouble or were harmed because of their online activities. Some, like a student not getting an internship (6), are understandable, but another is an extreme case that is dangerous and disturbing (9). Fleming details the various ways in which institutions have reacted to or tried to guide students on the use of these sites (10-14), and he transitions to his wishy-washy thesis, "a targeted review of online social networking sites can be a good thing" (15). To support his thesis, he argues from precedent by drawing the connection to how courts use online postings as evidence, and he states that "[i]t stands to reason then, that schools are free to use content from these sites in their own judiciary proceedings" (15) because they should "treat them like any other university activity, subject to the school's code of conduct and applicable state and federal laws" (17). The author interestingly brings up FERPA in the next to last paragraph, but relates the fact that students are freely putting their personal information on the Web for many to see; therefore, colleges and universities should be able to use that information for their safety or for judicial matters related to the college.
* Weaknesses of the argument: While readers might agree with the author's assertions that college administrators should review online postings to protect students from themselves and protect the general welfare of their campuses, Fleming offers a vague set of

Copyright © 2010, Pearson Education, Inc., Publishing as Longman

guidelines because "targeted review of online social networking sites" is vague, open to various interpretations and possible abuses. For example, some readers could take issue with the examples of swimmers losing athletic scholarships, the "Drunken Pirate" student, and the law student being reprimanded for activities that should be considered "free speech." Sure, they can put those thoughts and images on the Web, but that doesn't give those institutions the right to infringe upon their rights as citizens, some would argue. In addition, the analogy to evidence in criminal court referred to in paragraph 15 could be questioned since someone writing silly comments or venting anger on an online forum is quite different than criminal acts judged in the legal system.

- Appeals to ethos and pathos: The author provides a calm, third-person dominant tone to the argument, a voice that seems open-minded and thoughtful. Fleming uses emotional appeals in some of the examples in the piece, particularly the horrific one that relates the dangers of social networking sites—the danger of having anonymous "friends."
- Genre of the argument: Because it is written in an academic journal, the author refrains from using first-person and relies heavily on examples and use of precedent. His audience values *logos*, so he attempts to persuade them by examples and analogy/precedent.

Adam Sternbergh, "Hey There, Lonelygirl"

- Core of the argument: The video blog featuring "Lonelygirl15" is a fake because of a number of criteria—"[s]he's just a little *too* charming, her videos a little *too* well edited, and her story a little *too* neatly laid out" (paragraph 2). The author also argues that this mini-saga will, in turn, become a "brand-new art form" that he calls "WikiTV" (6).
- Major stases: This author's commentary begins with an evaluative claim and ends with a causal claim.
- Use of evidence and argumentative strategies: Sternbergh marshals evidence from his own observations of the "micro-soap" (1) coupled with the interactive commentary spawned by the YouTube serial broadcast. The author speculates that this episode on the Web is an example of a new type of marketing that will grow as the Web grows, and author uses his questioning of the credibility of the site as his main form of argumentative support. The assumption is that viewers are becoming more and more accustomed to interactive features with their entertainment programs, so the Lonelygirl example is a natural outgrowth of that phenomena.
- Weaknesses of the argument: As is the nature of columns about popular culture, the claims are based mainly on inductive leaps and observation, although it's clear that the author was on to what was going on.
- Appeals to ethos and pathos: The author presents himself in a light-hearted but snarky manner, appropriate of a column on pop culture. Sarcasm, such as "Lonelygirl 15 should be just as annoying as the rest of them" (1), "ultimate viral marketing technique" (4), among others, makes sense for his audience and subject matter.
- Genre of the argument: Apropos of column on this pop culture, the argument rests mainly on conjecture, hearsay, and observation.

Copyright © 2010, Pearson Education, Inc., Publishing as Longman

"A Message from the Creators"

* Core of the argument: Just as Adam Sternbergh predicts, "The Creators" of Lonelygirl15 argue that the reality of the videoblog is that it's really a fiction and represents "the birth of a new art form" (paragraph 1)
* Major stases: This argument is definitional in scope. The authors try to define the videoblog and now website as a different type of entertainment that connects a good story with the interaction of users.
* Use of evidence and argumentative strategies: The authors fend off the main line of questioning about the site (who is she?) with some rhetoric jujitsu. They take that interest and tell readers that it doesn't matter because what they really care about is the story and because Lonelygirl15 somehow represents all of us: "the portions of our personalities that we choose to show (or hide) when we interact with the people around us" (2). Moving from that ploy of "art for art's sake," the authors make a sales pitch about their upcoming "website" devoted to the Web-soap and attempt to appeal to their viewers with assertions of appreciation sprinkled throughout the piece: ""To Our Incredible Fans," "our tireless and dedicated fans" (2), and [y]ou are the only reason for our success, and we appreciate your devotion" (4). Their argument is that this story is a new medium based around traditional video storytelling that is "constantly evolving with the audience" (1).
* Weaknesses of the argument: To viewers of YouTube who value the authenticity of videos on that site, the skirting of the issue of who the person is might anger them, but the creators might effectively parry the "hoax" claim by their positive and upbeat expression of how Lonelygirl's story is just like everyone else's, revealing our common humanity since we might act differently around different people. But one could question if this was the original intent of the videoblogs, why weren't these important details put forth from the beginning? Viewers could appropriately think that Lonelygirl15 used YouTube as a way to hook viewers and then translated that good fortune into something larger and restricted if the Web site requires fees.
* Appeals to ethos and pathos: The authors use conciliatory language toward their viewers throughout the piece, so that is an attempt to put the reader in the frame of mind they want them to be in. And the authors also try to show themselves as just one of them with these words, "We want you to know that we aren't a big corporation. We are just like you. A few people who love good stories" (4). The assertion paints their work as not mainstream media, and they argue that the site enacts "the creator inside all of us" (4) since viewers comments are part of the story too.
* Genre of the argument: For the most part, this is a sales pitch, although not a traditional one. Because of this marketing genre, there is a great deal of care and repetition to show how the creators appreciate the fans of Lonelygirl15.

Yasuhide Fumoto, "The Thinker, Reimagined"

* Core of the argument: The act of thinking is being heavily influenced by our use of computer technology, to the extent that we are hemmed in by computer use, thereby limiting our creativity and depth of introspection. So we might be using the computer so

Copyright © 2010, Pearson Education, Inc., Publishing as Longman

much that we are losing our traditional ways of learning about topics and subjects via printed materials, face-to-face discussion, and isolated reflection free of technological influences.

- Major stases: Thinking in our postmodern world has become overly reliant on the use of computers to the extent that speed, convenience, and anonymous interactivity are valued over traditional reflection, face-to-face interaction, and deep thought.
- Use of evidence and argumentative strategies: The image of the laptop is foreboding in that it acts as a shield to the outside world, limiting the types of interaction and methods of knowledge gathering that people now use. The iconic image of the thinker is diminutive in comparison to the open but predatory-looking laptop along with the power cord circling around the "thinker." The image might suggest that our culture's belief that technology is a cure-all severely limits human potential. While we may have more information more readily available, the traditional aspects of thinking—thinking on your own, deep reflection—have been diminished in our culture.
- Weaknesses of the argument: Those who support the ever-increasing use of computers could argue that the technologies have not limited us or diminished traditional literacies, but they have enhanced self-expression (blogs, Web sites), convenience of finding sources (databases), and human interaction (social networking sites, online discussion forums). Rather than the laptop hindering the thinker, they would argue that the cartoon should show the thinker pondering as he sits in front of a laptop.
- Appeals to ethos and pathos: The image of the thinker is one that creates a certain credibility or even feeling about what an intellectual does, so Fumoto's use of the image appeals to emotions in a way.
- Genre of the argument: Like many effective visual arguments, this cartoon makes the viewer make his or her own connections to what "it means." Without copy, the cartoon invites the viewer to speculate on the positives and negatives of the relationship between the thinker and laptop.

Copyright © 2010, Pearson Education, Inc., Publishing as Longman

VIDEO GAMES AND THEIR INFLUENCE

Iowa State University New Service, "ISU Psychologists Publish Three New Studies on Violent Video Game Effects on Youths"

- Core of the argument: Repeated exposure to violent video games makes young adults more violent.
- Major stases: While this is a newspaper article, the claims are causal.
- Use of evidence and argumentative strategies: The article cites "concrete evidence" (paragraph 1) in its first sentence, so the weight of the argument is based on the three studies cited within the article. The first study had participants play violent and non-violent games and then play another game that has participants use "noise blasts" (6). The researcher found "significantly more high-noise blasts" by those who played the violent video games, concluding that the role of inflicting "intentional harm" in a game seems to the be what "increases aggression" among subjects (8). The second study of high school students examined how much exposure they had to violent video games and correlated that exposure to people who "held more pro-violent attitudes, had more hostile personalities, were less forgiving, believed violence to be more typical, and behaved more aggressively in their everyday lives" (9). The third study of grade school children tracked students who were exposed to violent video games early in the semester were, in turn, more aggressive five months later while finding "an apparent lack of 'immunity' to the effects of media violence exposure. TV and video games screen time was also found to be a significant negative predictor of grades" (16).
- Weaknesses of the argument: Like any causal argument, detractors can find other causes or flaws in the studies to question the accuracy of the researchers' findings. For Study One, opponents might question the "significance" of the data comparisons about the noise blasts. Also, how can playing interactive games really connect to the noise blast experiment since they are very different measures? One could also question why college students are used with 9 to 12 year olds. That's quite an age gap. For Study Two, opponents could simply chalk up those findings to the idea that people who have more violent tendencies are drawn to playing those games. In essence, the students seek them out because they're innately more violent—not video games making them more violent. That claim connects to the caveat that "trait forgiveness" makes people less affected since it sounds as though that trait is part of person's character or personality. For Study Three, opponents could question the findings because exposure to violent video games early in the semester is only *one* factor causing them to become more violent. There are many other factors that could lead grade school children to more violent behavior: child-rearing techniques, TV programs, personality traits, etc.
- Appeals to ethos and pathos: Since it's a news wire report, the article really calls upon the *ethos* of the researchers, who are cited in the paragraph two. The article does frame the study in a ground-breaking way though—"the first book to unit empirical research and public policy related to violent video games" (2).
- Genre of the argument: The article is a report that compiles the basic information about recent findings that appeal to a newspaper audience, which explains the short paragraphing and use of summary.

Copyright © 2010, Pearson Education, Inc., Publishing as Longman

Henry Jenkins, "Reality Bytes: Eight Myths about Video Games Debunked"

- Core of the argument: Video games do not cause people to become more violent in our culture; in fact, for the most part they are a positive force in American society.
- Major stases: This is an evaluative argument with *logos* as the embedded criteria. The argument also relies heavily on causal claims.
- Use of evidence and argumentative strategies: The whole article uses the pattern of myth vs. reality as its organizing principle. Jenkins' modus operandi within the piece is to debunk, complicate the causes or issue, and then sometimes provide a positive outlook on effects of video games. Like others who see video games as a symptom of a person's character, he refers to "mental stability" and "quality of home life" early on (paragraph 1) along with correlation rather than cause as more realistic explanation of violence (2). Threaded throughout his piece are various experts or artifacts that support his claims and assumptions, such as the U.S. Surgeon General's report (1), Gerard Jones (4), David Grossman (5), James Gee (6), Judge Posner (7), and Eric Zimmerman (9). He uses varied sources to support his cause, which is productive in showing a breadth of support. Jenkins uses statistics quite a bit to debunk perceptions by relating the sheer number of young adults who play video games, the majority of market being 18 or older, and the strong percentages that show gamers are not isolating themselves but connecting to one another. He adeptly concedes that advertising and marketing needs to be restricted to young adults (3), but turns that issue to the commonplace that familial support is crucial. His statement that "parents need to share some of the responsibility…" (3) provides a careful understatement that might make a reader become indignant and think, "They shouldn't share 'some;' they should have *most* of the responsibility." Jenkins also parries the argument of "The military uses video games to train people to kill" by people by relating the fact that the video games work in concert with shooting practice, hand-to-hand combat, etc. He offers the perspective that the military uses video games for learning, which then extends to his line of argumentation that they "are designed to be ethical testing grounds" that make viewers examine moral values (7). Using another commonplace, Jenkins employs the assumption that young adults and adults know the differences between "play" and real life.
- Weaknesses of the argument: While Jenkins does vaguely relate that females are playing games more often, his assertion that female characters "are often portrayed as powerful and independent" could be true, but one could question how their body images are portrayed with characters such as Laura Croft, among others. They're independent, sure, but they're still *killing* people and shaping perceptions about body image. While some might agree that video games can be used as learning tools and can connect people through gaming networks, others might cite that that much exposure to video games gives people a skewed view of the world since they rarely interact with the environment in traditional ways. While people may interact online, face-to-face interaction is decreasing. It's also possible that some games are "ethical testing grounds" (7), but detractors could certainly describe many violent games in specific and concrete detail and question how games like *Grand Theft Auto* are "learning experiences" testing ethics. Early on too he quickly dismisses studies on "methodological grounds" (2) without examining them, although he does admit that "video games may be one risk factor" (2). In addition, parents who see their children act out what they've done in video games could

Copyright © 2010, Pearson Education, Inc., Publishing as Longman

anecdotally argue against the idea that violence is merely "correlation" or a "'magic circle' of play" (9). Statistics and experts who support one's cause are powerful, but examples are quite persuasive also.

* Appeals to ethos and pathos: The author provides a straightforward and no-nonsense tone to his argument. His use of concession enhances his credibility because it shows how he's willing to admit that video games are factors. However, his repeated association with *Computer Games Magazine* might make some readers question his credibility, perhaps making them think he's a corporate shill.
* Genre of the argument: The essay has a rapid-fire approach to "debunking" perceptions about video games while using various sources to back his case.

Malcolm Gladwell, "Brain Candy"

* Core of the argument: To a large degree, Gladwell's argument is essentially presenting Steven Johnson's argument in his book. But the argument is that postmodern TV programs and video games present a different form of learning than traditional schooling; therefore, people's demonizing of reality TV and video games is misguided.
* Major stases: This is a book review, so it's an evaluative argument based on the *logos* of Johnson's book, but Johnson's argument is also an evaluative argument too.
* Use of evidence and argumentative strategies: Gladwell begins the piece in a savvy manner by relating the fact that IQ tests are calibrated constantly to keep the average at 100, which denotes that generation after generation is scoring higher on IQ tests (paragraph 1). To agree with Johnson's argument, the author gives examples of how TV programs now require greater interaction and "what Johnson calls 'filling in,'" (3) than formulaic programs of an earlier time, which coheres to their points that TV programs require viewers to become strong analytical thinkers as they view *The Wire* or *Big Brother*. Gladwell uses a similar comparison strategy by contrasting the rudimentary video games that were popular early on to the highly interactive video games that demand critical thinking and improvisation of players while thinking about "a longer-term strategy" (6). Then Johnson through Gladwell uses a "what if" contrast arguing strategy by showing how critics would discount traditional learning by reading books if reading books came after video games (7). To reinforce the gist of the argument, Gladwell (Johnson) defines his terms by relating that reading is "explicit learning," and interactive realms such as video games represent "collateral learning" (8). So Gladwell argues that both types of learning are valid and essential. Instead of only valuing "the explicit over the collateral," as he shows is the case with the example elementary school kids having less recess time, we are limiting our human potential.
* Weaknesses of the argument: Opponents of Gladwell/Johnson's argument might counter argue that while young adults can certainly learn a lot from video games because of their interactive and problem-solving focus, it's really about the amount of time that kids spend playing video games. Gladwell paints the use of video games as a natural outgrowth of learning, but many young adults, they would argue, do not spend enough time with "explicit learning" since they're unable to analytically read and unpack the nuances, assumptions, and logical support of written and visual arguments in our culture. Instead of testing hypotheses and thinking about our common good, they're being entertained into isolation. Sure, they interact with like-minded people who also like a

Copyright © 2010, Pearson Education, Inc., Publishing as Longman

certain TV program or play certain games, but do they branch out from there? Also, one could argue that the content of these video games provide disturbing images that really influence how children think about the world. If TV or video games are replacing how one might explore ideas and learn "explicitly" about concepts, places, and reflections while not interacting with one's family, who becomes the role models of young adults? Also, while both authors seem to critique the linear plot lines and rudimentary themes of both TV programs and video games, one could easily point to other programs and games that show those attributes.

* Appeals to ethos and pathos: Gladwell establishes his ethos early on with his contextualization of IQ tests within history, which makes the reader see that he's a serious and reflective writer. Gladwell uses Johnson's humorous but revealing "what if" strategy to perhaps make readers see their argument much more clearly, and he masterfully uses the example of how unstructured play, "recess," is being diminished to work as an emotional appeal for many readers since a lot of us probably look back at recess with nostalgia.
* Genre of the argument: Gladwell writes book reviews for the erudite *New Yorker*, where sometimes the author and book being reviewed merge in the piece of writing. In some reviews, the piece of writing centers more on the reviewer's ideas brought up by the book than the book itself. Since it's obvious that Gladwell agrees with Johnson, the review turns into a co-authored argument.

Michael Humphrey, "For a Virtual Dose of Reality, a Different Kind of Video Game"

* Core of the argument: Since video games can influence perceptions and attitudes, games with a social consciousness can do a lot of good in the world.
* Major stases: The makers of Games for Change are making a sales pitch that incorporates both resemblance and causal claims.
* Use of evidence and argumentative strategies: Since this is a newspaper article devoted to detailing this company, the article mainly relies on what the creators say about their games and what players relate. The thrust behind the social awareness games is the assumption that video games are an appropriate way to reach out to young adults in order to get them interested in certain issues or problems. The implicit argument is that since video games create effects in our culture (not merely an outgrowth of our culture), people can create games that will then be used as teaching tools for consciousness-raising.
* Weaknesses of the argument: One of the main counterarguments against the whole project can be found as paragraph 13 where the author asks the question, "But will ICED change attitudes toward immigration?" The project itself is based on the belief that video games can be used as teaching tools, so those who see them as sources of entertainment, not likely to create much of an impact, would question the efficacy of this product. Also, one could say that, yes, the games might raise social awareness, but whether that translates to people doing something in their corners of the world to address poverty, global warming, and other issues is specious. There are some causal links that need to be made.
* Appeals to ethos and pathos: The author of the piece uses a quasi-objective tone to relate the project, and the references to world poverty, immigration, and other issues probably evokes a bit of *pathos* for the readers of the *National Catholic Reporter*.

Copyright © 2010, Pearson Education, Inc., Publishing as Longman

* Genre of the argument: The document is traditional informational article devoted to profiling a new entity in a specialized newsmagazine.

William Lugo, "Violent Video Games Recruit American Youth"

* Core of the argument: The military's use of video games that offer simulated training and combat exercises is unethical because it hides the realities of war and being in the military.
* Major stases: This argument exemplifies a hybrid of evaluative claims (this practice is unethical) and causal claims (why the military is doing this, what's left out of the video games).
* Use of evidence and argumentative strategies: Lugo uses thick description of the military's games to paint a picture for readers. But his main strategies are finding criteria to evaluate the ethical nature of these games: price, realism/credibility of the gaming experience, and motivation/reason for the games. Throughout, one of his customary rhetorical ploys is to use rhetorical question to question an aspect about his phenomenon and then provide his reasoning to answer that question. So counterarguments are not grappled with much, if not at all. Lugo first notes that these games are free, which is counter to profit motive of video games, and he reasons that it's free because it's from the United States military, which attacks the credibility of the Army's motives (paragraph 2). In rich detail the author describes *Full Spectrum Warrior*, which is a simulation of Iraq that is highly unrealistic because the urban combat situation does not have women and children in the online environment, which he connects to making recruits not see the "gray areas" of combat or the potential for horrific destruction that combat entails (3). However, *Full Spectrum Warrior* is not a military game like *America's Army* but only uses the brand of the U.S. military to legitimize the combat experience that Lugo questions (no women or children in the line of fire). Lugo asserts that the military is using video games for recruitment because it's a much cheaper strategy than traditional recruiting and it makes basic training much eaiser than it really is by facilitating "do-overs" (6) or shielding recruits from hard ethical decisions that are part of combat missions since "virtually no women and children walk the streets. Thus, the possibility of killing innocent people does not exist" (7). Lugo further shows the contrast between typical load times of video games to the load times associated with the military's games in that America's Army's load times are much longer and capitalize on a captive audience by using the "Soldier's Creed" during load times (9-10). He then supports the propagandist element of the creed through the words of Colonel Keven A. Shwedo (10). While Lugo thinks the marketing strategy using video games is "brilliant" (12), he also calls it "unethical" based on his relation of the unrealistic simulations they provide and the assumption that "[t]eenagers have no idea they are being recruited and neither do their parents" (11).
* Weaknesses of the argument: While Lugo's point about the games being unrealistic is a solid point in criticizing these games, his argument that these games are "unethical" could be questioned. In fact, readers could point out throughout the piece his anti-military tone in the article, which could be a sign of bias against the military. One would need to know exactly how these games are "unethical." The author seems to think readers will agree with him. Just because the military is making these games doesn't necessarily mean that

Copyright © 2010, Pearson Education, Inc., Publishing as Longman

these video games are the only perspective they might have influence their perceptions about combat. Popular war movies or a mini-series such as HBO's *Generation Kill* could provide sobering critiques of the military that could influence them. Also, the statement that teenagers don't know they're being recruited is unsupported and rests on belief—not facts. And wouldn't people who are drawn to the military be drawn to games such as these anyway, so it's really just a matter of the American military more efficiently finding the recruits they would have had a good chance at anyway.

* Appeals to ethos and pathos: As noted, Lugo's tone could be seen as anti-military from the outset, so depending on one's leanings that tone could enhance or diminish the power of his argument. Much of the argument is an exercise in attacking the credibility of these games, so leading students to considering whether those attacks are credible is key for analysis
* Genre of the argument: This researched argument would resonate well with the readers of *Reclaiming Children and Youth*, whose mission connects with the appeal that Lugo uses in the last part of the argument—that young adults need to be empowered. So the argument is researched, but it doesn't really address counterarguments at all.

Copyright © 2010, Pearson Education, Inc., Publishing as Longman

THE NEW MEDIA: RESPONSIBLE PRODUCTION, RESPONSIBLE CONSUMPTION

William Powers, "The Massless Media"

- Core of the argument: Counter to how many critics lambaste how the news media is becoming more and more fragmented because of cable news networks, more prevalent niche news, blogs, and American citizens picking their news broadcasting more often according to the their political biases, Powers argues that the current situation in the news media is a sign of heightened political awareness and greater critical citizenship, which has historical precedents from 18th and 19th century America.
- Major stases: This argument exemplifies a resemblance/evaluative claim that derives much of its power from discussion of the news media in American history and causal claims that show how the media landscape has changed and is changing so rapidly.
- Use of evidence and argumentative strategies: Powers analyzes the media landscape by explaining that currently there is no true "mass media" anymore because of the explosion of technological advances that have catered to individuals' preferences for certain types of news rather than the days of three television networks that mainly presented the same information throughout the 50s and 80s. The author offers the realistic example of Fox News Channel's consumer base and how many viewers describe themselves as conservatives contrasted to CNN, the other main cable news channel, as being perceived as mainly serving a Democratic base. Ratings data supports this claim by the predominance of conservatives viewing coverage of the Republican Convention on Fox News and CNN placing first in rating for cable news channels during the Democratic Convention (paragraph 4). Many pundits, Powers comments, bemoan this politicization of the media (6, 10) and how there are so many diverse market segments that target specific niche audiences (7-9), but in Powers' opinion the fragmented and chaotic new news media is really more realistic than it was throughout most of the country's history because "the centralized, homogeneous mass-media environment… was really an anomaly, an exception to the historical rule. For two centuries before the arrival of television America has a wild, cacophonous, emphatically decentralized media culture that mirrored society itself" (11). He asserts that the new technology of television made the news a package that was shared by all and centralized (causal), but now with the advent and power of the Internet, bloggers, and 24/7 news networks these changes have democratized the media and are possibly a sign of good things to come.

  Powers provides a concise history understanding of the media post-1721, with the spark lit by the *New England Courant*, signaling a change for newspapers to be irreverent and highly critical of governmental power. Citing respected sources like Isaacson, Starr, and Tocqueville, the author suggests that the media in the 18th and 19th centuries reflected a turbulent time in America's history when citizens were deeply questioning the country's proper direction through newspapers, of which "80 percent … were avowedly partisan" (17). Rather than helping assimilate the diversity of Americans, Powers suggests, the media offered outlets for many different voices, which he links (resemblance) to today's news landscape that offers specialized news, bloggers of influence, sensationalized journalism, and partisan media squabbles—a news media that isn't so dependent upon having a "safe neutrality" that won't offend people (21). His evaluation of the historical causal chain posits that because leaders in postwar American

Copyright © 2010, Pearson Education, Inc., Publishing as Longman

had pretty much similar goals, the Cronkite era of three networks providing similar messages and news was created. He claims that the "Reagan era and the end of the Cold War dealt the old politico-media structure the final blows" (23). Through a diverse media now comprised of partisan reporting, blogs, and cable network echo chambers, American citizens pick and choose their news according to their ideologies (28) while still supporting larger national publications, as evidenced by the recent gains by the *New York Times*, *Wall Street Journal*, and *USA Today* (26). Powers questions the assumption that niche-based news hurts democracy; in fact, he suggests that because of the highly combustible new outlets and partisan bickering democracy is actually doing better as shown by the higher than normal voter turnout for the 2004 Presidential election (30).

- <u>Weaknesses of the argument</u>: Powers states in the final paragraph that there is "no substantive evidence yet that the rise of the niche is bad for democracy" (30), but an arguer can't offer the lack of evidence as evidence that the "niche" is perhaps positive for civic engagement (Appealing to Ignorance fallacy). Also, the single criterion of voter turnout isn't the only factor by which a properly functioning democracy is evaluated, and many would question whether the media climate is healthy just because there are supposedly diverse viewpoints out there. Some media analysts, in contrast, are quite worried about media ownership because a number of major corporations (see "Why Media Ownnership Matters…" by the Goodmans) own approximately 90 percent of the media outlets in the United States. People concerned about this issue could argue that while the media may look diverse and partisan it is really controlled by corporate interests that lack the fortitude and integrity to do true investigative journalism, which requires substantial funding rather than relying on recycled news stories by the newswire services. While Powers' relation of the media in the 18th and 19th centuries is instructive and perhaps comparable in some ways to our own, issues of corporate ownership, the immediacy of news, literacy factors, and the apathetic nature of American citizenry could be quite different from our own era, one could argue. Like any analogy, it's not an exact one-to-one match. Also, as many everyday citizens can write blogs and influence some people's opinions, where is the editorial filter and fact-checking that many readers demand? Powers tends to dismiss concerns over quality of information and how Americans citizens might be easy to manipulate through graphic images, unchecked claims by governmental officials, reliance on government sources, and well articulated and timely released "leaks" of information. In addition, what does the partisan news media do to argument as a whole when most outlets offer simplistic pro/con debates, biased analyses, and sloppy reporting? Where's respect for others' opinions? And what about argument as truth-seeking and persuasion for the greater good of the whole country, not just people who think like you do?
- <u>Appeals to ethos and pathos</u>: Powers' ethos is reflective and open to exploration of where exactly the new media culture is taking us. He doesn't address opposing viewpoints in detail—they are mainly used as a springboard from which to provide his own resemblance claim and evaluation—so that could hurt his credibility some.
- <u>Genre of the argument</u>: This short argument provides a "different take" that some readers of the *Atlantic Monthly* might welcome, a positive, upbeat view on how the media is becoming democratized in contrast to the logically-driven and very serious articles in the well-respected magazine.

Copyright © 2010, Pearson Education, Inc., Publishing as Longman

Yahoo! Home Page

- Having students evaluate the organization of the Home Page based on order, highlighted information, and advertisements could be very instructive and revealing to how an online provider tries to keep its clients happy. With this screen shot, leading students to question why the focus on body image and pop culture at the top supported by visual cues while "News" is pushed farther down the page. Showing the visual and organizational contrast between "real news" and "infotainment" could be a focus of discussion along with commentary what images are most prominent and why. Also, asking how this home page frames how they see the world or themselves might be an appropriate question since it relates to a definite "angle of vision" produced by a corporation and reinforced on a daily basis.

Dan Kennedy, "Plugged In, Tuned Out: Young Americans Are Embracing New Media but Failing to Develop an Appetite for News"

- Core of the argument: While news outlets are becoming more "Web 2.0," younger people still do not seem to have a desire for local, national, and world news. Therefore, a citizenry that is not well informed about the world around them is detrimental to our republic.
- Major stases: Kennedy makes a causal argument about how the younger generation's lack of initiative to read and discuss important national and world events creates a self-absorbed and uncritical citizenry.
- Use of evidence and argumentative strategies: Kennedy main organizing principle in this argument is to first show how younger people do not read newspapers or watch news programs or care much about hard news, and then he explores the causes and effects of this phenomenon that he finds troubling. Important to note in this argument is his extensive use of sources from the news media and people who specialize in new media. After beginning with a description of people no longer reading newspapers anymore (paragraphs 1-4), he asserts that those under 40 do not have a "news habit" like the generations before them, which is supported by a Harvard professor's comments (4-5). Citing an "aversion to *news* media," (6), Kennedy presents comparable statistics of news consumption now to consumption of the news in the 50s and 60s (6-7). The author concedes through Professor Patterson that a diversified media is one of the culprits, and Kennedy argues that a lack of "news habit" is damaging to the ideal of "civic life, the ideal of an informed citizenry, and our ability to govern ourselves" (9). Using an example of one of his students as an anomaly (10-11), Kennedy then brings in the popular book *Bowling Alone* to reassert the lack of interest in the news by younger Americans (12). Citing an expert on how "there is a direct correlation between voting and news awareness" (13) along with a survey by the Pew Research Center that presents young people's paucity of knowledge of current affairs, Kennedy works with the counterarguments that newer media sources—such as *The Daily Show* (15-19); online newspapers (25-26), blogs, interactive media outlets, and podcasts (27-32, 37); and social networking sites such as Blue Mass Group and Digg.com (35-36, 41-43)—are ways in which the news media has transformed to be more interactive and more enticing to younger Americans. Kennedy concedes that these are interesting developments that news

Copyright © 2010, Pearson Education, Inc., Publishing as Longman

media outlets are using and attempting to tap into the younger market; however, he counters that optimism by asserting that lack of interest in news by younger Americans is caused mainly by affluence and self-absorption. He further counters the feel-good marketing of participatory news sites by stating, "…for participatory news to work, you need participants. And the evidence suggest that young adults (most of them, anyway) are not using these new tools to learn about the world around them," an assertion that is supported by the data and surveys related earlier in the piece. Kennedy concludes the argument with the famous statement by Neil Postman about us "amusing ourselves to death" (47), which works as a maxim to reassert his thesis: younger Americans need to care more about the news and their democracy.

- Weaknesses of the argument: Readers could question Kennedy's use of experts because he uses a number of like-minded people to support his argument. Although Kennedy works with a common enthymeme, a commonplace in our culture that connects to Thomas Jefferson's assertion that "An enlightened citizenry is indispensable to the proper functioning of a republic," one could question whether our country has ever had a true informed citizenry who votes for good reasons. That assumption is the linchpin of his argument, so whether a reader agrees with it (most may, but some may not) affects the argument's persuasion. While Kennedy cites statistics about reading newspapers and watching newscasts, his sources point about how "…CNN executives think that we're idiots" could be another cause of younger adults' aversion to traditional forms of the news since both newspapers and newscasts (driven now more by the profit motive, shareholders' interest, and dominated by multi-media corporations concerned about cutting costs) regularly provide "infotainment" rather than hard news. Those factors might also cause "the cratering circulation of daily newspapers" (22). He also tends to depict younger Americans as self-absorbed, an assumption that can be debated.
- Appeals to ethos and pathos: Kennedy enhances his *ethos* in the argument by showing different perspective on the news media, how it's changing for the worse and for the better, and the various causes. At times his tone is exploratory, but at other times, he comes across as more cynical. Facts such as people not able to identify the secretary of state or the disparity of statistics about media consumption are meant to shock early on—to grab readers' attention.
- Genre of the argument: The argument is place-specific since it's written for a magazine devoted to Massachusetts, so that explains the multiple references to and examples from Boston. Since the magazine is devoted to public policy questions, which are usually discussed in the traditional media, the subject could be of particular importance to readers of this magazine.

Chris Shaw, "Should Killers Be Given Air Time,"

- Core of the argument: Like terrorists, mass murderers like Cho Seung-hui use digital media for self-aggrandizement and propaganda, but "news organizations did not have much of a choice about showing the material but the implications are quite scary" (paragraph 13).
- Major stases: This speculative argument is a combination of resemblance and causal claims.
- Use of evidence and argumentative strategies: Shaw draws a quick comparison of the

Copyright © 2010, Pearson Education, Inc., Publishing as Longman

Columbine killers and Seung-hui to terrorists and bomb attacks in Iraq (8-9). Shaw argues that the news outlets "did not have much of a choice" because, it's implied, that the video offers insight into the killer's mindset and explains his motivation, which is newsworthy and trumps the concerns of family members whose loved ones were killed by Seung-hui.

- Weaknesses of the argument: It's not exactly clear how terrorists and attacks on troops in Iraq are comparable to a mass murderer's YouTube moment. They both use digital images, but one could question how comparable these acts are. Shaw's thesis—that they "did not have much of a choice"—is debatable. Someone arguing against Shaw could provide numerous examples of how news outlets don't release content or names of victims to their audiences because images are offensive, violent, or insensitive.
- Appeals to ethos and pathos: Shaw attempts to strike a conciliatory tone by saying that "[f]ears of copy-cat killings … are not unfounded" (5), so he reaches out to possible readers who worry about how the video will cause others to follow the killer's example. And the author provides language that provides a tone of emotional concern with words and phrases such as these: "sinister," "disturbed," "ethical issues," "quite scary," and "massacre,"
- Genre of the argument: Since it's a short newspaper article, the author employs very short paragraphs for concision, paragraphs that get to the point quite quickly and succinctly.

Daryl Cagle, "Those Terrible Virginia Tech Cartoons"

- Core of the argument: Driven by a daily deadline and an art form that by nature is "negative" (paragraph 6), it's typical that many of the cartoons about the Virginia Tech tragedy were insensitive and knee-jerk. Political cartoonists and the media as a whole need to take more time to cover a story "until there is something constructive to say" (7).
- Major stases: This is a causal claim that ends with a soft proposal.
- Use of evidence and argumentative strategies: After establishing his authority as a cartoonist and head of cartoonist syndicate, he uses one subscriber's comments to highlight the effects of daily deadlines for political cartoonists: insensitivity and formulaic responses (2). Transitioning from the cartoonist to the news media as a whole, he belittles NBC broadcasting the killer's manifesto and reporter's inane questions to Virginia Tech students. He concludes that the media needs to learn how "to take a step back" and wait for more thorough and sensitive coverage of a tragedy to emerge with time.
- Weaknesses of the argument: While his proposal at the end is laudable, people could argue that it's very unrealistic. Media outlets, driven by getting the scoop and driven by their audiences who want information right away, are simply catering to their audiences. While NBC could be criticized for presenting the killer's video manifesto, one could argue that their duty is to present the killer with information that they have available so that people can see how disturbed he was. The playing of the video, one could argue, is to show his irrationality to better understand and hopefully stop future campus killers.
- Appeals to ethos and pathos: Cagle establishes his credibility thoroughly by referencing his experience as a cartoonist and his work as an owner of cartooning syndicate (2-3, 5-6). He expresses sympathy for cartoonists having daily deadlines (2) while relating that he's fortunate not to have them (6), which in a sense undercuts his argument. Cagle uses

Copyright © 2010, Pearson Education, Inc., Publishing as Longman

loaded language to show that he has sympathy for those who died by calling the killer a "lunatic" (1) and implying he was a "nut-case" (4).

- Genre of the argument: Apropos of a blog post, Cagle's argument is short, pulls from his experience, and offers soft proposal for readers to mull over.

Sydney Schanberg, "Not a Pretty Picture"

- Core of the argument: Growing government intervention and media self-censorship goes against the tradition of a true free press, one that reports the facts, requires transparency, and asks the difficult questions of our leaders and their actions.
- Major stases: This is a definitional claim because Schanberg evaluates the current news media as going against an idealized norm of behavior, essentially how the press should act and has acted in the past. The author makes an evaluation because he believes the move to "censor and sanitize" (paragraph 8) the news creates a weakened democracy that goes against ideals of full disclosure and critical citizenry.
- Use of evidence and argumentative strategies: Beginning with a shocking statement from the philosopher Hegel and incisive questions about why the news media does not provide coverage of the "slaughter" in Iraq (1-2), Schanberg proceeds to offer examples of how the American government has created preventative measures to let the American people see the effects of the war through the notable example of photographers not being able to take pictures of caskets at Dover Air Force Base, combined with his intimation (without support) that governmental officials intimidate and restrict the American press corps in other ways. Employing the raw data of soldiers killed and wounded in the conflict, he asks the reader, "And when was the last time you saw a picture of a single fallen American solider…?" (6) while claiming that visual images "have become sparser and sparser" (7). Addressing counterarguments, he provides the Bush's administration's rationale that the government's actions of not letting caskets be photographed is a result of honoring the dead and privacy of the soldiers' families along with a columnist's ideas that the use of horrific photographs is on the upswing and only helps the insurgency. Going against the latter claim, he offers an expert's opinion (Kurtz) that such photographs are actually becoming less frequently used (10). Schanberg implies that the columnist's call for restraint goes against the ideal of free press and smacks of censorship and media manipulation, as used by Rudolph Giuliani while conceding that he, like the columnist, abhors the sensationalism of the 24/7 media climate. However, he insists that a journalist's true role is to provide the reality of the situations about which he or she reports and offer diverse views about a subject—in his words, the "primary mission has to be one of getting the story right" regardless of considerations of shock value and sensitivity (12). He finally concludes, through a substantial statement by photographer David Leeson (14), that the main journalistic mission—reporting the story accurately—takes precedence over journalistic restraint.
- Weaknesses of the argument: To a skeptical reader, Schanberg's idealized journalist would be just that, an ideal that isn't reflective of reality. Some could say that to "support our troops" that journalists need to consider closely the messages they present about the Iraq war, especially since terrorist networks could exploit such images for their own purposes. The author provides these opposing viewpoints; however, he doesn't refute them effectively and with any degree of detail. He simply relies on the belief that the

Copyright © 2010, Pearson Education, Inc., Publishing as Longman

ideal of "reporting the facts" as supported by sympathetic sources who think like him. He boldly claims that "[t]he true reason" why the administration wants to use censorship and manage the journalists is because "an outcry … might bring down the administration" (8). That could be a plausible aim of the Bush administration, but Schanberg has no proof to support such a claim. Since he has an obvious anti-Bush frame of vision, his tone and claims about the administration wouldn't persuade those who have different perceptions of the president or beliefs about how the news media should work. His argument from analogy—restraint likened to Giuliani's time frame manipulation—is not a direct match. One could argue that journalistic restraint on sensitive subjects and images is different than a mayor releasing crime data for the sake of not getting bad press.

- Appeals to ethos and pathos: As a Pulitzer Prize-winning journalist and as someone who has covered wars and atrocities throughout his career, he refers to his own experience throughout the opinion piece. He supports his credibility and the use of the opening quotation about "slaughter" by the fact that he "served in the military" and has reported on many different wars (8). The reader knows that he's seen war first-hand, and a number of his sources are reputable, namely David Leeson and Cheryl Diaz Meyer. Leeson's powerful and emotional statement at the end of column provides a great deal of pathos by revealing that in regard to vivid photographs and realistic reporting, "'the greatest dignity and respect you can give them [the victims] is to show the horror they have suffered, the absolutely gruesome horror'" (14). The powerful style of Leeson's statement reflects the author's view that reporting must reflect reality.
- Genre of the argument: The avowedly liberal publication, the *Village Voice*, published this article, so the derogatory tone toward the Bush administration reflects the ethos of the journal. The *Village Voice*'s readers would not trust the Bush administration, so Schanberg's accusatory and derisive tone toward them would connect with the audience's beliefs and values.

Copyright © 2010, Pearson Education, Inc., Publishing as Longman

IMMIGRATION IN THE TWENT-FIRST CENTURY: ACCOMMODATION AND CHANGE

Francisco X. Gaytan, Avary Carhill, and Carola Suarez-Orozco, "Understanding and Responding to the Need of Newcomer Immigrant Youth and Families"

- Core of the argument: Because immigrant youth have a host of challenges to grapple with as they live in the United States but are still tied to their native culture through their families, it's crucial to provide after-school and mentoring programs that address the diverse needs of this large population.
- Major stases: Using results from their five-year study, the authors first make causal claims as to what challenges these young adults have, and then they offer a soft proposal that will address those challenges.
- Use of evidence and argumentative strategies: The authors first establish the sheer number and diversity of "newcomer families" (2.84 million) and assert that "many struggle to thrive in schools and communities that do not provide the resources they most need" (paragraph 1). The authors present the details of their impressive long-term study in paragraph 3 to establish a human context for their findings. The researchers' argumentative strategy in this journal article is to first use statistics in response to their questions and then insert colorful and emblematic quotations from respondents that reinforce their findings. Using this strategy, they come to these conclusions: separation from family members in the population is normal but presents tricky emotional concerns and familial politics (4-7); over time since young adults acculturate at a greater pace, one would expect conflict between youth and parents, but that was not the case (8-11); and since schools are places for "cultural change," thus making them learn English, youth usually don't have parental guidance with homework because of language barriers, and sometimes young adults take on work as "translators" for the older generation, which can hinder their education (12-18). Based mainly from their findings that lack of help with traditional schooling hinders their potential, the authors offers the proposal calling for more after-school activities and mentoring programs because "[o]ur ethnographic observations revealed that immigrant children and youth by and large do not have access to supportive after-school programs, mentoring opportunities, and community-based organizations" (18). Prior to the proposal pitch, the authors use statistics to frame it by relating that 37% of their 407 subjects were participating in after-school programs, and the higher-achieving students were more likely to participate in these programs.
- Weaknesses of the argument: Since this study is probably based in New York City, one could also argue that the researchers need to branch out from here and look at less cosmopolitan areas like medium-sized cities, rural towns, and small cities since this problem may be even more acute in those areas compared to a metropolitan area that has lots of resources. While some readers might empathize with these young adults' challenges, the standard counterargument to helping these young adults through programs paid for by taxes and other methods is one based on precedent. Some opponents would assert that these youths have the same challenges that many immigrants had in the late 19th century, and those immigrants acculturated and learned how to "cope" with their conditions. There is no reason to give these young adults special treatment now since many immigrants did quite fine learning English and contending with their multiple roles

Copyright © 2010, Pearson Education, Inc., Publishing as Longman

of translator, student, and adolescent, they would argue. In a similar vein, one could say that 37% using after-school programs is quite high, questioning the author's use of framing the figure as "[o]nly 37%" (18). Regardless, a comparison to native-born students or even at-risk students using after-school programs might be revealing or damaging to their proposal. In addition, since it's a soft proposal (one that doesn't discuss funding and other more detailed issues of implementation), opponents could question how these programs will get paid for, so cost and logistics and fairness are major counterarguments if the authors care to take this a step further.

- Appeals to ethos and pathos: The authors cite various sources but don't overly rely on them, which shows that they've done significant research, and past research works, in a sense, as "backup singers" to their own argument. While the article's statistics establish a degree of validity, the quotations taken from subjects paint a more human picture of the complexities and challenges of the immigrant experience, and many of those statements from respondents have significant emotional content.
- Genre of the argument: Typical of an academic journal article, the authors present their research in objective-sounding language and call upon sources when needed. Table 3.1 is typical of social scientific research. And the argument is problem-solving in nature, a hallmark of academic inquiry.

Matali Perkins, "A Note to Young Immigrants"

- Core of the argument: To be a young immigrant is a shifting role that has strong emotional and intellectual effects. To be an immigrant is to be a "stranger, pilgrim, sojourner, wayfarer" (paragraph 9)
- Major stases: Perkins explores the internal reactions that many young immigrants deal with as they navigate their two cultures, so being a young immigrant is being someone who consistently vacillates between the "foreign" and the "familiar" with a sense of loss coupled with reinvention.
- Use of evidence and argumentative strategies: Perkins uses thick description of the inner struggles from her experience to define the immigrant experience, which in a sense connects to the "common and universal" of humanity (8). Using a simile from cooking, she describes the way immigrants feel as "a pinch of chili into a creamy pot" (1). Unlike one's home country, she asserts that immigrants are always aware of race (2) while the first language starts "to feel foreign to lips, pen and mind" (3). Likewise, young immigrants become translators, buffers for the older immigrants because they understand the new country better. Countering the sense of loss in the first part of the essay, Perkins contends that "[t]here are gains to offset the losses" because the experience makes them discover themselves as they constantly shift between cultures and define themselves as people attempt to define them.
- Weaknesses of the argument: Since this is a belletristic essay, the author speaks from experience, which some readers could fault as only showing one perspective. Opponents of this definition of the immigrant experience could trot out examples of immigrants who aren't concerned about race or had parents who were quite helpful in grappling with their new countries. And some young immigrants quickly embrace American culture completely, shrugging past cultural traditions.

Copyright © 2010, Pearson Education, Inc., Publishing as Longman

* Appeals to ethos and pathos: The tone of the whole piece is expressive and emotive, so its main appeals are *ethos* and *pathos*, supported by Perkins' well-crafted metaphor of the "chili tossed into a creamy pot" (1) and emotional anecdotes that show how one feels as a young immigrant. The most prominent emotional appeal of this essay is its use of the second-person to draw the reader in, to make him or her feel like an immigrant. The use of "you" is the crucial ploy to make the reader see her perspective.
* Genre of the argument: Since it's an expressive essay written in *Teaching Tolerance*, the focus on understanding another's experience is appropriate and important to readers who would be reading the magazine.

Maileen Hamto, "My Turn: Being American"

* Core of the argument: Counter to the idea of all immigrants assimilating and being part of some monolithic melting pot, being an American involves honoring and remembering one's cultural roots. We all believe in the country, but we also honor our pasts and ethnicities.
* Major stases: This is a definitional claim about what it means to be an "American."
* Use of evidence and argumentative strategies: In this conversational and sometimes sarcastic piece, Hamto claims that those who have become Americans haven't shed off their ethnicities as they immigrate. Rather, they honor and remember their cultural heritage while believing in the American "tenets of hard work, sense of community, and a spirit of indpendence and self-sufficiency" (paragraph 10). Hamto, through relating her recent experience in a diversity seminar, takes issue with others who seem to think shirking off the past is a way to become an American. She offers short anecdotes about early settlement of North American by both whites and Africans ("forced migration"—5) and the hard work of other ethnic groups in America, Hamto contends that "mounds of evidence" show that the belief in a metling pot is delusional because of past immigrants who keep parts of their cultures alive still (7). Transitioning from those examples of Caucasian Americans, she implies that the recent consternation about "people of color" who are immigrants stems from apprehension about the economy—jobs—and because they look different—"the 'other'" (8). She offers up her response to the question about immigrants holding onto their cultural identities by stating that they believe in American beliefs but hold onto their cultural identities out of pride and to make a unique country. She counters the melting pot ideology by offering a different metaphor, halo-halo.
* Weaknesses of the argument: This expressive essay is based solely on her personal experience as an Asian-American. While she offers examples of European Americans as anecdotal evidence that people don't seem to have a problem with those people holding onto cultural traditions, she may not effectively grapple with the opinion of some people that even those European Americans shouldn't still have Irish or Norwegian pride. Their view is that they should be "Americans." Historical incidents about discrimination and persecution of German-Americans (during World War I, for example), Irish (in the late 19th century, for example), and other European Americans could be used too to show how history hasn't been kind to those groups too. Also, the metaphor of halo-halo may not be much different than the concept of "melting pot." Perhaps the idea of America as a multicultural mosaic is a better metaphor?

Copyright © 2010, Pearson Education, Inc., Publishing as Longman

* Appeals to ethos and pathos: To readers of *Asian Reporter*, they would probably be moved by her sardonic tone in this essay, especially the perceived double standard that she contrasts in paragraphs 7 & 8. Using the metaphor of halo-halo is particularly astute considering her audience.
* Genre of the argument: As sort of op-ed or columnist piece, this argument operates with the use of short anecdotes and personal experience to make its point. The column attempts to make a reader think, rather than bludgeon the audience with stats, studies, and numerous details.

Scarf Ace, "Miss or Diss?"

* Core of the argument: This implied argument contends that there is a bias in America against clothing associated with religions other than Christianity and Judaism.
* Major stases: This blog post is a mix of evaluative and causal claims.
* Use of evidence and argumentative strategies: Like many blog posts, the author begins with personal experience and self-expression. The first paragraph sets the tone for her "outlet" that provides her "mental rumblings." She lists the conflict she's dealing with by recounting why she doesn't want to wear the hijab and why she's still compelled to wear it. The following paragraphs then provide her inner monologue that she grapples with and the various realistic effects of how she perceives people looking at her, which range from puzzlement to outrage (2-6). These perceived thoughts of people provide realistic examples that many readers could see. Relating her own self-doubt, she lets the audience into how it feels to be "the other" in America," a persuasive technique of showing the author's frame of mind or angle of vision. Transitioning from her reflection, she uncovers what she wants to be in a place where head scarves are the "norm" but strongly asserts that "this kind of attitude is dangerous for America" (8) because it causes unthinking attitudes and knee-jerk statements that exemplify a frame of vision that doesn't embrace diversity. To show that contrast, she provides the example of how a Nun's Habit is not looked down upon or derided because of American culture's automatic bias toward Christianity by those who believe that Americans should look a certain way. The author further contends with an opposing audience by providing an anecdote about programs that equated brotherhood between Jewish and Christian brothers while she asks the pertinent question, "what about your Muslim brothers?" (8).
* Weaknesses of the argument: Like a number of good blog posts, this document offers self reflection from the author while also questioning the status quo and the country in which she lives. However, forms of support that could be labeled as "soft"—personal experience, her inner thoughts, the creative depiction of others' thoughts, the example of the Nun's Habit, and the program on a Christian Channel—could be called into question. This is just one person's viewpoint, one could argue. Creative writing isn't proof, others might say. And many folks could argue that a Nun's Habit is looked at strangely because they're more rare, and the "Muslim head scarf, a Sikh turban, or Hindu dot on the forehead" (8) are now more common because of the large influx of legal immigrants over the past few decades. The anecdote about being brothers could also be faulted in that the author is using evidence from a very biased source, creating a straw person effect, implying that many Americans are just like those who don't include Muslims in their "brotherhoods."

Copyright © 2010, Pearson Education, Inc., Publishing as Longman

* Appeals to ethos and pathos: The post is laden with *ethos* because the author is writing from personal experiences and self reflection. Her technique of putting the reader in her frame of mind and others' frames of mind is quite savvy in that it might emotionally move readers to feel her inner conflict about the hijab and how she is seen as the "other" in a country that some argue is a "Christian nation."
* Genre of the argument: As noted above, typical of blog post, the document draws from personal experiences and examples that cater to her viewpoint and purpose in the implied argument.

Fatemah Fakhraie, "Scarfing It Down"

* Core of the argument: Banning hijabs, as many have done, is an unlawful and "ignorant" practice (paragraph 2).
* Major stases: This argument mainly takes a stand on an issue in the news, but it makes evaluative claims coupled with a large causal claim about the media's coverage. In addition, the argument defines the head scarf as an example of "personal freedom" (4), and the author uses analogies in the final paragraph in an attempt to persuade.
* Use of evidence and argumentative strategies: Fakhraie begins the argument with a number of anecdotes about the banning of head scarves and then moves to her evaluative claim of "[t]he idea of banning the hijab is an exclusionary and ignorant one" (2). She bases that argument on the criteria of media coverage, in particular how Muslim women don't seem to have voices in this issue, and the criteria by how the hijab is defined. Instead of linking the head scarf to religious practice as she assumes the media always does, he counters with the notion that the hijab is worn out of personal preference, not for the sake of religious freedom (4). She ends with the analogies that help her definition of the head scarf as exemplifying personal freedom by asserting that the hijab is similar to "your best pair of jeans or your faded t-shirt" (5).
* Weaknesses of the argument: While the author provides a number of compelling examples of how head scarves have been banned, one could question how prevalent this issue is. And she assumes the reader agrees with how the media's portrayal of the controversy is biased against Muslims and particularly Muslim women, which is not supported by any details or examples—just her assertion. She concedes that some people wear the hijab as a religious obligation but then contradicts herself later by saying the head scarf should be defined as "personal freedom" (4). If a woman wears it for religious reasons, wouldn't such a case be one of personal *and* religious reasons or even just religious freedom? While the analogy to jeans and a t-shirt is clever, that comparison could be questioned also because of the religious factor.
* Appeals to ethos and pathos: Fakhraie entices the reader with a stunning example of a women being killed because of not wearing a head scarf, but other examples show some rather innocuous instances where the head scarf was banned for illogical reasons. That contrast works well to show the contrast of the extreme and the silly, which might move readers to her way of thinking. The appeal to personal freedom in paragraph four is savvy in that she attempts to redefine terms to suit her needs. And the comparison of the hijab to jeans and t-shirts provide positive connotations for the head scarf that frames the issue in a way that opens up the reader to see the hijab in a much more positive light.

Copyright © 2010, Pearson Education, Inc., Publishing as Longman

* Genre of the argument: Since this come from a Web site that is focused on "critiquing images of Muslim women," the use of short anecdotes and personal indignation conveys the spirit of a site devoted to critically reading the world and images presented by the media, which explains the author's statement that the "ignorance comes as much from the media's coverage of these bans as from those implementing them" (2).

Student Advocates for Immigration Reform

* Core of the argument: The DREAM would provide opportunities for immigrants to take advantage of the American dream.
* Major stases: The photo and the protesters represent a proposal—the DREAM act should be passed.
* Use of evidence and argumentative strategies: The use of diverse three diverse faces represent America and its tradition of including immigrants in empowering themselves through education. The poster, "Immigrant Students Excluded Not Included," works with the belief and assumption that America is an inclusionary country that offers hope for a better life through opportunities, especially opportunities via education.
* Weaknesses of the argument: The argument mainly rests on definition of "inclusion," so some would take issue with how alien minor should be included in the American dream since they are breaking the law or are living here because of their parents breaking the law. In this view, someone living in America because of illegal activity should not be rewarded with in-state tuition rates when legal citizens would have to pay the same tuition or out-of-state tuition.
* Appeals to ethos and pathos: The look of hope and sense of purpose of the two protesters conveys an emotional appeal. And term, "excluded," might resonate with viewers based on the assumption that the US represents a nation that welcome all who are willing to work, serve, or do well in school.
* Genre of the argument: It's a photo typical of those used to frame the message of a protest demonstration. There are close-ups of specific members of the group, and concise messages in the sign reinforce a simple message of inclusion.

Jay Nordlinger, "Bassackwards: Construction Spanish and Other Signs of the Times"

* Core of the argument: Instead of having a defeatist attitude about immigrants learning English as they get used to our country, America as a country should reinforce the idea that new immigrants should learn English just as others have in the past.
* Major stases: This is an implied proposal relating that we should expect immigrants to learn English.
* Use of evidence and argumentative strategies: Nordlinger deftly begins with a concession followed by an unsupported assertion by stating that the country "has always been a place of many languages, along with our common tongue, English" (paragraph 1). He then offers his theme for the argument, that "Spanish in today's America is something else: a language coddled, bowed to, enshrined," which provides his basic stance: immigrants should be expected to learn English just as others have, and those who cave in to learn "specialized" forms of Spanish are doing the country and those immigrants a disservice. Rather than going into the well worn debates about bilingual education and

Copyright © 2010, Pearson Education, Inc., Publishing as Longman

English/Spanish instructions, he takes shots at how those who employ immigrants are learning specialized forms of Spanish rather than demanding that workers assimilate and learn English (2-6). Using the rhetorical ploy of "in the old days it was different" (an appeal to tradition), he asserts that the "old deal" was that immigrants "assimilated" while still holding onto the language and customs from the old country if desired, with the second part working as a small concession about citizens' personal freedom to speak what they want to speak in their families. Nordlinger uses numerous examples to support his framing of the problem via an excerpt from *Spanish on the Job* (6), a Virginia official's statement (8), an assistant superintendent's words (9), and a supervisor's statement of defeatism—"I'm not saying I like what's happening. But I figure I can't fight it." (10). The author transitions to his argument that this type "of cultural defeatism" needs to stop (11) followed by another concession about how "[y]ou want to be considerate of the immigrant, who has enough challenges, without a new language; but you are not placed to see him trapped in a linguistic ghetto—barrio-ization…" (12). Then after offering personal experience about how he's dealt with this problem, he asserts that we all want immigrants to "join the American family" because they will limit themselves without learning English (14). This appeal is then supported by his relation of how many Latinos agreed with him after one of his columns, and he then quotes a former manager who thinks using Spanish is "condescending" to immigrants (17). Following up that support, Norlinger uses a personal anecdote how he gave janitor a bilingual dictionary and how he was thanked. In paragraph 24, he offers another concession that some immigrants don't care to assimilate through the relation of Korean-Americans who simply want to be called Koreans. Staving off a counterargument about how he could be accused of being a xenophobe (26), Norlinger uses a "famed linguist and politician" who presumably thinks as he does about this situation while closing with the open-ended statement that by using Spanish and not making immigrants learn and use English, "we will have lost a lot—all of us will" (28).

- ✹ Weaknesses of the argument: While Nordlinger does a fine job of making concessions and anticipating opponents' counterarguments, some might argue that communities using an English/Other Language naming system has been done for many years, if not centuries. One could easily bring in examples of small towns in various parts of the country where this is done, such as Concordia, Missouri where shops are named both in German and English or towns in Minnesota that also have Norwegian or Swedish with English labels. Also, although people are learning highly specialized Spanish, that fact doesn't necessarily mean that immigrants will not learn English eventually. And Nordlinger thinks of assimilation in only one way. Assimilation can also mean that immigrants keep parts of their cultures and languages while the non-immigrant learn other languages. And for those workers, they may already know "Survival English," but their bosses have simply tried to learn Spanish to make their businesses more efficient through more clear communication. Nordlinger's implication that we'll all lose a lot by doing this can be countered by saying that we could learn a lot by people with diverse cultures. He cites readers of the National Review Online, many of whom probably have a similar political frame of vision. What about those who criticized his column there? In addition, how do other linguists stand on this debate? Nordlinger only cites one, someone who thinks like he does.

Copyright © 2010, Pearson Education, Inc., Publishing as Longman

- <u>Appeals to ethos and pathos</u>: Nordlinger's tone surfaces as sarcastic at times, so that can appeal to people who have similar reservations as he does, but it can also distance readers who might feel differently. His concessions as noted above enhance his *ethos* since he seems willing to concede that immigrants do have many hurdles and that people do have personal freedom to speak how they want to in their homes. His strongest use of emotions are these parts of the argument: how he paints all of us as wanting "them [immigrants] to join the American family" (14), how he makes it seem like by people using "Construction English" they are talking down to immigrants (17), and his example of a janitor thanking him (23). Those points in the argument could move readers to his side through emotion.
- <u>Genre of the argument</u>: Nordlinger's column is emblematic of his right-leaning magazine, *The National Review*, but he provides some strong concessions while fleshing out the reasons that he values "assimilation."

Copyright © 2010, Pearson Education, Inc., Publishing as Longman

WOMEN IN MATH AND SCIENCE

Linda Chavez, "Harvard Prez's Admission: Men and Women are Different"

- Core of the argument: The backlash against Summers' conference presentation is symbolic of how feminists cling to beliefs that are unsupported by empirical evidence.
- Major stases: This op-ed piece combines causal claims and argues from sign since Chavez seems to aver that the reaction to Summers' comments symbolize an academic culture that is not open to differences of opinion.
- Use of evidence and argumentative strategies: Chavez uses the reaction to Summers' comments as way to take an opportune moment (*kairos*) to show her readers that people in academia have a bias have against views or evidence that goes against what they believe to be true, not what's true. Early on she cites "empirical evidence" to explain that women usually perform better on verbal tests and men perform better on visual-spatial tests. In addition, she mentions that more men are in remedial reading classes and outnumber women as being "gifted in math and science" (paragraph 2). Chavez attempts to counter opponents who think socialization is a larger factor by stating that "socialization alone can't explain the wide difference in ability," and she asserts that "most researchers" think that "biology plays a bigger role" than socialization (3). Chavez uses one example of an outraged "feminist" in her article to show how professors like Nancy Hopkins represent academics who are unwilling to examine and reexamine their own assumptions or beliefs about issues. To combat Hopkins' claims and her study about the discrimination at MIT, she brings in Summers to reiterate that the "overall size of the pool" of women candidates is small based on innate differences.
- Weaknesses of the argument: Typical of an op-ed piece, the article drips with sarcasm with such words, phrases, and sentences such as "So much for rigorous intellectual debate" (1), "surprise, surprise" (5), and "women-as-perennial victims set" (7). This diction will not win over people who consider themselves feminists or people who are simply open to the idea that socialization is a strong factor. The vague differences that she references early on in the article are not clear or specific, and one could seriously question how those differences come from innate differences and not socialization. She provides no proof for these "small but important differences" (2). While she concedes that socialization may be a small factor, she offers her own implied belief in innate differences supported with vague proof. She makes the same rhetorical move that she criticizes "feminists" for. The term "most researchers" (3) is one that warrants analysis since she doesn't provide any examples or evidence. Chavez also uses Hopkins as a strawperson—depicting her views in a slanted way—to paint people who question Summers' assertion as fringe participants in this debate, and it's unclear whether Hopkins deserves such derision. She accuses Hopkins of believing in a cause-effect relationship in an example of test-taking, but Chavez could be accused of the same logical leap in her belief in innate difference.
- Appeals to ethos and pathos: In this piece, "feminist" stands out as a term of derision, and Chavez's sarcastic tone colors the argument throughout. She paints academics as pointy-headed liberals who are unwilling to hear other perspectives. This tone of moral indignation would connect to her core audience in *Jewish World Review.*

Copyright © 2010, Pearson Education, Inc., Publishing as Longman

* Genre of the argument: Op-ed articles are tailor-made for pithy responses to hot issues in the news. Summers' comments provide an opportunity for this well-known conservative columnist to paint academics as close-minded and "liberal" (aka "feminist").

Brian McFadden, "Amazing Facts About the Fairer, Yet Equal Sex"

* Core of the argument: Lawrence Summers' provocative comments are sexist.
* Major stases: This cartoon exemplifies a resemblance argument.
* Use of evidence and argumentative strategies: McFadden uses hyperbole in order to paint Summers' conference presentation as exemplifying sexist assumptions and beliefs about women. The cartoon implicitly compares Summers' challenge to researchers to the sexist depiction of women being obsessed with hair, caring about pets, cutting sandwiches diagonally, an innate lack of humor, an association with the "cooties virus," and a penchant for shopping. The image of Summers giving the viewer a double-finger pointing pose symbolizes a discredited belief that women have limited capacities and interests coupled with the verbal tone of a lothario, "I hope that clears thing up. Don't forget. Larry loves you."
* Weaknesses of the argument: The mocking tone and extreme analogies paint Summers and his argument in a way that would make many discredit his remarks. The depiction of Summers essentially "poisons the well" in that one could argue that the cartoonist's portrayal is more agitprop than argument. Summers did not make such conclusions, and the cartoon limits its effectiveness by only delving into mockery and exaggeration. It may be humorous, but it's not a fair portrayal of what Summers argued.
* Appeals to ethos and pathos: The cartoonist trucks in using emotions in order to mock and perhaps anger its readers to see Summers as someone who sees women as not being equal or as intelligent as men.
* Genre of the argument: This cartoon presents a hot topic that had been in the news, so the artist seizes this opportunity to delve into mockery and exaggeration.

Nature Neuroscience, "Separating Science from Stereotype"

* Core of the argument: Summers and others' assertions that innate differences between genders make women less likely to become mathematicians and engineers is inconclusive. In fact, any neurobiological differences make minimal, if any, difference.
* Major stases: This is an evaluative argument that considers the validity of Summers' argument based on the criteria he used.
* Use of evidence and argumentative strategies: Based on what the writer of the editorial had heard from Summers' talk, the writer evaluates Summers' purported claims about gender differences and how they might cause more males to be in certain professions than others. After offering a context about the media's fascination about this event, the author provides the thesis of "[t]he evidence to support this hypothesis of 'innate difference' turns out to be quite slim" (paragraph 2). Citing first how SAT scores were used by Summers, the writer describes the differences are a "statistically small margin" while also relating that "cultural factors" could be quite important since in 16% (7 of 43) of the countries scores were comparable, with Icelandic women doing better than men (3). The author transitions from the idea of "innate difference" to the fallibility of test scores in

Copyright © 2010, Pearson Education, Inc., Publishing as Longman

predicting future success in high-demand and high-intensity professions. The author concedes that "male and female brains differ anatomically in subtle ways, but no one knows (or even if) these anatomical differences relate to cognitive performance," but relates the idea that media outlets like to report studies that show difference as opposed to studies that show lack of differences (5). The author does relate that male and females have cognitive differences in "spatial reasoning and navigation," and testosterone might be a factor, but the author proposes that such a minor hormonal difference is unlikely to "account for the dramatic overrepresentation of men in science departments at top universities" (6). To further support the author's assumption that "gender bias" is more instrumental in this gap between men and women, the writer uses examples of how male and female names affect value of articles and how SAT questions were adjusted to improve male scores (7). The writer concludes with the point that "humans cannot be examined in a culture-free state," and the "media hype" is just going to make things worse (8).

- Weaknesses of the argument: The author's relation that the highest performers in SAT math scores provides an entry for those who take Summers' side in this debate because the highest performers are the exact group of people he was talking about in that those high-performers are the most likely to take the high profile jobs at universities. While the averages show a "statistically small margin," the high performers are the ones who gravitate toward the difficult and high-intensity research. Likewise, 16% of countries having comparable scores for men and women does not offer a lot of confidence toward stating that gender differences don't matter. The author's point about men "tend to assess the euclidean properties of the environment" might help Summers' argument too since "euclidean" thinking, "spatial reasoning and navigation" that caters to geometrical principles, might help male mathematicians, engineers, and scientists in their fields.
- Appeals to ethos and pathos: The author provides a calm, dispassionate tone in the editorial, which connects with the lack of emotion in scientific discourse. The writer also establishes credibility by using five different sources in the short editorial, indicating that research was consulted. While this is a specialized field, the writer sprinkles in informal language like "hornet's nest" and "media hype" to create stylistic variety and emphasize how media coverage of Summers' speech is counterproductive.
- Genre of the argument: Unlike a number of editorials, this one is different in that it offers a cool and reasoned tone to the issue, but like most editorials it enacts kairic timing to comment on something in the news.

Deborah Blum, "Solving for X"

- Core of the argument: While Summers had some interesting and valid points about possible innate differences between genders, this belief in innate differences is detrimental to the issue at hand and might really reflect how many people cling to the belief that women aren't as good at math or the sciences.
- Major stases: The argument is primarily evaluative in that Blum looks at Summers' purported claims and analyzes them by the criteria of *logos* and in light of other studies that she presents.
- Use of evidence and argumentative strategies: While Blum intimates that she doesn't want to link Summers to Richard Lynn, in fact she does link the two by using him as an

Copyright © 2010, Pearson Education, Inc., Publishing as Longman

example to contextualize the brouhaha that Summers' comments created. And she also circles back to her experience with Lynn as a way to show her emotional reaction to Summers' comments. Blum says that she doesn't want to "yoke Lynn with Harvard President Lawrence H. Summers," but she really does (paragraph 6). Drawing from her own research and expertise, the author cites a couple of succinct examples of how people made excuses for "the often less-than-perfect status quo" (8). And Blum draws upon the wisdom of two researchers—Marlene Zuk (9) and Janet Hyde (16 and 18)—that support her overall aim in the argument, to discredit Summers' exploratory remarks. Along the way, she concedes Summers' anecdote about his daughter with a darkly humorous anecdote about her two sons in order to confirm that she also thinks that "[t]here's nothing like being the parent of a small child to convince you that biology is a powerful influence on behavior – and vice versa" (11). To combat view about innate differences, she makes the causal claim that nature and nurture work together in ways we still don't understand while relating that testosterone levels may have an effect on behavior but not necessarily the ability to do geometry, science, and engineering. Using Hyde's study from 1990 that claims to show neglible, if any, differences in math abilities between the genders, Blum also concurs with Hyde that the mindset of how women might not do as well in those disciplines could also impact women's performance.

- Weaknesses of the argument: Blum asks more questions than actually offering a conclusion in regard to the studies about "male variability" and what they actually show us, which is one of Summers' main claims—that more men in the higher range causes more men to take those high-intensity jobs in those disciplines. Other readers would also take issue with how Blum does "yoke" Summers with the author of "The Bell Curve." In addition, the two main forms of support for her argument are both female scientists, which some could argue creates a bias. Readers might have wanted to see a more recent study too, instead of an older one from 1990.
- Appeals to ethos and pathos: After relating her experience with interviewing a famous author, she also drops hints about her expertise by stating, "[s]pend any time at all study the biology of behavior…" (8). Her tone if open and conversational, but she presents herself as an expert. Her use of verbal irony about "the male brain" in the last paragraph ties in her opening strategy to compare Summers and Lynn, and she also uses a bit of self deprecating humor in an attempt to win over her audience.
- Genre of the argument: This well-known writer about sex differences uses this opportunity to comment on the hot issue of the moment—Summers' comments—and offer a different and at times light-hearted slant on the issue.

Steven Pinker, "The Science of Sex Difference: Sex Ed"

- Core of the argument: The firestorm of reaction in response to Lawrence Summers' claims about sex differences indicates something about human psychology. When someone goes against a taboo or politically correct beliefs, they will pay a price, as Summers has. Regardless, Summers' contentions connect directly to recent findings in the sciences and social sciences and should be considered if academia is truly open to diverse viewpoints.
- Major stases: This hybrid argument incorporates evaluation in that Pinker evaluates Summers and others' views on the issue via the criteria of *logos* and scientific findings.

Copyright © 2010, Pearson Education, Inc., Publishing as Longman

In addition, he makes a resemblance claim that Summers' comments are like uttering a "taboo" thought, and he employs causal claims throughout.

- Use of evidence and argumentative strategies: In his defense of Summers' ideas and his skeptical stance that this incident exemplifies an academic community that seems prone to shun those who harbor different ideas than the majority, Pinker begins his argument with a concession through an example of older scientific literature that certainly had prejudicial thinking within it. He then contrasts that outmoded thinking from *Scientific American* with certain people's colorful reactions to Summers' propositions, comments and connections that portray Summers' opponents as unthinking and close-minded. Pinker coolly depicts Summers as someone who simply is asking questions that are important, and he lays out the same argument of Summers' early on in the article (end of paragraph 3). He makes a number of concessions for resistant readers by stating that "[o]nly a madman could believe such things" and using a subordinate clause before he presents the same argument as Summers, "Although no one can deny that women in science still face these injustices…" (3). He calls for this discussion to be laid out by reason and not knee-jerk reactions of those very invested in certain beliefs while making the causal argument about parenting similar to Summers (5) and relating generalized "numerous statistical differences between men and women" (7). Following up on his depiction of the illogical comments of Dr. Hopkins, he questions the credibility of a number of academics who believe "that children are born unisex and are molded into male and female role by their parents and society is becoming less credible" and offers a study that confirms that there is little consistency in how sons and daughters are raised (8). Like Summers, he brings in the "greater variance" issue and connects that to evolutionary biology. Transitioning from his relation of scientific research, he fully develops his stance that the reactions to Summers' comments symbolizes "the mentality of taboo" (11) within academic culture, where people attacked Summers without hearing his speech or showing valid evidence to definitively prove him wrong since this episode represents how that "mentality of taboo" goes up against "the finding of science and the spirit of free inquiry," Pinker appeals to an espoused belief in academic culture—that research is done in a "spirit of free inquiry (13).
- Weaknesses of the argument: While Pinker concedes how socialization might be a factor, his comparison of this discussion to a "fatwa" is an emotionally-laden word choice that paints those who argue that factors of socialization and discrimination are dominant in negative light. Some readers would also question the veracity of his claims because he refers to his own book that Summers drew from, so it might have been more persuasive to simply to call upon the research that he used rather than Pinker intentionally or unintentionally painting himself as a defender of Summers. The use of word choices of "statistical differences" and "better" when Pinker discusses gender differences is quite vague. How much better? How extreme are the differences? Pinker also only cites one research article (dated from 1991) about the socialization of sons and daughters. There could be other studies that provide different results.
- Appeals to ethos and pathos: Pinker presents himself as someone who wants to cut through the media sludge and academic bickering. He questions the credibility of those who have chimed in about this media event, whether conservative or liberal, but in a sarcastic vein relates that "the quality of discussion among the nation's leading scholars and pundits is not a pretty sight" (6). He presents himself as defending logic and reason

Copyright © 2010, Pearson Education, Inc., Publishing as Longman

by bringing up studies that support his claims and by unpacking the reactions to Summers though the concept of taboo.

* Genre of the argument: This article is reflective of *The New Republic*, a magazine that is traditionally seen as a slightly left-leaning publication but one that is open to many other views. The journal article genre is one that provides an established scholar to dissect a socio-political controversy to a well-informed but layperson readership.

Ben A. Barres, "Does Gender Matter?"

* Core of the argument: In contrast to recent commentators who posited that innate differences between men and women are one of the causes to the disparity of men and women in the sciences and math, Barres advances that lack of self confidence and discrimination are the main causes of this discrepancy.
* Major stases: The argument is a hybrid in that it uses resemblance claims and causal claims while evaluating others' arguments and offering its own causal claims. It ends with a number of soft policy proposals.
* Use of evidence and argumentative strategies: Barres opens with a startling example to draw a comparison between racist views and views that he sees as sexist about women in the sciences, engineering, and math. Similar references to prejudicial thinking are sprinkled throughout the article, with notable examples in paragraphs 9 and 15. Barres characterizes his opponents' views as positing that innate difference is the main factor in the gender discrepancies in those fields and goes against the "Larry Summers Hypothesis" by first using his own studies to support the idea that innate differences in mathematical and reasoning abilities are minimal to nonexistent by using text scores, bias in academic culture, and "gender-blinding studies" (5, 6, and 7). Barres then uses the idea from the researcher Valian that "we all have a strong desire to believe that the world is fair" (8-9) while relating that men are actually more "emotional" than women based on violent crimes committed in anger (11). He also tackles the issue that some think that the harsh reaction Summers dealt with is a result of "taboo" thinking, and he agrees that all ideas should be thought about, a mild concession to those who agree with Summers and Pinker. The author's main claim is that "difference in self confidence rather than ability" is the main cause of the lack of high-power scholars in these fields (12), which leads to his collection of proposals: create more leadership diversity in institutions (17), provide young women and people from diverse backgrounds with "diverse faculty role models" while offering more pragmatic ways that women can compete in the academic marketplace (18 and 19), talk more about discrimination (20), and "enhance fairness in competitive selection processes" (21).
* Weaknesses of the argument: While the author makes repeated resemblance claims between racism and sexism, some could point out that gender is a biological matter whereas race is a cultural construct. The comparison is risky and unhelpful in some people's eyes. While both have been burdened by explicit and implicit discrimination, but gender and race are not the same. In addition, Barres implies that Summers' argument is that innate difference is the main culprit when Summers identifies three possible culprits that might be interrelated. And the author does not take on the "greater variability" sub-argument that people use when talking about how the elite schools have many more male scientists, mathematicians, and engineers.

Copyright © 2010, Pearson Education, Inc., Publishing as Longman

- Appeals to ethos and pathos: Barres uses his interesting perspective as a transgendered person to portray the differences in expectations or perception that he lived through. The tone of the piece if mostly cool and professorial with detailed and specific examples to color and detail the causes and effects of the problem that he addresses. The use of personal experience enhances the argument in that Barres argues from *ethos* in strategically significant spots in the argument.
- Genre of the argument: This commentary essay provides nineteen different footnotes to reference the arguments and research that Barres employs. For the esteemed journal *Nature*, use of sources is typical even is an article that is more conversational. Hard research and an objective look at issues are valued.

David Malakoff, "Girls = Boys at Math"

- Core of the argument: Based from a recent research study and research studies over the past twenty years, it's clear there is no logical reason why people should think males are innately drawn to math and sciences.
- Major stases: The article is mostly informative, but it offers causal claims about mathematically abilities of males and females.
- Use of evidence and argumentative strategies: The article's support is drawn from a older study by Janet Hyde that shows simply that the gap in test scores between males and females is "'trivial'" while males tend to be better at solving more complex problems. A more recent study conducted by the same researchers now shows, based on seven million students' scores, that there is no significant difference in ability to do math between males and females. Hyde's conclusion is that "cultural and social factors, not gender alone, influence how well students perform on tests" (paragraph 4) and the 7% higher average of males is countered by more females taking the test (5). The author and researchers see an alarming trend though—"neither boys nor girls get many tough math questions on state tests" because of influence of the No Child Left Behind Act (6).
- Weaknesses of the argument: The causal claim in paragraph 6 is unsupported; there are not explicit links between NCLB and the difficulty of questions. And the final comment by a psychologist is based on observation, not detailed study.
- Appeals to ethos and pathos: Apropos of a newswire report, the article uses third person, but the tone and diction of the article is conversational and to-the-point. The opening of "Zip. Zilch. Nada" (1) offers an opening and inviting light-hearted approach to an issue that has been researched for years, an approach that contrasts the professorial tone of the peer-reviewed journal *Science*, which *ScienceNow Daily* is associated with.
- Genre of the argument: The pithy title of the article connects well to the concise presentation and preview of a forthcoming study, and the report provides succinct information in a limited amount of space.

Copyright © 2010, Pearson Education, Inc., Publishing as Longman

FINDING SOLDIERS: THE VOLUNTEER ARMY, RECRUITMENT, AND THE DRAFT

Donald Rumsfeld, "New Model Army"

- Core of the argument: In this Pentagon brief, Donald Rumsfeld addresses both military commanders and the general public to argue for his and the Bush administration's vision of a "new more 'Modular Army'" (paragraph 8) that will be able to be more easily deployed and able to respond to conflicts with which the military is engaged. He argues that by enhancing the army's "interoperability" (8) American forces will be able to respond appropriately and swiftly without a need for increasing force levels through non-volunteer means but by retraining soldiers for "skill sets" (7) that are needed. Rumsfeld argues that the problem isn't necessarily an issue of how many troops are needed, but rather how these troops are deployed and "managed" (4).
- Major stases: This argument begins with evaluative claims about why the troop situation is as it stands now—multiple tours in Iraq and need for increased troop forces—and then argues for the proposal of a "modular army" that sounds more agile and not as cumbersome to deploy.
- Use of evidence and argumentative strategies: Rumsfeld provides quite a bit a data, and for an audience who is conversant in troop levels the numbers might add up appropriately. The fact that there are 2.6 million military personnel at the disposal of the Pentagon provides a weighty statistic that may persuade readers to his way of describing the troop level situation. He provides a savvy comparison of the forces needed in Iraq (115,000) to the greater whole (2.6 million) while conceding the fact that the Iraq conflict "has required that we temporarily increase the size of the force" (4). Later, Rumsfeld sets forth data in a positive light in that they "have not mobilized 60% of the Selected Reserve," and "58% of the current Guard and Reserve force have not been involuntary mobilized in the past decade" (6). It's important to note that he frames the data in what percentage *has not* been mobilized rather than what percentage has been called up recently or in the past decade (40 percent, 42 percent). Crucial to his proposal for a more agile military force is Schoomaker's metaphor of the rainwater barrel, which provides a vivid image that readers can grasp: the implication is that the problem of soldiers, reserves, and national guard troops returning to Iraq is that the workforce is not being managed properly because of the lack of supply of military members with high demand "skill sets" (5-7). The people that the army needs are being siphoned off early and then are being recycled, which is a very mixed metaphor.
- Weaknesses of the argument: A skeptical reader and members of the reserves or the National Guard could really question a number of Rumsfeld's assertions and assumptions. His argument is one of the management of troops from a cool, distanced perspective than one of empathetic reasoning for those who are doing the fighting. His assumption that the Iraqi security forces and Iraqi government will eventually be stable is a contention that many would argue with (3). His own admission one time that the war would be a "long, hard slog" seems to refute his very positive argument in this brief. In addition, he doesn't support the assumption that 115,000 soldiers are enough to provide stability and peace to the war-torn and insurgency-ridden country. Other commentators and policy analysts disagreed from the outset with how many troops are necessary to

Copyright © 2010, Pearson Education, Inc., Publishing as Longman

make Iraq stable, as Carter and Gastris detail in "The Case for the Draft." As noted, the rainwater barrel is a vivid metaphor but a mixed one. If one moves the spigot down, will the new troops drawn be able to fill the positions (the highly needed "skill sets") of the often-recycled troops? While he offers a great deal of data, a layman might have a difficult time keeping the numbers straight in his/her head—numbers seem to be thrown about without enough context. In addition, how exactly will this new modular army be implemented? How will these troops in the middle or bottom of the barrel receive proper training and how long will that take? The blank statement that "[w]e are taking military personnel out of civilian jobs to free them up for military tasks…. And we are fixing the mobilization process to make it more respectful of troops, families, and employers" might be accurate, but where's his proof for these statements? Some National Guardsmen could easily argue that their role is to protect the American homeland for national disasters and homeland security based in the US, and Iraq doesn't necessarily adhere to either role. How exactly have their methods been "respectful"?

- Appeals to ethos and pathos: Rumsfeld's argument employs a managerial, detached, and objective tone. Besides using a homespun metaphor from a colleague, his diction is at formal level and ventures into military jargon ("rebalancing skill sets," "peacetime statutory limit," "interoperability," et al.) that is germane to his colleagues but probably not most American citizens. The argument is logos-driven by numerous statistics, which might inundate a typical reader, but he does attempt in a small way to appeal to the values of "self-government and self-reliance" in regard to our mission in Iraq (3), reassure Pentagon brass of his commitment to the endeavor ("whatever is needed," paragraph 4), and keep in mind the lives of personnel (10).
- Genre of the argument: This formal brief was intended for military commanders and Congressmen, so that fact explains the highly jargon-laden diction and statistic heavy support for his argument. This short argument is concise yet needs to be supported. However, the fact that the brief was released for public perusal shows that this short argument was also intended to reassure American citizens that a draft is not necessary. The brief is intended to assuage fears and also provide a new vision of how the military should effectively coordinate its efforts in the "war on terror."

Philip Carter and Paul Gastris, "The Case for the Draft"

- Core of the argument: Carter and Gastris provide a detailed article that claims that the current all-volunteer army is both unjust and unrealistic since America is the lone superpower. Also, the authors make claims that the current conception of our armed forces doesn't effectively match the way in which America goes into wars because of unclear exit strategies and the need for much more plentiful troop levels to sustain wars in various theatres. In contrast to "five bad options" of how to solve America's foreign, over-extended military, Carter and Gastris offer the solution that students who wish to attend a four-year college or university will be mandated to serve their country in one of three ways: a twelve-month to two-year service term with some type of "national service program," "homeland security assignments," or the armed forces (paragraph 42).
- Major stases: This argument is a proposal; however, the detailed analysis of the problem and possible solutions employs numerous causal and evaluative claims.

Copyright © 2010, Pearson Education, Inc., Publishing as Longman

* Use of evidence and argumentative strategies: The authors provide a great deal of evidence to support their evaluation of the current issue, which they perceive as an overstretched military. Carter and Gastris, counter to Rumsfeld in "New Model Army," argue that a greater force is needed to create stability in Iraq, and they offer various experts and perspectives that run counter to those who felt that the security of Iraq could be created by a leaner and agile force. They provide perspectives from notable officials (Eric Shinseki, Thomas White, Colin Powell) and a major corporation that analyzes such projects (RAND) in paragraphs eight and nine. The authors make an evaluation of why exactly the Army and Marines cannot meet their the necessary troop levels to sustain stability in Iraq because of a number of factors: there are other places where the US military is committed (9, 11, and 17); Iraq is a "ground game," namely meaning that the conflict draws heavily from two of the four branches of the US military—the Army and Marines (10); the current military has many "specialized fields" that are not compatible to the conflict in the Middle East (12); the fact that there is a distinct difference between sending troops to overthrow a government and having troops there to nation-build while being cognizant that the morale of service men and women have to be accommodated (13); and the fact of the Pentagon's "stop-loss" measures to keep soldiers from leaving the service and what that strategy causes, a drop in recruitment for Reservists and the regular Army (16).

In the "Stress Test" section of the argument, Carter and Gastris exemplify their point through statistics (18), offer historical examples of how the US leads the "international community," based on work in Rwanda and Bosnia and Kosovo (19), provide the assertion that the current military paradigm is configured for "wars with explicit purposes, narrow parameters, and clear exit strategies" (20), explain how the strategy of "'total force' concept" was conceptualized to create an volunteer army without needing to mobilize American citizens or put soldiers there who wanted to volunteer (21 and 22), and that an all-volunteer army will not be able to secure longevity as a long-term occupying force. By citing the quick success of Operation Desert Storm, the authors provide a juxtaposition to the Iraq war: "Desert Storm did not break the all-volunteer force because that war was precisely the kind that the force had been designed to fight: a limited campaign for limited ends, of limited duration, and with a defined exit strategy" (24). In contrast, Carter and Gastris claim "Operation Iraqi Freedom" is a war not conducive to the current parameters of engagement, and having so many troops pulls necessary security away from other fronts and the homeland (25).

The authors then provide the five various "bad" options available to the US, and they oppose such measures with causal/consequences claims: 1. The US can convince other nations to share "the burden in Iraq" countered by the United States' reticence to "share decision-making" and the considerable public opinion against the war in other countries (28); 2. The US could use more military contractors countered by how such forces are more expensive, would plausibly hurt recruitment, along with sketchy ethical responsibilities and "legal grey areas" with such contractors (29); 3. The "radical" shift in the military to respond to different threats countered by the sheer need for troops and the possibility that a large-scale war may need to be fought, while intimating that such a shift is merely "playing a shell game" with personnel (30); 4. The Pentagon can simply increase troop force countered by questioning how such proposals would cost in the long-term, the authors supporting those points by relating the monetary commitment each

Copyright © 2010, Pearson Education, Inc., Publishing as Longman

soldier signifies—$99,000 per year (33), establishing the metaphor that what the military really needs is a "surge capacity of troops in reserve to quickly augment the active duty force in times of emergency" (34), and indicating reluctance of American citizens to financially support such a large military in the long term (35); and finally 5. The idea that "surge capacity" being fashioned with the reserves countered by the causal claim that raising bonuses for reserves would then raise the bonuses of regular military and also undercut "[t]he real advantage of the all-volunteer force," which "is its quality" (36).

Carter and Gastris afterward detail their proposal, which is a three pronged menu of mandatory service for those who intend to matriculate at a four-year college or university based on an appeal to tradition (40), an ethical claim that the military predominately draws its members from the "lower socioeconomic classes"—meaning that their proposal would lessen the burden on that social stratum in our country (40), and a causal claim that this new draft would create an "ethic of service" needed in our country while providing the pragmatic necessity of "surge capacity" (44).

- Weaknesses of the argument: While the argument is heavily detailed and does a fine job of refuting opposing viewpoints, it has its flaws. A resistant reader could really question whether the author paints the choices before the military in simplistic terms, especially their statement that exudes a logical fallacy: "America has a choice. It can be the world's superpower, or it can maintain the current all-volunteer military, but it probably can't do both" (7). The statement has the qualifier of "probably," but this depicts it as a very either/or proposition. Particularly flawed is their solution, one that they admit politicians want no part of, which begs the question of how plausible the solution really is. If the draft is the new "third rail" or American politics (37), will anyone realistically have guts to push this proposal forward? In addition, they assume that much of fighting boils down to "Islamic terrorism" (40), which is an assumption about the Iraq war that opponents could seriously question. Also, why only four-year college and university students? Why specifically do community college students get a pass on this proposed service requirement? How would this plan affect enrollments at both four-year schools and community colleges, and what are the assumptions within this proposal? Most importantly, although the authors question the ability to fund increasing troop strength of a number of "bad options" in their article, they ironically offer no real financial plan for how to pay for a massive number of young adults flooding the ranks of ambiguous "service programs," "homeland security assignments," and the armed forces (42).
- Appeals to ethos and pathos: Carter and Gastris offer an even-handed and analytical ethos in the argument, and they enhance their credibility by addressing opposing solutions in quite a bit of detail. The presentation and counter-argumentation of the five available options sets the stage for the unveiling of their somewhat taboo solution of reinstating a new type of draft, one which would bring some major consequences for young adults and those working in higher education. Some proponents of the "five bad options," however, could argue that their proposals were not analyzed conclusively enough. The authors appeal to ethics in part of their proposal by attempting to address the apparent class inequity that is inherent in the military. Carter and Gastris cast their proposal as a way to be fair for the greater good of America. Sections of the argument, and most notably the final paragraph, attempt to work with the emotions of readers in challenging them to make sure America remains the sole superpower by a statement and question that emotes guilt mixed with stereotypical male pride and a dash of appeal to tradition: "We have

Copyright © 2010, Pearson Education, Inc., Publishing as Longman

done it many times in the past. The question is: Do we have the will to do so again?"

- Genre of the argument: This policy proposal exemplifies the genre of high-level current affairs magazines, an argument that is heavy with sustained, well-supported reasoning and some could consider quite wonkish. The argument also exemplifies *kairos* in that the authors are trying to the seize the opportune moment—chaos and turmoil in Iraq and Rumsfeld's vision of a leaner and more efficient military—to propose a radical shift in how America supports its armed forces.

Selective Service System, "How the Draft Has Changed"

- Core of the argument: If a draft were enacted in the future, the procedures to select servicemen would be more "fair and equitable."
- Major stases: This argument is a proposal but also uses the old draft system as a contrast.
- Use of evidence and argumentative strategies: Possibly in response to the fear that a draft might need to be enacted to fight the "war on terror" after the attacks of 9/11, the selective service system present an argumentative assurance that if a draft is held, it will be more fair than the draft during Vietnam. To make this contrast, the author states that those selected, unless a senior in college, would have to enlist after the semester is over, and "a man would spend only year in first priority for the draft." Afterward, as the years go by, possible enlistees would have less of a chance to be selected. In addition, to assuage the argument that draft boards are likely to be racially or class biased, the Web site states that the boards are "required to be as representative as possible of the racial and national origin of registrants in the area served by the board."
- Weaknesses of the argument: A skeptic reading this Web site would find the argument for equal treatment to be specious. The requirement for the boards to reflect diversity sounds positive, but that doesn't necessarily mean that the boards still won't select men who disproportionately come from lower socio-economic backgrounds and minority groups. Also, one could wonder how much lower a "lower priority group" is after the twentieth birthday.
- Appeals to ethos and pathos: The site offers a calm and cool tone to deflect any fears that people may have in case there is a draft. And the text's presentation of a possible draft is one of stark contrast, whereas it really may not be much of a contrast.
- Genre of the argument: This hypothetical proposal is typical of government-sponsored presentation of policy. It is short on specific and long on vague and positive reassurances.

Lawrence J. Korb and Sean E. Duggan, "An All-Volunteer Army? Recruitment and Its Problems"

- Core of the argument: Despite the serious problems that the Army has had meeting recruitment goals and providing soldiers for wars on two different fronts, it is not prudent to institute a draft because the American people do not want one, and the military needs to simply shift priorities in how it allocates its resources.
- Major stases: This argument is a proposal—a draft should not be implemented—and it provides causal claims throughout.
- Use of evidence and argumentative strategies: This argument by Korb and Duggan is

Copyright © 2010, Pearson Education, Inc., Publishing as Longman

starkly realistic about the challenges of staffing the Army. However, they argue that "the all-volunteer model is the right one and should be maintained if at all possible" (paragraph 1). The authors detail that the main problem the Department of Defense is having is meeting the needs of the Army in Afghanistan and Iraq. They posit that implementing a draft will not help the problems that the Army is experiencing, particularly since a mix of draftees and volunteers "would be more expensive due to increases in turnover and, therefore, much higher training costs" (2). They support this assertion with statistics that draftees rarely reenlisted and that three years is typical of making troops fully competent in combat (3). To address the common argument that the Army pulls from certain economic and racial groups disproportionately, they relate studies that state that the makeup of the military is very similar to the U.S. demographics and better educated than average (5 & 6) coupled with visual logos supplied by a bar graph. The writers are realistic about the severe difficulties that the Army, in particular, faces by relating the various ways in which recruiters are compensating for recruitment problems: lower enlistment standards (9), using large monetary incentives (10), various methods of "coercion and manipulation" (11-13), and the "stop-loss" policy that brings soldiers back to the battlefields (14). Korby and Duggan then offer a perspective on the situation that looks beyond the issues of manpower but of technology and equipment. They detail examples of how soldiers and reservists are using dated equipment while the "Department of Defense apparently does not see the necessity of making difficult trade-offs" in regard to monies put toward weapons systems and equipment that are not needed (18). The authors conclude that a draft "does not seem to be an option supported by military leadership or the American people" (20), and they offer instead—quite succinctly—that the Army needs to focus more on the troops as opposed to "hardware," better recruitment methods, and a national service program.

- Weaknesses of the argument: To those who might argue for the draft, they would probably point out that the authors spend a great deal of their article making an argument that the pressure to meet recruitment needs is causing recruitment officers and the military to lessen standards, as evidenced by how the Army is perhaps pushing people through basic training and relaxing standards for enlistment. In addition, the role of reservists is not really addressed in their argument. To some in the regular military, the reservists and guardsmen who are sent to Iraq might not be as qualified or prepared as "regular military." So by the armed services using a large contingent of reservists on a regular basis, that effect of not recruiting enough volunteers is diluting the quality of the force there already, one could argue. Also, the "stop-loss" policy is not good for morale, and it creates situations where there are multiple deployments, which many American families may not agree with. The authors' argument spends more time on the negative situation in the Army than actually explaining a solution to the problem through an all-volunteer army. To that end, their proposal is perfunctory and not well developed. The generalization that a draft isn't favored by the military and the American people is not supported by any evidence whatsoever—it's belief or hearsay. Another bold assumption of the authors is that draftees, after a strong basic training regimen, are not as "qualified" to serve in the military. Vietnam veterans might seriously question that assumption.
- Appeals to ethos and pathos: The authors present an objective-sounding tone in the article, But the multiple examples in the piece provide emotional coloring from time to time, especially when they detail the negative effects of pressure put on recruiters. One of

Copyright © 2010, Pearson Education, Inc., Publishing as Longman

the main appeals in the argument is toward "quality" or "qualified" servicemen. And the authors end on a *pathos*- and perhaps cliché-ridden note: "… win the nation's wars and secure the peace. To do any less would endanger our national security" (23).

- Genre of the argument: Written for a magazine devoted to political science, Korb and Duggan's argument resonates with their audience since they address pressing needs of national security and policy matters. The journal article exemplifies an objective presentation while using copious examples from a wide range of sources.

Louis Caldera, "Military Service"

- Core of the argument: Caldera argues that we as Americans should help support interest in and "create workable opportunities" (paragraph 6) in military service because such service offers the benefits of developing young adults' leadership and physical abilities while fostering an ethic of service for one's country, which might in turn create people's "lifelong commitment to public service" like his own (6).
- Major stases: The argument uses many different stases, but essentially it is a short proposal based from personal experience, ethical claims of America's positive mission abroad, and causal claims about how military service can transform individuals.
- Use of evidence and argumentative strategies: After identifying the perceived problem of Americans not supporting the idea that military service is a valued endeavor, Caldera offers causal claims about how service in the armed forces creates leaders, fosters "moral and physical courage, and command presence and voice" (2). He makes an ethical claim in the same paragraph, implying that American forces work for the greater good of our nation and its self-interests. Drawing from his own personal experience, he relates anecdotal evidence that soldiers value the service they provide for their country and "they knew that they were making a difference," a claim augmented by examples of fairly recent nation-rebuilding tasks (3). The author assumes that the general public looks down on military service because there are very few veterans who are role models for young adults and there's a psychological hangover from the Vietnam era (4). Citing President Bush's recent proposal, Caldera offers a hopeful message that the country needs to further recruitment methods for the positive effects that military service can provide for young people.
- Weaknesses of the argument: A hostile reader may have some serious questions about Caldera's lack of support and assumptions. Although they might agree that there are some certain positive benefits of military service, they would question the means by which the armed forces develop leadership and confidence. Although Hurricane Mitch and Bosnia-Herzegovina are difficult historical examples to argue against, an opposing viewpoint could easily provide counter-examples of America's military corruptness, mass slaughter, immoral use of power, and nebulous or ill-founded goals: Mai Lai, Abu Ghraib, Viet Nam, etc. In addition, the assumption that there are few veterans as role models seems mostly based on opinion. Although he nicely qualifies America's motivation at times as "enlightened self-interest," the author seems to assume that America has a distinct moral purpose as a country; however, it seems to some that "moral purpose" is used quite selectively about where to send troops: Kuwait vs. Rwanda, et al. Caldera believes that military service causally leads to greater public service, which is a slippery slope fallacy. Military service can, but there are many factors that would lead to

Copyright © 2010, Pearson Education, Inc., Publishing as Longman

that positive end. The arguer doesn't grapple with opposing viewpoints at all.

* Appeals to ethos and pathos: Caldera's personal experience is pretty much the linchpin of this argument, which can be very powerful yet very flawed. The author assumes that people would agree with his positive slant on what the US military's role should be throughout the world, a watchman "on the world's hot spots" (3). He invokes a strong appeal to pathos through diction that portrays the American military as a moral force of good. He plays upon a reader's patriotic spirit.
* Genre of the argument: This is a short opinion piece, so the effectiveness of the argument is quite limited because the author neither contends with counterarguments nor offers a definitive plan to attract more recruits for the armed forces.

(Army)Wife, "Stop-Loss"

* Core of the argument: While many criticize the stop-loss policy as an underhanded way of keeping enough soldiers available for combat, the author argues that the policy is fair because soldiers signed a contract that includes the possibility of stop-loss, and the policy ensures that troops are properly trained in an adequate amount of time.
* Major stases: This is an evaluative argument that examines the fairness of the stop-loss policy.
* Use of evidence and argumentative strategies: (Army) Wife begins her post with a context about a recent movie and then argues that no one in the debate about the policy "will ever be fully right. However, in this issue, I side with our military and the need to use the stop-loss policy" (paragraph 3). To counter opponents' analogies of how the policy is counter to working in the "real world," she articulates the fact that being in the military is not similar to working in a business or a factory by relating that the military can be unfair based on the shared experiences of her audience's possible shared experiences (4). She asserts that the policy is part of the contract a soldier signs, thereby defining that being in the military is being at the behest of whatever the military wants a person to do (5). Using the example of "Stonewall," she asserts that the stop-loss policy is in place because commanders need to make sure that their soldiers are ready while soldiers seem to be frivolously suing the military about "improper training" because the National Guard is losing soldiers. She argues that the "Stop-Loss policy takes some of the pressure to deploy fully trained off of Stonewall and the other leaders of the unit and puts it on the rest of the unit" (11). Counter to the idea that the policy continually puts soldiers back into harm's way, (Army) Wife argues that the policy "protects the soldiers" (12) so they're properly trained and it connects to the legal contract that they signed.
* Weaknesses of the argument: The legal counsel of many soldiers who have been stop-lossed would disagree that the Army has the ability to use this policy. They might point out that the contract is valid only in regard to the time they signed on for, not for extended time beyond that contract. The author also asserts that the policy in turn protects soldiers, but one could argue that it simply extends their tours of duty, giving them more opportunities to be killed or wounded. Just because some policies of the Army seem "unfair," that doesn't necessarily mean that the policy is fair. From another perspective, legality should trump bad precedents.
* Appeals to ethos and pathos: It's clear that the author knows her readers and her conversational tone shows that she is experienced in the trials of being a wife who has to

Copyright © 2010, Pearson Education, Inc., Publishing as Longman

deal with the tribulations and heartbreak of being married to a military man. Consequently, her role as an army wife lends credibility to her appeals to tradition and loyalty within her post. Many readers might expect her to come out strongly against the policy, so there's an element of surprise here. And the fatalistic diction of "[i]t's part of being in the military" along with the nationalistic and cool-minded tone of "protect the soldiers," "[i]t is the reality all soldiers must face," and "it is what they agreed to do when they signed their contract" combine to provide a sense of loyalty and shared purpose.

- Genre of the argument: The informal tone and use of personal experience is typical of a personal blog, a site where citizens can comment on the mundane and the weighty.

Matt Carmody, "I Need You"

- Core of the argument: The US Armed Forces, and particularly the Army, are troubled and in a very difficult situation because of their inability to recruit young men and women to fill the troop levels needed for the various theatres on the "war on terror," namely Afghanistan and Iraq.
- Major stases: This is a causal argument relating that the recruiting situation is so dire that instead of "wanting" recruits the armed forces desperately needs them to fill their ranks.
- Use of evidence and argumentative strategies: Using the iconic image of Uncle Sam from the "I Want You" posters, the cartoonist creates humorous incongruity. Many viewers would recognize the famous image, and the cartoonist's Uncle Sam is much different. Instead of being a virile and aggressive figure that looks you straight in the eye, asking for help like the original image, Carmody's Uncle Sam looks bewildered, frustrated, almost emotionally wounded. He's pleading with the viewer, and his prayerful hands accentuate that emotional image.
- Weaknesses of the argument: Some viewers who support, say, the Iraq war, would not find this cartoon humorous. They could react very negatively because it paints a serious situation—lack of troops, "stop-loss" provisions, and America's role—in a sarcastic and playful light.
- Appeals to ethos and pathos: The cartoonist using the Uncle Sam icon certainly enhances the message: the credibility of America is in question, and the Pentagon is using measures to plead for and attract recruits. The obvious scrawling of "NEED" over "WANT" showcases the emotional context of the situation.
- Genre of the argument: This piece effectively sums up a dire and divisive situation with the simple manipulation of an iconic image and changing of one important word. It encapsulates the consequences of the lack of recruits—more aggressive and enticing measures to secure recruitment quotas.

Copyright © 2010, Pearson Education, Inc., Publishing as Longman

WAL-MART AND THE PUBLIC GOOD

Arindrajit Dub, T. William Lester, and Barry Eidlin, "A Downward Push: The Impact of Wal-Mart Stores on Retail Wages and Benefits"

- Core of the argument: The opening of Wal-Mart stores depresses the wages of workers in the grocery and retail industries while also lowering the rate of health care coverage in counties across the United States.
- Major stases: This research exemplifies a collection of causal claims.
- Use of evidence and argumentative strategies: Using data that the authors have compiled for the years 1992-2000, the authors state that their "research finds that Wal-Mart store openings lead to the replacement of better paying jobs that pay less. Wal-Mart's entry also drives wages down for workers in competing industry segments such as grocery stores" (paragraph 1). Since most arguments about the effect of Wal-Mart seem to rely mostly on anecdotal evidence and individual cases, the researchers did a long term study that tracked the economic effects of Wal-Mart. The "Executive Summary" of the article provides the synopsis of the argument and research (1-6), but the authors main rhetorical ploy in this article is to identify an issue or possible effect they want to track, they talk about the pitfalls of finding for those effects, and then they explain how they controlled for possible inaccuracies and the resulting hypothesis from their findings. In regard to wages, the researchers present that the company pays lower wages than comparable large retailers, 26% less (7). They bring up issues involved in comparing wages—stores located in more rural areas and Wal-Mart's large portion of the employees in that employment sector, but they "adjusted retails wages" to cohere with location and average wages in those areas (8). The gaps they found were quite large: 17.4 percent compared to general merchandise employees, 7.5 percent compared to grocery workers, and 17.5 percent compared to workers at large grocery stores (9). In explaining their research methods, the authors explain the problems associated with confusing correlation with causation (11) and then describe how they looked at the ripple effect of store openings in turn having their "estimates avoid the selection bias that can be a problem for similar studies. We also subject our results to a number of different test of internal and external validity, which all indicate that our methodology is robust" (13). Their conclusion is that the opening of Wal-Mart stores lowers retail wages in individual counties, specifically a 0.5 and 0.9 percent decrease in average retail wages (17). The researchers also address the issue of Wal-Mart depressing grocery store wage even though one researcher claims that these stores provide a "small net increase in jobs" (19). In contrast, they find that "[e]very new Wal-Mart in a county reduced the combined or aggregate earning of retail workers by around 1.5 percent" (19). They further support that data point with another researcher who states that there aren't any job gains. To provide another effect of Wal-Mart, the authors also confirm anecdotal evidence about Wal-Mart employees being less likely to receive employee-provided health insurance since the rate of health insurance in areas where new Wal-Marts located showed a significant drop (22-23). They also address a counterargument by discussing how they control for demographic factors that might unduly influence their findings. Overall, the researchers conclude that their research, which has now gone beyond the small case studies, "suggests that Wal-Mart entry lowers wages for employees in competing businesses" (28).

Copyright © 2010, Pearson Education, Inc., Publishing as Longman

- Weaknesses of the argument: A supporter of Wal-Mart could point out that the authors' assurance of how they have problem-solved for selection bias and controlled for other factors is quite vague in paragraph 13. That assurance is not specific at all. Furthermore, while the study only looks at the effects of Wal-Mart entry, the counterargument about lower prices is only minimally addressed in the final paragraph. To some, Wal-Mart represents a model of efficiency and economy of scale that is unparalleled. The corporation has taken the challenge of cutting costs and passed on those cuts to consumers at a fair price. In addition, one could also argue that retail and grocery workers are, for the most part, unskilled laborers, so the minimal loss in wages isn't all that important or noteworthy. A one or two percent loss in average wage is not much at all, some might argue.
- Appeals to ethos and pathos: The authors present an objective-sounding tone emblematic of social science research even thought they do use the first person plural. And the authors use some large numbers to shock, intrigue, or scare readers. Paragraphs 20 ($4.5 billion lost in total earnings) and 21 (10 percent wage reduction) are particularly notable.
- Genre of the argument: The peer-reviewed, research article presents a host of numbers and calculations while working with the methodological problems that social science research confronts. For each possible problem in doing the research, the authors specifically or vaguely assure readers that the data is true and well scrubbed. The article presents an extreme value on *logos* and almost derisively discusses "anecdotal evidence" in a few points of the argument.

Dan Piraro, "Bizarro, Greeter Gone Wild"

- Core of the argument: When Wal-Mart enters a market, the corporation drives out small retailers and drives down wages, thereby making Wal-Mart a monopoly in the community.
- Major stases: This comic presents a causal chain and argument.
- Use of evidence and argumentative strategies: Using the well-known elderly gentleman as a Wal-Mart greeter image, Piraro plays with the basic causal arguments that people present about the effects of Wal-Mart entering a town or city: the company drives out small businesses; it monopolizes the general merchandise and grocery market; and the "everyday low prices" of Wal-Mart come at a significant cost, the "downward push" of everyday wages and health care coverage. The copy of the strip gently mocks the common counterargument about the effect of Wal-Mart: that low prices compensate for the closing of other businesses. And the final sentence, "Enjoy shopping at Wal-Mart" drips with sarcasm, the calling card of comic strips that take on socio-political issues.
- Weaknesses of the argument: While it could be true that Wal-Mart hurts small businesses, one could argue that shopping at Wal-Mart is the consumer's decision. If Wal-Mart provides products and an experience that offers what the consumer wants, then it should benefit from its market research and efficiency. Someone could argue that the small business owner is a relic of bygone time, representative of business people who simply need to adapt and find their own niches in the changing retail and grocery markets in America. Essentially, a person could argue that we should not blame Wal-Mart. We should blame the small business owners with the unwillingness or lack of foresight to adapt.

Copyright © 2010, Pearson Education, Inc., Publishing as Longman

- Appeals to ethos and pathos: The comic appeals to emotion in that Piraro takes a typical image and relates the "back story" beneath the Wal-Mart greeter. In contrast to the happy person giving shoppers carts, Piraro's greeter is stoic while matter-of-factly relating how the corporation affected his life.
- Genre of the argument: The comic strip is typical in that it uses an everyday (and now somewhat iconic) image and plays with incongruity—what the "real" story is behind Wal-Mart through this fictional greeter.

Robert B. Reich, "Don't Blame Wal-Mart"

- Core of the argument: Reich claims that blaming Wal-Mart for its business practices is wrong because, in reality, "today's economy offers us a Faustian bargain: it can give consumers deals because it hammers workers and communities" (paragraph 6). Instead of following the status quo, Reich proposes some forms of "laws and regulations that make our purchase a social choice as well as a personal one" (10) such as "wage insurance" and stronger "labor standards" combined with fairer "trade agreements" for American workers and consumers.
- Major stases: Reich provides a soft proposal here, one that mainly works as an evaluation of why Wal-Mart is merely playing "the game" as it's refereed, and the US needs to make better rules.
- Use of evidence and argumentative strategies: Beginning with a successful scuttling of plans for a Wal-Mart in Queens, Reich portrays the corporation the way many of its detractors portray it, a heartless retail monolith that treats its workers horribly (1). Instead of going with that common perception, Reich argues that American consumers are really to blame because all we tend to focus on is price, and we rarely consider the social costs that go into products we buy. Wal-Mart, in his view, merely reflects post-industrial capitalism as we know it in America—products are built elsewhere and "American consumers get great deals" without a guilty conscience (4). Arguing from analogy, Reich introduces the idea that we would hold many companies to the fire for giving us cheap rates for books, airline tickets, and other products (5). Appealing to Americans' belief in consumer freedom to find the best "deal," Reich argues that the larger problem is that "the choices we make in the market don't fully reflect our values as workers or as citizens" (9). He provides possible solutions such as a "requirement that companies with more than 50 employees offer their workers affordable health insurance" and also "an increase in the minimum wage or a change in labor laws making it easier for employees to organize and negotiate better terms" (10). He argues that the pro or con Wal-Mart debate is hopelessly simplistic. Instead, US leaders and citizens need to consider measures to make our consumer decisions reflect social costs more accurately, and a "sensible public debate" is necessary (14).
- Weaknesses of the argument: While some readers would wholeheartedly agree with Reich's position that prices need to reflect social costs, they might question why Reich is letting Wal-Mart's notable flaws—meager wages, union busting activities, and poor health benefits—"off the hook" so easily. Certainly other companies treat their employees much better than Wal-Mart, and a corporation's business practices should be an important factor in consumer decision-making, one could argue. So Reich's claim that their objections are "paternalistic tripe" could be heavily contended. Backers of the

Copyright © 2010, Pearson Education, Inc., Publishing as Longman

corporate giant could also easily say that Wal-Mart does offer "affordable" health insurance, but its workers merely choose not to enroll. In regard to his proposal, how will it be implemented? And how much will those social costs drive up prices? If Americans are so price-conscious as the author depicts, why would they support higher prices?

- Appeals to ethos and pathos: Besides the "paternalistic tripe" comment, Reich's ethos is mostly calm and even-handed. He takes into account corporations' drive for profit while balancing American consumers' desire and expectation for cheap prices. He almost takes a Rogerian position in that he's arguing that both sides need to meet in the middle, a move for compromise in the US economy.
- Genre of the argument: This Op-Ed piece reflects the ethos of a major newspaper. Reich is a well-known associate of President Clinton's. The argument exemplifies a "New Democrat" frame of vision in that he respects labor unions and workplace equity while simultaneously embracing free market principles.

Steve Maich, "Why Wal-Mart is Good"

- Core of the argument: Maich asserts that much of the criticism directed against Wal-Mart is misdirected and reflects an agenda from "a well-financed, well-organized opposition." The author argues that, in contrast to its detractors' portrayals of the company, Wal-Mart is a godsend to communities by helping the local economies and individuals.
- Major stases: The argument mainly exemplifies the evaluative stasis through showing various reasons why Wal-Mart should be seen as a "good" company. The evaluation employs a number of causal claims to support its position by attempting to show that "most of what we've been told—about worker abuse, destroyed small-town economies, crushed suppliers and greedy management—is wrong" (paragraph 7).
- Use of evidence and argumentative strategies: Maich opens with a scene of a planned revitilizaton of a run-down area in Cleveland that has a retail development proposed, but some people oppose Wal-Mart being the "anchor tenant of Steelyard Commons" (4). Employing statistical data that shows the economic consequences of the whole mall (not Wal-Mart's impact alone), the author asserts that the mall is in jeopardy of large property and payroll tax revenues because of "a broad array of activist groups and unions" who have bonded together to stop Wal-Mart. Transitioning from Cleveland, Maich examines the community of Miramichi as an example to show how bringing Wal-Mart to that small town had some very positive effects: "new life" to the city through various other chains opening (10); the claim that "communities reached out to Wal-Mart" in Canada like Miramichi (12); a university study that says "opening a new outlet is generally an economic boon for the whole area," and the point that "[i]t is difficult to make that case that a Wal-Mart story actually puts retailers out of business" (14); and a study of business owners indicates that 16 percent have been negatively affected by large retailers like Wal-Mart, 5 percent claiming a negative impact, and the rest "little or no impact" (15).

  Addressing the director of Wal-Mart Watch and other anti-Wal-Mart groups, Maich concedes that being an associate is a "low-wage gig"; however, he compares profit per employee at Wal-Mart ($6,000) with GE ($54,000) and Microsoft ($143,000) in paragraph seventeen. Taking on the health care complaint by the company's detractors, the author relates that part of US companies' current problems (GM is cited here) are that they are hampered by "skyrocketing health care costs," that Wal-Mart shouldn't follow in

Copyright © 2010, Pearson Education, Inc., Publishing as Longman

GM's footsteps (18), and that many of its employees use their jobs as a secondary income and "only seven percent of its staff are supporting a family" (19). Using expert opinions from Utilizing Hewitt Associates (20) and a legal analyst from the National Right to Work Legal Defense Fund (21), Maich relates that Wal-Mart associates are "content" and many people apply for jobs there every day. Citing an example from a recent scuttling of a Vancouver-based Wal-Mart, the corporation finally pulled out after even proposing an environmentally sustainable store.

Relying on an analyst from a conservative think tank initially along with studies by the New England Consulting group, UBS Warburg analysts, and another consulting firms, the author claims, like others, that Wal-Mart's low prices do help low-income citizens by saving US consumers $100 billion annually or $600 per American family (27), offering groceries that are 10-15 percent cheaper (27), and the "'Wal-Mart effect'" that "was the biggest single contributor to the growth of economic productivity across the US between 1995 and 1999" (28). Maich portrays Wal-Mart as a friend of the impoverished and those who have to be cost-conscious, and he argues that Wal-Mart, according to *Fortune*, is an admired company. In the penultimate section of the argument, Maich contends with those who oppose Wal-Mart in more detail. Using the words of Tom Robertson against him—"'My mission is to keep them the hell out of town so they won't drive wages down…They just fuckin' destroy jobs, period'" (34), Maich portrays the anti-Wal-Mart forces as merely led by self-interest, a fight to keep unions and the money and organizations they generate. The cause, the author remarks, is that union membership is on the decline because of the decline in industry jobs and a boom in the service economy, "a larger trend unfolding throughout the continent" (37). In response, Maich asserts, the unions see retail and the service industry as the next place to unionize for self-preservation, and he supports that claim by using statements from a director of the AFL-CIO and an advocate for Wal-Mart who asserts that "'The union is looking for dues to finance their operations'" (40). Maich reasons that because the union forces merely want to get bigger in a changing economy, they must rely on a smear campaign that is also based ultimately on the fear that unions themselves will be rendered irrelevant (41). The author also paints the organizations who are against Wal-Mart as forces that see it as a "'societal fight'" (42) between the haves and the have-nots, which he dismisses as belief with "near-religious zeal that Wal-Mart is dangerous" (43). In the final section of the argument the author follows up on that depiction of zealotry by stating people see the situation in Cleveland as the mayor "selling out to the Great Satan of Corporate America" (45) while 78 percent of residents in a poll indicate that they want Wal-Mart in their community (46).

- Weaknesses of the argument: A skeptical reader could question how Maich frames his evidence and support in this argument for a number of different reasons. First, he tends to use data and statements that only fit his purpose, to laud Wal-Mart and make its opponents look like zealots with ill-founded beliefs, not reasonable individuals who are looking out for the greater economic good. The Steelyard Commons example is stirring, but one could question whether another company could anchor the development. The figures used to portray the worth of the development (5) look as though they reflect the whole development and not just Wal-Mart's financial impact. He offers Miramichi as a typical example of the beneficence of Wal-Mart; however, the Ryerson University study only indicates that "the *opening* of a new outlet is *generally* an economic boon for the

Copyright © 2010, Pearson Education, Inc., Publishing as Longman

whole area" (14), my emphasis. Perhaps the study is not a long-term analysis of the economic ramifications of Wal-Mart's bottom dollar pricing on independent businesses? Likewise, one could question the survey on the criteria used for the study. How is small business defined, did the study do a comparison of comparable business operations, and isn't 16 percent significant? Also, why are profits calculated "per employee" in comparing GE and Microsoft? Certainly both GE and Microsoft employ substantially less workers, so is it statistically accurate to compare an enormous retail company that employs many part-time workers to two large, entirely different companies? In regard to the studies used, many exhibit a right-leaning bias—a conservative think tank analyst and business analysts and *Forbes*—that doesn't really take into account the human factors of the working poor or perhaps even value independent businesses. His sources are extremely corporate-friendly. In addition, the statements he uses from union proponents put them into the position of seeming only to care about union membership, not the viability of working class families in the new service economy.

- Appeals to ethos and pathos: Maich's ethos is suspect, and many times his tone is pompous and disrespectful to those who disagree with him. He shows little respect for opposing viewpoints and portrays them as believing in a great machination of a PR campaign funded by forces supposedly out to get the free enterprise system and the working class who go to Wal-Mart because of low prices. The use of the Steelyard Commons and Miramichi examples are used to vividly show how Wal-Mart's detractors are misinformed and "wrong" (7). This argument would easily win over a compliant audience, but the constant rhetorical sniping against views different than Maich's own would work against his aim—persuasion. The final four paragraphs exemplify Maich's attempted depiction of Wal-Mart's critics—he and his biased sources see them as merely out of step with reality, and he argues in the end that their attempts will hurt "poor families" (48).
- Genre of the argument: This is a developed argument typical of the Canadian current affairs magazine, *Maclean's*. Maich's business-oriented perspective is reinforced by the sources he provides for both his support and opposing viewpoints.

John Tierney, "Shopping for a Nobel"

- Core of the argument: Wal-Mart is a company that has and could help people rise out of poverty.
- Major stases: This column combines causal and evaluative stases to propose that the major corporation could be beneficial to the world community.
- Use of evidence and argumentative strategies: Tierney argues that rather than bettering themselves through micro-loans, people in developing countries would be better off getting jobs in factories to sell products at Wal-Mart, thus lessening "poverty" in those countries. Jobs in those factories, which pay as little as "$2 per day—provide enough to lift a worker above the poverty level" (paragraph 8), an assertion that is supported by a study about Asian and Latin American countries. Tierney also cites two other authors—an economist (4) and a head of a non-profit that focuses on "entrepreneurship" (5). The counterpoint to Tierney's argument is that micro-loans are valid ways to alleviate poverty, but working in a factory is a quicker method of getting out of poverty (6).

Copyright © 2010, Pearson Education, Inc., Publishing as Longman

- Weaknesses of the argument: The column provides a sarcastic tone at times, especially for big names that are attempting to address world poverty, and the tone of the piece, while congratulatory toward Yunus and Grameen Bank, implies that micro-loans are more feel-good strategies than really helping people get out of poverty in a large and sustainable way. The sketchy assumption within Tierney's argument, however, is that people in the developing world want to live like Americans. And how is "poverty" defined? While it's possible that some people would want to work in a factory, Tierney is sarcastic about the nature of sweatshops since he puts quotation marks around the term. In addition, Tierney sidesteps the issue of Americans losing jobs to factories going overseas and does not account for what jobs those unemployed Americans will find. Tierney also assumes that Americans save money by shopping at Wal-Mart, a warrant that could be seriously questioned.
- Appeals to ethos and pathos: Tierney seizes the kairic moment by using the context of a recent Nobel prize recipient as an opportunity to discuss another way people in developing countries could rise out of poverty. His tone and points are meant to provoke discussion and surprise, which paragraph 2 does well when he refers to Sam Walton and Wal-Mart "lift[ing] people out of poverty" (2). The author attempts to turn the argument onto the angle that Americans already "are already far better off than most of planet's population" in order to use guilt to make readers think that factory work overseas will create a "rising tide that floats all boats," and the economic maxim goes.
- Genre of the argument: Tierney's column is conversational and works with a few sources while attempting to make readers of a liberal-leaning publication to think differently of a corporation that to many is an anathema and representative of what the American economy has become.

David Horsey, "A New World to Conquer"

- Core of the argument: Horsey's cartoon implies that the retail giant is so powerful and ubiquitous that they would take their worldwide dominance even further, comically expanding to Mars, a rural site for sure.
- Major stases: This is a comical causal/consequences claim, which relates and shows the effect of how expansive Wal-Mart has become.
- Use of evidence and argumentative strategies: Horsey employs the typical sign—"FUTURE SITE OF A NEW WAL-MART"—that many Americans see when the company constructs another store or one of its Supercenters. Using a NASA-like situation, the two people before the computer keep zooming in on the strange image they see, which creates a short plot line, and the situational irony of the sign surprises the reader, connecting with the startled expressions of the two characters. The comic depiction of the corporation being so powerful that they could expand beyond the Earth perhaps even implies that corporations are more powerful than government.
- Weaknesses of the argument: Those readers who tire of Wal-Mart bashing would chalk this up as just another overblown statement about the company's expansive and efficient nature.
- Appeals to ethos and pathos: Using situational incongruity to grab the reader's attention through Wal-Mart being on Mars, the cartoon uses that humor to comment to hopefully startle viewers into the sheer retail power that Wal-Mart holds. The depiction of NASA

Copyright © 2010, Pearson Education, Inc., Publishing as Longman

scientists look at the screens provides a kind of mock verisimilitude for the cartoon.

* Genre of the argument: The political commentary cartoon offers a story-like chain of images to create a storyline while using the typical Wal-Mart "coming soon" sign combined with the doomful sounding caption, "A New World to Conquer."

Copyright © 2010, Pearson Education, Inc., Publishing as Longman

SUSTAINABILITY: THE SEARCH FOR CLEAN ENERGY

Nicholas Kristof, "Our Gas Guzzlers, Their Lives"

- Core of the argument: Americans need to consider and be moved to action about greenhouse gases since our habits harm people living in countries that are poor, especially countries in Africa.
- Major stases: Kristof presents a set of causal claims in order to move readers to action.
- Use of evidence and argumentative strategies: The author begins with an emotionally loaded causal claim to begin his argument: "villagers here in Africa will pay with their lives for our refusal to curb greenhouse gas emissions" (paragraph 1). Kristof uses a host of experts to link the American lifestyle that creates carbon emissions to Africa's changing weather patterns (4-6), lakes receding with "unhappy" hippos (6-9), possible "water shortages and crop failures" (11), reduced yields of crops (12), and the possibility of failed states because of turmoil caused from climate change (13-14). The sources for these claims include an agricultural scientist, a representative of the World Food Program, a fisherman, the Intergovernmental Panel on Climate Change, a bureaucrat in the British government, Uganda's president, and a Care staff member working in Kenya.
- Weaknesses of the argument: Since the argument uses a number of experts, some experts could be questioned. While the UN Panel might be hard to challenge, other "experts" could be challenged because of their possible biases about Africa. Also, there are many causes for "changing weather patterns," so one could question whether there aren't other factors besides global warming that are making living in Africa at this time very difficult. The bold claim that people will die because of American lifestyles also might exemplify a slippery slope fallacy.
- Appeals to ethos and pathos: This column has emotional appeals interwoven throughout the whole piece. From "pay with their lives" diction (1) to "greenhouses gases are killing people here" (4) to unhappy hippos, the author uses the dire situation in Africa to open Americans' eyes about their effects on the world environment. Apropos of Kristof's plea, he ends with "[t]he cost of our environmental irresponsibility will be measured in thousands of children dying of hunger, malaria, and war" (17). Guilt is the modus operandi behind the marshalling of sources about causality.
- Genre of the argument: Like many newspaper columnists, Kristof uses a large issue and attempts to shrink it down to the audience's level—what they can do or should do.

Andrew C. Revkin, "Carbon-Neutral Is Hip, but Is It Green?"

- Core of the argument: People going carbon-neutral can be beneficial, but such moves really just justify bad environmental habits.
- Major stases: The article is mainly an evaluative claim that never comes to a definite conclusion, and it also uses a resemblance claim to color the evaluation. A reader could surmise though that he thinks they're a "gimmick" (paragraph 3).
- Use of evidence and argumentative strategies: Revkin analyzes carbon offsets through the implied criterion of how truly "green" they are or can be. After providing a context about carbon offsets and a comic that mocks the practice, his use of quotations around carbon neutrality also tips the reader that he has a skeptical and negative view of carbon

Copyright © 2010, Pearson Education, Inc., Publishing as Longman

neutrality. While Revkin provides a two-sided outlook on the offsets, he ends that important paragraph (4) with the idea that environmentalists think the practice is "easy on the sacrifice and big on the consumerism," implying that carbon offsets are merely a feel-good practice that don't make people change their environmentally destructive behaviors. To further support that view, he quotes an environmentalist who compares carbon offsets to the sale of indulgences in the Catholic Church (7), a resemblance claim meant to show that carbon neutrality is indeed a gimmick. While the author does provide a view from the NRDC (10) that offsets are helpful in a limited way, Revkin then supplies information about how the market for carbon neutrality is unregulated and unreliable (10-16).

- Weaknesses of the argument: The main counterargument that one might have against Revkin's implied argument is that he might not depict carbon neutrality in a fair-minded manner. He uses a spokesperson from the NRDC, but positive views on carbon neutrality are limited to one person. Revkin provides mostly a negative view of the practice through coverage and even organization. The NRDC spokesperson's quotation is buried toward the end and also, interestingly, leads to Revkin's discussion about the lack of oversight of the carbon offset market.
- Appeals to ethos and pathos: The visual image used in the article mocks the idea of carbon neutrality, and the author presents himself as skeptic who might be looking out for his reader's best interests since he implies that some carbon offsets could be a gimmick or sham. Revkin has a derisive tone toward what some would call liberal guilt about the environment, and uses glaring examples of how people may not change anything about what they're doing and merely use carbon offsets to assuage their guilt similar to buying indulgences.
- Genre of the argument: Revkin works in the kairic moment in that he takes a phenomenon/trend in American society that other people might notice. The article evaluates the trend for his readers and attempts to evaluate the validity of the practice.

Gwyneth Cravens, "Better Energy"

- Core of the argument: America should generate electricity through nuclear power as an effective response to global warming and the widespread pollution associated with coal-fired energy.
- Major stases: Cravens' argument is a proposal.
- Use of evidence and argumentative strategies: Using an example of a noted environmentalist who now supports nuclear energy, Cravens argues that nuclear power is the logical and pragmatic alternative to other fuel sources (paragraph 1). After using the credibility of James Lovelock, Cravens establishes that nuclear plants haven't been built in three decades while offering a recent example of projects that supply a great deal of energy in Texas (3). Using the startling amount of carbon dioxide that the US emits, the large percentage (70%) of electricity created by fossil fuels annually, and the fact that half of our electricity comes from coal-fired plants (4), Cravens further emphasizes the negative effects of how the use of coal for energy "kill[s] 24,000 Americans annually and cause[s] hundreds of thousands of cases of lung and heart problems" in order to paint coal—the largest rival to nuclear power—as something we need to move beyond very soon (4). To address the idea that alternative energy sources, such as wind, solar, and geothermal, will not meet the substantial needs of Americans, Cravens translates the large

Copyright © 2010, Pearson Education, Inc., Publishing as Longman

tract of land needed to address electrical needs through wind power to an area larger than Texas (5). Cravens concedes through a CEO's quotation that the cost of building of nuclear energy facilities is high and provides the negative views of various environmental groups. To allay the fears of environmentalists, she presents the two main concerns about nuclear power, but she argues that "[a] Chernobyl cannot happen here" (7) because of the state of the art reactor cores in the US. In addition, she says that the most famous of US nuclear fiascos—Three Mile Island—was only a "partial meltdown" (8). And she relates that in response to that crisis, US regulations have become more stringent, and the company who is building a new nuclear energy project has now created a design that will stave off nuclear meltdowns. To address the major issue of nuclear waste, Cravens cites an analyst from the Nuclear Energy Institute who compares the amount of nuclear waste (2,000 tons a year) to the "tons of toxic material" produced a year (100 million tons) (9). Cravens describes the process for transferring the nuclear waste and how it is kept securely at a Nevada test site. Cravens then concludes that the recent project that she refers to in the article "could signal the start of a nuclear renaissance and of substantial reductions in America's carbon footprint" (11).

- Weaknesses of the argument: While Cravens does cite an iconic environmentalist and the head of the Program for the Human Environment early on in her article, some of the sources and information she provides comes from strong supporters of or people within the nuclear industry—NRG Energy, David Crane, and David Bradish. Cravens also notes that "wind, water, and biomass cause serious environmental harm" but provides zero support for that assertion, a strange one since those energy sources rely on the natural world and closed-loop cycling for their sources of energy. In fact, many scientists have shown that those sources of energy could provide a large portion of energy in America, but the trickiest issue is storing the energy or converting it quickly for consumer use. Even the quotation that compares the amount of space needed to larger than Texas, that comparison frames the issue in unfair terms since Texas is a huge state, but also because the Texas-size of wind farms needed would be spread across the breadth of forty-eight states, not concentrated in one area the size of Texas. Cravens somewhat sidesteps the great costs involved in building nuclear power plants by using a quotation from an industry executive that informs us that construction is "not cheap," a vague and conversational way of not addressing the substantial costs of nuclear power plants (6). While Cravens does realistically portray the steps the nuclear industry has taken to combat partial meltdowns, the comparison of spent nuclear fuel to "toxic material" from coal-fired plants (9) is perhaps an unfair comparison since coal is a much larger power source than nuclear. And the waste from nuclear power is not only toxic but also radioactive. The site for nuclear waste, too, is under heavy debate because the Nevada test site rests on a fault line. Cravens also fails to comprehensively address the security surrounding nuclear energy plants along with the idea that more nuclear energy production might make more nuclear material available to nations that might use those sources to create weapons.
- Appeals to ethos and pathos: Cravens effectively uses the strong credibility of James Lovelock to put the reader at ease about nuclear power or at least interested in the argument for that type of energy. She also brings in her own experience that she "had a similar change of heart" (2) when she wrote her book, but the title of the book begs this question: Did she go into writing the book with idea that nuclear energy is a positive

Copyright © 2010, Pearson Education, Inc., Publishing as Longman

energy source? To aggressively counter the major emotional concerns that readers would have about nuclear power, Cravens smartly addresses their concerns—safety concerns and nuclear waste.

- Genre of the argument: *Discover* is a mass-market publication devoted to readers who care about science and are interested in current affairs. This article fits the audience perfectly since it addresses an enormous problem—global warming—with a proposal that draws heavily on logical claims.

Charles Krauthammer, "Save the Planet, Let Someone Else Drill"

- Core of the argument: The unwillingness of Democrats to let oil companies drill more in ANWR and outer continental shelf is short-sighted and creates a host of problems associated with relying on petro-states for gasoline.
- Major stases: This is a causal argument that asserts that not drilling in America has disastrous effects on our economy and the world environment.
- Use of evidence and argumentative strategies: Krauthammer's third paragraph provides the main claim for his argument—that the moratorium on oil-drilling has harmful effects on the planet. Using the drop in oil production since 1970 when American hit "peak oil," the author strikes a tone of urgency about the how "[w]e need the stuff to run our cars and planes and economy" (4). He uses the example of Nigeria as a place where corruption and an unstable supply can wreak havoc on the market (5), and Krauthammer provides other volatile states (8) to augment his point that Americans rely on unstable countries for their gasoline. The author also enacts a guilt by association ploy by lumping Sen. Chuck Schumer (and by extension Democrats) with OPEC, and how protecting caribou is destroying Arabian deserts (11). The author assures readers that through advanced technology we can now get to oil more easily than before. In addition, he depicts biofuels as "a devastating force for environmental degradation" (12) and links them to food shortages, higher prices at home, and the negative effects of traditional farming (13). Krauthammer further purports that drilling offshore is necessary since we import so much oil, higher gas prices, and our support of unstable and perhaps violent governments whose countries export oil.
- Weaknesses of the argument: The tone toward noted Democrats and those who disagree with lifting the moratorium on drilling are likely to only move readers who agree with the author. Democrats and the party's leaders are treated with scorn and derision, a move that simply limits the audience who Krauthammer might be able to persuade. The author references "peak oil," but what peak oil indicates is that production will naturally be drastically less after the peak hits, which was 1970. Many petroleum geologists would argue that hard-to-obtain oil costs too much to justify the expensive procedures and technologies to drill for it. Sure, many countries that have oil as one of its main exports are unstable, and the American economy is beholden to that supply, but one could argue that the main problem is our consumption of that non-renewable resource. We need to lessen our use of oil and move toward other systems of transportation, one could argue. Krauthammer also links biofuels to creating price increases, but that claim is unsupported and could be suspect. In fact, the volatile price of gasoline might be the greatest factor to

Copyright © 2010, Pearson Education, Inc., Publishing as Longman

price increases since most goods rely on gas-powered vehicles for shipping. So, with that point in mind, lessening dependence and the use of gasoline is the main culprit, not biofuels.

- Appeals to ethos and pathos: As noted above, the snarky tone against Democrats limits his audience, and the column exudes an ethos of disdain and frustration—not the type of character that usually persuades a fair-minded reader. He also uses word choices that create emotional coloring: "exploitation of the pristine deserts," "a gas tax (equivalent)," and "terror-supporting regimes," to name a few. The author also tries to seize the opportune moment to show why more drilling is needed since gas prices are so high.
- Genre of the argument: The negative view of a political party and unsubstantiated causal claims are the modus operandi of many op-ed columns, especially ones by this noted conservative columnist.

David Tilman and Jason Hill, "Fuel For Thought: All Biofuels Are Not Created Equal"

- Core of the argument: The world community should pursue "carbon-negative" biofuel sources as a method to combat global warming and for sources of renewable energy.
- Major stases: This article provides an implied proposal that uses causal claims, but it also evaluates the efficacy and "carbon footprint" of biofuel sources.
- Use of evidence and argumentative strategies: Using the backdrop of presidential candidates touting ethanol as a good source of energy, the authors explain the environmental and economic consequences of using specific types of biofuels. One core component of their argument is that most fertile lands are already being used or degraded or have strong competition for them for food production (paragraph 3). And they establish the direness of the situation by presenting the stark projections for population growth, which in turn increase food and energy consumption (5). The authors first evaluate the efficacy of corn-based ethanol by addressing these problems. They judge that corn-based ethanol has a miniscule impact on gaining energy since traditional farming is very energy- and gas-intensive (6-7), and the demand for corn-based ethanol has created a ripple effect that drives up food prices as evidenced from the protests and grumblings about corn in Mexico and the United States (8-9). Tilman and Hill then proceed to evaluate soy-based biodiesel, which, according to the authors, "may be about to follow corn's trajectory, escalating the food-vs.-fuel conflict" (10). The authors assert that the "net effect[s]" of corn- and soy-based ethanol both "increase atmospheric greenhouse gases," and those increases are only 15 and 40 percent less than gasoline and petroleum diesel (12). The authors then evaluate sugar cane-based ethanol in Brazil, which only exacerbates that country's noted problems with clearing rainforests for crops since those forests, when cleared, release enormous amounts of carbon into the atmosphere (14-16). Biofuel based from sugar cane, however, "releases 80 percent less greenhouse gases than gasoline" (13). They conclude, based on how forests would need to be cleared, that "[i]t could be harmful to both the climate and the preservation of tropical plant and animal species if it involved, directly or indirectly, additional clearing of native ecosystems" (18). Tilman and Hill end with information about their implied proposal concerning the use of native grasses for ethanol production. They cite their own long-term study published in a prestigious journal that relates native prairie plants can be grown on less than optimal land. They found their plantings "yielded 238 percent more

Copyright © 2010, Pearson Education, Inc., Publishing as Longman

bioenergy than those planted with single species" (21). Those cellulosic plants could be used in energy production as an adjunct or can be made into gasoline, but also they are perennials (23) that need very little pesticides or herbicides (21) and also make the land more fertile (24). Based on their analysis of the biofuel options, the authors conclude by choosing the best options for biofuels, we can move away from unsustainable choices.

- Weaknesses of the argument: Those who support corn- or soy- or sugar cane-based ethanol fuel sources might argue that the fossil fuel energy to harvest those crops at the beginning still rely heavily on traditional gasoline, but in the long term those tractors would use gasoline that is made mainly from corn, soybeans, or sugar cane, thus lessening the impact of our dependence on petroleum, a goal that America should target. Also, those who criticize grass-based ethanol aver that those sources of fuel are far from being ready for market. In fact, some people argue that cellulosic ethanol is a decade away from implementation. One could also argue that if farmers see great profits from growing these native plants and grasses, they'll turn a great deal of their farmlands to these perennials, which in turn would lessen food production.
- Appeals to ethos and pathos: The article exhibits a logic-centered, dispassionate tone throughout, and the authors' main emotional appeal is found when they discuss Brazilian ethanol since that product is linked to deforestation.
- Genre of the argument: This newspaper article presents itself as strongly informative, which it is, and also persuades simply through information and facts and figures. The evaluation of fuel sources based on logical claims proceeds to a *logos*-laden conclusion, which is an implied proposal.

Sustainable Forestry Initiative, "Two Ways to Show You Care About Our Forests"

- Core of the argument: The logo of the Sustainable Forestry Initiative (SFI) is similar in credibility to the iconic recycling symbol.
- Major stases: This is a resemblance claim that attempts to persuade the reader that the SFI logo provides sustainably harvested lumber or paper.
- Use of evidence and argumentative strategies: The visual argument makes the reader view the iconic recycling symbol first and then connect that image to SFI's logo. In addition, the copy of the ad provides a soft causal analysis that the consciousness created by the environmental movement in turn created organizations like SFI that verify the products from companies come from "well managed forests certified to the SFI standard."
- Weaknesses of the argument: It's unclear exactly what the "SFI standard" is. And it's also unclear whether SFI is a non-profit organization that really checks into how forests are managed, or whether SFI is a timber industry front that "greenwashs" products. While SFI may indeed "care about our forests," the symbol may be more of an attempt to make consumers feel good about the wood products they buy.
- Appeals to ethos and pathos: The direct comparison of the logos attempts to align the feel-good and very positive image of recycling with the SFI logo. The copy of the ad also uses emotionally-laden diction in order to sway the reader with "sustainable," "well managed forests." and "Good for you. Good for our forests."

Copyright © 2010, Pearson Education, Inc., Publishing as Longman

* Genre of the argument: Like any strong advertisement, the document has clean images and concise copy. The advertiser attempts to create a positive feeling about SFI through the association with the recycling icon and the copy of the ad.

Iain Murray, "Time to Recycle Recycling?"

* Core of the argument: Recycling paper is environmentally unfriendly because it is an inefficient process.
* Major stases: The author evaluates the short-term effectiveness of recycling paper.
* Use of evidence and argumentative strategies: After establishing that he takes a skeptical look at the environmental movement, Murray provides a typical list of things that people can do to reduce their carbon footprints from an advocacy organization (paragraph 3) and presents his main thesis—recycling paper doesn't make sense. He asserts that recycling paper is "a carbon positive process" (4). He further details that once paper is recycled the quality of its structure and fiber are reduced substantially, with figures provided that by the sixth time it's recycled, paper's strength is down to 38 percent of its initial value (6). Murray also lumps in the use of trucks to pick up the materials as another source of environmental degradation since, as he says, "[t]here are also air emissions, traffic and wear on streets from the second set of trucks prowling for recyclables" (8). The author also makes a mild concession in that cardboard makes sense, but "not so much in expensive consumer products like seventh-generation bath tissue" (9).
* Weaknesses of the argument: The tone of Murray's article likely will not persuade people who recycle passionately or people who consider themselves environmentalists. Other word choices—"global warming alarmism," "Contrary to received wisdom," "sacred cow", *et al.*—betray a rightward lean on this issue, which can be further gleaned by the sources he uses—the Corporate Forum on Paper and the Environment and a writer for the pro-business *Wall Street Journal*. For those who might support recycling, they might argue that recycling paper does make a difference in reducing the vast amounts of waste that could be recycled going to landfills. While recycled paper isn't as strong as non-recycled paper, some paper that we used doesn't need to be strong. His point about trucks coming to pick up the materials on a different day is a strong one, but many proponents of recycling would argue that woods shouldn't be treated like tree farms and that the majority of recycled materials actually make money once economy of scale is reached by the majority of citizens in a certain area participating in recycling programs. The last paragraph, in particular, drips with sarcasm that will only validate readers who have a similar frame of vision about the issue.
* Appeals to ethos and pathos: As noted above, the article has a bias against recycling. And the author smartly plays upon common arguments that environmentalists use in order to move people—that "gas-guzzlers" do a great deal of harm to the environment and energy-intensive processes create pollution.
* Genre of the argument: Written for the arch-conservative *Washington Times*, this article makes a lot of sense for its core audience since it takes on a "sacred cow" of the environmental movement while painting environmentalists as unreasonable and illogical.

Copyright © 2010, Pearson Education, Inc., Publishing as Longman

Al Gore, "Nobel Lecture"

- Core of the argument: Gore proposes that the world community needs to create a system that has "a universal global cap on emissions and uses the market in emissions trading to efficiently allocate resources to the most effective opportunities for speedy reductions" (paragraph 44) coupled with a tax on carbon dioxide.
- Major stases: This lecture is a hybrid argument that is a proposal supported by substantial resemblance claims.
- Use of evidence and argumentative strategies: After establishing the well known reason Nobel established the Peace Prize, Gore presents a clear statement about global climate change: "'We must act'" (6). He uses substantial resemblance claims in this speech: global climate change is "a planetary emergency" (8), our situation as a species is similar to Nobel's example of inventing something that has unintended but quite negative consequences (17), our habits have created a war on the planet's life support system comparable to the Cold War (23), the effect of global warming is eerily similar to nuclear winter (24-5), how our inaction is comparable to inaction about Hitler's power (28), and how our need to address global climate change should be addressed similarly to how Allies addressed the threat of fascism (39-42). The lecture has few logical appeals mainly because Gore assumes the audience agrees that global warming is real and needs to be addressed; however, he does reference our daily output of pollution (10) along with numerous arguments from sign—the melting polar ice caps (13) and various anecdotes about the consequences of global warming (15-6).
- Weaknesses of the argument: The resemblance claims can be questioned here. For example, global climate change is much more pervasive than facism was. Global warming involves all countries. And some have criticized the use of market-based systems to address pollution because some feel that stringent enforcement of caps will be more effective than a cap and trade system. And the cap and trade system that Gore proposes would be rather unwieldy since it involves the whole world, especially considering that developing countries such as China and India believe that they shouldn't be held back from their own industrial revolutions.
- Appeals to ethos and pathos: Since the lecture is a ceremonial speech that is intended to move people to action, it is full of appeals to emotion: invocation of God (2), Churchill's statement about inaction (8), the use of guilt through "We are what is wrong, and we must make it right" (12), the stylistic fragment of "Seven years from now" for rhetorical effect (14), the quotation from Orwell about "reality" (21), "mutually assured destruction" (23), "It is time to make peace with the planet" (27), the use of the phrase "moral purpose" (39) and "moral authority" (42), and the use of the next generation's questions at the end of the speech to make hearers/readers consider that their lack of action has lasting effects.
- Genre of the argument: Since this is a Nobel speech, there was no need to provide a *logos* laden speech about global warming since Gore and the IPCC's work has been officially recognized as outstanding research on global climate change. Because of this, Gore relies mainly on *pathos* in order to move his audience and people who may read his speech.

Copyright © 2010, Pearson Education, Inc., Publishing as Longman

BIOTECH AGRICULTURE AND THE ETHICS OF FOOD PRODUCTION

Jonathan Rauch, "Will Frankenfood Save the Planet?"

- Core of the argument: The outright dismissal of biotech agriculture by environmentalists and consumers is unreasonable. Instead, we need to pursue GMOs to "get through the next four or five decades with as little environmental damage as possible" (paragraph 13). The sheer severity of the world's environmental problems demands that well-thought out use of biotech agriculture should be part of the tool kit for righting environmental wrongs, saving water, conserving wilderness, reducing pollution, and hindering erosion.
- Major stases: Rauch's argument is a proposal in that he provides various methods by which the world could bring back overused farmland, lessen environmental degradation, and reduce erosion/pollution. There are prominent evaluation claims in the argument because he evaluates the efficacy of genetic engineering while providing substantial causal claims about its use and critics' resistance to it (with everything considered, GMOs are "good"). Rauch's argument also exemplifies a bit of Rogerian appeal; he takes a middle ground position, desiring "environmentalists" to look at some of the good of biotech agriculture.
- Use of evidence and argumentative strategies: Rauch relies quite heavily on the expertise and views of others to present his claims about genetically modified organisms. The various examples and experts he employs to provide a positive depiction of GMOs are these: the no-till framing used at "Good Luck Tract" in Virginia and Brian Noyes's claims that no-till farming could "'revolutionize' the area's water quality" (2-6); the Averys at the Hudson Institute (14-17, 23-5, 29); Bt cotton (25); genetically modified corn (26); Norman Borlaug's support for the "Green Revolution" and the ability of increased production to save habitat and its animals (28); David Sandalow at the World Wildlife Fund (33-5); and Don Doering at the World Resources Institute (42). From these experts and examples, Rauch makes causal claims about bioengineered crops: when used with no-till farming, farmers can reduce fuel/energy use, erosion, and water pollution while increasing crop yields; GMOs will help feed a increasingly populous planet because of increased production; these crops can drastically reduce use of irrigation and pesticides/herbicides; crops can be planted in soil mixes that have excess amounts of chemicals that reduce its fertility (high salinity in fields and aluminum, for example) and ward off pests that attack the crops; and the use of transgenic crops can stave off yet more habitat destruction. Rauch also appeals to and concedes certain points to potentially resistant readers. The no-till causal claim of reducing erosion and water pollution is interwoven throughout the article. He fleshes out the problem that "crop monocultures... make poor habitat and are vulnerable to disease and disaster" (9) while also relating that use of manure can cause quite an environmental impact also (10). He informs the audience of the plausible point that most of the land suitable for agriculture is already being utilized (17). Rauch also concedes that there are possible negative effects of biotech agriculture such as cross-pollination that would create "'superweeds'" (19), that there are "severe ecological disruptions" that might occur and "huge risks" with GMOs (34), and mentions the problem of how to distribute—the fact that "[b]iotech companies are in business to make money"—and educate farmers to use the crops properly (37-8). The author does make a strong appeal to environmentally-conscious readers though,

Copyright © 2010, Pearson Education, Inc., Publishing as Longman

especially where he offers a number of questions that quickly connect with the ethos of environmentalists, those who care about the environment and are willing to look for solutions contrasted with "Not politicians, for the most part. Not farmers. Not corporations. Not consumers" (41). Following up on the large ethical appeal, he offers Don Doering's perspective that transgenic crops can be used effectively in a "'design-for-environment'" capacity (42). After using these more compliant environmentalists' views on GE organisms, Rauch offers Greenpeace and the Sierra Club as environmental groups that resist the use of transgenic crops "[f]or reasons having to do more with politics than logic" because of their distrust in market-like mechanisms. He concludes the argument with a resemblance claim, noting that some environmentalists have "embraced market mechanisms—tradable emissions permits and the like—as useful in the fight against pollution," and that precedent should inform the debate about biotech agriculture in order to "transform American environmentalism" (47).

- <u>Weaknesses of the argument</u>: One warrant of Rauch's argument that some, like Altieri and Rosset, would question is that the "crunch" in regard to growing world population is really more a question of food distribution, not increased food production. In addition, the idea that most of the good land has been depleted or degraded is plausible, but is biotech agriculture the only suitable solution? In long-term studies, organic farming methods have shown to be as equally productive and effective as transgenic crops. Even though organic farming may use manure and other natural fertilizers, farmers often create buffer zones in conjunction with their fields to lessen run-off and erosion. Rauch does offer the counterargument of "superweeds," but he does so minimally, as though it's a small but easy concern to grapple with, one that will merely necessitate "government regulation," a proposal that is fraught with complications both politically and scientifically. His offering of Roundup Ready soybeans is reflective of farming in certain parts of the Midwest. However, some farmers who have refused to use those seeds have been sued by Monsanto once GE soybeans cross-pollinate with their fields (the company argues that the farmers are using Monsanto seed varieties without permission), and the cross-pollination of their crops also renders the crops as not being able to be certified as organic or able to be sold to the European Union. One could also question the effects of ingesting GE foods. Have they been properly tested? If certain products have pesticides and herbicides inherent in their genes, what effect do those genes have? Like the use of Roundup, he assumes that such chemicals are "relatively benign" (21). Are they? Where's the proof for that assumption? While Rauch relates that the companies are out for the bottom-line (money), he doesn't give another practical reason why these companies want to increase the amount of GE foods being grown. Do they have any other plausible motivation other than money?
- <u>Appeals to ethos and pathos</u>: The author uses a number of emotional appeals in the argument, many of which revolve around the depiction of the current, environmentally destructive methods of industrial agriculture, a portrayal that many ecologically-conscious readers would agree with. The facts about and description of pollution, erosion, degraded soil, and intensive monoculture farming would connect with many readers' values and beliefs. Rauch, although combative and dismissive to certain environmentalists (Greenpeace and The Sierra Club) either through word choice or use of their own statements, does show that he cares about the environment and world hunger. Although he portrays himself as listening to reason, he also uses emotional appeals to

Copyright © 2010, Pearson Education, Inc., Publishing as Longman

engage the reader—the vivid example of no-till farming and its effects, impoverished nations, the overuse of irrigation, et al.—to see that his audience should see biotech agriculture as a means to help the world's environment and citizens. One could question his ethos because of his use of sources; he could be selectively using ones that fit his purpose and suppressing some questions/claims that other scientists and environmentalists have about GE foods.

* Genre of the argument: This is a public affairs article that is heavily researched, and his argument is reflective of the readers of *The Atlantic*, a left-center magazine that both criticizes the left and right on public policy issues. Many of the readers of the magazine may be conversant with the GMO debate but might have easily taken a position that reflects membership with certain environmental advocacy organizations, so Rauch attempts to make them questions their reasoning and assumptions about genetically modified organisms.

Council for Biotechnology Information, "Would It Surprise You to Know that Growing Soybeans Can Help the Environment?"

* Core of the argument: Soybeans that are bioengineered are safe, and they help fight soil erosion.
* Major stases: This advertisement is an evaluation claim.
* Use of evidence and argumentative strategies: The product advertisement makes broad claims, such as "[p]lant biotechnology makes it easier to control weeds and plow soybean fields less—which means less soil erosion," connected to an appeal to tradition—that people have planted these crops for years—and an appeal to authority—that "three governmental agencies" have determined the plants to be safe.
* Weaknesses of the argument: Since it's a product advertisement essentially, the copy is short and to-the-point. However, skeptics could question the authority of the Department of Agriculture, the EPA, and the FDA since some people question how scientific their studies have been because detractors assert that those governmental entities are beholden to monied interests, specifically the giants of agribusiness and chemical companies that support biotechnology.
* Appeals to ethos and pathos: The ad appeals to positive values by claiming that bioengineered soybeans help the environment, so that claim attempts to counter environmentalists' concerns with biotechnology. And, as noted above, the Council attempts to yoke itself to reputable governmental agencies.
* Genre of the argument: With the inviting copy and serene color scheme, the design and copy attempt to sooth the concerns of those worried about bioengineered plants.

Miguel A. Altieri and Peter Rosset, "Ten Reasons Why Biotechnology Will Not Ensure Food Security, Protect the Environment, and Reduce Poverty in the Developing World"

* Core of the argument: The promotion and adoption of biotech crops world-wide is a poor and detrimental solution to the problems of agricultural productivity, food security, and dependence on herbicides and pesticides because it is based on false theories of "the gap between food production and human population density or growth rate" (paragraph 1); because genetic engineering of crops is "profit-driven rather than need-driven" (2);

Copyright © 2010, Pearson Education, Inc., Publishing as Longman

because genetically engineered foods pose potential health risks to those who eat them; because "Bt crops violate the basic and widely accepted principle of integrated pest management" (2, section 6); because biotech crops are being pushed by marketing interests before these crops have been adequately tested for short-term and long-term effects; because biotech crops with herbicide resistance may create superweeds; because biotech crops promote monoculture agriculture, which in turn causes environmental problems; because biotechnology is not needed to solve these biological problems that agroecological approaches can solve.

- Major stases: This researched article is an evaluation argument that uses categorical and causal reasoning for its criteria. In its final sections, it moves toward a proposal to pursue alternative agroecological principles and to devote money and attention to "people-centered agricultural research and development" (4, section 10).
- Use of evidence and argumentative strategies: This article, which gives a big picture perspective on the problems of genetically engineered food, is structured basically as a rebuttal to the main opposing views on this issue: "Our objective is to challenge the notion of biotechnology as a magic bullet solution to all of agriculture's ills . . ." (2). It begins by refuting the theory that there is hunger in the world because there is not enough food and that "genetic engineering is the only and best way to increase agricultural production" (paragraph 1). After mapping out their entire argument in their abstract, Altieri and Rosset work their way systematically through each main criterion, citing sources from their extensive list of references. Altieri's and Rosset's main move in each section is to lead off with an opposing view or a statement about one main problem with biotechnology and then offer a few telling statistics and facts as they explain their counter views. For instance, in paragraph 2, section 1, they debunk the connection between hunger and population by stating that even countries with sparse population like Brazil and Indonesia have problems with hunger. They then cite a numerical fact about the amount and kinds of food produced today, and they explain their counterargument that "too many people are too poor to buy the food that is available . . . or lack the land and resources to grow it themselves" (2, section 1). Even the points that are not developed in this article—for instance, the potential for creating superweeds—cite a source. Altieri's and Rosset's final move is to propose an alternative course of action: civil society should demand that universities and other organizations research alternatives to genetic engineering; the system of owning intellectual property rights in seeds and chemicals and dominating the market should be challenged; and focus should be placed on "agroecological principles that emphasize diversity, synergy, recycling, and integration; and social processes that emphasize community participation and empowerment" (section 10).
- Weaknesses of the argument: Some readers might say that in places Altieri and Rosset pass off claims as solid evidence. For instance, in Section 5, they say that "[r]ecent evidence . . . shows that there are potential risks of eating such foods . . . ." A source is listed at the end of this section, but they don't cite specific studies, experiments, or any concrete scientific findings. Resistant readers might note that Altieri's and Rosset's angle of vision comes through as an anti-corporate, anti-private, anti-WTO bias that guides them to focus on public interest, the small guy—the small farmer and the "people"—in the US and around the world, and what they call an "agroecological" vision of agriculture. Readers holding opposing views might question whether this angle of

Copyright © 2010, Pearson Education, Inc., Publishing as Longman

vision makes it difficult for them to explore and assess any of the potential benefits of biotech crops.

- Appeals to ethos and pathos: With professional affiliations and authorship of other publications in the field—an intersection of food policy, agriculture, environmentalism, and business—Altieri and Rosset write knowledgeably and authoritatively on the issue of GE food. In this piece, they have created a cerebral and logically structured argument that includes discipline-specific terminology (for example,"transgenic crops," "integrated pest management," "metabolic changes," "non-target organism," "conservation of biodiversity") that would be particularly meaningful to readers conversant with the field, yet the structure of this article and the highlighting of main points with individual sections make this argument accessible to general readers who have a basic understanding of the biotech food controversy. Preferring to contribute to the field by laying out a comprehensive case against biotechnology, they have not attempted to include any personal, experiential, or emotional content.
- Genre of the argument: This policy statement fits the content and format requirements for a scholarly, well-researched, article. Altieri and Rosset have grouped their points to make them comprehensible and memorable. Successful for its genre, this piece provides an illuminating overview of the anti-biotech position, at least one level of supporting evidence, and an array of sources for readers to explore for more depth on these points.

"Monsantoland"

- Core of the argument: The use of genetically modified organisms will bring disastrous results to our environment in a much similar way in which Monsanto introduced other harmful chemicals for widespread use.
- Major stases: This stark visual image is a resemblance claim that plainly links Monsanto and other chemical companies' checkered pasts to go against the perception that genetically engineered organisms are relatively benign products.
- Use of evidence and argumentative strategies: The main argumentative strategy is contrasting "From the People Who Brought You PCB's, DIOXIN, & AGENT ORANGE" to genetic modification and the company. The reasoning stands as: Monsanto is linked to these harmful chemicals in the past; therefore, GMOs are likely to be just as harmful. The causal claim of "You'll need to be genetically modified…" implies that such foods will in turn upset the natural balance of nature and the balance in humans' bodies.
- Weaknesses of the argument: The resemblance claim is quite a leap here. One with an oppositional or pro-Monsanto view could claim that even if the company is associated with those harmful compounds that doesn't necessarily mean that GMOs will do harm in the future. Perhaps testing has advanced quite measurably and genetically engineered products can been found to be safe by multiple, independent evaluators. Chemical companies, in this view, have learned from their mistakes.
- Appeals to ethos and pathos: Skeptical readers of this image could easily criticize "Monsantoland" for using overt, overblown scare tactics, but the image's coloring, layout, and copy are emotionally gripping, full of pathos. The Halloween-like coloring of the ad creates a horrific tinge to the piece—the fiercely auburn backdrop juxtaposed by the black field and barbed wire. The central image provokes an emotional response via a

Copyright © 2010, Pearson Education, Inc., Publishing as Longman

skeletal scarecrow looking directly at the reader, with the whiteness of the skull implicating death, which connects to past chemicals and by extension GMOs. The copy's coloring, black against the orange at the top and red-orange against the black, provides a simple color scheme that gets the reader's attention and holds it. The overall image equates Monsanto and GMOs with death, waste, and destruction—an altered world depicted in almost nuclear holocaust-like imagery.

- Genre of the argument: This advocacy ad uses simple language and claims to stir discussion and get the point across efficiently. The ad is not meant to contend with oppositional views; it is meant to provide a specific "take" on the current debate and do so in a visually disturbing manner.

Gregory A. Jaffe, "Lessen the Fear of Genetically Engineered Crops"

- Core of the argument: This argument answers the issue question: What steps would make agricultural biotechnology more safe and appealing to the public and therefore guarantee its further use and development? Jaffe's claim in response says that the government should implement "a mandatory approval process with specific testing and data requirements" (paragraph 6); should institute environmental reviews; and should focus on consumer benefits. He reasons that the public fears that biotech food is not rigorously tested—and, indeed, the current testing and regulatory system is flawed—and that consumers will support biotech food only if they, in addition to farmers and seed growers, begin to experience some concrete benefits.
- Major stasis: This article is a short policy proposal argument with three main parts to its claim.
- Use of evidence and argumentative strategies: Jaffe first sets up the problem that his policy proposal claims to be able to solve: the polarization between the biotech industry and it supporters, on one hand, and the anti-biotech activists and the resistant public, on the other. In the first four paragraphs, Jaffe also communicates the stakes and his moderate position in this debate. The stakes, he says, include the possibility that this new technology that has shown great promise so far with crops such as cotton and soybeans will lose its markets, its public and private investment, and therefore its possibility for use and expansion. Readers might note that this piece fits well with Stephen Milloy's argument about the fear campaigns against biotech food and in favor of organic food. Rather than attack the antibiotech activists and the advocates for organic food, Jaffe explores ways to make biotech foods more acceptable to the public. In paragraphs five and six, Jaffe admits the uncertainties and riskiness with the current safety review and environmental review process and calls for more rigorous, unbiased, and thorough testing. He suggests new steps for the FDA, the National Academy of Science, Congress, and the Environmental Protection Agency. In the final part of the argument, Jaffe mentions the need to show real benefits to consumers, and he proposes specific ways to gain world acceptance of biotech crops: help the scientists in developing countries and fund research there.
- Weakness of the argument: Readers might note that Jaffe only sketches ways to solve the problems. His proposal does not very thoroughly discuss funding or overcoming obstacles. For instance, he mentions the need to persuade consumers of the benefits of biotech crops, but he says nothing about what those benefits are or how they can be

Copyright © 2010, Pearson Education, Inc., Publishing as Longman

passed on to consumers. Highly resistant readers might say that Jaffe's angle of vision commits him to believing that genetic engineering of food is good and should be advanced. He assumes that tests can be devised to determine safety and future environmental effects. Opponents might counter that short-term consequences may be ascertainable, but how can we possibly know what will happen further down the road?

- Appeals to ethos and pathos: Jaffe's writing is concise, direct, and lucid. He speaks with authority from his position as co-director of the Project on Biotechnology at the Center for Science in the Public Interest. His rapid mapping of the current debate and his discussion of the flaws in the regulatory system as it is testify to his knowledge and rational approach to this controversy. This article is very cerebral, sensible, and neutral in its use of language. It does not use appeals to *pathos* other than in his quick initial description of the protesters against biotech foods in paragraphs 1 and 3: "carrying signs stating 'Biocide is Homicide'" and "[a]ctivists have burned fields and bombed labs." Even these descriptions are direct and factual.
- Genre of the argument: This article exemplifies the brief policy proposal. It is intended to sketch out a moderate position in the huge Frankenfood controversy and offer a reasonable way out of the stalemate that is gradually moving in favor of the antibiotech forces. The *Christian Science Monitor* is a moderate news commentary weekly that provides a forum for volatile current issues.

Froma Harrop, "Food Industry Should Modify Its Stance on Altered Food"

- Core of the argument: The biotech food industry and the government should support labeling of foods containing genetically modified organisms because labeling would please a large number of consumers; because it is important to the European market and would thus improve our international relations; and because it would bring more credibility to the biotech food industry and the government.
- Major stases: This proposal argument is supported by categorical and causal lines of reasoning.
- Use of evidence and argumentative strategies: In this short op-ed piece, Harrop moves quickly from reason to reason, briefly supplying a few pieces of evidence for each. She refers to the NBC News poll to show consumers' preference for labeling of GM foods; citing the case of Europe, Japan, and Australia, she refutes the claim that labeling would sizably raise food bills; she mentions Prince Charles' campaign against GMOs and discusses her concern about antagonizing Europeans over this issue; and then finally, she points out how untrustworthy the federal government and the biotech companies themselves appear to be. She supports this most disturbing point by asserting that both the Environmental Protection Agency and the National Academy of Sciences are staffed by people with direct ties to the biotech food industry. With this last point, she makes consumers think about the power of the profit motive in the government and industry resistance to labeling.
- Weakness of the argument: Resistant readers might say that Harrop's casual, slightly humorous tone suggests that she is making light of the scientific advances that biotech food represents. They might also say that both the cost of labeling and the government's involvement in promoting GMO food are more complex than she states in her quick refutation and accusation.

Copyright © 2010, Pearson Education, Inc., Publishing as Longman

* Appeals to ethos and pathos: In this op-ed piece, syndicated columnist Froma Harrop gives her personal response to the biotech food industry and the government's refusal to label food with GMOs, backed by the knowledge that she is speaking for a large group of consumers. She takes a stand as an adamant opponent, yet one who is still congenially using humor: "sit guard over my organic vegetable patch with a shotgun" (paragraph 4). She defuses some of her vehemence through her casual, breezy tone created by words such as "grub," "mucking around with genetic material" (1); "chow down on GMOs" (13); and "Why mess with success?" (14). She builds her ethos as an informed biotech food opponent by mentioning the ABCNews.com poll, the political fight that the biotech food industry sponsored in Oregon, and the European market's protest. Without using the word 'unnatural," Harrop implants in readers' minds the idea and image of nature that has been tampered with through gene splicing: "a tomato carrying fish DNA" (2); " GMO cows (the ones with rat genes)" (12); "moth genes into catfish" (14). She gradually feeds the readers' disgust, fueling their negative response to GMOS.
* Genre of the argument: This op-ed policy proposal speaks back directly to Milloy and Jaffe. Not allied with any particular organization or institute as they are, Harrop represents "old-fashioned" (2) consumers and liberals, the latter seen in her antagonism to Bush's "bullying" of Europe. In contrast to proponents of biotech agriculture, Harrop believes that the biotech food industry, not the organic food industry, is the tricky, manipulative one, and she admits that no amount of Jaffe's rational reforms will move her.

Sustainusa.org, "What Is the FDA Trying to Feed Us?"

* Core of the argument: We should work to stop the creation and sale of genetically engineered food because genetic engineering is producing food that is very artificial and unnatural; because GE is turning good food into potentially dangerous food; and because GE food is wrongfully being sold to us without our knowledge or approval.
* Major stases: This poster argument presents a proposal claim with implied definitional, causal, and ethical evaluation reasoning.
* Use of evidence and argumentative strategies: The only evidence in this argument is the image of an imagined, monstrous, hybrid strawberry and piranha. In the color version of this poster, the sickish red of the piranhaberry makes this freakish creature look especially menacing. The implication here is that the scientists involved in genetic engineering don't know what they are producing; it is all experimental and could easily get out of control This poster issues an urgent call to consumers to learn what is happening to their food and to resist these manipulations. The poster makers count on this image being alarming enough to motivate readers to go to the Web site of the advocacy group Keep Nature Natural to learn more about GE foods and how consumers can protest them. In other posters, these anti-biotech food advocacy groups emphasize the need to label foods so that consumers will know what they are eating; here the claim is broached but not developed.
* Weaknesses of the argument: Biotech food advocates would point out that images like this one are gross and ludicrous exaggerations and reductions of what genetically engineering does. Resistant readers would say that this poster is a prime example of the "scare stories" generated by those opposed to biotechnology and that this poster offers no

Copyright © 2010, Pearson Education, Inc., Publishing as Longman

evidence that such a freakish creature could be created or that biotech scientists are conducting cross-species experiments as drastic as the one depicted here.

* Appeals to ethos and pathos: This image, exemplifying the "Frankenfood" idea, works on the imaginations and emotions of readers by suggesting that when scientists combine the genes of one kind of organism with those of a different kind of organism, they are dangerously tampering with nature. With images of deformity and monstrosity, the anti-biotech supporters argue that these experiments have crossed the line between helping nature produce its best and playing with the fundamental features of nature: in other words, playing a God-like role. Anti-biotech supporters believe that "natural" is normal, healthy, and good and that tampering with nature is arrogant, disruptive, and short-sighted, especially when no one knows the long-term effects on the environment or humans. Just as the fictional scientist Victor Frankenstein finds that the creature of his invention turns out to be hideous and uncontrollable, Keep Nature Natural portrays its idea that genetic engineers will find that they have unleashed monstrous crops and animals into the world. This poster corroborates the theory of public relations strategist John Bissell that the general public does not understand scientific processes and therefore that fear and emotion work well in manipulating public opinion about scientific inventions. Like another anti-biotech image—the mouse with a human ear growing out of its back—the piranhaberry in this poster inspires fear and anxiety. It conveys the urgent need to act before such monstrous creatures are unleashed into the wild where they will be irretrievable, especially if they begin to pass on their altered genes through breeding and cross-pollination. For its ethos, this advocacy poster counts on the Web site address, directing readers to the advocacy group Keep Nature Natural, to give credibility to this anti-biotech food campaign.
* Genre of the argument: A poster argument must condense an argument into one or a few striking images and bold, memorable text. With the piranhaberry image, Keep Nature Natural found a potent symbol to express its view of GE food and GMOs. Students might want to discuss how this poster talks back to the pro-biotech food posters and how both those against genetic engineering and groups such as the Council for Biotechnology Information with its numerous pro-GE crops ads claim to understand, value, and preserve nature. The Council claims that biotechnology is working with nature to enhance nature; this poster claims that biotechnology is mutating and destroying nature.

Gerald D. Coleman, "Is Genetic Engineering the Answer to Hunger"

* Core of the argument: Because of the very pressing need to combat hunger, we should use GM foods because of the moral imperative to show solidarity with needy nations while ensuring that such nations do "not become dependent on G.M.O. seeds patented by a small number of companies" (paragraph 18).
* Major stases: This is a soft proposal argument that presents the three main positions (and their causal claims) regarding GMOs while making resemblance arguments. It also employs a delayed-thesis structure.
* Use of evidence and argumentative strategies: After providing a historical context about GMOs, Coleman provides concise analysis of proponents and opponents' reasons for supporting or rejecting the use of GE foods and sketches the three main positions in this debate: 1. Using "G.M.O.'s amounts to a moral obligation" (6); 2. Using "G.M.O.'s is

Copyright © 2010, Pearson Education, Inc., Publishing as Longman

morally irresponsible" (10); and 3. Using "G.M.O.'s should be approached with caution" (14). Responding to the latter position's "Precautionary Principle," Coleman relates the mass of hunger in the world through data and offers the sad example of African governments returning GE corn to the US in 2002 (15). Arguing from analogy via support from the Roman conference, he offers the idea that "organisms have been exchanging genetic information for centuries" (16). Additionally, he presents various Catholic sources (arguing from precedent) that support his assertion that we all have a moral charge to help poorer nations, while relating the qualifier that developing nations should "not become dependent on G.M.O. seeds patented by a small number of companies" (18) because to "promote and ensure the dignity of every human being is to enable them to have their daily bread" (19).

- Weaknesses of the argument: A skeptical reader, especially the detractors of GM foods as evidenced in paragraph four and those who rely on the "Precautionary Principle," would question his assertion that "G.M.O.'s are useful, healthful and non-harmful" (16). They would more strongly argue for a cautionary approach because they believe the tests for GMOs look only at short-term and not long-term consequences of GE foods. Also, companies such as Monsanto and Bristol-Meyers would defend their practices of patenting GM seeds because of their substantial financial investment in the products. One could ask, "If they spent millions of dollars on the seeds, why don't they deserve intellectual property rights for them?" Also, Coleman doesn't effectively refute the idea that the real challenges of hunger come from distribution of resources, not the mere production of foodstuffs. He simply attempts to refute that claim by overpowering the reader with the severity of the problem, supported by a deluge of numbers (15).
- Appeals to ethos and pathos: Coleman relies a lot on other viewpoints in his article, and part of that aspect of the article is a result of providing the distinct perspectives in the debate. The debate is framed in terms of morality and what is the greater good for all, and arguing from analogy/resemblance is integral for supporting his position: the Roman Conference's assurance about GMOs (16) along with Catholic Church's Catechism, In Populorum Progresso, Sollicitude Rei Socialis, Centesimus Animus, and support from both Pope Paul VI and John Paul II (17).
- Genre of the argument: The argument is written for a Catholic audience, so Coleman wields ethical support for his argument quite extensively. While concise, the article offers a moral frame of vision that focuses more predominately on the ethical implications of GMOs.

Copyright © 2010, Pearson Education, Inc., Publishing as Longman

CLASSIC ARGUMENTS

Martin Luther King, Jr., "Letter from Birmingham Jail"

- Core of the argument: The nonviolent demonstrations in Birmingham are justified and noble because they square with moral laws and represent an effective and ethical means for addressing injustice in America.
- Major stases: This is a hybrid argument. However, one could argue that that it's an evaluative argument because it examines the assumptions and arguments of the clergymen while providing its own evaluation of the non-violent demonstration and how African-Americans can't wait any longer.
- Use of evidence and argumentative strategies: This argument is a strong example of counter-argumentation because his letter is organized mainly around the arguments and assumptions of the clergymen while providing his own argument for change in the South at that time. He first refutes the idea that he's an outsider by explaining that he is part of an organization that has smaller groups throughout the South, and he "was invited here" (paragraph 2). King then works with the shared belief that there is injustice in Birmingham by then reinforcing his decision to come because he believes "the interrelatedness of all communities and states" because "[i]njustice anywhere is a threat to justic everywhere. We are caught in an inescapable network of mutuality, tied in a single garment of destiny" (4). This move is important because he preys upon the Christian principles of his audience, the belief that all humans are tied together through God. He further details examples of injustice (6) and also establishes the "broken promise" (7) that segregation in stores would be stopped. To refute the idea that civil right leaders need to negotiate rather than protest, King defines and proposes the reasoning behind their protest demonstrations by outlining the principle that non-violent protest creates tension that in turn will lead to important negotiations (24). He argues that these demonstrations are the best route to negotiation because they provide the only way of discussing issues because "[t]oo long has our beloved Southland been bogged down in a tragic effort to live in monologue [what whites say and deem appropriate] rather than dialogue" (11), which he also reinforces with his argument that it's "an historical fact" that those in the majority and those who have advantages rarely relinquish their "privileges" (12). King moves on to the implicit message of the clergymen of "wait" by counter-arguing that "wait" equates to lack of change, which is supported by a litany of examples that really provide a face to the prejudice and oppression that African-Americans face (14). To refute the idea that their protest might break laws, King defines terms to help his cause, relating that unjust laws are simply immoral laws that degrade human nature while also reminding his audience of the just law passed by the Supreme Court in 1954 (Brown v. Board of Education) (16). The author then explicates and expands on the differences and nuances of just and unjust laws (17-19) while arguing for the idea of civil disobedience as supported by evocative precedents that show the positives of civil disobedience and the negatives of not standing up to injustice: Shadrach, Meshach, and Abednago; Christians; Socrates; the Boston Tea Party; and Hitler (20-22). To contend with the assumption that their protests will create violence, King does a bit of logical jujitsu with the analogies of the robbed man, Socrates, and Jesus (25). To further reiterate the foreboding idea that African-American should "wait," King returns to the

Copyright © 2010, Pearson Education, Inc., Publishing as Longman

element of time with a call to action that they can't wait any longer (26) while painting his movement as a golden mean between complacency (middle class) and hatred ("Elijah Muhammed's Muslim movement") (27). He grapples with the extremist label by comparing his movement to the Black Nationalists who are not Christian and espouse hatred and perhaps even violence. King further shows that being perceived as "extreme" is a force for change because of the numerous examples of "extremists" he provides (31). He contrasts his desire for "creative extremists" by appealing to members of the white community who have supported his movement and also reaches out to certain audience members by complimenting them on taking perhaps controversial stands in their communities. At this point in the argument, King turns the letter into a call for action to argue that religious leaders need to join his movement because it is both lawful and moral, but he also expresses his disappointment in church leaders, directly implying that the church shouldn't be places to enforce the status quo. Rather, he sees churches as creators of moral change in communities rather than asserting conformity and immoral behavior—injustice (34-43). King then draws upon the belief that America is a nation of redemption by insisting that the legacy of race relations in America is linked to the country making right on the past, providing change for past mistakes that are still with us. And he calls on clergy to do something about these issues now. In the end, he reasserts the theme of injustice by refuting the pastors' implication that the Birmingham police are a source of good by giving vivid examples of violence (45) and implying that they don't see a lot of chaos and injustice inflicted on the black community (46). Instead, he declares that history will be on their side since they are on a noble cause for justice, as exemplified by James Meredith and Rosa Parks (47). And King reinforces the theme of injustice by reminding his readers that he's writing this in jail, a fact related early on—he "was arrested on a charge of parading without a permit" (19). His circumstances are an implicit argument that there is injustice and America needs to change.

- Weaknesses of the argument: To some, King's argument from principle that we're all linked together (4) does not square with their ideas that individuals should seek their own freedom and self-interest. His definition of unjust law could be questioned because it's premised on the idea of "moral law," which can be defined differently because of varying value systems. And while he paints civil disobedience and extremists in a positive light, his examples are decidedly slanted toward his frame of vision. Also, his repudiation of the Muslim movement could be seen as prejudiced, but his audience is mostly Christian, however. But many in that movement might not condone violence or view whites as "devils." One could argue that he's presenting that movement as a stawperson.
- Appeals to ethos and pathos: The letter is sprinkled full of appeals to *ethos* and *pathos*. To build and assert his credibility and character in the text, he often refers to Jesus, early Christians, important historical figures, and uses Scripture and quotations by philosophers. He presents himself as a scholar. All of these examples carry a great deal of rhetorical weight and persuasion because these figures directly connect to the values and assumptions of his audience. The use of "creative extremists" in paragraph 31 is a defining moment in the argument because he connects his cause to religious and patriotic figures that most readers would value, trust, and have positive views of. The latter part of the argument relies even more heavily on his identification with the church—his disappointment and hope for what churches can do in American society. He establishes early on that he's traveled the South and is one of them; however, he also questions

Copyright © 2010, Pearson Education, Inc., Publishing as Longman

leaders on their complacency in a very condemnatory tone in paragraph 42, for example. The examples of injustice and violence are the most compelling emotional appeals, as can be seen in paragraphs 14 and 45. Loaded language pervades the text too, with such terms as "hope," "sacred," "injustice," "broken promise," "tension," "violence," "nonviolence," "Wait!," "brothers," "moral," "eternal law," "tragic," "faith," "extremist," "love," and "destiny."

- Genre of the argument: The argument is obviously a letter written to clergymen, but King intended the text to be disseminated to other people than them. So it could be fruitful and interesting to have students analyze how King appeals to the clergymen and a more general audience in the piece.

Garret Hardin, "Lifeboat Ethics: The Case Against Aid that Does Harm"

- Core of the argument: Instead of having a spaceship mindset, we should think of the earth's available resources and carrying capacity through the metaphor of a lifeboat. Rich countries that benefit from strong planning and less population growth should be rewarded, whereas poor countries should pay for their poor decisions. Bailing out poor countries and offering limitless immigration only fosters a mindset that shirks personal responsibility and private property rights.
- Major stases: Hardin's highly speculative argument uses a strong resemblance claim/analogy while mixing in various causal and evaluative claims. But, essentially, it's a counter-proposal stating that a world food bank and limitless immigration are misguided and illogical ideas.
- Use of evidence and argumentative strategies: The author begins by presenting the controlling metaphor of the text, the lifeboat full of rich countries with poor countries wanting let in and they swim around. Using this analogy he attacks the idea that richer counties have a social responsibility toward countries that aren't as well off by using the decision that the lifeboat has ten more spots. If we follow the Christian or Marxist ideals, he argues that it leads to "[c]omplete justice, complete catastrophe" (6) because the lifeboat has a limited amount of resources. He first introduces the implicit theme of responsible government in the "Adrift in a Moral Sea" section (8) but then the typical counterarguments to his idea—that not helping people in need is immoral. To answer his possible critics, Hardin inserts the issue of reproductive rates of rich and poor countries with statistical data—"doubling in numbers every 87 years" (rich) contrasted to "doubling, on the average, every 35 years" (poor) (11). Hardin appeals to the fear that people in poor countries are multiplying more quickly, and his example (12) posits that "[e]ach American would have to share the available resources with more than eight people" (14). He asserts, though the use of numbers, that such growth rates are unsustainable, which he later connects to the idea that implication that "the rate of their population growth would be periodically checked by crop failures and famines," which is a coded way of saying that these crises will curb population numbers through death (26). Hardin then connects his counter-proposal to his point that we shouldn't think of world resources as a "commons." Rather, those who live in countries with smart leadership should prosper, and those who don't, shoudn't not prosper. The author also argues against the humanitarian argument for helping poor countries by examining the vested interests that companies and the government have in a world food program (19-21). Next, he

Copyright © 2010, Pearson Education, Inc., Publishing as Longman

provides an evaluation of how poor countries should "learn from experience" rather than depending on rich countries to bail them out periodically (24). Hardin, without any detail, says that the "concept of blame is simply not relevant here" (25). He argues that citizens of countries with poor leaders who fail to account for their own crises should pay for them—the theme of responsibility again but an argument against of entitlements and social welfare based on emotional appeals, not logical ones. He ties the idea of a world food bank to the idea of a commons, one that he sees is fundamentally flawed because he believes we should see ourselves as individual states and not world citizens. Hardin derides the public relations about the "green revolution" through a source's words (30-1), and the argument turns to immigration. To support his anti-immigration stance he relates that all humans have environmental footprints on the world, and the earth has a limited carrying capacity (32-33). He wisely points out that anyone who goes against the tradition immigration policies in American is usually perceived as a bigoted for voicing concerns about letting more people into our country. He coolly pleads with his readers that we should at least question they way immigration happens in America because immigration makes a significant impact on our resources and quality of life. Further reinforcing his logic-focused *modus operandi*, he declares that quantity is important to the argument and "charges of bigotry and chauvinism become irrelevant" (37) even though people fear being perceived a bigoted, and many times those charges stifle arguments for change in immigration. Hardin argues against tradition by arguing for *kairos*, effectively asserting that our arguments and rationales have to fit the time and place, not simply what's been done before because that's what's been done previously (41). In the end, he argues that we need to be generous with own self-interest (care about our country first), not always helping others based on emotional appeals and guilt, which connects to his example of Native Americans (42). Since the UN is ineffective in producing change and ruling the world commons, he avers that countries simply need to worry about themselves more than other countries' crises and problems (46).

- Weaknesses of the argument: This well known argument is ripe for counter-argumentation, so what's provided are some examples. There are certainly more to be found. First, the lifeboat metaphor could be questioned because it's provides a false dichotomy—rich versus poor countries. One could argue that it's not too simple, and poverty and famines happen even if countries' governments are not corrupt or well managed. Also, an opponent could argue that our common humanity is important—we are all tied together, and we need to help others. You could also question his stress on population growth because that's seems to be the main criterion for his reasoning. Population growth is important, but if immigrants adapt won't they assimilate the dominant culture and have less children? Wouldn't providing humanitarian aid also provide opportunities to show other societies the benefits of birth control? His implication that death is a positive result of famines and crop failures, to some, could be beyond the pale. They could label such an assertion as unethical and bordering on genocidal. Those who support humanitarian aid could also argue that what they're doing through a program like the world food bank actually gives them an opportunity to help other countries build sustainable systems of agriculture, a point he dismisses through a source's words. And just because [w]e are all descendents of thieves" (44) doesn't justify

Copyright © 2010, Pearson Education, Inc., Publishing as Longman

the unequal distribution of wealth and resources throughout the world. Some would argue that it's our moral obligation to help others in need, rather than focus only on our self-interests.

- Appeals to ethos and pathos: This argument is much like a counter-statement against *pathos*. Hardin seems to believe emotional appeals and broader ethical concerns shouldn't even factor in when thinking about these issues. His character in the article is one of hard-edged logician who cares more about numbers than people, an *ethos* that might not persuade readers except for those with similar core conservative beliefs.
- Genre of the argument: This is an argument that represents a journal article that honors and cherishes logical over emotion. His speculative claims are meant to invite conversation and also question readers' beliefs and assumptions.

Pablo Picasso, *Guernica*

Since interpretations of this piece of art vary, probably the best method for analyzing this painting is to simply have students analyze the Cubist images within the painting after providing an introduction about the aerial bombardment of Guernica. Since as *Writing Arguments* relates, "[t]he utter destruction of Guernica has come to symbolize the atrocity of modern warfare," having students work in small groups divided by *ethos*, *logos*, and *pathos* might be helpful to unpack the images within the visual argument. Or small groups of students could be assigned to do short presentations about various art critics' interpretations and analyses of the work for a class day.

Rachel Carson, "The Obligation to Endure"

- Core of the argument: The use of insecticides and herbicides is detrimental to the welfare of our environment; therefore, we should show much greater caution and care with using these toxic chemicals and avoid them whenever necessary.
- Major stases: This is a hybrid argument that provides causal claims about the use of pesticides, but it also provides a soft proposal that care and prudence is necessary if we continue to use these chemicals.
- Use of evidence and argumentative strategies: Carson provides an argument that exemplifies caution and reflective thinking about how we are ecological citizens. While she argues against the use of chemical pesticides and monoculture farming, she does offer two concessions to frame the reader's mind to think that she's not an absolutist. The concession that there are insect problems (paragraph 12) and her statement that "[i]t is not my contention that chemical insecticides must never be used" (24) provides active engagement with readers who might be skeptical of her motives. Carson provides a broad view because she's sketching the overarching arguments against the use of pesticides and the simplistic thinking that sustains their use. She evocatively describes how chemicals cycle through our environments (2) and broadly describes evolutionary change (3) while contrasting how chemicals introduced into the environment go against the natural cycle of nature since they are introduced so quickly: "The rapidity of change and the speed with which new situations are created follow the impetuous and heedless pace of man rather than the deliberate place of nature" (4). Much of her argument is philosophical and based on premises from basic ecological principles, but she also provides specific some

Copyright © 2010, Pearson Education, Inc., Publishing as Longman

facts and figures to back her claims, such as 500 new chemicals each year (5) and the sheer number of invasive plants (18). Various sources are used to indicate the strength of her claims and ecological philosophy: Darwin (8), Charles Elton (17 and 20), Paul Shepard (22), and Jean Rostand (26). Her causal claims about how chemicals stay in the environment are described in abstract ways (8, 9, 11), and she also asserts the idea that these chemicals destroy indiscriminately (10) while invasive species are detailed and exemplified by the destruction of elm trees in monocultures (16-19). Carson argues from principle in the sense that she feels that "nature knows best" because the end of a truly natural state is biodiversity, not monoculture, which she derides (15). Those points about monocultures and invasive species cohere with her assertion that insects will adapt and eventually become resistant to each newly introduced chemical through natural selection (8) while humans continue to douse the environment with harmful chemicals with "fanatic zeal" (23). In the end, she calls for greater care and investigation into the harmful effects on "soil, water, wildlife, and man himself" so there is prudent implementation of chemicals, rather than indiscriminate use of pesticides that will harm the environment

- Weaknesses of the argument: Critics of Carson frequently cite that the use of DDT could have saved many humans from dying of malaria, which she anticipates later in the argument (14). To modern farmers, her argument against monoculture farming wouldn't make sense because experts from universities and other entities have told them that's the most productive way to farm, which she alludes to in a few spots. Her advice about having diverse croplands is hopeful but not practical to some readers. Farmers would have to intensively change how they work the land. Also, some would argue that there has been enough scientific study about the effects of various chemicals, while others would say the traces amounts of pesticides in humans are not harmful. Their experts could contradict her experts.
- Appeals to ethos and pathos: Carson establishes her credibility through her source materials, and the character of this essay is reflective, abstract, and philosophical. The argument offers many loaded terms that attempt to persuade readers to see her frame of vision about the use of these chemicals. Some examples are as follows: "chain of evil" (2), "poisoning and death" (2), "war against nature" (6), "violent crossfire" (8), "incredible potential for harm" (9), "buying time" (20), "chemical death" (21), "fanatic zeal" (23). A language of violence pervades the argument to make readers feel that the environment is under attack for astounding unsound reasons.
- Genre of the argument: Taken from *Silent Spring*, Carson's Chapter 2 lays out her philosophical foundation for her well documented research about the effects of pesticides and herbicides. The tone is elegiac in order shock, question, and motivate.

Stanley Milgram, "The Perils of Obedience"

- Core of the argument: Even when faced with tasks that are violent and could be seen as unethical, humans tend to obey authority because they want to please superiors or feel that simply following orders justifies their actions.
- Major stases: Milgram's article makes evaluative and causal claims.
- Use of evidence and argumentative strategies: Milgram uses a great deal of factual evidence from studies of this nature but also provides detailed examples of how subjects responded to the experiments. Early on in the argument, he provides an overview of the

Copyright © 2010, Pearson Education, Inc., Publishing as Longman

role of authority in human societies and offers his general thesis: "The extreme willingness of adults to go to almost any lengths on the command of an authority constitutes the chief finding of the study and the fact most urgently demanding explanation" (paragraph 3). After detailing the parameters and setting of the experiment, he offers a detailed example (Gretchen Brantt) of where a subject refused to continue, which connects with the predictions of many people who believed "that virtually all the subjects would refuse to obey the experimenter." So Milgram creates a surprising-reversal pattern for this argument because he provides the common view of what would happen but then provides what really happened and his causal reasoning why. To contrast the common perceptions, his point that 25 of the 40 followed the experiment to the end is surprising. Within the argument, he also contends with a few counterarguments: that Yale undergrads are "a highly aggressive, competitive bunch who step on each other's necks on the slightest provocation" and that people believe that he's using only the "sadistic fringe of society." He counters those claims by relating that as the experiments progressed and were refined that they pulled people from all walks of life and professions—"they represented ordinary people drawn from working, managerial, and professional classes." What many readers may find very persuasive are the dialogues between the subjects and "experimenter" along with the pleadings of the person acting as though he's being shocked. The description of Fred Prozi, Morris Braverman, and Bruno Batta's sessions are used as typical examples to show how regular people can easily submit to authority. Prozi referencing to "authority" especially drives home the point that people are willing to take orders and commit heinous acts as long as though they feel they're "covered" in a sense by someone higher than them. Milgram then makes the inductive interpretation that these various signs—the behavior of humans in tightly controlled experiements—lead to the generalization that "ordinary people, simply doing their jobs, and without any particular hostility on their part, can become agents in a terrible destructive process," which squares with Hannah Arendt's conclusion about Eichmann. So Milgram provides a positive evaluation of Arendt's claims backed by social scientific studies he's conducted. The "Duty Without Conflict" section of the article sketches his main causal argument that people submit to authority and do horrible things to others because they no longer feel responsible because the "self" is not involved directly. People submit their sense of self, but "[m]orality does not disappear—it requires a radically different focus: the subordinate person feels shame or pride depending on how adequate he has performed the actions called for by authority." While Milgram concedes and provides that there are ways in which submission to authority can be disrupted—no physical presence of authority, conflicting orders, and peer pressure—people tend to care more about pleasing an authority figure than the moral implications of the acts, especially "when one is only an intermediate link in a chain of actions." Milgram concludes by making the claim that by people thinking of themselves as workers or consumers they rarely think of themselves as citizens and morally responsible agents in society.

✸ Weaknesses of the argument: Milgram's last claim about "division of labor" could be questioned because that point is not fully supported in his argument. It is more speculative than substantive. It could be true, but it's not supported with enough depth. Some could also question his conclusions because they are highly controlled experiments that don't replicate everyday life where there are conflicting messages from authority figures at times and collaboration and human interaction happens all the time.

Copyright © 2010, Pearson Education, Inc., Publishing as Longman

* Appeals to ethos and pathos: Milgram establishes his credibility early on with the strong description of the experiments and the factual data from the experiments done across the globe. The argument exudes a dispassionate tone, but the examples of Prozi, Braverman, and Batta provide startling examples of the "socially organized evil in modern society." When reading the dialogues, people could possibly put themselves in those situations and think about how they would react, and the pleadings from the person being shocked reinforce Milgram's overarching claim at the start of the argument, "obedience is a deeply, ingrained behavior tendency, indeed a potent impulse overriding training in ethics, sympathy, and moral conduct." The detailed examples work to disrupt common assumptions and beliefs through emotions, or rather the subjects' lack of emotions.
* Genre of the argument: Appropriate to where it was published—the erudite *Harper's* magazine— the article provides a thought provoking and detailed argument that questions assumptions and beliefs we have. In particular, this article shows that it's part of a scholarly conversation that is going on by publicly defending Arendt's work.

Copyright © 2010, Pearson Education, Inc., Publishing as Longman

X. SELECTED BIBLIOGRAPHY OF WORKS ON ARGUMENT

Barnett, Timothy, Ed. *Teaching the Argument in the Composition Course: Background Readings*. Boston: Bedford/St. Martin's, 2002. Print. [Provides a collection of influential articles about teaching argument from diverse sources.]

Berthoff, Ann E. *Forming/Thinking/Writing: The Composing Imagination.* Rochelle Park, NJ: Hayden, 1978. Print. [Influential work that articulates the "new rhetoric"; stresses writing as a process of making meaning.]

Bitzer, Lloyd F. "The Rhetorical Situation." *Philosophy and Rhetoric* 1:1 (1968): 1–14. Print. [Emphasizes that rhetoric is pragmatic, situated, and intent on effecting change in the audience's thoughts or actions.]

Bruffee, Kenneth A. *A Short Course in Writing*. 4th ed. Cambridge, MA: Winthrop, 1993. Print. [Uses various four-paragraph shapes as heuristics; gives practical advice on collaborative learning.]

Brunk-Chavez, Beth L. "What's So Funny about Stephen Toulmin? Using Cartoons to Teach the Toulmin Analysis." *Teaching English in the Two-Year College* 32.2 (Dec. 2004): 179-85. Print. [Outlines ways in which instructors can use cartoons to teach Toulmin's terminology and the complexity of visual argument.]

Childers, Pamela B., Eric H. Hobson, and Joan A. Mullin. *ARTiculating: Teaching Writing in a Visual World.* Portsmouth, NH. Boynton Cook, 1998. Print. [Provides practical pedagogical discussions of approaches to teaching visual literacy with ideas for assignments.]

Corbett, Edward P. J. and Robert J. Connors. *Classical Rhetoric for the Modern Student*, 4th ed. New York: Oxford UP, 1998. Print. [Comprehensive introduction to classical conceptions of argument.]

Crosswhite, James. *The Rhetoric of Reason: Writing and the Attractions of Argument.* Wisconsin: U of Wisconsin P, 1996. Print. [Re-presents the teaching of argumentation as dialogic conflict of alternative views—of claims and counter-claims—as an ethical means "to conduct learning and inquiry, and to create change and newness" (Introduction 9).]

Crowley, Sharon and Debra Hawhee. *Ancient Rhetorics for Contemporary Students*, 3rd ed. Boston: Longman, 2003. Print. [Grounding argument in the desire to enter conversations based on difference of opinion and to influence human events, this important textbook "reclaims both the theory of knowledge and the argumentative strategies built into ancient rhetorics" (preface, xiii).]

Copyright © 2010, Pearson Education, Inc., Publishing as Longman

D'Angelo, Frank J. *A Conceptual Theory of Rhetoric.* Cambridge, MA: Winthrop, 1975. Print. [Theorizes that linguistic structures, including formal paradigms, match innate conceptual structures of cognition.]

_____. "Paradigms as Structural Counterparts of Topoi." In *Linguistics, Stylistics, and the Teaching of English Composition.* Ed. Donald McQuade. (Akron, OH: U. of Akron Department of English, 1979.) Print. [Presents a sense of form as a heuristic: formal paradigms, analogous to the classical *topoi*, guide invention and arrangement.]

Elbow, Peter. *Writing Without Teachers.* New York: Oxford UP, 1973. Print. [Explains freewriting and the "believing /doubting game."]

Emmel, Barbara, Paula Resch, and Deborah Tenney, Eds. *Argument Revisited, Argument Redefined: Negotiating Meaning in the Composition Classroom.* Thousand Oaks, CA: Sage, 1996. Print. [Offers a diversity of perspectives on the argumentation, particularly examining the ways in which teachers should present argumentation.]

Fahnestock, Jeanne, and Marie Secor, "Teaching Argument: A Theory of Types." *College Composition and Communication* 34 (Feb. 1983): 20–30. Print. [Rationale for approaching argument through *stases*.]

Fulkerson, Richard. *Teaching the Argument in Writing*. Urbana, IL: NCTE, 1996. Print. [Offers a solid background for teaching argumentative writing, especially in regard to stasis theory, marshalling of support for an argument, accessible analytical tools for evaluating arguments (STAR and GASCAP), and logical fallacies.]

Fulkerson, Richard, "Technical Logic, Comp-Logic, and the Teaching of Writing." *College Composition and Communication* 39 (1988): 436–52. Print. [Strong critique of traditional textbook methods of teaching argumentation, especially their confused and confusing explanations of induction and deduction and formal logic.]

Fulwiler, Toby, and Art Young, eds. *Language Connections: Writing and Reading Across the Curriculum.* Urbana, IL: NCTE, 1982. Print. [Promotes the value of expressive writing.]

Gage, John T. "An Adequate Epistemology for Composition: Classical and Modern Perspectives." In *Essays on Classical Rhetoric and Modern Discourse.* Eds. Robert J. Connors, Lisa S. Ede, and Andrea A. Lunsford. Carbondale, IL: Southern Illinois UP, 1984. Print. [Argues that an awareness of audience precedes purpose; the dividing issue is not "the rhetor's invention" but "the outcome of his presence in a conflict of belief."]

_____. "Teaching the Enthymeme: Invention and Arrangement." *Rhetoric Review* 2 (Sept. 1983): 38–50. Print. [Reveals the enthymeme as a powerful heuristic and shaping device.]

Copyright © 2010, Pearson Education, Inc., Publishing as Longman

Garver, Eugene. *Aristotle's Rhetoric: An Art of Character*. Chicago: U of Chicago P, 1994. Print. [Provides a detailed analysis of Aristotle's *Rhetoric* in relation to its historical context; offers helpful analysis and discussion of *phronesis* ("practical wisdom") and *pistis* ("belief, persuasion, et al.).]

George, Diana. "From Analysis to Design: Visual Communication in the Teaching of Writing." *College Composition and Communication* 54:1 (Sept. 2002): 11–38. Print. [Very helpful overview of ways to teach visual communication and of the changes in this pedagogy toward more integrated and productive practices.]

Hillocks, George Jr., Elizabeth A. Kahn, and Larry R. Johannessen. "Teaching Defining Strategies as a Mode of Inquiry: Some Effects on Student Writing." *Research in the Teaching of English* 17 (Oct. 1983): 275–84. Print. [Presents empirical evidence in support of hypothesis that teaching systematic defining strategies leads to cognitive growth and increased fluency.]

Johannessen, Larry R., Elizabeth A. Kahn, and Carolyn Calhoun Walter. *Designing and Sequencing Prewriting Activities*. Urbana, IL: NCTE, 1982. Print. [Series of cognitive exercises for teaching definition—formulating positive, contrastive, and borderline cases.]

Kinneavy, James L and Catherine R. Eskin. "'Kairos' in Aristotle's 'Rhetoric.'" *Written Communication* 11.1 (Jan. 1994): 131-42. Print. [Examines the ancient concept of *kairos* by evaluating the ways the term is used in Aristotle's *Rhetoric* and presents how the concept is still vitally important.]

Klausman, Jeffrey. "Resurrecitng the I-Search: Engaging Students in Meaningful Scholarship." *Teaching English in the Two-Year College* 35.2 (Dec. 2007): 191-96. Print. [Argues for the use of the "I-Search" essay as a means for students to explore complex issues and problems.]

Kneupper, Charles. "Teaching Argument: An Introduction to the Toulmin Model." *College Composition and Communication* 29 (Oct. 1978): 237–41. Print. [Useful introduction to Toulmin system.]

Kress, Gunther, and Theo van Leeuwen. *Reading Images: The Grammar of Visual Design*. New York: Routledge, 1998. Print. [Presents a comprehensive semiotic exploration of visual communication; helpful for theoretical background.]

Lamb, C. E. "Beyond Argument in Feminist Composition." *College Composition and Communication* 42 (1991): 11–22. Print. [Helpful feminist critique of the argument-as-combat metaphor, which Lamb associates with a male-dominated rhetoric; proposes argument as dialogue and negotiation as more productive than win-lose debate.]

Copyright © 2010, Pearson Education, Inc., Publishing as Longman

Lunsford, Andrea A., and Lisa S. Ede. "On Distinctions between Classical and Modern Rhetoric." In *Essays on Classical Rhetoric and Modern Discourse*. Eds. Robert J. Connors, Lisa S. Ede, and Andrea A. Lunsford. Carbondale, IL: Southern Illinois UP, 1984. Print. [Excellent overview of differences between classical and modern conceptions of "truth" and hence of argument.]

Messaris, Paul. *Visual Literacy: Image, Mind, & Reality*. Boulder, CO: Westview Press, 1994. Print. [Helpful background on visual literacy and cognition.]

_____. *Visual Persuasion: The Role of Images in Advertising.* Thousand Oaks, CA: Sage, 1997. Print. [Influential discussion of the compositional features of photos and drawings.]

Perelman, Chaim. *The Realm of Rhetoric.* Trans. William Kluback. 1977; South Bend, IN: U of Notre Dame P, 1982. Print. [Landmark text of the "new rhetoric"; stresses tentativeness of argument—arguers don't prove; at best, they increase adherence to a point of view.]

Perelman, Chaim, and L. Olbrechts-Tyteca. *The New Rhetoric: A Treatise on Argumentation.* Trans. John Wilkinson and Purcell Weaver. 1958; South Bend, IN: U. of Notre Dame P, 1969. Print. [In cataloguing ways that arguments can work, this text has had a major influence on contemporary discourse theory.]

Raymond, James C. "Enthymemes, Examples, and Rhetorical Method." In *Essays on Classical Rhetoric and Modern Discourse*. Eds. Robert J. Connors, Lisa S. Ede, and Andrea A. Lunsford. Carbondale, IL: Southern Illinois UP, 1984. Print. [Excellent explanation of the relationship between an enthymeme and the values of an audience.]

Roberts-Miller, Patricia. *Deliberate Conflict: Argument, Political Theory, and Composition Classes*. Carbondale, IL: Southern Illinois UP, 2004. Print. [A thorough examination of the political theory of argumentation and how epistemologies affect rhetorical practice; supports perceiving argument as exploration and using personal experience along with traditional support to effect change.]

Sipiora, Phillip and James S. Baumlin, Eds. *Rhetoric and Kairos: Essays in History, Theory, and Praxis.* Albany, NY: State University of New York P, 2002. Print. [A compendium of articles about the ancient rhetorical concept of *kairos*.]

Silberstein, Sandra. *War of Words: Language, Politics, and 9/11.* New York: Routledge, 2002. Print. [A fascinating analysis of how rhetoric and image have been shaping the national response to 9/11.]

Tannen, Deborah. *The Argument Culture: Moving from Debate to Dialogue.* New York: Random, 1998. Print. [Opposing the current climate of public debate that features polarized positions and combative debate, Tannen suggests alternative approaches to argument based on listening, negotiating, and finding middle ground.]

Copyright © 2010, Pearson Education, Inc., Publishing as Longman

Taylor, Tim N. "The Research Paper as an Act of Citizenship." *Teaching English in the Two-Year College* 33.1 (Sept. 2005): 50-61. Print. [Suggests that students should use research-based arguments to connect with and create change within their communities.]

Toulmin, Stephen. *The Uses of Argument.* New York: Cambridge UP, 1964. Print. [General theory of argumentation and basis for *Writing Arguments'* approach to invention.]

Tufte, Edward R. *Envisioning Information.* Cheshire, CT: Graphics P, 1990. Print. [Useful for raising rhetorical issues about visual displays of quantitative and scientific information.]

_____. *Visual Explanations: Images and Quantities, Evidence and Narrative.* Cheshire, CT: Graphics P, 1997. Print. [Although Tufte takes a positivist approach to visual information, he foregrounds key issues in visual communication and provokes important discussion.]

Wiener, H.S. "Collaborative Learning in the Classroom: A Guide to Evaluation." *College English* 48.1 (1986): 52–61. Print. [Helpful discussion of criteria needed for evaluating a teacher's use of small groups in the classroom.]

Young, Richard E., Alton L. Becker, and Kenneth L. Pike. *Rhetoric: Discovery and Change.* New York: Harcourt, Brace and World, 1970. Print. [Influential articulation of the "new rhetoric" and Rogerian argument.]

Copyright © 2010, Pearson Education, Inc., Publishing as Longman